Bernard Gauthiez

The Production of Urban Space, Temporality, and Spatiality

SpatioTemporality / RaumZeitlichkeit

Practices – Concepts – Media /
Praktiken – Konzepte – Medien

Edited by / Herausgegeben von
Sebastian Dorsch, Bärbel Frischmann, Holt Meyer,
Susanne Rau, Sabine Schmolinsky,
Katharina Waldner

Volume / Band 8

Bernard Gauthiez

The Production of Urban Space, Temporality, and Spatiality

Lyons, 1500–1900

DE GRUYTER
OLDENBOURG

ISBN: 978-3-11-061963-8
e-ISBN (PDF) 978-3-11-062306-2
e- ISBN (EPUB) 978-3-11-061972-0
ISSN 2365-3221

Library of Congress Control Number: 2020934841

Bibliographic information published by the Deutsche Nationalbibliothek
The Deutsche Nationalbibliothek lists this publication in the Deutsche Nationalbibliografie; detailed bibliographic data are available on the Internet at http://dnb.dnb.de.

Cover image: Landscape of Lyons along the River Saône seen from the St-Vincent footbridge. (Photo: Thiérry Egger, 2019)
Printing and binding: CPI books GmbH, Leck

www.degruyter.com

Foreword

This book originated in a research project I began in 1999 with my colleague, the historian Olivier Zeller, from Lyon 2 University. Our goal then was to understand how the space of a given city changes at the highest level of resolution, the scale of the building, and over long time frames, as well who the agents of the transformation are, and its social dimensions. The project is innovative in two ways. Firstly, it takes account of all the buildings produced during the period studied and within the perimeter of the city, in our case the French city of Lyons, which requires access to relevant archival sources and an appropriate mapping system – hence the use of a GIS. Secondly, it maintains the same level of detail over the entire period studied, in our case three centuries, from about 1600 to circa 1900. This approach was developed by drawing on existing methods used in quantitative history as developed by scholars like Pierre Chaunu, Jacques Dupâquier, Jean-Pierre Bardet, Olivier Zeller and others, and on the French urban history of Jean-Claude Perrot.[1] These methods were adapted to the study of the production of buildings, and completed with a geographical and architectural approach I developed during my PhD on the transformation of the urban space of Rouen, another big French city.[2] The English school of urban morphology, particularly with M.R.G. Conzen and Jeremy Whitehand, was also a strong source of inspiration.[3] The GIS software made it possible to fully integrate these innovative methods. The problems of spatiality and temporality have led me to deal more thor-

1 Pierre Chaunu. *Histoire quantitative, histoire sérielle.* Paris: Armand Colin, 1978; *La mort à Paris (XVIe, XVIIe siècles).* Paris: Fayard, 1978; Jean-Pierre Bardet. *Rouen aux XVIIe et XVIIIe siècles, les mutations d'un espace social.* Paris: SEVPEN, 1983; Jacques Dupâquier. *Histoire de la population française.* Paris: Presses Universitaires de France, 1988; Olivier Zeller. *Les recensements lyonnais de 1597 et 1636: démographie historique et géographie sociale.* Lyons: Presses Universitaires de Lyon, 1983; Jean-Claude Perrot. *Genèse d'une ville moderne, Caen au XVIIIe siècle.* Paris-La Haye: Mouton, 1975. In *Räume der Stadt. Eine Geschichte Lyons 1300–1800* (Frankfurt/Main: Campus Verlag, 2014), Susanne Rau develops another fruitful approach on Lyons, based on the study of practices.

2 Bernard Gauthiez. La logique de l'espace urbain, formation et évolution, le cas de Rouen. PhD dissertation. Paris: Ecole des Hautes Etudes en Sciences Sociales, 1991.

3 M.R.G. Conzen. The use of town plans in the study of urban history. *The study of urban history.* Harold James Dyos (ed.). London: Edward Arnold, 1968; Jeremy W. R. Whitehand. Background to the urban morphogenetic tradition. Jeremy W. R. Whitehand (ed.). *The urban landscape: historical development and management. Papers by M.R.G. Conzen.* London: Academic Press, 1981, 1–24; Recent developments in urban morphology. Dietrich Denecke, Gareth Shaw (eds.). *Urban historical geography, recent progress in Britain and Germany.* Cambridge: Cambridge University Press, 1988, 285–401.

https://doi.org/10.1515/9783110623062-001

oughly with the questions involved and to treat the data available in a more precise way. This was an ambitious undertaking, which sometimes appeared unattainable, but the results are certainly rewarding.

Once the feasibility of the project was ascertained, the field of possibilities it opened developed progressively. This was mainly thanks to the opportunity to locate information from the written record at the scale of the building, which had previously only been possible for a few buildings, but not for an entire city. Once dealing with the entirety of urban space at this level of resolution became a reality, many new investigations emerged.

The progress of the project was marked by several important steps, notably the building of the necessary databases from the archival record, the conceptualization of the units to be mapped (this is where the books begins), and the building of the methodology of the GIS (geometry of the plan, layers, spatial address system). The contribution of Olivier was crucial in identifying serial sources on the building scale, and in the constitution of several databases. Three of the papers published over this twenty year project here form the basis of Part I and Part II, where the arguments of the articles have subsequently been greatly developed.[4]

The project was made possible by funding from several institutions. Initially, it was financed by the Ministère de la Recherche through its Action Concertée Incitative Ville, which allowed me to build the first phase database on the building permits from 1645 to 1763, and to carry out tests of the mapping methodology (which greatly evolved thereafter). There then followed funding from the Région Rhône-Alpes over several years through its Cluster 13 and ARC 5 research projects, when the main bulk of the work was carried out.

This book would not have been possible without funding from several other institutions: Université Lyon 3 Jean-Moulin and its subsidiary Lyon3-Valorisation; the research unit of which I am member (Unité Mixte de Recherche du Centre National de la Recherche Scientifique n° 5600 Environnement, Ville, Société) and its sub-unit within Université Lyon 3 (Centre de Recherche en Géographie et Aménagement). Henry Dicks has done an indispensable job in correcting and editing my original text, making sure the English is correct and reads fluently. Finally, I am grateful for the help of the Erfurt Space-Time Research Group housed

4 Bernard Gauthiez. Des unités pertinentes pour mesurer la ville concrète. *Histoire et mesure*, XIX-3/4 (2004): 295–316; Typologie architecturale et démographie. L'habitat collectif à Lyon à l'époque moderne, 1500–1800. Mathieu Grenet, Yannick Jambon, Marie-Laure Ville (eds.). *Histoire urbaine et sciences sociales. Mélanges en l'honneur du professeur Olivier Zeller.* Paris: Garnier, 2014: 19–48; Le temps dans l'espace des villes, ou l'espace des villes comme accumulation des produits matériels de phénomènes sociaux. *Géocarrefour*, 89, 4 (2014), 283–296.

in the University of Erfurt, led by Professor Susanne Rau, and for the opportunity the editors have given me to publish this book as part of the collection Spatio-Temporality / RaumZeitlichkeit.

Contents

Introduction — 1
Intro 1: Decomposing urban materiality — **4**
Intro 2: Historicizing and 'geographizing' — **8**

Part One: Spatializing and historicizing materiality — 13
I.1 A historicization based on the decomposition of space into production units: the planned developments and the construction-units — **13**
I.1.1 The production units and their scale — **13**
I.1.2 What is a construction-unit? — **14**
I.1.3 Dating issues — **18**
I.2 Dating, use-lengths, inertia: analyses of the urban space of Lyons — **22**
I.2.1 Dating planned developments (Level 1 and 2 production units) — **22**
I.2.2 Dating the plot pattern — **26**
I.2.3 Dating construction-units (Level 3, 4 and 5 production units) — **28**
I.2.4 Dating public space — **35**
I.2.5 Coherence between buildings and planned developments — **39**
I.3 From materiality to remanence: the nature of the transmitted facts — **45**
I.3.1 Traces and remanence: transmission, multiple substitutions — **46**
I.3.2 Time and lines: the origin of 'lines' and of property limits — **51**
I.3.3 On the history of land property and material limits — **54**
I.3.4 On the development of by-laws with respect to the built-up fabric and urban space — **60**
I.3.5 Substitution and reconstitution: the particular temporality of the historical monuments — **62**
I.3.6 The omnipresence of the new — **65**
I.4 Conclusion — **66**

Part Two: Demography and building typology — 68
II.1 The 'cells' of urban space: thinking building typology — **68**
II.1.1 Building the historical Geographic Information System — **73**

II.2 The building typology of Lyons from the fifteenth to the nineteenth century — **81**
II.2.1 The Middle Ages — **82**
II.2.2 The Renaissance: from the mono-familial house to the multi-familial — **85**
II.2.3 The relationship between occupation mode and form of the building — **91**
II.2.4 Seventeenth century: the invention of a new building type of multi-familial housing (or apartment-building) — **102**
II.2.5 Typological variations and evolutions — **108**
II.2.6 The new type and its assemblage properties — **112**
II.2.7 The typological adaptation of older buildings — **115**
II.2.8 The origins of the building types present at Lyons — **120**

Part Three: Temporalities of urban fabric production — 125
III.1 Temporalities and urban morphology — **125**
III.1.1 A ‘film’ of the building production over three centuries — **126**
III.1.2 Space, time and social scales — **128**
III.1.2.1 The year scale — **129**
III.1.2.2 The several year cycle and the grouped rebuilding of neighboring houses — **135**
III.1.2.3 Long duration periodicity — **138**
III.1.2.4 Long-term trends and demography — **144**
III.2 The social agents of change: who builds, for whom — **150**
III.2.1 From the late fifteenth century to the mid-sixteenth — **152**
III.2.1.1 The group of five houses under construction in Rue Grenette: an example of renewal — **158**
III.2.1.2 The subdivision of Chanu’s garden, illustrating the extension of urbanization — **158**
III.2.1.3 The investment logics of major proprietors in the late fifteenth century — **161**
III.2.2 The seventeenth and eighteenth centuries — **166**
III.2.2.1 The series in seventeenth- and eighteenth-century production — **173**
III.2.2.2 The production of buildings in the late eighteenth century — **175**
III.2.2.3 For whom were new buildings produced at the end of the eighteenth century? — **181**
III.2.3 Elements of building production in the nineteenth century — **188**
III.2.3.1 Rue Pierre-Blanc: a singular development of 1820 — **193**

III.2.4 The growing distance between the dwellings of proprietors and their properties — **199**

Conclusion and discussion — 205

Conclusion 1: Temporalities and spatialities of the production of urban space — **205**

Conclusion 2: Temporalities of urban space production compared to temporalities in other scientific domains — **211**

Appendix: 27 images from the film of building activity at Lyons from 1620 to 1830, one image per 10 years — 217

Abstract — 231

List of Figures, Graphs and Tables — 233

Tables — **233**

Figures — **233**

Graphs — **235**

References — 236

Index of persons and places — 247

Subject index — 254

Introduction

In space we read time.[1]

How to discern time in space?[2]

The analysis of the dispositions of the lay-out of the buildings, squares and streets of a town tells us if its constructions were, from the beginning, submitted to a regular and symmetrical order, or if, as the haphazard result of fortuitous causes and accidents, the town's shape developed according to many individual and isolated decisions.[3]

The material form of cities is the product of social phenomena, but it can also be questioned as to its morphology through the analysis of the successive transformations of a historicized materiality at relevant spatial and temporal scales. This implies an appropriate approach in urban morphology, which can profit by its development in recent decades,[4] and an appropriate historicization, i.e., its study at the right temporal and process scales.

I am deeply indebted to Olivier Zeller, who has given me access to numerous databases he made using archive sources, especially for 1636, 1698, 1789. This book could not have been realized without these sources. I thank him as well for our rich and sometimes animated discussions. See Bernard Gauthiez, Olivier Zeller. Lyon aux XVII-XVIIIe siècles, la fabrique de la ville. Emilie Bajolet, Marie-Flore Mattei, Jean-Marc Rennes (eds.). *Quatre ans de recherches urbaines, 2001-2004.* Tours: Presses Universitaires François-Rabelais/Maison des sciences de l'homme "Villes et territoires", 2006, 464–466.

1 "*Im Raume lesen wir die Zeit*", Friedrich Ratzel cited by Karl Schlögel. *Im Raume lesen wir die Zeit. Über Zivilisationsgeschichte und Geopolitik.* Munich, Wien: Carl Hanser, 2003, 269.
2 [Comment discerner le temps dans l'espace?], François Dagognet. *Une épistémologie de l'espace concret, néo-géographie.* Paris: Vrin, 1977, 107.
3 [C'est effectivement au plan d'ensemble des bâtiments, des places et des rues d'une ville, qu'il appartient de faire juger de ses dispositions, et de nous apprendre si les constructions ont été soumises, dès le principe, à un ordre régulier et symétrique, ou si, résultats primitifs de causes fortuites et de rapports accidentels, l'ordonnance et les distributions de cette ville se sont combinées au gré d'une multitude de convenances isolées et particulières], Antoine Quatremère De Quincy. *Dictionnaire historique d'architecture.* Vol. 2. Paris: Adrien Le Clere et Cie, 1832, 672. De Quincy doesn't develop this idea. Nonetheless, he implicitly places the study of urban form in the wider context of debates in geology: Barry J. Cooper. *Changing reflections on the history of geology.* London: Geological Society, Special Publications, 442, 9 Nov. 2016, 63–67, https://doi.org/10.1144/SP442.23; François Ellenberger. *Histoire de la géologie, 2 vols, Technique et documentation.* Paris: Lavoisier, 1994. A major French contribution to this discussion was: Georges Cuvier. *Discours sur les révolutions de la surface du globe et sur les changements qu'elles ont produits dans le règne animal.* Paris: Dufour et d'Ocagne, 1825.
4 Even if it often seems to overlook the production of objects present in material space, great progress has been made in that direction. See Bernard Gauthiez. The history of urban morphol-

https://doi.org/10.1515/9783110623062-002

This essay is intended as a contribution to thinking the historicization of urban space, and it proposes conditions and tools for a better understanding of it. As an illustration, an empirical study is carried out of the area of Lyons that developed until the beginning of the nineteenth century, today the center of the city. Studies dealing with these issues tend to oscillate between an archaeological approach in which historicization is often a goal in itself, at times reduced to mere dating, and an approach to urban history that gives pride of place to the uses of space and to written sources, often the only sources explicitly described as 'historical'.[5]

First of all, the material phenomena have to be associated with social processes and explicitly characterized as such. They can then be individually analysed, using "appropriate concepts to discern relatively precise historical forms".[6] Urban physical space will not be considered here as a philosophical idea or as an ontological reality. It exists as it is only the result of the many individualizable anthropic processes that produced it. The articulation of these processes has also to be exposed and disentangled if we are to understand the empirical materiality. According to Bachelard, "only a relentless awareness can deal with this field of obstacles".[7] It is also necessary, though this is a point I will not discuss, to extricate urban studies from idealistic orientations, so frequent when one speaks of 'urban space' as a concept grounded on slight empirical data and propitious to mythologies, of which some have been analysed by Barthes.[8] Everyone is free to see in urban space poetic opportunities.[9] But a scientific approach designed to understand its materiality has to free itself from poetics and ideologies and to avoid stating the obvious. The aim here is to go

ogy. *Urban morphology, Journal of the international seminar on urban form*, 8/2 (2004), 71–89. The following paper is very useful: Whitehand, Recent dvelopments.

5 Michael Robert Günter Conzen. The use of town plans in the study of urban history. *The study of urban history.* Harold James Dyos (ed.). London: Edward Arnold, 1968, 113–130; Rémy Allain. *Morphologie urbaine. Géographie, aménagement et architecture de la ville.* Paris: Armand Colin, 2004; Jean-Luc Arnaud. *Analyse spatiale, cartographie et histoire urbaine.* Marseilles: Parenthèses/Maison Méditerranéenne des Sciences de l'Homme, 2008. See also the articles and debates in *Urban Morphology.*

6 [Cerner par des concepts appropriés, des formes historiques relativement précises], Louis Bergeron, Marcel Roncayolo. De la ville préindustrielle à la ville industrielle, essai sur l'historiographie française. *Quaderni Storici*, 27 (1974), 827–841; 858–876, 875.

7 [Champ d'obstacles que seule une conscience opiniâtre peut aborder], Gaston Bachelard. *Le matérialisme rationnel.* Paris: Presses Universitaires de France, 1953, 11.

8 Roland Barthes *Mythologies.* Paris: Seuil, 1957. Barthes on "Semiology and Planning": *L'aventure sémiologique.* Paris: Seuil, 1985, 261–271.

9 Gaston Bachelard. *La poétique de l'espace.* Paris: Presses Universitaires de France, 1957.

beyond mere description and to contribute to constructing the conditions of a deeper understanding, putting aside poetics, mental and cultural representations, and mythologies.[10] Following Roncayolo,[11] it is necessary to put aside the 'social morphology' developed by many French geographers,[12] which still dominates geography in France and in Europe, and is sometimes also very present in archaeology.[13] The social morphology school considers materiality principally as a functionalist expression of societies. The overall result is that many researchers have studied societies, giving great importance to ideas taken from Weber, Durkheim, Halbwachs and others, but very few have studied the material fabric itself, or – and this is a major point – its production.

This book will offer a successive examination of three different and complementary aspects of the production of urban space:

PART I: Concepts, spatiality of time, production and construction units, anthropological origins of lines.

PART II: Building typology, the meaning and configuration of the production and construction units.

PART III: Temporality and spatiality of the production of space, its agents and its markets.

---

10 Bertrand: [Le paysage n'en est pas moins une structure matérielle, concrète et 'objective', c'est-à-dire indépendante de l'observateur], he insists as well to "renounce to an idealist approach and to its principal corollary, the analysis of the lived or perceived space" [Renoncer à la démarche idéaliste et à ce qui constitue, au moins dans la pratique actuelle, son principal corollaire, l'analyse sectorielle du paysage 'vécu' ou 'perçu'] (Gilles Bertrand. Le paysage entre la nature et la société. A. Roger (ed.). *La théorie du paysage en France (1974–1994).* Seyssel: Champ Vallon, 1995: 88–108, 96, 98.

11 Marcel Roncayolo. La morphologie entre la matière et le social, interview by Guy Burgel and Philippe Genestier. *Villes en parallèle*, 12/13 (1988), 42–59.

12 Marcel Poëte. L'évolution du plan des villes. *Bulletin du Comité international des sciences historiques*, 20 (1933), 526–537; Maurice Halbwachs. *Morphologie sociale.* Paris: Librairie Armand Colin, 1938; Michel Lussault, Jacques Levy (eds.). *Dictionnaire de la géographie et de l'espace des sociétés.* Paris: Belin, 2003. There is no entry for "urban morphology" in this dictionary.

13 [Concrètement, l'analyse fonctionnelle est considérée comme l'outil le plus adapté à décrire le processus de fabrique d'une ville avec, pour référence, des critères économiques et sociaux], Henri Galinié. *Ville, espace urbain et archéologie.* Tours: Presses Universitaires François-Rabelais, 2000, 82. Galinié introduces the production of urban fabric, but does not examine it as a process. He also does not deal with the physical inertia of material productions, which means that a city is not only a social product. Marlies Heinz. *Der Stadtplan als Spiegel der Gesellschaft, Siedlungsstrukturen in Mesopotamien als Indikator für Formen wirtschaftlicher und gesellschaftlicher Organisation.* Berlin: Dietrich Reimer Verlag, 1997, 1–2.

To implement this project, I will first investigate how the phenomena can be conceptualized, and then illustrate some of them by means of a case study. This approach in turn requires:

a. The decomposition of materiality into objects corresponding to processes that can be individualized, i.e., a *geographization.*
b. An appropriate historicization.

Intro 1: Decomposing urban materiality

The various elements of urban materiality have to be decomposed into pertinent objects. This is a necessary condition for a mapping to make sense. As will be amply demonstrated below, mapping is central here, for it makes it necessary to break materiality down into discrete items issuing from social or natural processes. The scientific fields in which this requirement to break items down in this way first arises are, if one follows their historical development, geology, archaeology (with social processes), and later astronomy, in which mapping is also central.

There can be no geology without units like layers, formations, and the generative processes that produce them. Likewise, archaeology cannot proceed without a decomposition into structures, to which are attributed a succession in time and an emergence process, which nowadays often uses the Harris matrix.[14] Astronomy and cosmology rely deeply on the role of time, and are also historical sciences. Urban space is often decomposed into blocks, buildings, and public spaces, but, if we are to understand its genesis, production processes, and transformations, these notions are generally inadequate. They result from the amalgamation of varied spheres of reality, used in simplifying and idealizing technical approaches linked to planning practice, even if they are considered with a morphological mind-set,[15] one more interested in the evidence of forms and in their social role than in their morphogenetic processes. Many scholars, from Kretzschmar,[16] and Schwartz, with his “solidifications of the past”,[17] to

14 Edward C. Harris. *Principles of Archaeological Stratigraphy.* London & New York: Academic Press, 1979&1989.
15 Jeremy W. R. Whitehand. Background to the urban morphogenetic tradition. Jeremy W. R. Whitehand (ed.). *The urban landscape: historical development and management. Papers by M.R.G. Conzen.* London: Academic Press, 1981, 1–24, 13.
16 Johannes Kretzschmar. Der Stadtplan als Geschichtsquelle. *Deutsche Geschichtsblätter,* 9 (1908), 133–141.
17 Rudolf Schwartz. *Von der Bebauung der Erde.* Heidelberg: Lambert Schneider, 1949, 41.

Roncayolo,[18] have evoked urban materiality as petrified history, but their decomposition is arguably too simple, as in the case of the *Stadtteil* of Keyser,[19] and even the *plan-unit* of Conzen.[20] I have investigated in a previous paper the history of these ideas and how they progressed through the fields of geography, history and urban planning, and in different countries, mainly Germany, England and Italy.[21]

The social processes responsible for the genesis of the forms are not, in these authors and others, explicated as processes of production or realization. Space is separated into entities expressing the particular social conditions of given societies, which are indeed placed in time. But the production of space is never or rarely examined. This was particularly true in the French studies that relied on the concept of social morphology.[22] Henri Lefebvre published a brilliant book in 1974 on the production of urban space.[23] Reading it, the precision of his intellectual project is clear. He argues for a knowledge that cannot rely on an inventory made of descriptions, as this decomposition would produce, to use his word, only a "discourse".[24] But his solutions, based on a complete account of the concepts of *space* and *space production* (which are never precisely defined), combine "on the one hand formal abstraction (logico-mathematical space), and on the other hand the practico-sensible and the social space".[25] His thought is impregnated with a Marxist vision of society and the structuralism of Lévi-Strauss. This approach is a long way from the present focus on materiality, and one is puzzled, when contemplating his ideas, how one might go about studying concrete urban space using such vague ideas. When Lefebvre deals with the concrete process of material production, he avoids this difficulty and

---

18 Marcel Roncayolo. *La ville et ses territoires*. Paris: Gallimard, 1997, 143.

19 E. Keyser. Der Stadtgrundriss als Geschichtsquelle. *Studium Generale*, 6 (1963), 345–361.

20 Michael Robert Günter Conzen. *Alnwick, Northumberland: a study in town-plan analysis*. London: George Philip, 1960, 5, 108: "A plan unit may be identified in any part of the town plan that is morphologically different from its surroundings – in terms of its streets, plots and buildings. This may be undertaken at differing scales from layouts to individual morphotopes and applies to any area that exhibits internal homogeneity and morphological disunity with neighbouring plots".

21 Gauthiez, History.

22 Maurice Halbwachs. *La population et les tracés de voies à Paris*. Paris: Alcan, 1928.

23 Henri Lefebvre. *La production de l'espace*. Paris: Anthropos, 1974.

24 Lefebvre, *La production*, 14. The meaning of 'discourse' is not clear here. This is probably opposed to 'scientific discourse'.

25 [D'une part avec l'extrême abstraction formelle (l'espace logico-mathématique) et, de l'autre, avec le pratico-sensible et l'espace social]. Lefebvre doesn't develop. Lefebvre, *La production, 23.*

takes refuge in the imprecision of an undefined social space whose geographical dimension escapes him because it is too difficult to grasp, or rather because he has no conceptual tools to study it, and he instead refers to a rather elusive 'morphographic' mathematization, which is not defined either.[26] For him, there is an ontological disconnection between social space and physical materiality.[27] The ideas of Lefebvre have been developed by historians in the "spatial turn" taken two decades ago. Practice was emphasized as forming a triangle with perception and production.[28] Susanne Rau added to this general view of the production of space richer considerations about its technical conception and the need to investigate this aspect of the domain.[29] This view is nevertheless still probably blinded by the idea of social morphology as enunciated by Halbwachs. According to Halbwachs, urban space is the expression of a society in space, an idea, as seen above, which is still very present in recent French geography,[30] be it by means of a detour via Brazil, as when Claval cites Milton Santos and Abreu.[31] This idea relies on the supposition that reality is the immediate fruit of social space, in association with a functionalist credo. This is obviously not true, as material reality changes at a rate that is much slower than the social one, as Lefebvre acknowledged, and because its transformation is due to particular agents within the society, not to the society as a whole. As a consequence, only a tiny part of material reality can be changed in the scale duration of a year by a given society, and all societies must always deal to a great extent with what they inherit from the past. Further, it is also important to recognize that only a small part of a given society can effectively produce new space. This point was made forcefully by Whitehand who emphasized its importance (in 1988) for fu-

26 Lefebvre, *La production*, 103. The word 'morphographic' was coined by Whitehand, Background, 13.

27 Lefebvre, *La production*, 36.

28 Sebastian Dorsch. Introduction. Sebastian Dorsch and Susanne Rau (eds.). Space/time practice and the production of space and time. *Historical Social Research/Historische Socialforschung*, special issue 38 (2013), 7–21, 9.

29 Susanne Rau. Die Vielfalt des Räumlichen – Stand und Perspektiven der frühneuzeitlichen Raumforschung. *Frühneuzeit-Info*, 28 (2017), 75–86; 82: [jede Gesellschaft ihre eigenen Räume produziert], 84: [Wird der Blick zukünftig noch stärker auf Raumpraktiken verschiedenster Art (Zeichnen, Bauen, Passieren, Kartieren, Exponieren etc.) gerichtet, kann dadurch auch der prozessuale Charakter der Konstruktion von Räumen unterstrichen werden]. She develops in: *History, space and place*. London-New York: Routledge, 2019.

30 Lussault, Lévy, *Dictionnaire*.

31 Paul Claval. Géographie et temporalités. Philippe Boulanger, Jean-René Trochet (eds.). *Où en est la géographie historique? Entre économie et culture*. Paris: L'Harmattan, 2005, 43–62, 54. On the ideas of Abreu see S. G. Pereira. *A réforma urbana de Pereira Passos e a construçao da idendidade carioca*. Rio de Janeiro: Universidade Federal de Rio de Janeiro, 1998, 24–25.

ture research in urban morphology.[32] The rest of society, mainly if not exclusively, uses urban space as it is, this is to say, as it is inherited. I will consider the changing rates of space in PART III of this book, using empirical data.

To answer the need for a clear approach to the link between materiality and social space, I proposed in 2003 the concept of the 'construction-unit' (*unité de construction*) defined as the *realization of a conception unit*, i.e. the material fruit of a project.[33] Developing this idea at the right scales, it becomes possible to decompose the space of a given city into objects closely related to their production processes, as they are the material result of these processes. To give a very concrete example, one can establish a correspondence between a social process like the issuing of a building permit and a material object, such as a building, an ensemble of buildings, or a part of one. In this way, a straight connection can be made between the space of the individuals or of their various associations and organizations,[34] the social and economic relations, and the material space of the realizations produced by these social spaces, including the space of conception (to which Lefebvre accorded great importance). This connection does nevertheless leave room for a certain amount of autonomy of these different spaces, resulting from varying comportments and properties, especially if time is taken into account. For example, a building can stay standing for centuries, although a social context lasts a much shorter time (even if the building, to stay standing, needs deliberate maintenance). Later on we will have to consider the singular moment of material production to fully understand this difference.

---

32 Whitehand, Recent developments, 288: "a serious deficiency in previous work was the virtual absence of analytical studies of those who initiated and designed changes to the physical fabric, whether it be the construction of new buildings or the variety of changes to existing buildings".

33 Bernard Gauthiez. *Espace urbain. Vocabulaire et morphologie*. Paris: Editions du patrimoine/ Monum', 2003, 112. For Caniggia and Maffei a building is a product (*prodotto*), but they do not perceive the particular historicity and nature of the production processes. Gianfranco Caniggia, Gian Luigi Maffei. *Lettura dell'edilizia di base, nuova edizione*. Florence: Alinea, 2008, 52.

34 Translation of "Vergesellschaftung", Max Weber. *Wirtschaft und Gesellschaft. Grundriss der verstehenden Soziologie*. Tübingen: Mohr, 1972 [1922], 41.

Intro 2: Historicizing and 'geographizing'[35]

A second matter which is necessary is the precise dating of the objects in order to understand the chronological relations between them. The idea is simple, but the investment required to obtain the necessary data for a given space or city can be huge, as thousands of objects have to be researched in detail (see I.1.3). This precision is however indispensable if we are to understand the chronological relations, including whether these relations were produced at a single time or at different times, according to differing logics. The existence of multiple scale levels can also have a substantial impact on the amount of investment required: less if one is studying a small number of larger objects, greater if one is studying a large number of small objects, though even in this latter instance the investment may well prove necessary for a full understanding of the present, concrete, and lived space.[36]

The scientific fields interested in materiality, whose phenomenology is first of all spatial, accord great importance to time, as is the case in geology, archaeology, and astronomy. Research programs in these fields are typically well identified and methodologically well defined. To cite a number of French scholars, Lefebvre has written that: "historicity breaks definitively with naturality, establishing on its ruins the space of accumulation";[37] Dagognet evokes: "the decisive interest of chronology and of dating";[38] and, more recently, Benoist affirms that, "temporality will certainly be discovered ... in the de-obstruction of all sorts of spatial metaphors hindering comprehension, and [which] prevent us from staying loyal to what it [temporality] can tell us as about what is truly important for the understanding of phenomena".[39] Grataloup agrees: "a geohistory of territories makes it necessary to historicize space, and conversely to spatialize the period".[40] The program expressed in these citations is clear: to understand space

35 Geographers usually use the word 'spatializing', but with a meaning generally limited to location and mapping. Hence the need of a word to signify the categories of geographical objects, geotopes, and their organizations.
36 To give an example from the early nineteenth century in Lyons: every year a few dozen building permits were issued for entire buildings, and around a thousand for small modifications.
37 Lefebvre, *La production*, 60.
38 Dagognet, *Une épistémologie*, 24.
39 Jocelyn Benoist. Rompre avec l'idéalisme historique: re-spatialiser nos concepts. Jocelyn Benoist, Fabio Merlini (eds.), *Historicité et spatialité. Le problème de l'espace dans la pensée contemporaine*. Paris: Vrin, 2001, 97–116, 102.
40 Christian Grataloup. Géographie historique et analyse spatiale: de l'ignorance à la fertilisation croisée. Philippe Boulanger, Jean-René Trochet (eds.). *Où en est la géographie historique? Entre économie et culture*. Paris: L'Harmattan, 2005, 33–42: 40.

requires a good knowledge of its chronology, but this, I would add, is only possible thanks to the dating of pertinent objects and processes. In what follows I will apply this program to the urban space of Lyons. In this way, the present essay may be considered to fall within the scope of a "continued geography" that studies materiality in a way "from which a new history could follow", as Marcuzzi has proposed.[41] Benoist also insists on the importance of empiricism in the study of materiality.[42]

It is important to make clearer what the dating of reality actually signifies. Age is a sort of chronological depth, established from the present time (or another time, like, conventionally, the birth of Christ, to which is added the elapsed time between this moment and the present), itself in continued displacement. All objects have an age and, if they have not disappeared, constitute the present material space. All configurations of objects also have an age.

Dating the objects consists in measuring them with respect to a time of reference, generally the present (although this is not very practical because of its constant shifting), or in relation to the birth of Christ, the present being a cut in the arrow of time, and the future being largely unknowable. Dating an object makes it extant on a given duration in respect to the time of reference. This allows for the reconstitution of the materiality at a given moment – a present moment – cutting the time lines of all the objects whose existence is encountered at that moment. This is a conception of time that differs greatly from how time is often considered in urban history studies, where a succession of presents is adopted, reconstituted or made possible by extant maps and plans, and which is obviously made easier by the nature of the available historical documentation, especially maps. The hypothesis of a shifting present made of all the objects present at a given date has been tested here on the space of Lyons in its modern extension. This allows one to see phenomena that would otherwise be difficult to identify. In recent publications dealing with cosmology, the history of the universe is often represented with the shape of a sausage, with an origin point corresponding to the Big-bang at one extremity, and a transversal cut, the present time, at the other extremity. In the context of urban space, a material object like a construction-unit is equivalent to a piece of space and a time segment, a 'fibre' of the sausage, as it were, with a beginning point when its production

41 Max Marcuzzi. L'écriture de l'espace dans la Géographie physique de Kant. Jocelyn Benoist, Fabio Merlini (eds.), *Historicité et spatialité. Le problème de l'espace dans la pensée contemporaine*. Paris: Vrin, 2001, 117–139: 122; Jocelyn Benoist. En quoi la géographie peut-elle importer à la philosophie? Benoist, Merlini, *Historicité*, 97–116.

42 Benoist, Rompre, 226–227.

occurred, and an end point occurring when the object is destroyed, whether before the present or perhaps also in the future.[43] To model reality in this way makes it possible to produce a film of the lives of objects in a given perimeter and of the transformation of a material space, made of the production and appearing with new elements and from the destruction of previously existing ones.[44] Temporality, from this perspective, is made from a gathering of all the material objects present simultaneously in a geographical space.[45]

Time is investigated here with a view to drawing a parallel between a still poorly developed field of knowledge, the production of urban space, and other domains that have been formalized to a much greater extent, and are now considered 'hard' sciences, like biology, the sciences of evolution, and geology. Physics may have a different conception of time.[46] In what follows, I will present various empirical elements necessary to make this comparison. They will deal in a thorough way with aspects like cycles, relations between scales of time and scales of space, and the possibly shifting temporalities of separate domains of reality. My hypothesis is that some properties of the temporality of urban space can be better understood in the light of the natural sciences, and that, if this is confirmed, there is a continuity between the social science of urban space as human artefact and some natural sciences. In order to reach this goal, it is necessary to decompose the urban fabric into units that may be precisely located in time and space, and corresponding to clearly identifiable causal processes.

This analysis of urban space allows for the identification of phenomena that are otherwise difficult to discern and for a new understanding of the processes involved.[47] Urban material space is a continuum, but it is also made of discrete

43 Schwartz, *Bebauung*, 41: "A horizontal cut through history is a sort of concrete made of the remains of the past" cited in French translation ("une coupe horizontale à travers l'histoire est une sorte de béton constitué des restes du passé"), by Panos Mantziaras: Rudolf Schwartz et l'aménagement du territoire. Des principes topologiques pour une herméneutique de l'histoire. Benoist, Merlini, *Historicité*: 43.

44 Dagognet employs the film metaphor about geology, *Une épistémologie*, 107.

45 Schlögel, *Räume*, 48; 50.

46 Christophe Bouton, Philippe Huneman (eds), *Temps de la nature, nature du temps: études philosophiques sur le temps dans les sciences naturelles*, Paris: CNRS Editions, 2018 [*Nature of Time and the Time of nature. Philosophical Perspectives of Time in natural Sciences*, Cham: Springer International Publishing AG, 2015].

47 Bernard Gauthiez, Olivier Zeller. Lyons, the spatial analysis of a city in the seventeenth and eighteenth centuries. Locating and crossing data in a GIS built from written sources. Ekkehard Schönherr, Susanne Rau (eds.), *Mapping spatial relations, their perceptions and dynamics. The*

elements. Hence there is no continuous evolution, but only the accumulation of isolatable and singular facts, of some sort of *quanta* of produced space, showing acceleration, slowing down, and stasis moments in their production, all occurring at different scales. A better comprehension of this complexity is evidently one of the main aims of historicizing objects. The metaphor of cut fibres is of course imperfect. Two aspects at least are lacking in this image: the three dimensions of the material elements, and the fact that material space is not made just of material objects, but also of their properties, both physical and social. This will be clarified, notably when dealing later on with plot patterns and typology.

Another important fact about materiality is that we are very perceptive to its superficial or surface features. In our perception of things, the presence of recent objects is very strong: new coatings, tags, shop fronts, posters, urban furniture, asphalt paving, and so on. Considering a tree is quite interesting from this perspective. In an old tree, the oldest parts are hidden behind the annual growth rings and bark and may even have disappeared as the core rots away, whereas the more recent parts are generally the only ones visible. Similarly, in the case of urban materiality, some facts are only legible by the hole they have left behind; although they have disappeared, they are still very present (as examined in I.3.1).

Material space is not a succession of times, but an accumulation through time of material events that we have to individualize and discover, and which, once known, must be placed in relation to other events. The production of space has been poorly considered by philosophers, historians, geographers, with the notable exceptions of some individual objects generally considered to be particularly remarkable (castles, monuments, works of famous architects...), probably because of the particularity of the production moment. In the near absence of epistemological reflection on these subjects, I will begin by placing in time the empirical objects, before going on to question their relations to one another at pertinent times for the production urban material space, the complexity of which will be explored.

'Geographizing' in this context means the adoption of adequate concepts to map physical reality, in this instance a city. One should discard notions like that of a 'building',[48] or 'zone' because they are too vague and cannot always be mapped without ambiguity or attributed to clear causal social processes. As we will see, the choice of units that establish correspondences between social processes,

city of today and in the past. Cham, Heidelberg, New York, Dordrecht, London: Springer Verlag, 97–118.

48 This word is inescapable, unfortunately, so it will be frequently used below, with the meaning of functional unit or construction-unit.

constructed objects – parts of, whole ones, or groups of –, construction-units at the architectural scale, and planned developments at the urban planning scale, defined firstly as perimeters in which the materiality is transformed according to a given project, allows for such a precise and unequivocal mapping.[49] The concept of *plan-unit*, defined by Conzen in 1960, is still too morphographic to be unequivocal.[50] Scholars have produced maps based on it, but the precise limits of a plan unit are difficult to define. These maps may decompose urban space into units ranging from the very tiny to the rather large. This is why it is necessary to elaborate more fully the concept of the plan-unit. It is based on formal coherence and geometric differentiation from its surroundings, but one also has to take into account the material production of space generated by a dedicated social process, generally with precise spatial limits. The plan-unit includes units issued from single production processes, which have a form generally expressing their designed project, and units due to metamorphism and to a multiplicity of small events on a given area, like in the accretion process. The transformation of urban space requires examining its production-units, particularly at the scales of the planned developments and of the construction-units.

Other geographical objects appear from the mapping of these units, and these correspond to phenomena associating several constructions or planned developments over a period of longer duration. These objects can be qualified as emergent and will be examined in PART III.

The present study takes its principal source material from the city of Lyons, where I have lived for a long time and which I have used as a case study; but parallels will also be made with other cities and contexts. These parallels will help underline the fact that, while the source material can be very different depending on the varying contexts and cultures from which they are drawn, the conceptual construction can be applied to any urban site regardless of the historical period or culture.

---

49 Bernard Gauthiez. Des unités pertinentes pour mesurer la ville concrète. *Histoire et mesure*, XIX-3/4 (2004): 295–316.

50 Whitehand, *Background*, 13.

Part One: Spatializing and historicizing materiality

I.1 A historicization based on the decomposition of space into production units: the planned developments and the construction-units[1]

I.1.1 The production units and their scale

The materiality of urban space is produced at different scales corresponding to projects of varying nature. These scales can be classified in levels, which are, from the largest to the tiniest:

- Level 1:
  Planned developments (large) and big facilities: new towns, transport infrastructures (motorways, ports, railways, canals, airports, leisure resorts, etc.). Objects that can also be made of sites separated in space (examples: urban walls built on the orders of the King of France in April 1346 to fortify cities at Rouen, Tours, Lyons; the fortifications of the *Pré Carré* in northern France in the seventeenth century by royal military engineers like Vauban; linear technical networks like canals or motorways. Reference scale: between a few kilometers and several hundred meters.
- Level 2:
  Planned developments (common): new developments, redevelopments, housing estates, subdivisions, ZUP and ZAC in France (*Zones d'Urbanisation Prioritaire* and *Zones d'Aménagement Concerté*, acronyms that signify both the administrative procedure and the realized product. The same is true for *lotissement* in French and *subdivision* in American English). Reference scale: from the hectare to several hundreds of hectares.
- Level 3:
  Construction-units (large): ensembles of constructions issuing from a single process and conception, terraces,[2] facilities like schools, hospitals, etc., industrial plants, commercial centers. Reference scale: from one tenth of a hectare to a few hectares.

1 The expressions *construction-unit* and *building-unit* are here equivalent.

2 Several buildings constructed according to a same architectural project, and forming a construction-unit.

https://doi.org/10.1515/9783110623062-003

- Level 4:
  Construction-units (common): individual buildings, multi-familial dwellings, mono-familial houses, office buildings, generally mono-functional programs. Reference scale: from one are (100 m^2) to the hectare (10,000 m^2). The limit between Level 3 and Level 4 is often around 3,000 m^2 of site area (0.3 ha).
- Level 5:
  Construction-units (small): transformation of extant buildings: raisings, extensions, façade modifications, shop fronts. Reference scale: several meters in length, width, and height.
- Level 6:
  Big maintenance works: modification of openings, coating, rehabilitation, local technical networks.
- Level 7:
  Ephemeral and small objects: temporary settings, posters, awnings, cable fixings, street furniture, etc.

Some objects comprise several levels. This is especially true for the *grands ensembles*, large groups of buildings built in France and elsewhere in Europe after 1945, generally for social housing, which combine levels 2, 3, and 4 in the same conception and construction, thus integrating architectural and urban designs.[3] This was true as well in rarer previous realizations, examples of which are the town of Richelieu in 1631–35,[4] or the renewal of the Rue Impériale/de la République in Lyons, built in 1855–57.[5]

I.1.2 What is a construction-unit?

As we saw in the introduction, the construction-unit (a category of production unit) is the material object resulting from a building production process. In the built space, the duration of the building production process is determined largely by its complexity, the numbers of persons and institutions involved,

3 Paul Landauer. *L'invention du grand ensemble. La Caisse des dépôts maître d'ouvrage*. Paris: Picard, 2010. On the planned developments around Lyons from 1945 to 2005, Nicolas Ferrand. Approche morphologique de l'urbanisation: Lyon et son agglomération de 1945 à 2005: données, outils et méthodes. Lyons, Université Lyon 3 Jean-Moulin, 2010 (unpublished PhD dissertation).
4 Christine Toulier. *Richelieu, le château & la cité idéale*. Châteauroux: Berger M. Editions, 2005.
5 Bernard Gauthiez. *Entre Terreaux et Bellecour, architecture et urbanisme à Lyon au XIXe siècle*. Lyons: Editions lyonnaises d'art et d'histoire, 1999.

and the size of the object. To get to the production moment, a decision is necessary, associated with a project and a mental image that will eventually be drawn on a sheet of paper or a computer screen. The decision bears in mind the utility of the project, a utility that can be functional, i.e., with a view to meeting some need; this, in any case, is the explanation generally given for a new production of space. But other utilities are rarely absent, even if they are less often evoked and sometimes left unsaid:

- *Profit-making, material or financial.* Without profit, very few material productions would have occurred. Forms of profit-making include: rents and leases, returns on invested capital for a private developer, and the facilitation of economic exchanges and attraction of private investments for public authorities.
- *Symbolic profit or capital.*[6] This may be defined as the glorification of a person or of a group and may be achieved through various techniques: aesthetics, the use of particular technologies, imagibility and visibility,[7] or the simple fact of realizing something considered as an end in itself. Consider the following examples. To put a viaduct on a motorway is an engineering decision, but it also gives prestige to its designers and makers (and is therefore often used in the communication of the company involved).[8] The design of an architectural façade shows the know-how of an architect and his aesthetic orientation, thereby advertising his skills both to potential investors and to the public. Visibility in public space can also be an important aim. A construction is potentially exposed to the eyes of anyone, and may thus give public existence to a politician, a developer, a designer, an architect, the contractors, or a common proprietor. This inscription in public space sometimes has a very high cost and may even be the underlying aim of the production, with functionality being merely the pretext for the project: high-rise offices magnifying a company, buildings that resemble sculptures,[9] as is the case in the Guggenheim Museum in Bilbao and others, immense castles like Versailles, public buildings that express the nation as in Washington, magnificent temples like at St Peter's in Rome and in antiquity.

6 Pierre Bourdieu. *Raisons pratiques.* Paris: Seuil, 1994, 161.

7 Kevin Lynch. *The image of the city.* Cambridge, Mass.: The MIT Press, 1960.

8 For examples the bridges of Gustave Eiffel or "the Titans motorway" ("Autoroute des Titans", Motorway A 40 between Lyons and Geneva) made of several impressive bridges and tunnels across the Jura Mountains. See Samuel C. Florman. *The existential pleasures of engineering.* London: Souvenir Press, 1994 [1976], 119–126.

9 Robert Venturi, Denise Scott-Brown, Steven Izenour. *Learning from Las Vegas.* Cambridge, Mass.: The MIT Press, 1977.

The rationality of production is never dictated only by need and utility. It always includes aesthetic and material choices, and a semiotic and symbolic dimension that can be predominant.[10] Discerning the respective role of these generally entangled dimensions can be very difficult. As we have just seen, for some productions the dimension of functionality becomes secondary and their semiotic dimension comes to dominate, in association with important technical means and financial investment. When this concerns public buildings and constructions financed with questionable funds, their irruption in public space becomes a political question that can give rise to strong debate or opposition. The balance of powers between groups with divergent interests thus appears in urban space through the expression of different programmatic conceptions of the same object or through the juxtaposition of objects with opposed or contrasting meanings. The erection of an electrical pylon in a mountain range and its taking over of the landscape will be considered by its designers as a source of pride, because their professional culture gives value to technicity and building difficulty, but groups keen to limit anthropic intrusions in areas that have thus far been minimally modified and are thus perceived as natural will see in the same realization a social and aesthetic violence, the symbol of a technocratic domination. Many productions express just such a domination, and its attending symbolic, political and economic violence, simply because they are realized for the material and/or semiotic profit of some persons, groups, or institutions, having at their disposal the means to impose a new entity in space. Even a banal bourgeois building carries a semiotic charge, and can be perceived – and indeed will be perceived – by a poor person as the expression of an unjust domination or appropriation of wealth. To all power there corresponds a particular expression in space, often thanks to the appropriation of means used to maintain or enhance symbolic capital. This is sometimes clearly legible in the city space, as is the case regarding the Fourvière Hill in Lyons where, from the 1870s onwards, the Catholics erected a huge basilica to express their strong position in urban society (the same thing occurred in Paris with Montmartre Church and in Barcelona with the Sagrada Familia Church), soon to be countered by the laics, who in 1894 promoted the building of a nearby tower made of metal, copying at a reduced scale the Tour Eiffel in Paris. In the last analysis, our societies are permeated with this need to express an identity, and couldn't function as they do without their semiotic expression in architectural and urban space.

---

10 Barthes. *L'aventure sémiologique*, 261–271. Soja associates functionalism to a historicism that can be qualified as too univocal (Edward W. Soja. *Postmodern geographies. The reassertion of space in critical social theory.* London, New York: Verso, 1989, 32).

Once the project is decided, secondary processes take place to assure its financing, its conception, and the finding of space, when needed. These stages have to be accomplished and each of them determines some aspects of the final realization:

- *The conception/design* is made of aesthetic choices, but also of technical and functional ones, depending on the financing secured.[11] Financing, as Wilk has observed, is crucial if we are "to understand decision-making in housing".[12] In complex projects, the conception is a long process and the initial drawing is often modified, sometimes through competitions. In the La Défense business quarter near Paris, many projects were drawn and discussed over several decades from 1919 (a first competition), until the realization eventually began in 1958. When this phase occurred, the rest of the still undeveloped area was again and again redesigned to answer the needs of a changing real estate market and of changing architectural fashion, until the entire quarter was completed in the late 1980s (even if some replacements and densification have occurred since then, and the perimeter has been extended).
- *The development or building site* may already be available, providing an immediate opportunity to develop, or it may need to be found and acquired. It has a cost and constrains the possibilities because of the shape of the plot, the nature of the ground, and of the built and natural environments located within and around it. The zoning and planning by-laws must be respected, but in certain circumstances they can also be adapted to the project provided the right political will is present (planning laws in France nowadays allow for such modifications to take place quite easily, for example, in order to build a tower or to facilitate a redevelopment). The constraints of the extant surrounding buildings and environment limit the possibility of working with the tabula rasa dreamed of by the moderns. The larger the area available, the more this is possible, and the juncture with the surround-

---

11 These means can consist, in societies that are less technically developed, and that are either weakly monetarized or not monetarized at all, in the labour force, know-how and time, and material resources of all sorts.

12 Richard R. Wilk. The built environment and consumer decisions. Susan Kent (ed.). *Domestic architecture and the use of space, an interdisciplinary cross-cultural study.* Cambridge: Cambridge University Press, 1990, 34–42: 35: "To understand decision-making in housing, we should not begin with a grand, overarching theory of the complex balance of function, aesthetics, meaning, and social position. Instead we should study the full range of human factors that affect decisions to buy, design, build, alter, improve, sell and destroy houses, to see people themselves achieve a balance through an interaction of cultural knowledge and pragmatic action".

ings is, even today, rarely an important consideration in new developments. Moreover, a project can require secondary realizations within its perimeter (demolitions, de-pollution, etc.), as well as beyond it (water mains and other networks, a new road for a dam, housing for building workers and other staff, etc.).

- *The technical means* also have a cost, which constrains their use. They also require know-how, available materials and competent builders. Their choice depends on the construction in question: traditionally buildings were realized in earth, wood or stone, but metal was in the nineteenth and twentieth centuries often favoured for its elegance in America, and raw concrete was the material of choice in twentieth-century France.

It is important to insist on the remarkable moment when the production is carried-out, when a material object emerges from abstract considerations. This singular moment cannot occur without the following:

- A form dictated by typology (see Part II) and/or designed by a professional.
- An energy investment, whether in financial form or as a workforce.
- The materials gathered and prepared.
- A site or plot.
- A social organization and its temporalities capable of carrying out the production process.
- Various types of know-how.
- And, of course, people, with their varied personalities.

This explains why urban space does not evolve in a continuous way, but in small or large quanta.

I.1.3 Dating issues

Building works all have their particularities. They often require the temporary use of public space, sometimes with great intensity, which is a cause of nuisances and ephemeral installations.

The production of a new object in urban space is a very singular moment in the transformation of material space, but one that has been inadequatly studied as such.[13] It involves specific agents answering a particular decision (discussed

13 Susan Kent. Activity areas and architecture: an interdisciplinary view of the relationship between use of space and domestic built environments. Susan Kent (ed.). *Domestic architecture*

or not) and implies the disappearing or clearing of a space section, which is to be filled with a newly configured materiality. To measure the importance of a new production and its actual effects requires each process to be individually identified, located precisely in time, and compared to the given space section before and after its modification. This is probably why the systematic study of urban space in this way is difficult and time-consuming, and has only rarely been carried out.[14]

Henri Lefebvre had recourse to the forces of social groups and of politico-economic systems to try to explain the production of space, but he put aside the real people and organizations at work and the analysis of circumstances. Moreover, if one keeps analysis at this level of generalization, the mechanisms present in the individual processes do not appear, and neither does their complexity or the fact that the production of space is carried out by only a fraction of a given society, with its own interests. This will be studied in Part III.

The production duration of a construction-unit or of a planned development, a concept I will soon examine, is not a point on a time line, but it is nevertheless generally perceived as a short moment. In a given area, the urban fabric is on the whole essentially immobile most of the time and changes only by fractions at limited moments. The transformation occurs by units on limited portions of space. Sometimes, these portions are so large as to be impossible to grasp in their entirety in the field, as in the case of a motorway, for example. The duration of the production phase is about one year or two for a simple building, and a few years for a transportation facility. It can last a few decades for a planned development or redevelopment, but here the whole is produced by elements corresponding to separate processes, concerning only a part of the whole area. In total, the proportion of time dedicated to transformation compared to immobility is about 1/100 – 200th for a building (one or two years of construction compared to one to three centuries of life duration), 1/10th for an urban setting like the Ter-

and the use of space, an interdisciplinary cross-cultural study. Cambridge: Cambridge University Press, 1990, 1–8. In her otherwise very well informed and profound review of the study of the relations between architecture and the use of space, Susan Kent maintained a common view of architecture as a given, never as a produced environment, and never questioned its production. This view is also still widely accepted among anthropologists.

14 Whitehand, Recent developments, 288; Gauthiez, Zeller, Spatial analysis. Alongside my study of Lyons, I have also investigated the Piazza Navona area in Rome. The comparison of the two sites, smaller in Rome, very large in Lyons, allowed for some interesting improvements to the questions asked and the methodology employed, Bernard Gauthiez. Les logiques multiples de la production de l'espace d'un quartier: l'exemple de la place Navone à Rome, 1450-1870. Jean-François Bernard (ed.). *Du stade de Domitien à la place Navone, histoire d'un quartier de Rome.* Rome: Ecole Française de Rome, 2014, 325–383.

reaux square in Lyons (buildings constructed from 1646 to about 1675, redevelopment of the west side in 1858–1859), and 1/20th for medieval subdivisions still extent today, as in the case of Florence.[15]

The production process, as we saw above, can be decomposed into several secondary processes, which are chronologically separate and which can overlap, but obey the same command chain, and which possess their own logics. Ideally, each of these secondary processes has to be characterized by means of archival recordings of past realizations. Recent projects can be characterized through the planning documents made by the builders, the plans and sketches of the architects, as well as material from other technical design offices and consultants, but also from the contractors. Hence, mapping the date of production requires one to make a choice, as the duration of the production process is not zero. Pragmatically, for the construction-units, I opted mainly for the date of the building permit, as it was generally the only systematic information available, because the issue of the permit was with only a few exceptions rapidly followed by the construction (the duration of the process will be examined Part III), but also because information regarding the duration of the construction process is available in only a very limited number of instances. Another possibility available in the case of Lyons is, starting in 1840, to use the dates recorded in the cadastre registers, where new buildings are annotated as 'CN' (*construction nouvelle*, meaning 'new construction').

As the building authorization corresponds to the moment just before construction and the cadastral date to the moment just after it, they are usually only one or two years apart for any building before the twentieth century, though sometimes more, for some large buildings are usable only several years after the beginning of the construction work. Others are built in distinct phases which can be dated separately and individualized on the map. It is also possible to take into account the authorization of the new planned developments.

The sources for dating the construction-units in Lyons in the seventeenth-twentieth centuries are:

- Before construction:
  1 – Architecture and construction projects.
  2 – Property changes that often intervene prior to the modification/construction, notarial archives: Archives Départementales (Rhône Département's archive, hence ADR).

15 Giovanni Fanelli. *Firenze*. Laterza: Rome-Bari, 1980. The houses in the subdivisions were built over a duration of several decades.

- Before construction (a few days or weeks before):
  3 – Building authorizations (changing denomination in time: *autorisation d'alignement* before the twentieth century): Archives Municipales de Lyon (Lyons Municipal Archive, hence AML), continued series from 1617 to the present, with some interruptions in the record between 1763 and 1789. Rare plans bearing building permits for dates before 1852 (AML, 1774–1790). *Permis de construire* from 1943 (AML and ADR).
- Construction under way:
  4 – Progress of works, given every month in the review *La Construction Lyonnaise* (1879–1914).
  5 – Compensation for setting back, as is owed by the city when one has to reconstruct a building according to a set-back frontage line. The creation of new land separate from the plot to enlarge public space is generally paid for when the ground-floor is built (AML, varied series, seventeenth to nineteenth centuries).
- During and after construction:
  6 – Comparison of aerial photographs, for example from the French Institut Géographique National (IGN, mainly after 1945) and from Google Earth (from circa 2000).
- After construction:
  7 – Censuses which indicate when a building is inhabited and used, as sometimes already begins when the first floors are built (municipal annual censuses AML, 1814–1847; state censuses every five years, ADR, 1831–1936).[16]
  8 – Epigraphy, generally when the building is finished (rare remaining occurrences before the mid-nineteenth century, more frequent later).
  9 – Newly constructed and demolished buildings, when the change appears in the register of built properties for taxation purposes (cadastre: ADR, at Lyons registers from c.1840).
  10 – Comparison of successive maps. This gives the *terminus post quem* an object was constructed (Plan Topographique de la Ville de Lyon and its successive versions after 1860, scales of 1/5,000th, 1/2,000th and 1/500th; topographical maps: Military, Institut Géographique National, scale of 1/20,000th before 1945, 1/25,000th afterwards).
  11 – Rare plans of urban areas in archives bearing a date relative to the con-

16 The state censuses from 1951 to the present are not available because the administrative record at the building's scale is open to the public only after 70 years.

struction or the buying of the land determined by a new alignment to enlarge public space.

I.2 Dating, use-lengths, inertia: analyses of the urban space of Lyons

This conceptualization of both materiality and production processes, carried-out in reality and described in the written record, has determined units which can be used to break down and understand the role of time in the space we live in. To illustrate the understanding of the place of time in space, (i. e., the constitution of materiality made of pieces produced at given moments and the simultaneity in the present of objects produced in the past and still extant) several mappings are possible. As we will see, these mappings lead to new elements of comprehension of the present space and to new questions. In a way, the maps are a test of the hypothetical model developed above. As the quantity of data necessary to do the mapping are huge, I have limited the analyses to the Level 2 and Levels 3–4–5 of production units, which commonly correspond to urban and architectural scales.

I.2.1 Dating planned developments (Level 1 and 2 production units)

A planned development is here considered as the portion of space produced in a planning at the Level 1 or Level 2 scale. A planned development can be defined spatially by:[17]

- A perimeter (this is generally easy to recognize for a housing estate or subdivision, but can be more difficult, for example, if one deals with the buildings drawn according to a given by-law or an alignment plan).
- An area of transformation of the previous reality within the perimeter.
- A design and a program: composition of the plot-pattern, of the streets and public space, eventually the production of the buildings in a single conception (for example, by the same operator as the planned development), or when a by-law fixes the dimensions and other elements of the buildings produced: height, dimension in regard to street width, regulation of projecting balconies, and so on.

17 The categories of planned developments are defined in Gauthiez, *Espace urbain*, 53–87.

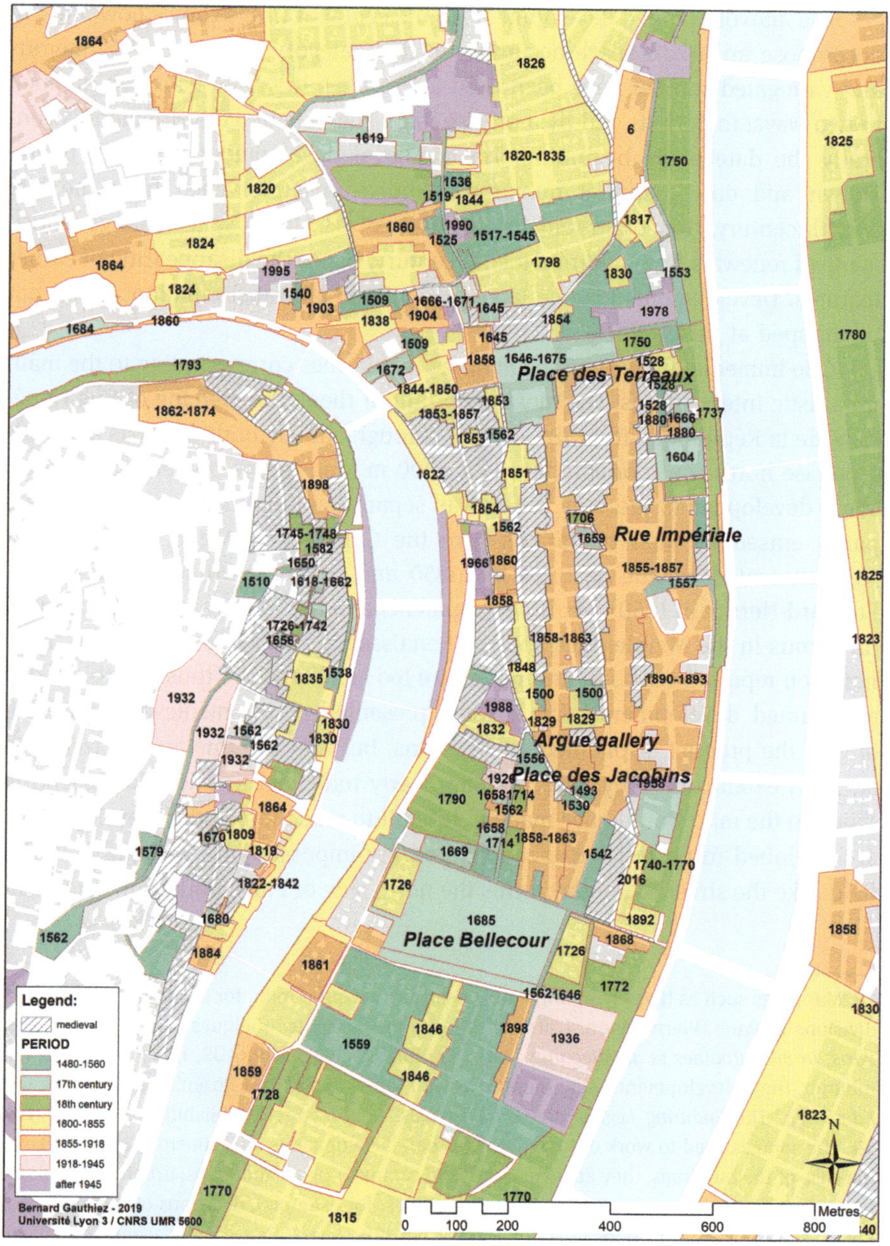

Figure I.1 Dating of planned developments in the center of Lyons, present state
The planned developments are mapped according to their area. The main part of the city may be decomposed in such objects. For the period before 1480, the urban fabric can be qualified as metamorphic, as planned developments of that period remain only as vestiges and as buildings produced in their perimeters have generally been reconstructed once or twice.

The map of planned developments in the center of Lyons shows how one can decompose an urban space according to this category of objects.[18] Numerous and variegated sources have been used to establish it.[19] Date has been mapped in two ways: in periods and by a precise date. The date of a development is generally the date of its beginning. The medieval developments are still poorly known and dated, and, if numerous subdivisions intervened from the late twelfth century, they often remain only as vestiges. Urban space change is also made of renewals from mid-nineteenth century, hence the disappearing of earlier features. Developments may be large or small, so all transformations could not be mapped at this scale.

One immediately sees on the map the regularities corresponding to the main urbanistic interventions. The most important of them, the piercing of Rue Impériale/de la République from 1853 to 1857 through already built-up areas and with a precise north-south orientation, is a 1,200 m long redevelopment.[20] However, some developments are only present as separate remnants because they were partly erased by later operations (like the Galerie de l'Argue, completed in 1832, truncated by Rue de Brest in c.1850 and cut into two segments by Rue Edouard-Herriot in 1860). Many developments anterior to the eighteenth century, numerous in the Middle Ages and the Renaissance periods (see Fig. III.8), have not been represented, as their remains are too small and are thus illegible today as planned developments. The areas represented as of 'medieval origin' are largely the product of planned subdivisions, but they are 'metamorphized'[21] to such an extent that they have become nearly indistinct as such. Representing them on the map would have made it difficult to read. Some other developments are englobed in posterior realizations and are impossible to distinguish in the field, like the street that today forms the north side of Place Bellecour, establish-

---

18 Mappings such as these have only rarely been carried out. Pinon, for example, mapped subdivisions in Paris (Pierre Pinon. L'archéologie des lotissements: quelques exemples parisiens. *Paris, formes urbaines et architectures*. Paris: Editions Recherche/IPRAUS, 1998, 15–28). In Edinburgh, the redevelopments were mapped by Jim Johnson and Lou Rosenburg. *Renewing Old Edinburgh. The Enduring Legacy of Patrick Geddes*. Argyll: Argyll Publishing, 2010, 138–139.

19 The sources used to work out the date of urban developments are numerous and, unlike in the case of the buildings, they are generally quite complex: plans and maps, urban morphology, plan units, files in the municipal archives (street files, for example), decisions of the municipal board, series of authorizations of subdivisions from 1919, later Zones d'Aménagement Concerté (ZAC), Zones d'Urbanisation Prioritaire (ZUP), etc. (AML, ADR, Archives de l'Equipement, Archives du Grand-Lyon after 1969).

20 *Rue* in French means street in English, and *Place* means square. From now on, the French words will be used throughout the text.

21 Here, the buildings have been either deeply transformed or rebuilt once or twice.

ed in 1562 at the latest, whose north side became the limit of the square established in the late seventeenth century, or like Place des Jacobins, created in 1557, enlarged in 1822 toward the south, and again in 1860 to the north and north-east when the Rue Edouard-Herriot was built. Each realization is conceived with a certain amount of spatial autonomy that sometimes makes it possible to propose a date through consideration of its aesthetics (width, disposition of squares, symmetry, etc.), its geometric properties as a plan-unit, and its more or less articulated connection with the surrounding conserved space. Rue de la République runs north-south, a characteristic that makes it quite distinct from its direct urban environment, and probably obeys a principle of universalism, as it is not fully determined by the local constraints. This orientation also dictates the lines, parallel and perpendicular, of the other minor streets traced in the same development (Rue de la Bourse, Place de la Bourse and Place des Cordeliers, Rue Childebert, Rue Jean-de-Tournes, Rue Sala).[22] At the same time, it is also carefully articulated with the remains of the blocks through which it cuts. It is also carefully articulated with Place de la Comédie, with an opening to the north right between the Grand Theatre and the City Hall. The intention here was to connect the new street, planned as an extension of the business center, with its extant heart around Place de la Comédie. To the south, its bending after Place de la République is due to the fact that on this segment it is made of a widening of Rue Bellecordière, an extant street, conserving its east front but considerably enlarging it to the west. In doing so, the new street aperture proceeds towards the east side of Place Bellecour, which continues the same line.[23]

As time passes, new realizations tend sometimes to continue and develop patterns already established by previous developments. Rue Hippolyte-Flandrin, a subdivision realized in 1509, was prolonged in 1844 to the south between Rue d'Algérie and Rue de Constantine by the Rue d'Oran. To the north, its axis, with a change of orientation after the demolition of the Déserte convent in 1822, became the axis of the Place de Sathonay development area, prolonged in 1858 to the north through a part of the Jardin des Plantes (botanical garden) by the Rue du Jardin-des-Plantes and a monumental sculpture in the remaining part of the garden. Place de Sathonay was established on the site of a women's convent, *La Déserte*, whose south church portal had dictated the axis of Rue Hippolyte-Flandrin when it was developed in 1509. This complex composition, made of

---

22 Immediately after, in 1858–1860, Rue Edouard-Herriot was pierced exactly parallel to Rue de la République.

23 Hence the presence in this place of older buildings, and the transfer of the street name Bellecordière to the Rue Bourchanin, whose name disappeared.

carefully thought out articulations, is important in the current urban landscape. It is a good example of a composite object made of successive realizations reinterpreting the previous elements to which they are attached and giving then a new signification and a new utility.[24]

The size of a development tells us about the means available at a given time to intervene in extant or new urban space. For every development, we have to uncover information about its aims, the operators, the program in terms of plots, functions and architectural content,[25] the technical and financial input, and the symbolic profit in terms of image improvement and political gain.

I.2.2 Dating the plot pattern

As we will see (I.3.3), in its legal and social nature, the plot pattern in not visible, for it is not in itself a material object. But this legal and social nature induces very strong material effects because of its strong social significance, defining as it does the limits of distinct properties. Its inertia is very high through time, because, once established, it is controlled by its tenants and proprietors, and therefore all new urban modifications have to respect it. Fusions and divisions of existing plots conserve its general pattern. This is why it is often used, and is of a great value, for the studies of the transformation of space in urban and rural studies. It can be, on rare occasions, fully erased on a given area, the plot pattern of which may then be reconfigured. Regroupings of properties (*remembrements* in French) are rare events and exceptionally occurred more than once in the same place in the long-term.[26] Urban renewal provides another occasion for erasing plot patterns. This occurred in many cities after World War I in northern France and World War II in Europe. The Barbican Estate in London is a case in point.[27] Transforming the plot pattern became possible in modern Europe only when a suitable legal framework had developed. This happened in France

---

24 Gauthiez, *Espace urbain*, 267.

25 This can include the production of buildings, the conception of which is included in the program of a planned development, or drawn according to specific regulations, and the general frame of urbanistic by-laws.

26 For example, when some medieval areas have been erased to build a new fortification belt around a city in the modern period, a space again redeveloped in the late nineteenth century or early twentieth like at St-Quentin in northern France (Jean-Louis Collart. Saint-Quentin. *Revue archéologique de Picardie* 16 (1999). Special issue: Archéologie des villes, démarches et exemples en Picardie, 67–128, Pl. IX), or in the famous Ring of Vienna.

27 Jennifer Clarke. *The Barbican Sitting on History.* London: Corporation of London Records Office, 1990.

for the first time at Rennes, after a large urban fire in 1720, when over ten hectares were erased and fully redesigned.[28] A little earlier, the Great Fire of London in 1666 (15,000 houses burnt),[29] and the fire that destroyed Dieppe in France in 1694 after a joint English-Lower Countries bombing (1,800 houses burnt),[30] led to only slight adjustments of the city layout, with streets made regular in width through setbacks and compulsory use of bricks or stones in the frontages and party walls.

All new buildings and developments in our societies are framed in and by the plot pattern, and this has been so for centuries. This is due to by-laws, legal constraints in relation to neighbors, jurisdictional use limitations in the context of aristocratic or religious estates or long leases.

To date the plot pattern means actually to date the plot limits, and not the plots themselves. The proprietor may change, but, morphologically, only the limits are subject to change. Excepting re-developments, new limits appear only when there occurs a subdivision (secondary limits) of an extant plot, whose previous perimeter limits are kept (primary limits). Limits disappear only when a fusion of plots occurs. New subdivisions may appear after a fusion/regrouping, thus offering scope for reorganizing the spatial setting. To study the plot pattern change, one generally uses the cadastral maps or similar documents, like the Ordnance Survey maps or the nineteenth century Tithe maps in England, which describe a synchronic situation at a given moment in history. By comparison with successive maps one may identify the changes. A more precise dating can only rely on the notarial documentation and deeds. To obtain information pertaining to all the changes occurring to the plots in a given area in a given period is a huge task, which can be especially long and difficult when the notarial records are not in the same place and when no map is available to represent the

---

28 Claude Nières. L'Incendie et la reconstruction de Rennes. Jean Meyer (ed.). *Histoire de Rennes*. Toulouse: Privat, 1972, 213.

29 Neil Hanson. *The great fire of London: in that apocalyptic year, 1666*. Hoboken: John Wiley and Sons, 2002.

30 Jules Thieury. *Projets de M. le maréchal de Vauban pour fortifier la ville de Dieppe (1694-1699)*. Chez A.Marais, 1864. The bombing of Dieppe prompted the bombing of Brussels by the French in 1695, which likewise gave rise to a fire that destroyed about 4,500 houses. The city was rebuilt according to the same plot pattern (Frank Daelemans. Les répercussions du bombardement de 1695 sur la population. Arlette Smolar-Meynart (ed.). *Autour du bombardement de Bruxelles de 1695, désastre et relèvement, Bulletin du Crédit Communal*, 199 (1997), 54; Maurice Culot, Eric Hennaut, Maris Demanet, Caroline Mierop. *Le bombardement de Bruxelles par Louis XIV et la reconstruction qui s'en suivit 1695-1700*. Bruxelles: Archives d'Architecture Moderne, 1992.

transformations.[31] This is certainly why nobody, to my knowledge at least, has ever attempted to map the changes over a large area and a long period at the plot and year scale. The number of deeds on a single area, corresponding to the changes arising from transactions, is considerably higher than the number of construction-units, even if the actual plot changes are smaller in number, for many deeds correspond only to changes in tenancy and ownership.

On the whole, the duration of the limits of a plot can be considerably longer than the duration of the construction it bears. But this remains to be statistically established. In European cities (in Italy, France, England), scholars consider that the plot pattern was generally rather well conserved from the Middle Ages to the redevelopments of the nineteenth and twentieth centuries. Conservation on a period approaching 1,000 years is documented for some areas, such as Dublin.[32] The cadastre maps only depict states of the plot pattern, generally separated by a long space of time (in France, the first cadastre maps were drawn in the early nineteenth century following a law in 1807. They were in some instances replaced by new maps in the 1930s, and new cadastres were established from the 1970s, and are now fully digitalized). They represent good examples of cuttings in our time sausage, although only the notarial record allows for the reconstruction of the plot 'fibres'. I know of no mapping of the precise dates of a given area's plot limits. A dating covering three periods has been made for the Geneva Canton and for the River Giers Valley near St-Etienne in France, using cadastre and topographical maps from about 1800, from 1945 or earlier, and late twentieth or early twenty-first century maps.[33]

I.2.3 Dating construction-units (Level 3, 4 and 5 production units)

Dating the built-up fabric is difficult when one wants to consider only a 'principal date', which is what many have done previously. This is because the urban

---

31 In some rare cases, a plan may exhibit the plot limits at two different dates, like on the *mappes* of the area around Geneva made in the mid-eighteenth century (Archives d'Etat du Canton de Genève).

32 Anngret Simms, *Howard B. Clarke*, Raymond Gillespie (eds.). *Irish Historic Towns Atlas, vol. II: Maynooth, Downpatrick, Bray, Kilkenny, Fethard, Trim*. Dublin: Royal Irish Academy, 2005.

33 André Corboz, Alain Léveillé, Yves Cassani, Marie-Paule Mayor, Isabelle Toumi-Overney, Paul Hirschi. *Atlas du territoire genevois. Permanences et modifications cadastrales aux XIXe et XXe siècles*. Geneva: Georg, 1993-99, 4 vols. Guillaume Sodezza. Héritage et patrimoine dans l'aménagement de la vallée du Giers, vers la définition d'une nouvelle politique patrimoniale pour l'espace stéphanois. Lyons: unpublished PhD thesis, Université Lyon 3 Jean Moulin, 2014.

fabric is then considered as an accumulation of integrated units,[34] generally defined as *édifices* (a unit adopted by the French *Inventaire*).[35] This unit is certainly quite useful for understanding the functionality of a territorial unit made of buildings and accompanied by open spaces and outbuildings,[36] but its unity is fragile, as it is subject to architectural and functional modifications, as occurs when a new use replaces a previous one or when the material difference between an ideal first edifice and its descendants grows significant over time. The pioneering urban study of the Quartier des Halles in Paris in the 1960s opted for this structuralist and functionalist approach. But this led to a dead-end when the dating of the building was attempted.[37] Another difficulty also emerged: it is often very difficult to identify events affecting constructions which are obviously old, but which are coated with plaster and lack decorations. This is particularly the case when the archival record of the building authorizations has disappeared or never existed, as is the case when such authorizations were not compulsory.

The difficulty of the *édifice* concept is overcome when one dates the construction-unit, and of course when the latter can be inferred from written or archaeological data. An *édifice* is principally defined by its function, which may require varying spaces and may vary itself. A construction-unit is defined by the material realization of a project of building, part of building or group of buildings. Therefore, the construction-units, when appropriately documented, are spatially identifiable without ambiguity, which is not the case for an *édifice*. The mapping of the construction-units is particularly effective at making visible those units whose perimeter is different from one another, as I have chosen to do

34 Such a dating was attempted in Françoise Boudon, André Chastel, Hélène Couzy, Françoise Hamon. *Système de l'architecture urbaine. Le quartier des halles à Paris*. Paris: Centre National de la Recherche Scientifique, 2 vols, 1977, 66 – 68, but the sources did not allow for detailed results. See also Bernard Gauthiez. Un inventaire, des inventaires. *Secteurs sauvegardés, ZPPAUP et PLU patrimoniaux, actes du séminaire de Chinon*. Paris: Association nationale des villes et pays d'art et d'histoire et des villes à secteur sauvegardé et protégés/Ministère de la Culture et de la Communication, 2007, 121 – 128.

35 An equivalent is the National Inventory of Architectural Heritage in Ireland, or the National Monuments Record in England.

36 The *édifice* is "a building or a group of buildings used for the same function and constructed on the same plot or tenement" (*L'édifice est un bâtiment ou un groupe de bâtiments affectés à une même fonction-destination et construits sur un terrain d'un seul tenant qui constitue le fonds*), Michel Melot, Hélène Verdier (eds.). *Principes, méthode et conduite de l'inventaire général*. Paris: Ministère de la Culture et de la Communication, 2001, 29.

37 Boudon, Chastel, Couzy, Hamon. *Système de l'architecture*, I, 67.

Figure I.2A Dating of construction-units, center of Lyons, present state
A: dating by periods

here.[38] Another difficulty emerges when one wants to map the addition of floors (raisings), as in that case two construction-units can be perfectly superimposed. Here the solution is to use a more precise scale, and to classify the raisings in a different layer in the Geographic Information System (see II.1.1), mapped for example by hatched superimposition. On Figure I.2B, the scale doesn't allow for the legibility of the superimposed units, so they have been indicated only by adding a complementary date to the area concerned. The mapping of tiny modifications, including multiple raisings (fortunately quite rare), can be complex; but then complex mapping only translates a complex material reality.[39]

The map of the construction-units in the central area of Lyons reveals various salient features. The largest construction-unit in the center of the city is exceptional in size. It is made of the buildings constructed by the Société Anonyme de la Rue Impériale along the Rue de la République (then Rue Impériale) in 1855 to 1857, constituting about 4,000 meters of frontages (of which only 670 meters, i.e., seventeen percent, were built by other operators). It was conceived and produced as a sophisticated whole by the same operator, under the planning direction of the architect Benoît Poncet, and it involved the fusion of architectural and urbanistic levels (Levels 2, 3 and 4). This urban construction-unit is possibly the largest produced in France in the nineteenth century. Conversely, the smallest construction-units in this area of the city have an area of only a few tens of square meters, comprising whole new buildings and new frontages with a thickness of two-three meters built after the cutting of previous façades as the consequence of a setback. To understand these differences, it is important to realize that the circumstances of these productions, their social and economic scope, and their aesthetic impact, is in principle independent of the size of the produc-

38 See the dating of the buildings in the atlas of Vienna, to which the present work on Lyons is comparable (Manfred Wehdorn (ed.). *Baualtersplan Wien-innere Stadt.* Vienna: Freytag&Berndt, 2011).

39 In the map Figure I.2, the date is when the authorization was given, or when the works were achieved. XV means a gothic style before 1540, XVI a classical Renaissance style between c. 1540 and 1599. Somme additional information is given: (/) = a time lag between different works; (–) = the duration of works; (s) = a raising of one floor or more; (r) = repairs (notably after the siege of 1793); (f) = a transformation of the façade; (m) = an unspecified important modification; (av) = a construction at the maximum a few years before the date. The main sources utilized are:
- AML, DD registers; AML, 315 WP series (building permits by street, 1850 – 1900), 316 WP series (building permits 1790 – 1848), 321 WP series (censuses).
- ADR: registers of the cadastre.
- Epigraphy (dates; initials of the owners).
- AML, suppressed commune of La Guillotière, 4 WP80 series, building permits before 1852. A few dates are from bibliographical sources.

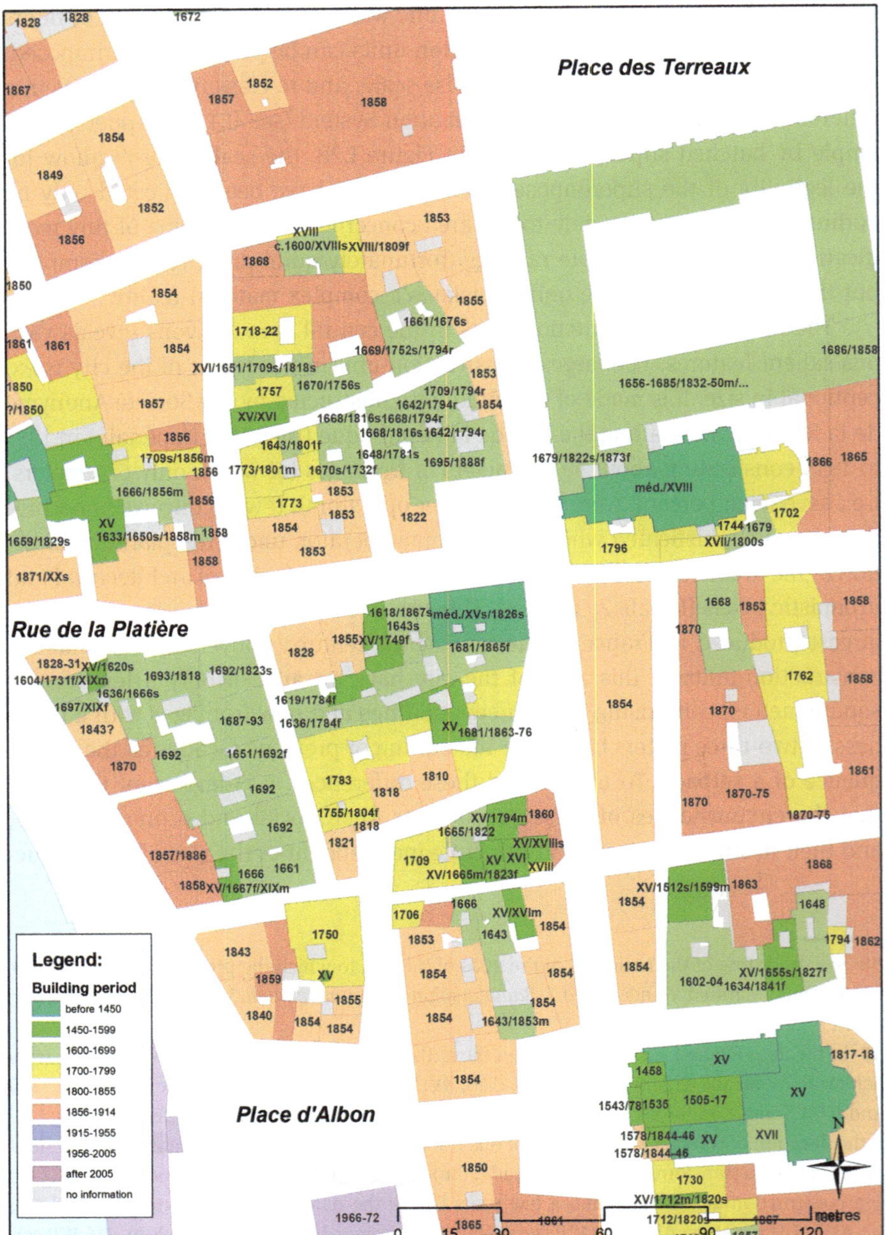

Figure I.2B Dating of construction-units, center of Lyons, present state
B: detail with explanation of the modifications
Each construction-unit, and its principal transformations, has been dated according to the data collected. To understanding these modifications, a characterization of the transformations is given between brackets. This a state of the knowledge, as the visits in old buildings and a closer examination of some frontages can make identify older phases or construction.

tion, and it is necessary to invidualize it if we are to understand both the past and present materialities of urban space.[40] Of course, the huge scale of some construction-units has to be fully understood and analysed. Part III will deal with the complexity this implies.

It is not always possible to establish very precisely the dates of a building made of several construction-units. The archaeology of the building tells us that, when studying an old building, one can often find older structures, for example medieval ones, hidden by more recent ones. The later transformations have often led to the modernization of an older construction, in order to give it functional adequacy and a contemporary look. This is particularly true when the façades are coated by plaster, which certainly makes analysis more difficult. The dating of the load-bearing elements, often the oldest, is impossible without peeling away their skin. The only material datum then available to estimate the date, in the absence of archival records, is the form of the building and the technical aspects of the construction.

Variable piers between windows and variations in the layout of the windows at different floors of the same house can suggest a succession of units, the addition of floors for example, or, when the spacing of the windows varies in different parts of the façade, the fusion of neighboring buildings covered by a new homogeneous façade. This occurred in many buildings in Rome, which were united and enveloped in a new façade so as to produce aristocratic mansions (*palazzi*). Transformations can also concern old prestigious buildings. The example of many municipal buildings in the Italian communes is well known, some of which have been extensively restored and homogenized in the late nineteenth and early twentieth centuries. On the whole the uniting of separate extant buildings behind a common new façade impacts properties whose owners did not have enough money to carry out a new and total construction, or didn't want it. This sort of transformation is absent from recent new developments, as it is generally only carried out on buildings more than 150 years old.[41] Nevertheless, it is still very common in developing countries.

---

40 This necessity of informing all objects in a given space, being small or large, prestigious or humble, has also guided the research on the Piazza Navona area at Rome (Gauthiez. Les logiques).

41 Bernard Gauthiez. La logique de l'espace urbain: formation et évolution. Unpublished PhD dissertation, Paris: Ecole des Hautes Etudes en Sciences Sociales, 1991, 2 vols. Research into the rhythm of building rehabilitation is lacking. At Rouen, extensive rehabilitation projects statistically occur, in the modern period, more or less 150 years after the initial construction, and rebuilding on average about 300 years later.

Figure I.3 Place Meyssonnier and Rue Chenavard corner, a building made of many construction-units, originally medieval
The fact that the c.1500 windows at the second and third floors (with gothic decors) do not superimpose on the windows of the first floor imply that they correspond to a raising of a conserved anterior building with a high probability built in the Middle Ages. This medieval house was the property of Cretin Maclet, one of the few wealthiest inhabitants of Lyons, in 1376. The shop bays at the ground floor were modified in 1698 and adapted in 1808 and 1817. A new raising intervened in 1826, accompanied by the modification of the decors of the façade. A workshop was established in the roof for a photographer in 1878.

The building at the corner of Rue Chenavard and Place Meissonnier in Lyons is a remarkable case in point (Fig. I.3). Its transformation, featuring new decorations, the suppression of the previous cross mullions at the lower floors, and the addition of two floors in 1826, are all clearly visible and make up much of what we can see today.[42] An earlier addition of two floors occurred circa 1500 (the second and third floors).[43] These floors are identifiable from the form of the window

42 AML 315 WP 022, building permit.
43 By first-floor (*premier étage*), I mean the floor immediately above the ground-floor. The word 'floor' is used throughout the text to signify the storeys over the ground-floor, like the French word *étage*.

frames, which bear late-gothic motifs.[44] The shop fronts at the ground floor were probably modified in 1698, when the Public Weight was moved from the building, and a photographer's atelier was inserted in the roof in 1878.[45]

When assessing the façade of this building, one is struck by the fact that the second floor windows are not regularly placed above those of the first floor. This never occurs in a building conceived as a whole; it is therefore highly probable that the two floors added around 1500, which may be identified by their proper decor, were superimposed on a previous construction. In addition, the walls of the ground floor are unusually thick. That tells us that this part was certainly built during the Middle Ages, when the building is documented as the house of a family that was among the richest in the city.[46] The windows of the first floor were also modified in 1826, but their general layout was probably only slightly altered, and some elements of the medieval decorations, possibly hidden by nineteenth-century plaster, will perhaps be uncovered when a future rehabilitation occurs. This house, which has been decomposed here into five distinct construction-units (one new construction at Level 4 and six modifications at Level 5), including two additions of new floors, and one shop-front modification (both Level 5), is a good example of a general phenomenon: the older a building is, the more likely it is to have been transformed, and the harder it is to identify its older features, embedded as they are in the later modifications.

I.2.4 Dating public space

The public space of the city of Lyons has a complex history, comprising, amongst other things, the addition of new squares and streets during the Renaissance, street widenings and the addition of further squares during the modern period, streets established in new subdivisions in the early nineteenth century, the redevelopment of streets and squares in the later nineteenth century, and then further redevelopments in the twentieth. The streets in white on the map (Fig. I.4) are generally of medieval origin.

Public space is understood here as the space of the streets and squares, accessible to the public and maintained by the public administrations. Dating the

44 One of the windows built at that time was later closed. It is only perceived when the morning or evening sun light makes the irregularities of the façade plan visible.

45 AML 315 WP 77.

46 The frontage is fifty meters long, compared with only five meters for the more modest neighboring houses to the west, whose plots were also extant in the Middle Ages. In 1376, the proprietor was Cretin Maclet, one of the richest citizens of Lyons, AML, CC 13/1, f° 15v°-16r°v°.

Figure I.4 Map of public space dating, center of Lyons
The date is indicated only by period. The enlargement of streets appears at the end of the sixteenth century and becomes standard in the seventeenth, but the set-backs are only slightly legible at the scale of the figure. The widenings and opening of new streets in the nineteenth century are much more easy to see, like the new quays on the river banks. When no date is given, the street is generally medieval. Note: here only the public spaces are dated. The neighboring buildings may be more recent.

appearance of streets and more generally of public space has already been carried out on the scale of a city a few decades ago by Françoise Mallet for the center of Marseilles and the Quartier des Halles in Paris.[47] To do this she compared successive plans of the relevant areas. The present dating of the center of Lyons is precise to the year, and gives the detail of even the tiniest widenings, arising generally from the reconstruction of buildings or frontages with a setback whose dimensions is given in the building permit. It follows that the dating is not made first according to chronological periods, even if the graphic expression also uses this representation, in order to make the maps more legible and easier to compare. It is mapped according to the units of transformation, decomposed and individually dated. Events like the opening of squares and streets are clearly visible, and some neighboring constructions are present with a common setback frontage line. There was a systematic trend, during the modern period, to widen the streets, clearly favoring the reconstruction of groups of buildings. The map makes evident a general increase in street width, resulting mainly from a municipal policy in place between 1630 and the end of the eighteenth century, with some forerunners in the late sixteenth century (observed in the field, but still not encountered in the written record), and implemented with efficiency and tenacity. The period between 1620 and 1710 was remarkable in that regard, as it saw hundreds of reconstructions of which the frontages were set back from 30 cm to 6 m behind their previous line. Several small squares were also created thanks to the widening of a street or the demolition of one or several houses.[48] The reconstruction of the buildings throughout the city followed a very coherent scheme, consisting of the re-definition and regularization of public space, as the dates of the modifications show. New constructions allowed for a better and more efficient circulation of traffic and for an improved architectural landscape along the widened streets and new squares.

Unfortunately, the spaces produced at the time subsist only partly, because of later alterations corresponding to other needs and logics. These setbacks created a streetscape characterized by the general widening and regularization of urban space. The main aims were to improve urban aesthetics and functionality, as is frequently alluded to in the written record. Wider streets were considered necessary in Lyons from the late sixteenth century onwards. One may consider the role of such a systematic transformation in creating propitious conditions

---

47 Françoise Mallet. L'âge des voies du centre de Marseille. *Bulletin de l'association des géographes*, 395/396 (1972), 33; Boudon, Chastel, Couzy, Hamon. *Système de l'architecture*, II, Pl. 2.
48 Bernard Gauthiez, Olivier Zeller. Beautifying the city and improving the streets with building permits: Lyons, 1580-1770. Terry S. Slater, Sandra M. G. Pinto (eds.). *Building regulations and urban form, 1200-1900*. London-New York: Routledge, 2018, 177–200.

for the Industrial Revolution, as it allowed for a more fluent circulation of carts and coaches in a city were the production of silk-wares had considerably increased in the seventeenth century to the point where it became the city's main economic activity.

Nevertheless, the precise dating of the transformations of public space only helps us understand places that are for the most part today only seen, by default, as 'old' in a general and banal way, even though their modification was considered urgent and important in the eyes of their contemporaries.

Using a projection on a vertical plan instead of on a horizontal one, it would also be possible to map the modifications made to the façade of a given building, as the public records keep the permits given even for the changing of a door or a window, the recoating or whitening of a façade, changes to the shop signs, and so on. This could be complementary to the method commonly used by the archaeologist of the built environment, who typically studies the transformation of the vertical structures.[49] I have not tried such a mapping here, and not all the necessary information is available in the permit record, as public facilities like street lighting, ties for the cables of the tramways, street-name plates, and so on, were not subject to authorizations.

The change of the facades is an example of a domain that is very poorly studied, partly because of the lack of information and the difficulty of obtaining it from archival records, but also because these objects have not been considered as sufficiently noteworthy to merit scientific consideration. One could also examine with rigor the transformation of the street furniture and surfacing, which is today often removed and replaced to facilitate access to underground networks, as well as the history of the underground networks themselves (gas, electricity, drinking water, wastewater...), whose presence is often perceptible through spyholes and manholes. The precise dating and mapping of the shop fronts, all subject to administrative procedure and authorization, could help understand the story of retail commerce, but also how some types of businesses spread through the city and later declined or were further developed. All these categories of objects can lead to an urban morphology that would also be a social morphology.[50]

49 For example: Caroline Bolle, Geneviève Coura, Jean-Marc Léotard (eds.). *L'archéologie des bâtiments en question. Un outil pour les connaître, les conserver et les restaurer. The Archaeology of Buildings in Perspective. How to Better Understand, Preserve and Restore Buildings.* Namur: Service Public de Wallonie, 2014.

50 Examples in Whitehand, Recent developments, 290 – 294.

Figure I.5 The street surfacing, rue Longue
The streets and squares can be historicized as well as 'geographized'. The image depicts various alterations: stone paving, asphalt, repairs, sign paintings, spyholes for networks, and street furniture.

I.2.5 Coherence between buildings and planned developments

Once a precise knowledge of the date of the buildings and of the production of the planned developments is available, it becomes possible to cross-examine the temporality of urban space. In what follows, the focus will be on the chronological coherence between the architecture of the buildings and the phenomenon of urbanization.

Table I.1 Number of buildings per period in the city center in 2019 (excluding public and religious constructions)[51]

Period	Total buildings	Percentage of total production still extant[52]	West bank of River Saône	East bank of River Saône	Buildings located in new planned developments and re-developments	Buildings in series	Large buildings
Middle Ages[53]	6	Less than 1 %	4	2	0	0	0
1450–1599	300	12 %	225	75	40	0	0
1600–1699	390	16 %	170	220	13	18	0
1700–1799	305	25 %	55	250	53	17	0
1800–1855	600	95 %	100	500	475	41	2
1856–1918	400	95 %	35	365	260	110	3
After 1918	52	100 %	7	45	23	0	4
Total	2,050	26 %	590	1,460	860	186	9

The high levels of building production before 1700 are poorly represented in today's urban fabric. Putting aside the medieval production, which is still extremely difficult to estimate, only about twenty five percent of all the buildings produced between 1450 and 1700 in the central area of Lyons are now still

51 The figures are rounded because of some uncertainty. Reconstructions of a façade only are not taken into account. The area considered is equivalent to more than ninety percent of the urbanization before the end of the eighteenth century, so only a few dozen buildings do not appear in the table.
52 Evaluated in comparison to the buildings actually built and known from the authorizations and the extant constructions.
53 This figure is conservative, as some medieval structures are probably hidden by later transformations. The list of remaining medieval houses in Lyons is short: the large house Place Meyssonnier, a house in a passage Quai Pêcherie, two houses Place du Change, one Rue St-Jean, one Rue St-Georges.

there.[54] Concentrating only on the changing pattern over time of the urban landscape (logics of investment and production will be dealt with in Part III), some significant features clearly appear. The sixteenth and seventeenth centuries were very active, and many buildings of this period are conserved, especially on the west bank of the River Saône, today called "Vieux-Lyon".[55] Production levels diminished thereafter, but, as the buildings were newer, more propitious to ulterior capital gains, and more adaptable to later technological needs, a greater proportion of them have been conserved. From the early nineteenth century onwards, nearly all new buildings have been conserved.[56] Another prominent fact is the progressive abandonment of the west bank by investors. This is probably due largely to the displacement of the business center from the Rue Juiverie and Change area where it was located until the mid-seventeenth century to an area centered on the City Hall. The east bank of the River Saône was also much larger and offered more possibilities. From the 1820s, and markedly from the 1840s, the new developments around the city occurred outside the area mapped in this book, in the suburbs to the north at La Croix-Rousse, and increasingly on the eastern bank of the River Rhône, where the main bulk of the agglomeration is nowadays located. These shifts explain the decreasing proportion of remaining houses per period on the west bank of the River Saône.

The proportion of buildings of a given period still extant in the then new urban developments where they were built tells another story. Only twelve percent of all the Renaissance buildings (from 1480 to 1560) are preserved, of which thirteen percent are contemporary with the new developments in which they were produced (Fig. III.8). This is especially true in the lower part of Rue Grand'Côte and Rue des Epies, where the remaining houses had one main floor (plus a low attic). In Rue Garillan, developed in 1512, several houses have also been conserved, with three floors (ground-floor plus three). In the developments closer to the center, around the Jacobins and the Augustinians convents, and in Rue Thomassin developed in 1500, it is generally the case that no houses have been conserved, probably because they were too low, and so were rebuilt with several additional floors in the seventeenth and eighteenth centuries

54 The suburbs are not considered here.

55 This name has no real historic root, as urbanization in the area developed exactly in parallel to urbanization on the east bank of River Saône. It appeared after the renewal in the 1850s to 1860s of the areas between the rivers Saône and Rhône, which had urbanized at the same time in the Middle Ages.

56 Which is not true in the suburbs developed after 1800 to 1820, where many buildings were subsequently replaced.

to maximize capital gain. No series of identical houses from the fifteenth and sixteenth centuries, built according to a single plan, have been conserved.

The situation in the seventeenth and eighteenth centuries is significantly different. First, the proportion of houses conserved is higher, especially for the eighteenth century. Many houses dating from the sixteenth century and the early seventeenth were rebuilt at that time, although in the seventeenth century the houses demolished to be rebuilt were probably mainly medieval (see Part II for a discussion of the relationship between architectural typology and demography). The proportion of new houses present in the developments of the time is low, but the new Quartier St-Clair to the north-east, built from 1750 onwards, and Rue Vaubecour to the south, constructed in 1728, were the beginning of a new trend which later became more pronounced. New constructions began to replace older ones throughout the city. Some buildings were produced in series of three or more (seven at Place Bellecour by Perrachon de St-Maurice in 1669, of which six remain, with 130 m of frontage),[57] and a series of about ten was constructed by Rigod (or Rigaud) de Terrebasse between Place Bellecour and the Rhône Quay in the 1770s (260 m of frontage). In these cases, a common design was given to the groups of buildings produced in a single production operation.

The first half of the nineteenth century is essentially marked by the great importance of the new planned developments on the precincts of former convents, suppressed during the French Revolution. In these areas, which concern about 350 new buildings, a certain coherence has generally been maintained between architecture and urbanism, and as a consequence they constitute a very coherent city-scape. On some occasions, the investors opted to build newly subdivided plots as well, which led to remarkable groupings of identical buildings. Examples include the *Façades* reconstructed on the east and west sides of Place Bellecour (from 1812, they are equivalent to contemporary English terraces such as in Bath), the new buildings on the east and west sides of Place Sathonay (1822), Rue Burdeau (from 1822), Rue Sala (1830), and all along Rue de l'Ancienne Préfecture (1830). The architect and developer Benoît Poncet opted for the same solution for Rue Chenavard in 1850 for the block between Rue du Plâtre and Rue Longue, and the same year a society of entrepreneurs, the Sécurité Générale, also used this solution for a block located between Rue d'Algérie and Rue de Constantine.[58] This last realization was a variation of a big building erected in 1830 on the Rue St-Claude by Lenoir and Miège, two merchants who had

57 Françoise Bayard. Villes et campagnes dans la fortune de Pierre Perrachon, noble lyonnais, de 1642 à 1688. Françoise Bayard, Pierre Cayez (eds.), *Villes et campagnes, XVe-XXe siècle*. Lyons: Presses universitaires de Lyon, 1977, 105–131.

58 AML 321 WP 35–37; AML 3 P 123–7.

made their money broking silk-wares in New-York. A large majority of the buildings produced both in this period and in the second half of the nineteenth century are still there today.

The chronological and design coherence between buildings and developments is also much higher in this later period. Fewer buildings were produced in the city-center, the majority in new developments, but it is striking that nearly one third of them belong to series and featured homogeneous architectural design. This is exceptionally true for Rue de la République, an operation already alluded to, which had about 4,000 meters of new frontages, conceived in a very sophisticated way by Benoît Poncet, who also directed its construction. In order to vary the architecture, he asked the young architects he employed to individualize the façade of each building (defined as a use unit by an entrance), thus creating an aesthetically harmonious block in each interval between two streets, while at the same time industrializing the production of the whole, thus giving it a strong sense of unity. Rue de la République, where all the buildings were erected in the space of two years (1855–1857), is well conserved, even if three of its constructions have already been pulled down and replaced. This way of designing the façades was copied when the Rue Grolée area was redeveloped from 1890 by the entrepreneur Stanislas Ferrand. Here each block is also architecturally individualized. Several large buildings bear testimony to the growth of big finance: Massif des Terreaux and the Massif du Parc, two adjoining full blocks, by the Société Anonyme de la Rue Impériale and the Hospices-Civils, both began in 1858; one building, Avenue Adolphe-Max, from 1864; the Mangini Building Quay Pierre Scize from 1888 (110 m of frontage length); and two large buildings Rue de la Charité from 1898.

This analysis reveals three levels of coherence between architecture and urban developments in todays's urban fabric. The lowest one occurs when, as time passes, the buildings once accompanying a new development are replaced, maintaining the line of the street, but with no relationship to its former history. The urban fabric thus finds itself metamorphized by the transformation and replacement of its components.

The second level of coherence involves the continuation of existence of a new development and of the constructions built when it was realized. Earlier occurrences of this sort of coherence include various early sixteenth century developments, such as those of the Rue du Garillan and Rue Grand-Côte St-Sébastien, some of whose houses are still extant, thus forming a rare case of a well-preserved Renaissance street-scape. None remain from the Middle Ages, although the various series of small houses owned by the same proprietor or institution, mentioned in the fourteenth-century *Nommées*,[59] make one think that such series were probably frequent before the modern period. The largest example of this sort of coherence is Rue Edouard-Herriot, a re-development began in 1858 and completed in 1864. Remarkably, all of its buildings are still extant but one. Although constructed at the same time as the street, the architectural designs of the buildings have the particularity of having been intended, in many cases, to showcase the skill of the best architects in the city, who had previously been denied permission to participate in the design of Rue de la République.

The third level of coherence is the fullest. This occurs when the buildings comprising a new development all are designed according to the same plan and façade, be it with individualizations, as became common practice in Lyons after the construction of Rue de la République. This particular street epitomizes this level of coherence, but other examples abound in the city, like the series of similar buildings drawn and realized in the seventeenth and eighteenth centuries at Place Bellecour by Perrachon de St-Maurice and Place Antonin-Poncet by Rigod de Terrebasse, or Rue de l'Ancienne-Préfecture, lined with about 296 m of regular façades repeating the same motif with no variation. Architectural discussions developed in 1855 regarding the precise place to be given to variations, some pleading for starker continuity, others for a strong individualization of the functional units identified by the entrances, a solution which had the upper hand until the 1920s.

Table I.2 Surfaces occupied in the same central sector, by period, and including religious and public buildings

Middle Ages:	26 construction-units	surface occupied	1.0 ha
1450 to 1599:	370	"	4.7 ha
1600 to 1699:	590	"	12.8 ha
1700 to 1795:	410	"	12.5 ha
1796 to 1855:	720	"	21.0 ha
1856 to 1914:	680	"	28.0 ha
1915 to 1955:	35	"	4.5 ha
1956 to 2018:	90	"	6.0 ha (car-parks excluded)
TOTAL:			90.5 ha of constructions

59 The *Nommées* are cadastral and/or fiscal records, depending on their nature: either a visit in the field recording all inhabitants, or a list of tax-payers.

So, the central area of Lyons is composed of:

A few medieval construction-units,	1 percent of the built-up area
1,400 construction-units before 1796,	33 percent "
1,400 construction-units of the long nineteenth century,	53 percent "
130 construction-units after 1914.	14 percent "

Table I.3 Average area of the construction-unit (bridges and car-parks excluded)

1450–1599:	125 m^2
1600–1699:	215 m^2
1700–1795:	310 m^2
1795–1855:	295 m^2
1856–1914:	410 m^2
1914–1955:	1,125 m^2
1956–2005:	690 m^2

I.3 From materiality to remanence: the nature of the transmitted facts

Some aspects of the often very complex material reality, understood in terms of construction-units and identified according to different scales and categories, have already been examined. To understand urban material space requires to explain this complexity, and one should not be surprised by the amount of research investment needed given the large number of events that have shaped that space. But understanding material space does not just imply the identification of its pertinent components. Explaining their social nature and production processes is important as well.

Urban space is also much more complex than the current way of seeing it would lead us to suppose. The example of the house at Place Meissonnier, examined above, allowed us to see one aspect of this complexity, beyond the identification of the change of the joineries and of the things attached to the façade, and whose history and logics do not belong directly to the building itself.[60] The comprehension of a building requires it to be decomposed at different levels of

60 Bernard Gauthiez. Les fenêtres à Lyon, espace urbain et anthropologie, 1650-1900. Aldo Casamento (ed.). *Il Cantiere della Città.* Rome: Kappa, 2014, 221–248.

analysis and information. To reach this comprehension, and because the building may have a remarkably long history, the quantity of information may be very high, even when one considers only the most significant events. In what follows, the focus will turn to the rapid replacement of the visible surfaces of the objects of the city.

I.3.1 Traces and remanence: transmission, multiple substitutions

The longer the duration, the more complex the reality is likely to become, except in those cases where replacement and urban renewal occur, erasing all previously existing spatial objects. Consider the new development of an urban area: once completed, all will be coherent and nearly synchronic, including streets and public space, street furniture, buildings, facilities, painting, claddings and coatings. This may be contrasted with a piece of an old city, for example Rue St-Jean in Lyons (but it could be Cheapside in London, Via dei Coronari in Rome, and so on), where many of these objects have different dates and obey different historical logics. Moreover, Rue St-Jean existed in the Middle Ages, at least in the mid-twelfth century, though the date of its appearance is not known exactly. It was made larger through multiple instances of building setbacks in the seventeenth to nineteenth centuries. Its paving was laid in the 1980s. What can be seen of the buildings that run along it has been constructed from the fourteenth century to the nineteenth; and the older they are, the more likely they are to have been modified.[61] The windows, both the stone frames and the joineries, have been modified several times in order to adapt to new technologies and because their 'life expectancy' generally does not exceed a century or two. Many joineries put in when a large-scale rehabilitation of the quarter occurred in the 1980s are currently being replaced, because of their unsuitability to the growing heating costs of the apartments. The shop fronts are rarely older than the late nineteenth century, a lot of them were remade in the late twentieth century and after, and the surveillance cameras are newer still. In this complex urban materiality, objects coexist whose utility is easily understandable, like the buildings and the shop fronts, but their design is more difficult to grasp, as we see this landscape as a 'historical' one, meaning ancient, although every object, when produced,

---

61 The oldest remaining one, n° 2 Place du Change, was built around 1300. One floor was added a few decades later, then two more around 1500 with, in addition, an extension covering a lateral alleyway (it was then named Maison des Bestes because of its decor of sculpted animals). It was refurbished in the seventeenth century, then again in the early nineteenth, and a last time in the 1990s when its medieval origin was discovered on removing the nineteenth-century plaster.

was an expression of the present. The image is also blurred by the frequent imitations of the past, in part compulsory in an area now protected because of its high heritage value, but never exact and always adapted to recent needs. We also see remains of more or less erased and suppressed objects, sometimes only subsisting as minute traces, like the materializations of plot limits established many centuries ago, yet conserved thanks to much younger buildings and a street that was remade much later. Some elements were even reused in later reconstructions one or several centuries later or displaced, thus further confounding our capacity to understand. A case in point is house n° 38 Rue St-Jean. Its frontage was set back one meter in 1728, but its proprietor decided not to build a façade designed according to the contemporary architectural style (*à la française*), as his neighbors did, but rather to reuse the old sixteenth-century late-gothic façade, previously disassembled with great care.[62] Let's not forget that this comprehension is only possible when all the present material phenomena are correctly identified and characterized.[63] In the case of this street, the ancient configurations of space and morphological structures have only been partly transmitted, as they have been altered by many subsequent transformations. Its original state, if ever there was one 'origin', subsists as a sort of ghost, but a powerful one because of the inertia of the plot pattern and the durability of the buildings.

This history, made of the successive production of space fragments affecting an older spatial framework, may be more thoroughly assessed. Rue St-Jean is mentioned in the twelfth century in the written archival records.[64] Thanks to the inertia of the plot pattern and of the buildings, we can be sure that its location is the same today, nine centuries later. No known phenomenon can account for the displacement of a street already limited by constructions, and the oldest houses along the street are late medieval. A street is materially defined, first of all, by its fronting buildings and fences. Its displacement can only follow the destruction of the buildings and their replacement along another line. A street can be a distribution of space planned from the beginning, for example in a subdivision, or the consequence of buildings allowing for a passage between them. Nevertheless, an important proportion of the houses in Rue St-Jean had their

---

62 Bernard Gauthiez. Pourquoi les remplois visibles dans l'architecture civile à Lyon aux XVIII-XIXe siècles. Entre architecture savante et identité locale. Dany Sandron (ed.). *Le passé dans la ville*. Paris: Presses universitaire de Paris-Sorbonne, 2016, 145–168.

63 This is approximately what André Corboz calls a palimpsest (André Corboz. *Le territoire comme palimpseste et autres essais*. Genève: Editions De l'imprimeur, 2001).

64 In 1167 as *Rua Palacii* [Palace street], Bibliothèque Municipale de Lyon, Fonds Coste, ms 1388, f° 79.

frontage constructed in the modern period, in line with setbacks. We have no indication that older houses were set back in this way (if this information still exists, it would be made of hidden foundations under the street paving, which sometimes appear during work on underground networks), so one can suppose that the line of the numerous façades built before the mid-sixteenth century was established according to a limit that was already present in the thirteenth to fourteenth centuries. As a consequence, the precise lines of the initial medieval street were probably conserved when the present buildings were built, some time before the mid-sixteenth century, but they disappeared when the frontages of the houses were rebuilt later, as can be identified from setbacks mentioned in the archives and visible also in the field. The dimension of the setbacks of these houses is given in the building permits, so the line can be reconstituted, generally a few feet further forward than the present one, which of course implies that the street was previously significantly narrower.

The present level of the street paving is higher than the medieval one. As it is today more or less the same as that of the buildings produced after the fifteenth century, which is ascertainable in the field from the current level of the ground floors of houses built in that period, it was probably kept and stabilized during the fifteenth century. But the previous, medieval level was certainly lower, if the streets of Lyons evolved like those of other medieval cities. We have only occasional bits of information pertaining to the evolution of this level.[65] The present paving is at a level that stayed more or less stable from the late Middle Ages, in conformity with the levels of the oldest conserved houses, but, as Rue St-Jean is in a protected heritage area, it is today made of stones cut in the nineteenth century and taken from ancient stocks, as well as of some others cut around 1980 to fit the new design of the paving. One can't help but think that putting nineteenth-century stones in the street of a quarter said to date back to the Renaissance (though it is in fact much older) is a little incongruous, but actually no knowledge of how the early sixteenth-century paving was made is available. Nineteenth-century stones, now worn by the passage of crowds of touring visitors, are enough to give the feeling of age.

So, to sum up, Rue St-Jean is a street at least nine centuries old, its present day materiality made of neighboring buildings produced from the fourteenth century to today, and its form has been modified to the point where its initial lateral limits and surface level are largely unknown. But, undoubtedly, the street we

65 Examples of an elevation between one and three meters from the eleventh century to the fifteenth are not rare in western cities. The street surface elevation in Rue des Prêtres in Lyons was, in the twelfth century, about two meters under the present day level, bearing in mind that after the fifteenth century the street level generally stabilized.

now see is the evolution of the medieval street, at the same place in the city. People were then walking at a lower level, between closer frontages, on a different paving (or on earth), in an ambience impossible to reconstitute entirely (including, for example, the height of the former houses, which would probably have had only one floor, and which, before the fifteenth century, would also have been gabled).[66]

Other examples illustrate the conservation of a form or of some of its features and can help us understand the processes at work in their permanence. Continuity through time exists despite little or large transformations affecting parts of the initial materiality, which in this case is never fully replaced, but which nevertheless leads progressively to the emergence of a new form. The chain of these modifications has to be reconstituted to understand the process well.

To provide another example from Lyons, the Guillotière Bridge crossing the Rive Rhône has retained the same location as its predecessor, built in the early thirteenth century,[67] although no material element in the area today dates back further than the first half of the nineteenth century. But the location of its accesses on the banks of the River could not be changed. They were widened, the river was straightened and made narrower, but its crossing place, once its accesses were materialized by standing buildings, could not be altered. So they constituted a constraint leading to the replacement of the bridge on the same spot. Interestingly, this also occurred for the bridge over the River Saône in the center of the city, at least until its nineteenth-century version was destroyed in 1944. It was not replaced, but the forms of its accesses are still visible, constituting a material shape that cannot be understood if their previous role is not known. Another interesting example is the conservation of the Roman streets in cities like Turin and Piacenza. The processes involved are the same as for Rue St-Jean, though they span a longer period of time, including a period of ruralization in late antiquity. At that time, the streets were mainly lined with gardens and fences, as archaeology tells us.[68] The conservation of such streets can only be explained by the permanence of an authority controlling and forbidding possible encroachments on public space. But the successive reconstruction of vegetal fences over

---

66 The earliest conserved houses originally had one floor. Only one of them had been raised, by one floor, in the fourteenth century. Houses built around 1500 have three to five floors in the center of the city.

67 Its earliest known representation is in a manuscript of Mathieu Paris, from around 1250 (British Library, Ms. Royal 14 C.VII, f° 3r°).

68 Gian Paolo Brogiolo, Sandro Gelichi. *La città nell' alto medioevo italiano, archeologia e storia.* Rome-Bari: Laterza, 1998.

long periods of time, associated with the rising of the street level through the accumulation of organic deposits and the circulation of people and beasts of burden, led to an evolution of the street shapes toward wavy lines.[69]

The partial conservation of the form through time can be qualified in these cases as a remanence. The materiality of the original configuration doesn't exist anymore, but, through a chain of successive transformations making its former materiality disappear, another materiality is produced. The initial spatial structure is thus partly transmitted and its functional logics may also endure.

The social perception of these spaces largely ignores their real temporality and materiality, constituting them instead as united entities. Sometimes, a particular event can erase all elements of a previous materiality, but a remanent space can nevertheless appear when social continuities lead to the re-materialization of the lost space more or less in the same location. An archaeologist, Gerard Chouquer, supposed that a special geographical property of a place must exist to explain how a property limit can keep more or less the same line as a more ancient one, although it is materially separated from its predecessor by a thick alluvial deposit making a direct material transmission of the limit impossible. How can this continuity of the plot be explained when no material continuity is present? And how can one explain the continuation over several centuries, up to two thousand years, of a rural Roman limit despite material deposits amounting to a thickness of several meters?[70] In both cases, the explanation is not material, or only partially material, and the spatial remanence is not due to a particular geographical property of a given space, but simply to the continuity of the property pattern when the owners survive the space-erasing event, in the present case a flooding. The owner remains the proprietor of a plot after its material limits have been erased, as does his neighbor for the adjoining plot. A new material limit was simply given to the same plot after the previous limit was destroyed, be it one meter or so higher and perhaps exhibiting a minor horizontal displacement. Evidently, when all spatial marks have also disappeared, the plot limit can move slightly because new bearings have to be established, which certainly happened following the flooding event in question.

Continuity in this instance is due to the tenants or owners of the space. The plot is first of all a social, economic and legal object. The catastrophic event of a

---

69 Bernard Gauthiez. La transformation des rues à la fin de l'Antiquité romaine, contextes, processus. Pascale Ballet, Nadine Dieudonné-Glad, Catherine Saliou (eds.). *La rue dans l'Antiquité, définition, aménagement, devenir.* Rennes: Presses universitaires de Rennes, 2008, 141–150.

70 Gérard Chouquer. Ce que le temps fait aux formes planimétriques: du péché originel de l'analyse de la morphologie agraire à sa réhabilitation. *Géocarrefour*, 84/4 (2009), 217–228.

flooding is overcome by the recreation/reproduction of the previous state when the afferent rights and practices continue to exist. The same process also leads to the conservation of the layout of a city after a fire, as nearly always occurred before the early eighteenth century, at which point the regrouping of plots became possible thanks to new administrative, legal and financial tools. After the Great Fire of London in 1666, several new plans were proposed for the city, but it was only possible to modify the street structure slightly, including a general regularization thanks to a moderate widening of the streets, and only two or three new thoroughfares pierced through the old urban fabric. So the inertia of the spatial form is due partly to the physical properties of its components (buildings, fences, etc.), which materialize the individual properties, but also to the social modalities of space occupation, including property rights and control of public space.[71] In addition, the conservation of the material limits of a property has always played a major role in the continuity of forms, regardless of the social control exerted. All new production, as we already saw above, is strictly constrained within precise limits, both material and social.[72] The use and utility of the spaces is also a factor of continuity, at least when they are maintained and evolve only gradually, but it is much more difficult to ascertain exactly how this works.

I.3.2 Time and lines: the origin of 'lines' and of property limits

It is often considered, and even unthinkingly accepted, that plot limits have always existed as such. This idea is so ingrained that some archaeologists often tend to consider a fence, or a ditch, or any other linear material structure forming an obstacle, as a property limit. As we will see, this is not necessarily true, and these lines have another origin, becoming property limits only when property rights developed. Actually, lines, often materialized as limits of varied natures or as determinations produced by the form of an object, are central to our way of being in space. To elucidate this important point, it may be useful to recapitulate the origin of the forms present in urban space, their determinants, and the role of time in their genesis, from the more concrete to the most abstract. Here, then, are the principal origins of lines in human space:

A. New lines in material space are determined by a material object when it is produced. But these lines have their origin in social processes of generating

---

71 Jan Heeling, Han Meyer, John Westrik, Eugène Sauren, Maarten Jan Hoekstra. *Het ontwerp van de stadsplattegrond.* Amsterdam: SUN, 2002, 16–20.

72 Roncayolo, La morphologie, 47–48.

space: definitions of lots used in agriculture, of plots and subdivisions in various contexts, of building typologies leading to regular dimensions and sizes. Abstract social determinations of these particularly important figures in space lead to their materialization in buildings and fences.[73] This occurs thanks to the transcription of a building type into a material object through processes of conception and production, or to the production of a fence to materialize the limit of a use unit or property right.

B. Some lines are determined by the constraint given by a material structure to its neighbors. A house cannot encroach on its neighbor, for example. The origin of these lines may either correspond to one of the possibilities set out above (A.), or it may be natural (the bank of a river, a cliff, etc.).
C. Remanent lines, i.e., those that originated in a materiality whose shape was indirectly transmitted (originally A. or B.).
D. Lines determined by considerations of proxemics.[74] An example is provided by the way houses are arranged in the Amerindian village of Yalimapo in French Guyana. No property limits or fences are extant, but the intervals between the houses and their orientations are culturally determined. And it is actually impossible for an intruder from a foreign community to be allowed to build a house of his own in such a context. These lines may not be materialized themselves, but they nonetheless exist in the anthropological practice of space.[75]
E. Lines determined by use. These are more elusive when not materialized by limits between, say, public and private domains. An example of which would be a limit between two fields cultivated separately.
F. Lines determined by by-laws and similar constraints.

It is important to underline the extent to which anthropological and social structures are intertwined with material ones, each with its own properties, inertia included.

73 Randal M. MacGuire, Michael Brian Schiffer. A theory of architectural design. *Journal of anthropological archaeology* 2/3 (1983), 277–303: 278.
74 Edward T. Hall. *The hidden dimension. New-York:* Garden City, 1966.
75 These lines also express the Amerindian way of life much better than would materialized fences marking the subdivision of land.

Table I.4 The decomposition of lines

Type of phenomenon	**Logical category**
Spatial need, occupation, flux, systems of activities[76]	Usage, needs
External line and/or margin, symbols	Semiotics, proxemics
Property limit, typology of occupation, spatial settings, systems of settings[77]	Social, legal
Buildings and fences, fixings and features	Physical/material (through a production process)
Induced spatial constraint, immediate	Material implications/morphogenesis
Induced spatial constraint, mediated	Remanence

To go a step further, this could suggest the following evolutionary schema of the human relation to territory over time:

a. A possible,[78] but empirically elusive, phase of free land that was just occupied and used.[79]
b. A social and anthropological organisation of space, based on use units and semiotic dimensions.
c. The invention of property as a delimited and reserved section of space with particular rights. This invention gives a new value to the use units, which become inheritable.
d. Then later, or as part of the same process, the materialization of the property rights, formerly often use-unit delimitations.[80]
e. The consequences of this new delimitation of space. As it grows and comes to cover all available space, it becomes the main spatial framework in our societies.

---

76 "Activity systems are inevitably organized in space and time". Amos Rapoport. Systems of activities and systems of settings. Susan Kent (ed.). *Domestic architecture and the use of space, an interdisciplinary cross-cultural study.* Cambridge: The Cambridge University Press, 1990, 9–20: 12.

77 Rapoport, Systems, 12[18].

78 It is actually difficult to imagine a context of human use without an anthropological dimension. But the availability of free space may have had consequences on the human mind, and so induced anthropological developments.

79 Typically, but with nuances, maybe in Paleolithic times.

80 For example, the "Celtic fields" in Great-Britain, where many field limits were materialized by stone walls.

f. The emergence of a space (the present one) that is the fruit of many layers of spatial constraints, both social and material, as well as the emergence of by-laws and planning laws that create new limits.

I.3.3 On the history of land property and material limits

This can be considered further through the examination of some archaeological and written data. The common view among historians of law is seemingly that property rights with respect to land appeared during the Neolithic and that the materialization of the field limits were a proof of their existence.[81] The affirmation of legal property was nevertheless probably not the direct origin of fences around fields or pasture. The code of Hammurabi,[82] written in Mesopotamia in the eighteenth century BC, gives some interesting clues as to the processes involved. More than ten times, it alludes to *house, garden and field* or *field, garden and house* as a single unit (§ 30 – 31 – 36 – 37 – 38 – 39 – 40 – 41 – 181 – 182). The unit described in these words is obviously of socio-economic nature, corresponding to the needs of a single family, which is reinforced when considerations about the storage of corn and the usufruct are added (§ 137 – 150 – 178 – 180). The house is also a household (§ 130 – 133 – 136 – 145 – 168 – 172 – 193) and an economic unit (§ 134 – 135 – 141 – 151 – 152 – 177). It is also a value linked with inheritance and dowagers (§ 161 – 163 – 170 – 183), an estate that can be divided in an abstract manner, in thirds, for example (§ 176 – 166 – 167 – 180). It seems probable that the property of a house in that period in Mesopotamia was a legal expression of a socio-economically functional unit attached to a family. This unit could be precisely defined spatially and materially, had a functional unity and coherence, could be inherited, thus warranting its continuity, but also divided through inheritance, which could hinder its viability. It follows that the materialization of the field and garden limits is not a direct implication of a property right, but the consequence of the functional setting of the rural production unit, associated with an anthropological organization. The materialization of a limit between two fields may also result in part from such needs as piling up unwanted stones on the side of the area in use, or protecting it from the wind, wild animals,

81 Elias T. Earle. Property in prehistory. Michele Graziadei, Lionel Smith (ed.). *Comparative property laws global perspectives*. Cheltenham: Edward Elgar Publishing, 2017. Robert Rowthorn, Paul Seabright. Property rights, warfare and the Neolithic transition. *TSE Working paper series*, 2010, 10 – 207.

82 Leonard William King. *The code of Hammurabi*. 1915. Paolo J.S. Pereira (ed.). http://www.general-intelligence.com/library/hr.pdf, accessed May 2018.

or even pasturing beasts.[83] Neolithization doesn't in itself imply the production of materialized limits. The Amazonian village evoked previously testifies to the fact that sedentarization over long periods and affirmation of agricultural production units were probably major factors favoring the production of fences. The equation 'property = fence/material delimitation' was a later consequence of this process. The Germanic law of the Visigoths in the seventh century can be placed in this historical sequence, as it insists on maintaining the boundaries and the landmarks that demarcate properties.[84] But the boundaries were still strongly linked at the time with familial succession,[85] and the functional unit was still the determining factor. Further, a property right could not be asserted after fifty years of abandonment.[86] All this makes one think that property appeared after use units, when families asserted themselves as fundamental to the continuity and stability of the community. The progressive occupation of all available space was a strong incentive in the process.[87] The use units needed an overarching protection, which was introduced through rights.

A property market probably only developed when the monetary economy appeared in the Eastern Mediterranean, associated with writing and formal legal systems,[88] but also with the development of an administrative and fiscal system using and based on the registering of properties and wealth, leading in the Roman period to the first cadastral plans.[89] The comparison between Çatalhöyük, a Turkish site 6,000 years BC, and the Greek city of Olynthos, 400 years BC, clearly expresses the evolution from a system where each family possesses a house much like its neighbor's, without the possibility of spatial expan-

---

83 For example, in the French Alps many occurrences of stone fences separating an interior closed zone of culture from an exterior zone for pasture, such as at an altitude of 1,250 to 1,300 meters, Plaine-Joux, village of Onnion (Département of Haute-Savoie), not dated, but probably medieval.

84 S. P. Scott. *The Visigotic code (Forum judicum).* Boston: The Boston Book Company, 1910. http://www.documentacatholicaomnia.eu/03d/0506-0506,_AA_VV,_Leges_Romanae_Visigotorum_[Scott_JP_Curatore],_EN.pdf. Book X, Title III, Law I.

85 Katherine Fisher-Drew. *The Burgundian code: book of constitutions or law of Gundobad.* Philadelphia: University of Pennsylvania Press, 1972.

86 Scott, Visigotic, Book X, Title II, Law I. The situation was similar in Japan until the introduction of a new property right inspired by the West in 1872 to 1873 (Harada Sumitaka. Notion de propriété. Traits caractéristiques du droit japonais. *Revue internationale de droit comparé*, 51 (1999), 449–52.

87 This could also be part of the explanation for the passage from rounded houses to square angled ones, the last area to adopt the square angle plan being, in Europe, Great-Britain.

88 Earle, Property, 23.

89 Emilio Rodriguez-Almeida. *Formae Urbis antiquae. Le mappe marmoree di Roma tra la Repubblica e Settimo Severo.* Rome: Ecole française de Rome, 2002.

sion because of tightly occupied space,[90] to a monetary economy where buying one neighbor's land is possible and, indeed, leads to the differentiation of house sizes through time, from, in the case of Olynthos, the identical square plots of the city's initial layout, to, a few decades later, rectangular properties made up of square plots to which fractions of other plots had been added.[91] The establishment of such real property rights was certainly not a clean break process, as overarching institutional rights could continue to exist and allow for modification of properties at the household level. This was true in the case of foreigners in the Roman Empire, and also, in that same period, when the rural landscape was reorganized according to the very regular *centuriatio* grids. Conversely, the remodelling of some sections of the city of Rome was only possible after fire destroyed them during Nero's reign. Different property regimes coexisted in the Roman Empire, one in a context of conquest allowing for a *tabula rasa* of previous property rights, another where the rights of citizens made redevelopment impossible, at least in normal times.[92]

So it is clear that the property of plots and spaces, delimited or not, derived from functional socio-economic units, based on usufruct, and that it later became based on its exchange-value.[93] Such a system was probably still extant in the Middle Ages, when, in the town of Pont-Audemer in Normandy, a Count could in 1118 destroy and relocate some houses in order to clear a space for a new planned development, in this case a market square.[94] It was at the time still possible for a Lord to displace dwellings and relocate people thanks to a spatial transfer of their – mainly use – rights. This was probably still possible also because the houses were made largely of movable materials. The Middle Ages probably saw a transition from a situation when seigneurial overarching rights could still be used to modify the material space and its limits to a more

90 Ian Hodder. *Çatalhöyük, the leopard's tale, revealing the secrets of Turkey's ancient 'town'.* London: Thames and Hudson, 2006, 95–102.

91 Between the extension of the new town founded in 432 BC and its destruction by King Philip of Macedon in 348 BC, the new polis lasted a period of about 80 years, during which time this phenomenon occurred. Nicolas Cahill. *Household and City organization at Olynthus.* Yale: Yale University Press, 2002, 197.

92 It was nevertheless easier to impose a reorganization of the plot and street pattern in the destroyed areas in Rome than much later in 1666 London.

93 Alain Testart. *Avant l'histoire, l'évolution des sociétés, de Lascaux à Carnac.* Paris: Gallimard, 2012, 407–410. This is what Testart calls the "propriété usufondée" (usu-founded property), which became later "propriété fundiaire".

94 Bernard Gauthiez. Verneuil-sur-Avre, Falaise, Pont-Audemer et Lisieux en Normandie. Bernard Gauthiez, Elisabeth Zadora-Rio, Henri Galinié (eds.). *Village et ville au Moyen-Âge: les dynamiques morphologiques.* Tours: Presses de l'Université François-Rabelais, 2003, 35–95: 64–65.

rigid urban space resulting from the development of more solid constructions and bourgeois property rights. This evolution probably also implied the affirmation of the public domain in the streets and squares, which from the late twelfth century led to more fixed street networks and limits, as well as to the introduction of building authorizations for all structures bordering the street space. This in turn explains why in north-western Europe it is impossible to infer the shape of cities before this period with any great certainty.[95]

Furthermore, property in the Middle Ages and the modern period is often (but not always) still split between the soil and the usufruct materialized in the buildings or tree(s).[96] In some medieval towns in north-west Europe, however, the soil was sometimes already freed from all seigneury (in Flanders and Normandy, for example). This probably explains, at least partly, the hesitation in materializing the limits between neighbors in the Middle Ages. In Turin and Pinerolo, in Piedmont, two walls were compulsory, one for each neighboring house, separated by a gap, probably to limit the extent of fires. But who owned the gap? In Rouen, two neighboring houses each had their own wall, but without a separation space. In many cities (London, Lyons, Dijon, Paris, Rome, Regensburg ...), the party-wall was common and the property limit was located in the middle. This explained the *mi-mur* (half-wall) right in Lyons, which meant that each neighbor was allowed to build over the same separating wall, possessing half of it each.

The dialectic between law and materiality was still strong in the modern period. A comparable difficulty was introduced by the porticoes, so frequent in the Italian and Swiss medieval cities, but whose ownership was sometimes difficult to establish.[97] At times, their space was attributed after the Middle Ages to the fronting house, which would mean a sort of encroachment of private space on public space, despite a public right for free movement retained on the ground-floor, or they were later destroyed to fully become part of public space. They were maintained only because rights could be clearly established: the private plot over (floors) and under (cellar) the portico, as well as a public use for the portico itself, generally at more or less the street level. Materiality was also prom-

---

95 Franz Verhaeghe. L'espace civil et la ville. Pierre Demolon, Henri Galinié, Franz Verhaeghe (eds). *Archéologie des villes dans le Nord-Ouest de l'Europe (VIIe-XIIIe siècle).* Douai: Société archéologique de Douai, 1994, 145–190: 169–170.

96 Olivier Faron, Etienne Hubert (eds.). *Le sol et l'immeuble, les formes dissociées de propriété immobilière dans les villes de France et d'Italie (XIIe-XIXe siècle).* Rome: Ecole Française de Rome, 1995.

97 Aurelle Levasseur. *Définir la rue publique du bas Moyen Âge, contribution à l'histoire du droit administratif des biens.* Dijon: Presses universitaires de Franche-Comté, 2017, 137–141.

inent when dealing with the aesthetics of public space and its functionality. The *Réglement général d'alignement* in Lyons in 1680 strongly constrained the lines of the façades in the form of precise setback dimensions,[98] but it was not accompanied by a plan, and the desired shape of the city was not conceived as a plan to be respected, but as a city-scape to establish progressively. In Rouen in the early eighteenth century, the aesthetics and functionality of the new alignments were also controlled in the field, and so not from a reference plan.[99]

A new chapter in this story began when, from the late seventeenth century onwards, seigneuries began to map their domains precisely, especially abbeys and estates controlled by Lords, or in some rarer cases like that of the French city of Toulouse in 1680.[100] The properties were then mapped according to their physically recognizable limits, measured in the field and confirmed by witnesses. This process accelerated in the eighteenth century, when systematic cadastral maps were established for entire territories, exemplified by some Swiss cantons like Bern, the kingdom of Denmark, and slightly later the kingdom of Piedmont-Sardinia around 1730. The French followed with a special law under Napoleon the First in 1807.

The final touch to the construction of the property rights we know today was arguably introduced during the French Revolution.[101] As Blaufarb has observed, this was when "formal public power" (in fact seigneurial property) was removed "from the sphere of property", drawing a neat line between property and political power. This was, in any case, the main idea, but exceptions were still possible, as occurred, for example, in the nineteenth century when the Hospices Civils of Lyons (the united hospitals of the city) allocated leasehold lots for durations of twelve to fifteen years in long leases, which only allowed for movable constructions made of posts and beams, which could be – and sometimes were – easily displaced to clear some blocks where the plot pattern could be fully re-designed, which happened for several full blocks around 1900.[102] Furthermore, an important point that Blaufarb doesn't allude to is that the seigneury rights of the Ancien Régime were generally transferred to the State.

---

98 AML DD 56.

99 Gauthiez, La logique, 511–512.

100 Aurélie Monroziès-Blanchard. Le cadastre toulousain de 1680: étude historique et statistique. *Annales du Midi: revue archéologique, historique et philologique de la France méridionale*, 115/244 (2003), 515–534.

101 Rafe Blaufarb. *The great demarcation: the French revolution and the invention of modern property.* New-York: Oxford University Press, 2016.

102 Anne-Sophie Clémençon, Shunichiro Koyanagi. Construire la ville en louant le sol. L'exemple français des Hospices civils de Lyon (de 1781 à 1914). *Dokkyo Law Review*, 2008.

These elements of the history of property point to a rather complex evolution. The modern property right was progressively established, and it was not implemented everywhere at the same time, for many local variations persisted. In a first phase there was the usufruct of some places, already present in the Pacific North-West in sedentary hunter-gatherer peoples,[103] and which later became standard in the Neolithic period. The usufruct was closely associated to the social unit which used and later owned it, generally a family, and this in turn led to the materialization of its limits by markers and fences. A complication was introduced when inheritance implied a division into several shares, and this is why many societies sought to avoid this difficulty by designating only one heir, generally the oldest son. The complication grew when monetarization and administrative records appeared, allowing for an abstract conception of property, partly detached from its physical basis. But the physical limit, especially in towns where buildings became conjoined as density increased, and where the frontages marked the limit between private and public spaces, was still important (even increasingly so), as a material constraint for the builder. The development of cadastral maps allowed for a neat recognition of the physical limits, but it also contributed to making them both more fixed and more abstract. Their control became possible on the basis of a reference plan, standard from the early nineteenth century in France, though control in the field was sometimes still a legal obligation. The transformation of urban space did, however, become possible in a fully abstract way, by reference to a precisely measured plan, without requiring controls in the field of the material situation, which was handed over to subsidiary professionals.[104] In parallel, the disappearance of the overarching right of seigneuries (which, as we saw, in France was generalized and transferred to the state) led to the development of legal tools to deal with space and especially to allow for expropriation. It had become nearly impossible, before 1789, to expropriate outside the cases of royal edicts, except for fortification needs.[105] In France, this was clarified in laws of 1807 and 1810 and many later texts.

To summarize, it would seem that property rights developed in several, overlapping steps:

- Usufruct, functional and social units (the rural farming unit).

---

103 Testart, *Avant l'histoire*, 209.

104 This led also from the eighteenth century to the development of urban aesthetics drawn and determined on the plan and growingly distanced from the field reality, which is overwhelmingly dominating today.

105 François Monnier. La notion d'expropriation au XVIIIe siècle d'après l'exemple de Paris. *Journal des savants*, 3/1 (1984), 223–258.

- Materialization of limits.
- Monetarization and fiscalization through public and seigneurial records.
- The development from case law to codification.
- Complete abstraction through mapping.

The transition from property rights towards material realization of property rights in the form of physical limits occurred in the West only after an abstract legal system developed, first in classical antiquity, and again in the high Middle-Ages. This process reached maturity after mapping became standard, as occurred in the Roman state, and again more than a thousand years later in Europe. Previously, only the social and functional unit, and the material limits it implied, were present.

I.3.4 On the development of by-laws with respect to the built-up fabric and urban space

The Romans adopted many legal constraints for buildings, particularly in Rome. Destroying a building could be forbidden because the material could be put up for sale or because of the need for dwellings: the intention of the law was that an existing house had to remain available and habitable. An abandoned space could be reoccupied without the acceptance of its owner. This was clearly intended to keep a unit functional. Other by-laws dealt with the dimension of the jetties, overlooking and privacy, the height of the buildings to limit the risk of collapse and of fire, with distances sometimes required to be respected between constructions. In Rome, at least from the time of Nero onwards, the line between the private space of the buildings and the public space of the streets was to be strictly observed. It seems that this had already been a law around other parts of the Mediterranean for centuries, at least in cities in the ancient Middle East and the Greek world, because archaeology shows that the limits between the streets and the private plots did not move during this period.[106] The control of the law

106 Léon Homo. *Rome impériale et l'urbanisme dans l'Antiquité.* Paris: Albin Michel, 1951. James E. Packer. *The insulae of imperial Ostia.* Rome: Memoirs of the American Academy in *Rome*, 1971, vol. XXXI. Catherine Saliou. *Les lois du bâtiment. Voisinage et habitat urbain dans l'Empire romain. Recherches sur les rapports entre le droit et la construction privée du siècle d'Auguste au siècle de Justinien.* Beyrouth: Presses de l'Institut Français du Proche Orient, 1994. https://books.openedition.org/ifpo/6125. Isabella Baldini Lippolis. Private space in Late Antique Cities: Laws and Building procedures. Luke Lavan, Lale Özgenel, Alexander Sarantis (eds.), *Housing in Late Antiquity, From Palaces to Shops.* Leiden, Boston: Brill, 2007, 197–237.

was seemingly carried out only *a posteriori*, after the construction. No public office was responsible for its implementation and there is no hint of building permits. Roman law became highly sophisticated in the Near-East, where its developments are well known in the sixth century,[107] but it largely disappeared from the Empire thereafter, at least as far as common practice was concerned.

Dedicated by-laws reappeared from the late twelfth century in the West.[108] They dealt mainly with the risk of fire, which explains the distances to be respected between buildings in many towns, and later the standard obligation from the thirteenth century onwards to build at least the party-walls in stone, the limits imposed on the dimension of the jetties, and the use of tiles for the roofs. This is, in some ways, the expression of an overarching law with respect to private property, not in the name of a seigneury, but for the common good, and it was carried-out mainly by the newly developed municipal authorities. This way of dealing with urban materiality led to the development of many of today's by-laws and legal codes relating to urban space.

One aspect of the control of urban space, namely the limit between public and private domains along the streets and squares, was formalized only later. The control of the frontage lines was (re)affirmed under Nero at Rome, and encroachment on public space was prohibited. But this only maintained already established lines. In the absence of building permits, modifying the street width was certainly difficult, but it seems to have occurred at Rome and Ostia. In the latter city, the widening of the *Decumanus Maximus* occurred in several phases, materialized in the reconstruction of several buildings in the late first to early second centuries, probably over a period of a few decades. So this was not a single operation, but a process carried out continuously by several administrations. To achieve such a goal without building permits implies action prior to each reconstruction, and the imposition of new frontage lines with setbacks.[109] This sort of improvement through setbacks was probably rare in the Roman Empire. It is also present in Pompeii, but it arguably developed during the mid-imperial period. It is present in exceptional circumstances, an example being one of the main thoroughfares in Ostia, a very dense and active city. One

---

107 Catherine Saliou. *Le traité d'urbanisme de Julien d'Ascalon. Droit et architecture en Palestine au VIe siècle.* Paris: De Boccard, *1996.*

108 Terry R. Slater, Sandra M. G. Pinto. Building regulations and urban form. Terry R. Slater, Sandra M. G. Pinto (eds.), *Building regulations and urban form, 1200-1900.* London, New York: Routledge, 2018, 1–21.

109 The setback is evident on the plan, and archeologically documented for buildings III-II-1, III-II-2, IV-VII-1, IV-VII-3, IV-V-1 (Carlo Pavolini. *Ostia, guida archeologica.* Rome-Bari: Laterza, 1989, 145, 179, 186.

other occurrence is known at Lyons in the first century AD, and for an important street as well.[110] Such a practice was nevertheless rare and, probably because of the lack of building permits making it difficult to carry-out, temporarily disappeared. It re-appeared only much later in the West.

In the Middle Ages, the legal notion of public ownership of the street developed very slowly (even if a street was already often named *via publica*), although evidence seems to show that in practice it was necessary to keep the streets in a fit state for traffic.[111] Encroachments were still frequent and were only properly dealt with from the end of the period and in the sixteenth century. In the French context, the building permit appears in a significant number of cities from the late twelfth century and the beginning of the thirteenth century onwards.[112] It was at first intended only to enforce respect of the public domain, the width of the established streets and their lines in new developments.[113] The dimension of the jetties was limited from the late thirteenth century and in the fourteenth. The next step was the introduction of the setback. In Lyons, where one finds the earliest occurrences currently documented in France, setbacks appear after 1550 (Rue du Boeuf), and became standard practice in the early seventeenth century, when traffic jams developed in the city, partly because of the increasing numbers of private coaches.

I.3.5 Substitution and reconstitution: the particular temporality of the historical monuments

The conservation of spatial form is due to two processes. One is its intrinsic inertia, which arises from its materiality, produced at a given time, and from social factors. The other is the constraint spatial form exerts on its environment, and the reciprocal constraint exerted by its environment on spatial form. Let us

---

110 Armand Desbat. Suppression ou élargissement de rues à Lugdunum au Ier siècle apr. J.-C. Pascale Ballet, Nadine Dieudonné-Glad, Catherine Saliou (eds.). *La rue dans l'Antiquité, définition, aménagement, devenir.* Rennes: Presses Universitaires de Rennes, 2008, 231–236.

111 Levasseur, *Définir la rue*, 45–51.

112 Bernard Gauthiez. Le rôle du contrôle de l'espace public et l'urbanisme au XIIIe siècle en France. Guy De Boe, Franz Verhaeghe (eds), *Urbanism in Medieval Europe*, 'Medieval Europe Brugge 1997' conference papers vol. 1, Zellik: Instituut voor het Archeologisch Patrimonium, 1997, 193–198.

113 For Levasseur, *Définir la rue*, 141, the (regular) alignment along the streets was primarily due to the cohesion prompted by community uses. One wonders how this could act.

now examine a specific aspect of the conservation of spatial form which developed in the nineteenth century and is still active today.

Art history often considers a material object in terms of the stylistic ideas it represents, normally expressed in its materiality. This explains a still predominant interest, at least arguably in France, for the buildings that most fully express a project, when the construction fully mirrors the architectural conception. So, ideally, it must remain unmodified, 'legible', not denatured, kept untouched and eventually with the patina of age (in French: *dans son jus*). This traditional approach does not deal adequately with old buildings, for the number and scope of potential transformation grows with time, and may include additions or removals of parts, modifications of windows and doors, changes to the roof, adaptations to modern technologies, as occurred when gas, water and electricity networks appeared in the nineteenth and twentieth centuries. To these one must add modifications caused by nature: the effect of microorganisms, algae and lichens, weathering by wind, rain, frost, and temperature changes, and exposition to sunlight. And lastly, one must also consider the wear and damage caused by use, and the effects of pollution (soot, chemical alterations). Considering these points, the dilemma facing restorers of historical monuments is clear:[114]

- Either historical materiality is preserved (preservation)
  The building is kept in its present state, retaining the effects of transformations, including weathering, use, and so on. The conservation is carried out through new transformations assuring only the permanence of the building and its adaptation to modern demands and security. The history of the building is preserved and displayed, as much as possible, which implies keeping the transformations. Its materiality is conserved as a principle, but the full legibility of the building's former aesthetics and functionality is forever altered.
- Or legibility is restored (conservation/reconstitution)
  The damaged parts are restored according to what is known (or imagined) of their pristine shape, the transformations and additions are suppressed in order to restore an ideal object, in the spirit of art history as exposed above. The building is afterwards easily comprehensible but has lost its history, which is now limited to two points: what is kept of its initial construction, generally much altered and limited, sometimes even hidden, and what its present restoration has brought to it, through replacing as many parts as necessary and suppressing the transformations and alterations. The history

114 Paolo Marconi. *Materia e significato, la questione del restauro architettonico.* Rome-Bari: Laterza, 1999.

> and richness of the events that affected it materially are erased. An interesting example of this is buildings damaged by bullets during a war or other violent event. One can choose to re-establish the building's previous state, or one can keep the damage to help retain the memory of a historically important event. As the case of the restoration of the Rouen Palais de Justice (Justice Building) after 1945 shows, this may even concern buildings already restored in the spirit of reconstitution (in this case a nineteenth-century extension).

In the case of preservation, the wealth of information and testimony carried by the object is retained, but in a complex and sometimes painful way. In the case of reconstitution, the building is reduced to an ideal made of modern material, as the damaged older materials had to be replaced (a good example being that of Notre-Dame in Paris, where a rapid examination clearly reveals that the proportion of original stones in the façade and towers is very limited). Bearing this in mind, the observation of restorations since they became common practice, i.e. in the mid-nineteenth century,[115] produces striking results. In the more recent period, reconstitution is more and more frequent in France, and carried out in a growingly idealizing way, which also implies a growing material transformation of the object, even if it is intended as a restoration.

This trend also leads to a profound renovation of the surface of old buildings. An emblematic old church can no longer stay darkened by soot and pollution; it cannot bear any mark of wear or weathering, and will be cleaned of its lichens and mosses (independently of the anti-pollution treatments), and even coated by a sort of whitening, making any externally analysis by the art historian and the archaeologist impossible because the ashlar work becomes illegible (see St-Jean Cathedral in Lyons). The effects of the passing of time are erased and refused.

Incidentally, no cleaning of the exterior of any church, cathedral or other religious building, is mentioned in archives, to my knowledge, before the restorations of the nineteenth century (we know of whitening of the insides). They had thus remained stained and darkened for centuries. When one whitens a building, the reality of the past and its meanings are willingly distanced to realize the idea of a sort of timeless object that is intended to express the conception of pure art. This way of dealing with objects introduces a strong paradox: an ancient building is on the one hand canonized by its age and eventually main transforma-

115 Many restorations were carried-out previously, already in Roman times. The restorers generally opted for modernization, using esthetical solutions of their time.

tions, but on the other hand it is actually made into a modern one, giving it the aspect of an avatar of the material shape it probably never had. It tends to be always repaired and restored to retain, as much as possible, this timeless and ever-young ideal. A comparison with the goals of cosmetic medicine and surgery comes immediately to mind. This trend also implies a concentration of means on a limited number of buildings, sometimes qualified as 'iconic', because of its costs. The consequence is the refusal of history, reduced in its richness and reconstituted in mythic and simplistic images.

I.3.6 The omnipresence of the new

Newness is actually a rather radical novelty in the space of our cities. What is perceived, the buildings' skin, the street paving and furniture, is extremely young, at most a few decades old. The oldest elements are covered over and more and more difficult to identify, so rapid has been the replacement of the joineries and of the urban decor. Never has so much money been made available to maintain and replace things, and this places a heavy pressure on old things, at least when they are considered to possess no meaning, even if this is generally only the result of ignorance. The structures are still there, as are the walls and public spaces, but only under the younger materiality of surfaces, both new and short-lived.

The effects of ageing are systematically combatted and with great force. Age is culturally valued, but only if it appears under a modern guise, or is reconstituted in order to make it presentable. What we see in urban spaces has never, in comparison with the rest of history, been so new. This newness is evident when a direct comparison is made between the present city-scape to what we know of it in previous periods, for example the seventeenth century. At that time, the façade surface was often in a bad condition. In Lyons, permits were only asked for to whiten and redo the plaster of the frontages of buildings every 100 to 150 years, and many houses were never re-plastered between their initial construction and the nineteenth century.[116] This implies that in the meantime the façades were increasingly weathered, which would have been especially visible when the quality of their construction was mediocre. The streetscape was made of new façades in limited number and of some recently restored frontages, both bright white, which would have stood in stark contrast with many more or

116 The building authorizations between 1600 and 1830 at Lyons mention only white, except in one sole case grey (AML, DD registers, 315 WP series, 316 WP series).

less damaged surfaces characterized by traces of water and leaking gutters, lichens and mosses, general dirt and soot, plaster partly falling down to reveal the stones of the masonry-work, teared oiled paper at the windows, flaking paint, and so on. The street paving would hardly have been in a better state: holes and irregularities were common, along with stagnant water, and refuse and mud after rain. The effects of time and decay would have been perceptible everyday phenomena.[117]

I.4 Conclusion

The chronological decomposition of material space through the dating of production units corresponding to particular social processes allows for a better comprehension of urban space. It provides new ways of understanding the temporality of perceived space, associating in a comprehensive image diverse phenomena of varying chronological depth. A building produced in the seventeenth century can exist today, but its roof will likely have been remade two or three times, its windows modernized about as often, its façade repainted and re-plastered also two or three times, including once in the four decades before the present. The shop fronts will also likely have been remade recently. It will stand along a street that could be of the same age, but will usually be older, whether medieval or from the sixteenth century. In this case, the age of the street will not be recognizable, because a medieval street will have been widened and straightened when the neighboring houses were rebuilt with a setback and not always following exactly the same line. In the present, we perceive objects of different ages, but with a skin or surface that is generally much more recent than the structure hidden behind it.[118] The understanding of this material reality implies the dissociation of the successive events and modifications that have given rise to it.

Three distinct temporalities have been identified in this analysis:

- *Superficial temporality:*
  This concerns the surfaces covering the structures, including the painting and plaster on a building, and the paving and asphalt on a street. It also includes the joineries, the tiles of the roofs and the shop fronts, as well as the

117 This is also true of people. In the urban space, thanks to medicine, people retain a young aspect much longer in life. Hair dyes and cosmetic treatments, still rare a few decades ago, have become quite common.

118 People often take the age of the skin for the age of the building.

annual vegetation. It is the skin of what we see, indeed what we see first. It is generally not older than a few decades.

- *Structural temporality:*
  This concerns the construction-units and their architectural structure, the materiality of the streets, the trees and the stones. It directly determines the form of what is perceived.
- *Remanent temporality:*
  This concerns the shapes determined by material productions that have since disappeared, but which remain partly visible through the constraints they have imposed on later constructions and the spatial continuity they generated in the process. This temporality is perceived either indirectly thanks to an informed analysis of space, or thanks to cultural representations which can be very imprecise.

Part Two: Demography and building typology

II.1 The 'cells' of urban space: thinking building typology

The first part of this book dealt with the temporality of material space and with the units into which it can be decomposed. This approach was applied to the study of the anthropological origins of the material facts, like the materialization of property limits, which assumes such great importance for the inscription of our societies in space.

This second part considers another aspect of this fundamental anthropological dimension, one which is necessary to understand the material city space: the architectural typology, not seen here as just the categorization of building forms, but also as the result of the construction processes of a given society. An architectural or building type is actually the materialization in discrete architectural and urban planning forms, material choices, and aesthetic modalities, of a way of functioning proper to a given group or society.[1] Therefore, its analysis must deal with the inscription of this group or society in space, but also with the way it, or rather the part of it making its living from the economic branch of building, produces an adapted space. The typology actually contributes to the determination of the forms of the urban fabric, and in two ways.

Firstly, it determines planning choices. One draws a new planned development according to a building program that generally follows a typological form, a type called "*tipo portante*" by Caniggia,[2] which can be translated as 'dominant building type'. A dominant type is the way buildings are generally conceived and produced at a given moment in time, by a given society. A planned development can potentially be drawn for or made of several building types, in order to realize a more or less complex project. The examination of the changing typology through time, presented below, will provide clear examples of the nature of dominant building types. Building plots are conceived according to these types and what I propose to call their assemblage properties. The concept of assemblage property is fundamental to understanding the materiality of urban space and the genesis of the urban fabric. An assemblage property is what de-

1 As developed PART I, it is not only functioning that is important here, for the semiotic dimension is also highly significant.

2 Caniggia, Maffei. *Lettura dell'edilizia di base*. Peter J. Larkham, Andrew Jones. *A glossary of urban form*. London: Historical Geography research Series 26, Institute of British Geographers, 1991, 'type'. Johnson, Matthew. *Living space*.

https://doi.org/10.1515/9783110623062-004

fines the juxtaposition of individual buildings (or *édifices*, defined in PART I as buildings with a given function along with their associated built and unbuilt spaces). For example, a detached suburban house is today assembled in relation to neighboring buildings of the same type, with a fence delimiting its plot, and is part of a continuous line of development along a street. This determines a rhythm of modes of access, fences, buildings with similar dimensions and shapes, repeated over and over, all respecting the same by-laws, and produced in similar circumstances. Characteristic of the old centers of the European cities is the urban house or multi-familial building assembled along with its neighbors by a blind wall (generally a party-wall), which is intended to be hidden – and used – by an adjacent building of the same type, the whole forming a unity on a specific section of a street. This common organization gives rise to a linear frontage alignment and strictly determines the public space of the street. Private space branches off the public space through a doorway and then on towards the upper floors and the back of the plot, which is often occupied by a garden area, a courtyard, or service buildings. The back of the plot forms an assembly with other plot-rears, depending on another street or streets, repeating the same motif in another direction.[3] This organization is associated with the plot dimensions within which the buildings are placed, with a variable number of floors, i.e., over the ground-floor, and with the lateral polarization of private and public space, as well as with choices of materials, roof shapes and architectural details, thus producing a recognizable urban fabric (*tissus urbain* in French, *tessuto urbano* in Italian).

This fabric is homogeneous when the buildings are of the same type. As new planned developments are conceived with a particular typology in mind, the size of the plots also tells us about the nature of the social and economic project. In a subdivision planned today around a sprawling city, this size corresponds to the

---

3 Interestingly, this is a part of the definition of urban space in the *Encyclopédie*. Denis Jaucourt, Denis Diderot (eds.). *Encyclopédie ou dictionnaire raisonné des sciences, des arts et des métiers*. Neufchâtel: 1751-1772, vol. 17: 277: "Il faut […] que la distance d'une rue à celle qui lui est parallèle, soit telle qu'entre l'une & l'autre il reste une place pour deux maisons de bourgeois, dont l'une a la vue dans une rue, & l'autre dans celle qui lui est opposée. Chacune de ces maisons doit avoir environ cinq à six toises de large, sur sept à huit d'enfoncement, avec une cour de pareille grandeur: ce qui donne la distance d'une rue à l'autre de trente-deux à trente-trois toises". Edition numérique collaborative et critique de l'Encyclopédie (1751–1772), enccre.academie-sciences.fr/encyclopedie/article/v17–449–0/ (accessed 8 april 2018). [*The distance between two parallel streets has to leave room for two bourgeois houses, one fronting onto a street, the other on the other street. Each house must have a width of about 5–6* toises (10–12 m), *and a depth of 7–8* toises (14–16 m), *with a courtyard of similar size: which gives the distance from one street to a parallel one of 32–33* toises (about 65 m)].

market aimed at, and, in given circumstances, corresponds to the given level of wealth of the builder, tenant, or buyer. This was no different in the cities of the modern period, where the size of a plot also corresponded to the wealth of the acquirer or investor. Planned developments are often modified, during their implementation, in order to answer unanticipated demands, such as the reuniting of several plots to build a larger building or to sub-sell in secondary subdivision,[4] or sublet, so as to increase profit through speculation. The possibility of uniting several plots, or buying plots that have not yet been defined, are adjustment variables between the planned development, defining the street and open space pattern, and the production of the buildings.

Urban fabric is heterogeneous when the urban space is old and the buildings of the first period of urbanization have been replaced in part or in totality by others of differing types, as occurs when, in the suburban subdivisions that first appeared in Paris in the 1920s to 1930s, individual detached houses (*pavillons:* detached houses built in that case often with *meulière* stone) are today replaced by multi-familial buildings which are small because of the limiting plot size. Houses then coexist with larger buildings. The ancient urban fabric can have been transformed or 'metamorphized', during successive periods corresponding to different building types, thus giving rise to potentially quite different assemblage properties, producing juxtaposed fragments of landscape with differing ages and shapes. The constraints which are exerted by the extant fabric on the new productions, in accordance with the new types, lead to particular adaptations of the buildings constructed according to past types.

These constraints can be so powerful that the incentive to produce new developments will make it all but impossible to remodel the old fabric and developers will thus choose instead to build in new spaces free of constructions, generally rural or garden spaces around the built-up areas. This incentive was, for example, very strong in big cities like London, Paris, Edinburg and Lyons in the first half of the nineteenth century, when it was much easier to produce new buildings, following the contemporary multi-familial housing type in new allotments (*lotissements*, subdivisions), rather than in the older quarters. The difficulty of building in old quarters had become significant, because acquiring adequate building sites by uniting of two or more plots was not easy, but also because of the high demand for such building sites in booming economies. After the developments of new areas outside the old urban centers, this led to the re-developments of large sectors of the historic centers of Paris and Lyons from the mid-1840s to the end of the century, in a move that in France is gener-

4 A secondary subdivision is a subdivision of a plot issued from a subdivision.

ally – though in the case of Lyons somewhat improperly – called "Haussmannism".[5] The erasing of the old fabric allowed for the creation of fully new and typologically adapted plot patterns and quarters. The urban renewals of many other large French cities, including Toulouse, Marseilles, Bordeaux, Rouen, and Nantes, followed on a few years later, albeit sometimes without a great deal of dynamism, a result of insufficient investment capital and potential for capital gains on the part of investors. Similar developments occurred with great intensity, however, in other countries, such as Italy in the 1880s (Rome, Palermo, Naples ...), and in the European cities after World War Two, especially in the 1960s and 1970s. The change was not only morphological, however, because the old quarters scheduled for demolition were generally, before the appearance of heritage politics, inhabited by poor people. Thus it was that re-development answered the need for a plot pattern adapted to the dominant contemporary building types, while also fulfilling a political objective of replacing poor inhabitants by members of the growing middle-classes. The possibility of high capital gains, while generally not made public, was often a major aspect of these projects.

Building typology has mainly been studied by architects, geographers and art historians, producing in the process a very rich literature; but it has been somewhat overlooked by historians.[6] Existing research for the most part, and sometimes even exclusively, deals with the form of the constructions, categorized according to their size, place, interior distributions, materials, decors, and building techniques. The more magnificent elite constructions have often been privileged in these studies,[7] but more socially oriented considerations, the study of social housing aside, are somewhat rare, and certainly do not correspond in quantity to the proportion of buildings for the poor and the middle classes.

---

5 As the transformations occurred at the same time in the two cities and were elements of a single project, Paris was not a model for Lyons. So, to use the word *Haussmannism* for Lyons is historically wrong: Bernard Gauthiez. La transformation de Lyon et Paris au Second Empire: le projet du ministre de l'Intérieur De Persigny, les exécutants Haussmann et Vaïsse. Aldo Casamento (ed.). *Città nuove fondate in Italia e in Europa dal medioevo al Novecento.* Rome: Kappa, 2012: 323 – 344. François Loyer. *Paris XIXe siècle. L'immeuble et la rue.* Paris: Hazan, 1987.

6 See Gauthiez. The history.

7 For example: Boudon et al., *Système.* History of art is the most present discipline in the literature addressing these questions, at least since the pioneering studies of Lille (Paul Parent. *L'architecture civile à Lille au XVIIe siècle.* Lille: Emile-Raoust, 1925) and Rouen (Raimond Quenedey. *L'habitation rouennaise, étude d'histoire, de géographie et d'archéologie urbaines.* Rouen: A. Lestringant, 1926). On the city of Toulouse (Michèle Eclache. *Demeures toulousaines du XVIIe siècle: sources d'archives (1600-1630 environ).* Toulouse: Éditions du Centre National de la Recherche Scientifique/Université de Toulouse Le Mirail, 2006).

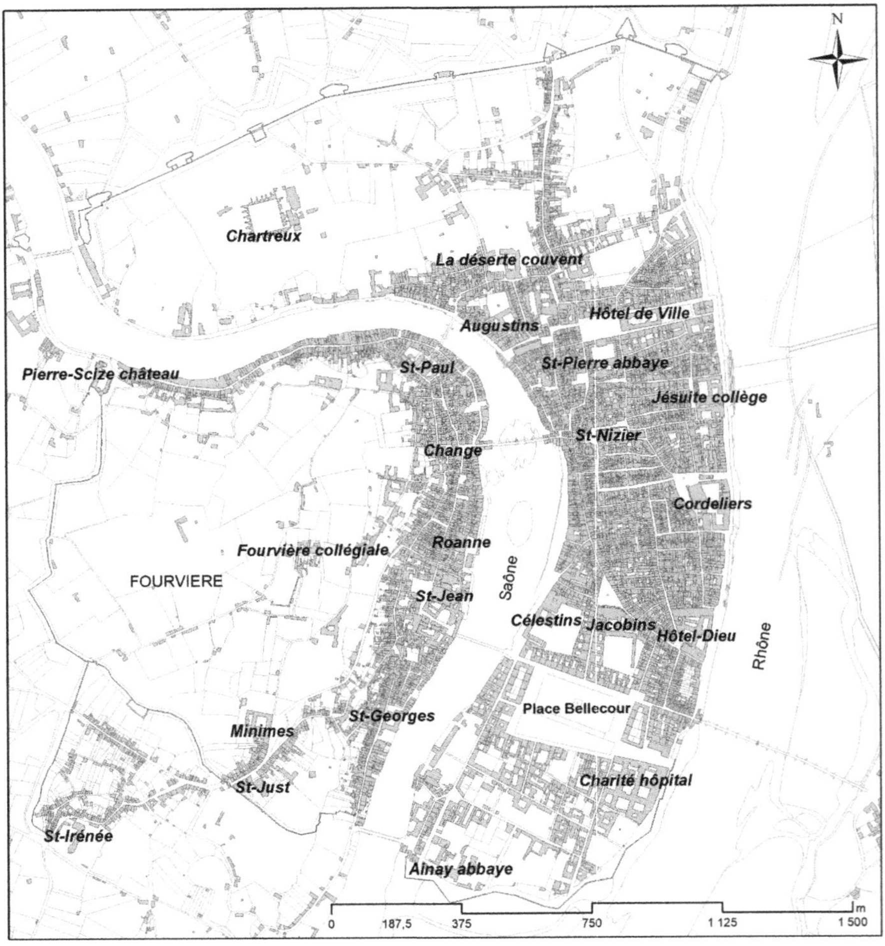

Figure II.1 Lyons circa 1745. A map from the Geographic Information System

The link between building type and plot pattern is sometimes taken into account, be it with a possible confusion between these two realities.[8] The assemblage properties are generally absent from these studies, which do not consider

8 Françoise Boudon. Tissu urbain et architecture: l'analyse parcellaire comme base de l'histoire architecturale. *Annales. Économies, Sociétés, Civilisations*, 30/4 (1976), 773–818.

many of the factors that together determine the type, such as financing, production processes,[9] management, and demographic determinations.[10]

This last point doesn't seem to have ever been considered closely, with little or no attention having been paid to the relation between population censuses and constructions, something which can only be achieved by means of a close comparison between construction and population entries in serial sources. In the present study, this was undertaken for the city of Lyons using a Geographic Information System (GIS).[11]

II.1.1 Building the historical Geographic Information System

A GIS is a very useful tool for dealing with a wealth of data of varied natures, associated with features in space, such as buildings. In the present context, this implied the constitution of many databases, the reconstitution of a vector map of plots and buildings thanks to nineteenth-century cadaster plans, and earlier tax rolls, an analysis of the extant buildings, as well as the mapping of other available data. The precise mapping of each new construction, development and transformation of public space, in time and according to their real extents, has made possible the maps presented in PART I. This leads also to the identification of processes that are otherwise difficult to discern: group rebuilding, for example, was very frequent. Change at different space scales becomes clearer, including individual buildings, neighborhoods, quarters, and even the city as a whole (studied in PART III). Time scales also clearly appear in space: yearly cycles, economic ups and downs, trends over decades and centuries.

To build such a GIS, one with a sound topographical basis, the following method has been developed. Firstly, a vector plan of the city was drawn, based on the first cadastral plans of 1830 – 31. The geometry of the plans was corrected to make the same objects correspond exactly with their present locations on the vector plan used today by the City of Lyons and the Grand-Lyon Metropole council. Direct geo-referencing of old maps and rubber-sheeting are clearly not

9 There are exceptions: Roberto Fregna. *La pietrificazione del denaro, studi sulla proprietà urbana tra XVIe–XVIIe secolo.* Bologne: CLUEB, 1990; Jean-François Chauvard. *La circulation des biens à Venise, stratégies patrimoniales et marché immobilier (1600-1750).* Rome: Ecole Française de Rome, 2005.

10 Gauthiez, *Espace urbain,* 110 – 112.

11 Bernard Gauthiez, Olivier Zeller. Un SIG historique sur l'espace urbain de Lyon aux XVII-XIXe siècles. Marco Panzeri, Andrea Farruggia (eds.). *Fonti, metafonti e GIS per l'indagine della struttura storica del territorio: verso il networking.* Turin: Politecnico di Torino, 2009, 39 – 49; 114 – 117.

appropriate methods, because the geometry of the old town maps proceeds from measuring in the field, which was generally not sufficiently accurate before the early nineteenth century and thus gives rise to discordant angles and locations, but also because each new plan was made thanks to a new measuring campaign in the field, never (before the nineteenth century) reusing the measures of the previous one(s). Any two plans therefore differ because their topographical structure is never exactly the same, and because of that superimposing representations of the same objects make them appear discordant. So I adopted as a reference geometry the vector plan used today,[12] a plan with a very small margin of error, redrawing the historical maps in order to obtain a precise superimposition with respect to the present day situation.[13] In this manner, the same object could be represented at exactly the same location and following exactly the same contour, as long as it still exists. Three main layers of shapes were drawn: plots, buildings, and lines, including other topographical features such as bridges, river banks, stairs, etc.[14]

A second step was to draw a vector plan of Lyons in about 1745 on the same topographical basis, also in three layers, and using more than three hundreds partial eighteenth century maps of the city,[15] such as seigneury plans.[16] Then, a system was needed to locate the alignment authorizations. As the only systematic information available was the proprietor's name, mentioned in the authorization deeds and in fiscal serial sources covering the city in its entirety or large parts of it, the system was based on the successive owners of the buildings,

12 Bernard Gauthiez. Lyon en 1824-32: un plan de la ville sous forme vecteur d'après le cadastre ancien. *Géocarrefour*, 83/1 (2008): 57–67.

13 The principles of the method, already followed by many scholars, drawing manually, from the nineteenth century to study the town's transformation, has been exposed by Schatti and Viaccoz de Noyers à propos the *atlas historique de Genève, Nicolas* Schätti, Anne-Marie Viaccoz De Noyers. L'Atlas historique de la ville de Genève, vieilles méthodes, nouveaux outils. *Patrimoine et architecture*, 14–15 (2005): 58–64.

14 See Ian N. Gregory. *A place in history: a guide to using GIS in historical research.* Oxford and Oakville: Oxbow books, 2003; Ian N. Gregory, Paul S. Ell. *Historical GIS: techniques, methodologies and scholarship.* Cambridge: Cambridge University Press, 2007.

15 For example AML 2 S 26, *Atlas de la rente noble de l'archevêché*; ADR 10 G 2338, seigneury of St-Jean chapter; ADR 15 G 188, seigneury of St-Nizier chapter.

16 This plan was first drawn by hand in the early 1990s. It was vectorized and its geometry corrected in the mid-2000s in reference to the vectorized plan utilized by the Grand-Lyon Metropole. The date of 1745 was chosen because detailed plans exist for parts of the city from the mid-eighteenth century, covering an important proportion of it, but are very rare before, but also because 1745 is before the big transformations of the city which often occurred a little later (renewals in the early nineteenth century, the destruction of the buildings along the River Saône bank in 1793, and so on).

which was the only precise information given in the records and deeds before 1790, along with the street name and some orientation elements like the neighbors (though not always) given generally according to the cardinal points.[17] This system based on property was the only one possible on the basis of written and sometimes cartographic sources, because the record of the successive owners is the only more or less complete one available in the archives. Two complementary methods have also been used to ensure the success of the mapping process:

From the 1830 to 1831 cadastre, and using the numeration system (even and odd numbers) established around 1810, it was possible to map the proprietors in 1814 to 1815, known from this year's census.[18] The first complete census was made in 1808, but the numeration system was different at that time (following a system in use from 1790 to around 1810). As the owners were often the same in 1808 as in 1814, it was possible to map 1808 by keeping the names where they were documented at both dates, and by filling in the gaps from the 1808 census, in which houses are numbered in numerical order (1, 2, 3 … 148, for example) for each quarter.[19] The numeration system of the French Revolution period could thus be reconstructed and mapped with accuracy. This made possible the location of data associated to this numeration system, notably the building authorizations.

The second phase involved the use of the listing order of older tax documents to reconstruct the spatial sequence of properties in the actual streets. It was possible to prove that this registering order had been very stable through the eighteenth century, even from at least the mid-seventeenth century, each quarter being surveyed according to a particular spatial order and with only small variations to the tax agent's route.[20] When compared to the 1808 census made according to numerated buildings, and bearing in mind that some thirty percent of the proprietors were the same, the route and proprietors in 1789 given in the 1/20th (*Vingtième*) tax list could be reconstructed with a fair degree

---

17 The orientation is generally correct, but, when a street like Rue De Flandres-Rue Puits du Sel-Rue Bourgneuf-Rue Pierre Scize (successive names of the same street) turns progressively east-west although its initial axis was north-south in the city center, the error due to a same compass reference kept for one side can be as much as 90°.

18 AML 921 WP 023–025.

19 AML 921 WP 005–010. The numeration system established in 1790 is an evolution of a previous one, determined according to a lesser number of quarters and attributing a number to a given building, rather than to the order place of a proprietor in a succession of registered entries.

20 Bernard Gauthiez, Olivier Zeller. Ordre textuel et ordre spatial à Lyon à l'époque moderne. Du parcours de visite au rôle nominal, une spatialité implicite. *Histoire et Mesure*. XXV-1 (2010): 197–230.

of certainty.[21] Then, the 1/20th tax list in 1766, preserved for half the city, could be mapped rather easily thanks to the high proportion of common names of proprietors compared to 1789. Unfortunately, the remaining sources (i. e., the identified ones, as some unexplored archives may contain new ones) do not allow one to go back earlier in time using on the basis of annual tax records, but other sources can still be very useful and help fill the gap for earlier dates. The lantern tax list of 1698 has been mapped relying on corner proprietors given in the *Règlement Général d'Alignement* of 1680 as landmarks.[22] This *Règlement* is a text detailing street by street the line of the façades to be respected if a building were to be reconstructed, and it mentions nearly all the proprietors of houses located at corners, which numbered about 800, which is 23 percent of their total number.[23] From this source and the lists established in 1677 for a city loan, which was unfortunately partial if one considers the whole city but complete for several quarters, it was possible to redraw the sequences of the route of the tax agent and to map the properties.[24] The great stability of these routes greatly facilitated the mapping process.

These reconstructed proprietor locations, fairly reliable for 1814, 1808, 1789,[25] 1766,[26] 1698,[27] and 1677 (when the data is available),[28] can be extended to other dates, but only partially, in conjunction with other partial sources, for example to 1744, 1723 and 1636. It has been successfully extended to 1493 as well, thanks to a

---

21 The 1/20th tax is annual and based in principle on one twentieth of the rent value of a property, generally a single building, but sometimes a group of, or a part of, a single building. As the annual rent value is itself also about 1/20th of the real estate value of the building, the 1/20th tax amount equals more or less 1/400th of the total value of the building (or group of them, or part of it). This was in principle, for, as can be seen comparing the tax amounts to the value given in selling transactions, the actual amount was, in 1789, closer to one fourth or one fifth of 1/20th.
22 AML DD 56.
23 The *Consulat* decided in 1698 to establish a public lighting system in the streets, which was financed by a tax based on the building's value, AML FF 0754–0755. The 1680 *Règlement Général d'alignement* is a by-law adopted in December 1680 to determine for all streets and squares the façade lines each new building had to respect. Its goal was to regularize the street width in a context of rapidly growing traffic and to organize the embellishment of the city, Gauthiez, Zeller, Beautifying the City.
24 The *Consulat* went bankrupt in 1677. Among various measures, it was decided to impose a loan on all rich people in the city. An inquiry followed in every quarter, but half of the results are unfortunately lacking, AML CC 4187. The mapping of wealth in the city, despite being partial, is quite interesting.
25 AML 3 C 52.
26 AML 2 II 160.
27 AML FF 0754–0755.
28 AML CC 4187.

source which proved of an extraordinary wealth,[29] and which was without equivalent until the first municipal census in 1808 and the cadastre in 1830. The system can also be strengthened by identifying the location of building permits. Once a permit can be located according to the name of the proprietor involved, its neighbors, generally mentioned in the deed according to their compass location (North, South, East, or West), can also be easily located, thus providing some new proprietors names. This is of great importance as about 50 percent of the re-buildings and façade modifications were carried out by series of neighbors in spatially continuous sequences.

These locations could be matched with the still extant seventeenth- and eighteenth-century buildings, which were documented in another vector layer in the GIS.[30] About 30 percent of the buildings extant in 1800, excluding religious ones, still exist today. Iconography, despite being rather scarce, can also be sometimes of some help.[31] Each source forms a particular layer which can be matched with the other ones by crossing data, which proved to be extremely informative. The description and approximate dating of buildings using art history methods, including the survey of urban signs and of the proprietor's initials, which were often placed over the main door and match with the building authorization, constitute another very useful layer.

Years of mapping and crossing the available information from many sources have produced reliable knowledge of the location of the proprietors, and thus also reliable knowledge of the location of the building authorizations (or *permis d'alignement*), the locations given in the GIS matching with the information of the extant ancient buildings. The certainty is more or less total for central streets, which are better documented, and when many buildings are still extant. Locations in the areas that have been later demolished, re-developed and along the longest streets (Grande Côte, Rue Pierre-Scize running for more than one kilometer), where the sequences of proprietors may slightly shift, generally retain some uncertainty. The location of the authorizations concerning only the modification of a frontage (change in the bays, windows and doors, signs, awnings ...) is generally more difficult to ascertain, because in these instances the neighbors were rarely mentioned.

---

29 AML CC 4 to 12, *Nommées.*

30 Some rare dates are still legible on the buildings themselves. These were identified by means of a systematic field survey.

31 Iconography does, however, tend to represent the same places over and over again. And it is somewhat scarce at Lyons. Rouen provides an interesting comparison. The city still conserves about 15 percent of the buildings extant in 1800, but a total of a little over 30 percent can be characterized thanks to ancient iconography (Gauthiez, La logique, 414–15).

It seems that the city was administered quite seriously and conscientiously, as the alignment permits were, with only a few exceptions, systematically respected by the actual transformation or construction of a building, and those who tried to escape authorization, or simply ignored its necessity, were fined. Some even had to demolish what had been erected without authorization, or to rebuild according to a different façade line imposed by the City, which was quite expensive.

Some areas are a little less well documented, mainly the St-Jean Cathedral area, where the jurisdiction of the religious precinct was not controlled by the City. So there the St-Jean chapter was master of the building permits, for which the record is not complete. The St-Irénée and St-Just quarter was also a distinct jurisdiction, with the same results. The military administration had jurisdiction over the area of the fortifications, its records seem to have been lost. In addition, the *Ponts et Chaussées* royal administration was responsible for the authorizations on the roads outside the city gates, of which only a few deeds have been conserved, and, lastly, the main public buildings were treated separately, like the Hôtel-de-Ville (City Hall), whose construction began in 1646, but which was not subjected to the alignment authorization. Of course, in this case, an alignment plan was nevertheless drawn.

The results of research carried out in many important archives was recorded in databases and then vector layers associated with each database were drawn. Each tax list, for example, was depicted in a vector layer.[32] Once the layers have been created, they can be superimposed and allow for the cross checking of information.

One of the major difficulties involved in taking demography into account is that it requires one to consider the numbers of inhabitants of dwellings, of buildings, and of households in a given entry of a given source,[33] all in a context where

32 Technically, the 'obvious' method would have been to make a 'juncture' between a layer of polygons and a database, but, as the entries in the tax database do not systematically correspond to single buildings, but sometimes also to a part of a building or a group of them, each entry had to be reexamined. For instance, the 1789, 1/20th of the tax list contains 3,821 entries, but only 3,431 buildings existed in 1786 [according to François P.S. Brac. *Mémoire lu par M. Brac, avocat au parlement et aux cours de Lyon, ancien échevin de la même ville, dans l'assemblée de Messieurs les anciens échevins de la ville de Lyon, tenue le mercredi 30 août 1786 dans l'hôtel des exercices de la Flèche, avec quelques notes ajoutées par l'éditeur.* Manuscript, La Perrière private archive, 1787. (I gratefully owe this source to O. Zeller)]. In that case, it means that the properties are listed, among them parts of buildings or apartments.

33 Ennio Concina, in his remarkable study of Venice, does not fully deal with this difficulty, as he sometimes appears to confuse the number of property units with the number of households

mono-familial and multi-familial buildings may co-exist, and without a perfect correspondence between use and architectural typology, for a given building can during its history become multi-familial when subdivided, without changing its appearance, as occurred regularly in modern times, or, more rarely, be modified so as to become mono-familial (which nowadays happens when two or more apartments are joined together to form a larger one). It can even be included in a living place regrouping several previous living units or houses. The aim of PART II is precisely to better understand the relationship between architectural typology and demography at the quarter and city scales.

Understanding how the production of buildings, their adaptation to new needs, and demography relate to one another is central to the more general comprehension of the transformation of cities and theirs dynamics. A 'demography' of building production is even possible and will be examined in PART III.[34] The aim here is instead to compare building uses with census data, using notably the data gathered and studied by Olivier Zeller for the years 1597 and 1636. This documentation is particularly precious because in Lyons the development of multi-familial housing occurred during precisely this period, which is in fact very early compared to the majority of big cities in Europe. Current terminology is poorly adapted to describing this, however, for a house is usually assumed to be mono-familial, whereas a building (*immeuble* in French, and *maison* in the French of Lyons) is generally assumed to be multi-familial.

To understand this development, two points have to be clarified:

1. The development of multi-familial dwelling in the same building was initially independent of any new architectural type. In the Middle Ages, some houses were already subdivided to allow for several households, without any modification to their shape other than an interior partition. This was common in the largest cities, and present at Lyons also, but to a much lesser extent than in Paris or Rouen, as we will see. Originally, a perfect equivalence existed between house and household, at least in principle, and this holds true for Lyons in 1446, when there were about 1,700 houses for about 1,700 households.[35] It is probably because multi-familial housing developed at first as a way of using a formerly mono-familial house that the

and/or houses. See Ennio Concina, *Venezia nell'età moderna: struttura e funzioni*. Venice: Marsilio, 1994, 193–195.

34 Gauthiez, Des unités.

35 One has to be prudent in this case, as the period was a demographic low point, and the source only gives taxpayers and so does not take into account the poorest people. Nevertheless, at that time, few people were dwelling in several united houses, and few others were dwelling in a part of one.

name *maison* ('house') was, until the nineteenth century, retained in Lyons even to describe the later architectural type of multi-familial housing. I shall hence in consequence generally call the Lyons multi-familial constructions 'buildings' or 'houses'. The 'building' can be defined as a single construction-unit, or a part of a construction-unit corresponding to the spaces distributed by a single entrance.

2. Even if the building is intended for mono or multi-familial use, other uses, or functions, are present. The building is always meant for different functions, at least until the end of the nineteenth century or the early twentieth, when functionalism began to prevail. These other activities can be trades, handcrafts, services, or even proto-industries. The silk-weavers, so numerous at Lyons in the modern period, worked and lived with their family and employees in the same space, often a single room. Spaces for living and spaces for other activities were generally the same for the majority of the population. The distinction appeared probably first when the shops developed in the late fifteenth century, replacing benches placed in the public space of the street. The commercial space became interior instead of exterior, which created an incentive to add a new floor to the house, and was therefore an important component of typological change from the late fifteenth century onwards.[36] Later, from the late seventeenth century, the shop ceiling or vault was raised in order to create room for a mezzanine (*entresol*), used generally as a dwelling space for the tenant or warden of the shop.

The functionalist conception of buildings, as it emerged from the late nineteenth century and early twentieth century and later attained a position of dominance, as of today, was based on the consideration that each building should have only one function. This blinds us to their other important properties, and, unfortunately, this correspondence in principle still dominates the historiography of buildings. The average urban building in the modern period, both in Lyons and elsewhere, was designed so as to be able to accommodate several uses, thus exhibiting significant plasticity. It was equipped for living and cooking thanks to fire places,[37] but it was intended first of all – except when it was

36 Bernard Gauthiez. La transformation des villes au bas Moyen Âge entre Valence et Pise. *Rodis, journal of medieval and post-medieval archaeology*, 1 (2019), 23–49.

37 Only the dwellings of the wealthiest and of the religious were actually heated during the cold seasons. The dwellings of the middle classes and of the poor could be regularly heated only when coal became affordable, from the beginning of the nineteenth century. This explains why, in the seventeenth-century buildings, the windows of the heated rooms are few and widely spaced, though this is rare (examples include the houses built by Perrachon de St-Maurice Place

the dwelling or premises of the owner – to be rented, whatever the profession of the tenants, and to make a profit. This explains both the great sameness of the buildings produced in a given period and their great variety of uses, as evident in the written record. This also explains why, in a multi-familial building, a single floor often comprises several rooms which can be rented either separately or as a single unit; why each one is provided with, when possible, its own access to the staircase; and why they can be connected thanks to doorframes in the separating walls, which can be either closed by a thin wall or equipped with a door. The building structure, thanks to this modular conception, can be adapted to particular and varied demands. This accounts for why tenants sometimes rented rooms on different floors in the same building.[38] If plasticity can be achieved in principle thanks to possible openings between rooms on the same floor, it is often difficult to take advantage of this possibility simply because the rooms will generally already be rented. Overall, then, the conception of buildings in Lyons before the twentieth century is remarkably adaptable to variegated needs and the buildings are equipped accordingly, with fire-places, privies (common in the back-yard and beside the staircase, but also, from the seventeenth century onwards, sometimes specific to a single dwelling), and decorative elements expressing the values and tastes of the social milieu for which the building was intended. Moreover, the ground-floor was optimised from an economic perspective, with minimum space occupied by the load carrying structures and the staircase, and potential to accommodate extremely varied activities. Indeed, the design of the ground-floor was, given the means available at the time, as close as possible to the 'free plan' dreamed of by the twentieth century modernists.

II.2 The building typology of Lyons from the fifteenth to the nineteenth century[39]

The form of the buildings in Lyons has been studied in a number of respects, but no research into its evolution and the relationship between form and use has

---

Bellecour c.1670, or the Capuchins convent in the 1620s). The average building was abundantly lit by large windows in order to facilitate economic activities.

38 Olivier Zeller. A l'enseigne du Chameau, manières d'habiter, manières de gérer à Lyon au XVIIIe siècle. *Cahiers d'histoire*, 38/1 (1993): 26 – 54.

39 This chapter draws on and develops from Bernard Gauthiez. Typologie architecturale et démographie. L'habitat collectif à Lyon à l'époque moderne, 1500-1800. Mathieu Grenet, Yannick Jambon, Marie-Laure Ville (eds.). *Histoire urbaine et sciences sociales. Mélanges en l'honneur du professeur Olivier Zeller.* Paris: Garnier, 2014: 19 – 48.

been carried out. The existing literature on the subject in Lyons deals mainly with art history and architecture, particularly in the period from the late fifteenth century to the first half of the sixteenth,[40] and with a specific focus on the west bank of the River Saône (the quarter named Vieux-Lyon today).[41] A study, mainly architectural, has dealt with the nineteenth century.[42] Françoise Bayard has produced a summary of the modern period,[43] and archaeological research has provided some very useful elements for understanding the evolutions of the Middle Ages, notably thanks to the work of Catherine Arlaud, as well as excavations at the Place des Terreaux, Rue Monseigneur-Lavarenne and Place de la Bourse.[44] These contributions can now be reassessed in the context of a wider, extended and more systematic theoretical framework.[45]

II.2.1 The Middle Ages

Existing medieval buildings are very rare in Lyons, maybe because the majority was built with rammed earth, and those which are present do not offer many possibilities for obtaining knowledge of the overall nature of medieval Lyons. Nevertheless, the available data suggest a rather radical evolution of the dominant building type during the fifteenth century.

Excavations at Rue Monseigneur-Lavarenne made by the Service Municipal d'Archéologie have revealed a spatial organisation that predates the fourteenth century. The street was bordered by modest mono-familial houses, with a façade width of 5–7 m, each possessing a cellar. The houses were separated by lateral

---

40 Maryannick Lavigne. Lyon, le quartier Saint-Jean. Jean Guillaume (ed.). *La maison de ville à la Renaissance. Actes du Colloque de Tours (1977).* Paris: Picard, 1983, 37–41.

41 Nathalie Mathian, Francis Martinuzzi. Lyon, histoire architecturale et urbaine de la rive droite de la Saône. Lyons: Ecole d'Architecture/Agence d'urbanisme pour le développement de l'agglomération lyonnaise, 1999 (unpublished paper).

42 Dominique Bertin, Nathalie Mathian. *Lyon, silhouettes d'une ville recomposée: architecture et urbanisme, 1789-1914.* Lyons: Éditions Lyonnaises d'Art et d'Histoire, 2008, 154–330.

43 Françoise Bayard. *Vivre à Lyon sous l'Ancien Régime.* Paris: Perrin, 1997, 212–244.

44 Catherine Arlaud. Contribution à l'étude de l'habitat médiéval dans le quartier St-Jean à Lyon: analyse archéologique d'un immeuble n° 58 rue St-Jean. Lyons: Mémoire de maîtrise, Université Lumière Lyon 2, 1983 (unpublished paper).

45 John Schoffield. *The building of London from the Conquest to the Great Fire.* London: British Museum Press, 1993; Paolo Maretto. *La casa veneziana nella storia della città.* Venice: Marsilio, 1986; Boudon et al., *Système*; Bernard Gauthiez. Les maisons de Rouen, XII-XVIIIe siècles. *Archéologie medievale*, 23 (1993): 131–217; Gian Luigi Maffei. *Firenze, la casa fiorentina nella storia della città.* Padova: Marsilio, 1990.

passages giving access to the back part of the plot. There were no cellars under these passages.[46] The area was described in an early eighteenth-century survey as badly built and in very poor repair.[47] It was inhabited by very poor people and this probably explains why the houses discovered in the excavations were not rebuilt before their destruction in the mid-nineteenth century, long after other archaic forms had disappeared from other parts of the city. A very old wooden house structure with two floors does still exist nearby at n° 13 Rue Ferrachat.[48] We may be certain that it was constructed before the late fifteenth century, because wooden structures were forbidden from that point onward, and a second floor would appear to have been added to it in the early seventeenth century. It was clearly a dwelling for the poor, with a frontage width of just 4.2 m. Such a house probably represents the typical type of dwelling occupied by poor people, and it was very common outside the city center, as may be inferred from the *Nommées*, a sort of cadastral survey conserved for the years 1376, 1388, 1406, 1446 and beyond.[49] These buildings measured about 4–6 m in width along the street, a little more in length towards the back of the plot, sometimes had a first floor, and were built with rammed earth over a stone wall situated on the ground-floor.[50] The houses were aligned along the street, as ascertained by the rare alignment authorizations dating from the thirteenth-fourteenth centuries kept in the municipal archives.[51] The internal layout of the houses is unknown. It is possible that the staircase, when one was needed, was internal.[52]

The large stone house already alluded to at Place Meyssonnier (PART I) corresponds to the highest level of the social scale and, as such, would have been occupied by a member of the city's controlling oligarchy and his *maisonnée*. Members of this oligarchy would have belonged to families owning several dozens of houses, lodging many households throughout the city. The two or three late thirteenth- to early fourteenth-century houses still extant at Rue St-Jean and Place du Change are probably typical of the rich or very rich bourgeoisie of the time. They are also aligned along the street, forming a continuous line.

---

46 Emmanuel Bernot, Éric Bertrand, Thierry Argant, Stéphane Carrara, Jocelyn Laidebeur, Tony Silvino. Document final de synthèse de fouille archéologique, rue Monseigneur-Lavarenne – avenue Adolphe-Max 69005 Lyon. Lyons: Service Archéologique de la Ville de Lyon/Service Régional de l'Archéologie, 2006, vol.1, fig. 128, cross-section n° 66; vol.2, fig. 51, cross-sections n° 100–100bis and 109 (unpublished paper).

47 ADR, 10 G 596, expert assessment, 28 April 1724.

48 This is the eastern part of an actual property reuniting two former houses.

49 AML, *Nommées*, CC series.

50 For example at n° 58 Rue St-Jean, Arlaud, Contribution, 204.

51 Bernard Gauthiez, Le rôle du contrôle, 184.

52 Lavigne, Lyon, le quartier St-Jean, 37–41.

Their frontage width is about 11 m, probably without lateral passageway, but, at n° 29 Rue St-Jean, it is clear that there was previously such a passage, later built over to enlarge the house.[53] It is possible that as early as the fourteenth century some buildings had been added at the rear of the plot, probably belonging to the same address. The lateral passageway was therefore probably intended to access a second building at the rear of the building away from the street, and it became a building hallway (*allée d'immeuble*) when it was built over in the densification process which began in the late fifteenth century, at which time the number of floors also grew significantly, from one or two to three or more.[54]

The inclusion of the space of a former passage within a house probably lies at the origin of what is called at Lyons a *traboule*, a passageway leading from the street to the backyard, or to the rear building, as well as to a staircase leading to the upper floors, and allowing for circulation through a block when interconnected to another building's passageway.[55]

It is also probable that the law of the *mi-mur* (half-wall), which concerned the compulsory common party-wall between two neighboring houses, appeared when the open spaces still extant between the houses along the street were englobed in the reconstructed and enlarged houses. No example of a separation between two buildings consisting of two distinct walls (one for the structure of each building) has been identified in Lyons. This probably means that the common party-wall is a very ancient feature of the city, unlike in Turin for example, where double walls were seemingly prevalent until the end of the Middle Ages. This feature made it possible to save about 60 cm of wall thickness for each separate building, and was probably a consequence of a by-law. It nevertheless had complex legal consequences when a neighbor reconstructed or raised the height of their house.[56] The raising of a house over a party-wall also often implied its reinforcement, notably when the number of floors was significantly increased, as was common from the late fifteenth century.[57] This probably explains two features which became constant from the late fifteenth century onwards: a growing

53 Two lateral passageways still exist Rue du Doyenné, not far from Rue Monseigneur-Lavarenne, and Rue Lanterne.

54 The same phenomenon occurred at Rouen and in other cities in the same period.

55 Gauthiez. *Espace urbain*. 176. *Traboule* is a word employed mainly in Lyons.

56 This right was fully taken into account when the subdivision of the area to the south of Place Bellecour occurred in 1559 to 1560. The plot width was determined at 22 feet, that is, 20 feet between the party walls and 2 feet for two half shared party-walls, Bernard Gauthiez. La topographie de Lyon au XVIe siècle. Jeanne-Marie Dureau (ed.), *Lyon, les années Rabelais (1532-1548)*. Lyons: Archives Municipales de Lyon, 1994, 23–32; 26.

57 Catherine Arlaud (ed.). *Lyon, les dessous de la presqu'île*. Lyons: Ministère de la culture et de la Communication, 2000, 250.

and henceforth compulsory use of stone for the party-walls and the frontages, and a roof parallel to the street, as previous gable roofs were generally associated with buildings placed perpendicular to the street.

No house before the fifteenth century had more than two floors above the ground-floor. The few known medieval houses had only one floor or none, except one, which had two. A loft floor was probably present on every house, which would have resulted in the general description of the houses as being *hautes, moyennes et basses* (this would mean: high with two floors, middle with one floor, and low when only a ground-floor was present). The majority of the houses were mono-familial before the late fifteenth century. There were about 1,700 houses in 1446 and as many households (with maybe 7,000 to 10,000 inhabitants in the city).[58]

II.2.2 The Renaissance: from the mono-familial house to the multi-familial

The number of still extant buildings erected in Lyons between the 1480s and the 1560s is much greater. The period was among the most active, in construction terms, of the city's entire history (see Graph. III.5). By contrast, only a few houses had been built before 1450. The result was that the urbanscape changed dramatically. In some areas the built-up fabric of today still dates predominantly from this period, as is the case around the Rue St-Jean. This period of very intense construction activity is comparable to what occurred in large cities like Rome, Rouen and many others at the same time. It was a European-scale phenomenon.

The existing houses can therefore be used to document the architectural typology of the period, and in significant detail. In addition, the first known plan of the city, drawn in 1544 and published probably a few years later, provides some complementary information, even if it is misleading as regards the real height of the houses, as some still extant houses may have several floors more than on the drawing.[59] If the houses at Rue St-Sébastien are represented with great accuracy, with one full first floor and a second low floor under the roof, those of Rue St-Jean are described as having only two or three floors, although

58 A number of people per household figure of about four is likely to be accurate in this period of demographic low, although this figure could have risen above five in boom periods. The poorest people are not included in this record, but the houses are all counted.

59 Jacques Rossiaud. Du réel à l'imaginaire: la représentation de l'espace urbain dans le plan de Lyon au XVIe siècle. Jeanne-Marie Dureau (ed.). *Le plan de Lyon vers 1550.* Lyons: Archives Municipales de Lyon, 1990, 29–46.

Figure II.2 Renaissance type buildings of the late fifteenth century and early sixteenth, Rue Juiverie

they actually had four or five.[60] The overall design of the buildings are well documented both by measured horizontal plans stored in archives and through their preservation in the form of the extant houses.

The architectural typology of the house – even if the word 'house', as we will see, henceforth covers many multi-familial buildings – is remarkably consistent,

60 Bernard Gauthiez. Les plans de Lyon de 1544-1555: la cartographie des villes au XVIe siècle à repenser? *Le Monde des cartes*, 205 (2010): 119–132. The reason for this difference is probably the difficulty of representing the façades of the houses on a horizontal plan. The real height was reduced to limit distortion.

Figure II.3 A building of the Renaissance type, early seventeenth century
Place de la Trinité (authorized on 18 Jan. 1626 to Jérôme Chausse, Doctor of law, AML DD 44).

varying little between the modest ones constructed in that period in the subdivisions around the city, like Rue St-Sebastien, to the large bourgeois buildings of, say, the Rue St-Jean. A dominant building type clearly dictated the design of the constructions, with variants arising as a result of size according to plot size, of adaptation when the location was at a crossroad, of real estate value in the proximity of the street to the city center, and generally of the social context.

Some rare constructions do not conform to this dominant type, and may be considered as palaces, like today's Musée d'Histoire de Lyon (previously named

Musée Gadagne), a very large residence made by uniting several large houses and new constructions around a wide courtyard.[61]

Compared to the previous medieval period, all available information points to a considerable change in the way houses were conceived and built, after the near complete absence of any new construction in the period following the 1390s.[62] Nothing compares with the large one floor house at the Place Meyssonnier, which is reminiscent of the type of medieval palace inhabited by high ranking aristocrats, burgesses and maybe ecclesiastics.[63] The modest medieval houses were systematically replaced, after 1450, by small buildings keeping the same plot width, but with several floors, like at n° 20 – 22 Rue de la Platière.

The houses built according to the new dominant building type fully occupy the width of the plot along the street. An inside passageway (*allée*) placed along the side of the house on the ground floor[64] – the former open passageway is now fully included in the construction – leads to the courtyard at the rear, where another building stands, and sometimes to a second courtyard and a third building. There was generally a well in the courtyard, many of which survive today, and some are extremely well decorated.[65] The construction was made of stone. Some rare occurrences of wooden beams in the façade, like Rue St-Jean, bear testimony to a progressively abandoned technical solution. Wooden structures also

61 Christine Becker, Isabelle Parron-Kontis, Sophie Savay-Guerraz (eds.). *Le musée Gadagne, archéologie et histoire au cœur d'un projet patrimonial à Lyon*. Lyons: Association de liaison pour le patrimoine et l'archéologie en Rhône-Alpes et en Auvergne, 2006.

62 In the *Nommées*, no new houses are mentioned in 1406, only one in 1446, but more than 200 in 1493.

63 There is unfortunately no information about the large houses or palaces of the high Middle Ages other than that contained in this building.

64 When the passageway is placed at the center of the façade, this is generally because the house is made from the joining of two formerly separate houses, whose structures are nevertheless maintained in the new grouping.

65 These wells sometimes had a sophisticated Renaissance decor, differing from that of the houses around them. They could have been built with a new style after the construction of the house (itself in the gothic style), or, if they were contemporary to the house, they would have discreetly adopted the classical style. The gallery built in 1536 by the architect Philibert de l'Orme in a courtyard built on the Rue Juiverie as an adjunction to a recently built house well illustrates this phenomenon (Dominique Bonnet Saint-Georges. La galerie de la maison Bullioud. Jeanne-Marie Dureau (ed.). *Philibert de l'Orme, Lyonnais*. Lyons: Archives Municipales de Lyon, 1993, 39 – 60). The building had already, in the same rear courtyard, been adorned after 1532 with door frames bearing a design probably inspired by examples from Rome, which were in fashion in the early sixteenth century. The Renaissance decors were adopted in Lyons several decades after Tours or Rouen and were initially private manifestations placed in remote locations.

became rare inside the plots, obeying strong regulations aimed at preventing fires and promoting urban aesthetics. The staircases, protruding from the rear façades, were spiral, built generally of stone, though often in wood in the poorer areas, for example around what is today Place de la République, the sector of the now lost Rue de l'Hôpital.[66]

The staircase was placed in the rear courtyard either directly behind the part of the house that bordered the street, sometimes partly englobed but generally fully protruding, or attached to a second building in the backyard.[67] This placing was probably due to the chronological succession of the constructions. An indication of this chronology is also given by the depth of the buildings, from the street to the courtyard, which was about 8.5–11 m in the medieval houses. This depth, when still measurable on the plan, means that the building probably had a medieval origin, because the full circa 1500 reconstructions had a depth of about 15 m. So the alternative location of the staircase may reveal the chronological order of the building's various moments of construction. For example, in the newly built houses of Rue Noire, from 1519, the staircase was attached to the back of the front building (Figure II.4).[68] In that case, the rear construction was probably added later, with a gallery placed on the lateral side of the courtyard, linking its apartments to the staircase.

The densification of the built up fabric led to the reconstruction and addition of buildings on a single plot. When an extant medieval building was replaced along a street, or when in a new development a new single building was constructed on the street, the new construction was accompanied by a spiral staircase. When a second building was constructed at the rear of the plot, a gallery was then built to join the old construction to the new one. Sometimes, a new multi-floor building was constructed at the rear, though the front house, dating from the Middle-Ages, remained standing. In that case, the new spiral staircase was attached to the new rear building. As we saw, the medieval front buildings nearly all disappeared during the process of reconstructing houses from the mid-fifteenth century.

The earlier galleries and spiral staircases would have been made of wood. Later, stone was the material of choice, which over time would have systematically replaced wood. The rapid densification of the fabric of the city between

66 Mentioned in the survey of several buildings which were to be demolished for the new Rue de la République made in 1853, AML, 925 WP 70.

67 Claire Seneclauze. Inventaire des escaliers à vis du quartier Saint-Jean à Lyon. Lyons: Université Lumière Lyon 2 (Mémoire de maîtrise), 1975 [unpublished paper, abstract in *Travaux de l'Institut d'Histoire de l'Art de Lyon*, 4 (1978)].

68 Plan AML 2 S 0432.

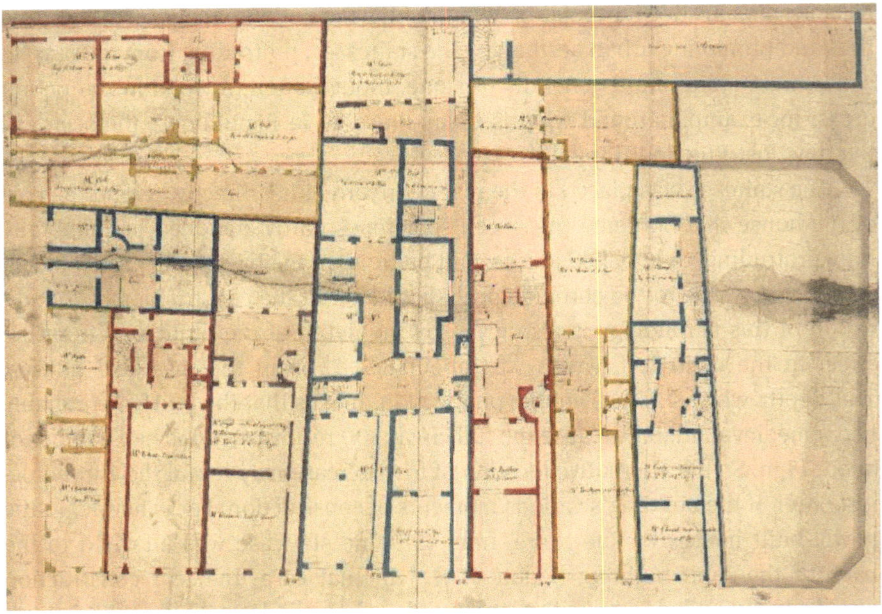

Figure II.4 Measured plan of the houses on the south side of Rue Noire, made before their demolition in c.1890
The subdivision was made in 1519 and the houses built soon afterwards (Arlaud, *Lyon les dessous*, 231). They were drawn according to the dominant building type of the sixteenth century, with a spiral staircase attached to the part of the building that fronts the street, but on the courtyard side (© AML 2 S 0432). Each colour on the map indicates a property unit.

1480 and 1560 was often a complex process at the scale of the house or the plot. Nevertheless, it led to a great regularity of the urban fabric, which shows the force of the dominant building type, to which all modifications and reconstructions had to conform. The Consulate (municipal government) banned several medieval features in the wake of fires, though also for aesthetic reasons: jetties, the prohibition of which was re-affirmed in 1551 (but they were probably rare already, as only one is documented in Rue St-Jean),[69] wooden frontages in the late fifteenth or early sixteenth century,[70] and wooden staircases in 1614. In

69 We do not know when this ban on jetties was first affirmed, though it was probably at the end of the fifteenth century.

70 The later replacement of wooden or rammed-earth façades by stone ones could explain why the remaining early sixteenth-century frontages are so rare in the houses found in the subdivisions Grand-Côte St-Sébastien, built in the early sixteenth century and significantly modified later.

1520 the placement of awnings overs the streets in summer was prohibited, so as to allow for a better circulation of air, but also so as to avoid bad smells and excessive heat in the streets.[71]

The number of floors, in rapid augmentation at the end of the fifteenth century and in the early part of the sixteenth, is a good marker of both centrality and demographic pressure; it may be explained by the higher real estate values in the center. The new houses in the peripheral subdivisions had only one main floor and a loft, like those at Rue Grand'Côte in 1505 to 1525. They had two floors on Rue Pierre-Scize, a suburban street of earlier origin, and four around the St-Nizier church of Rue Longue as well as at Rue St-Jean, where an exceptionally large house with five floors is still extant.

The buildings in the center of Lyons do not conform to a typology particular to the city, as much the same typology is visible in the houses in Geneva and Chambéry in the neighboring Alps region.[72] The houses of Paris and Rouen were not so different, but probably less multi-familial.

II.2.3 The relationship between occupation mode and form of the building

The number of four to five floors of the buildings in the center of Lyons did not increase significantly over the seventeenth and eighteenth centuries, whether in the form of new constructions or through the addition of one or two further floors. Given the known demographics of the city, this number does not make sense if we suppose mono-familial use. This is all the more clear when one compares the houses of Lyons to the houses in London and Rouen (where the period is documented by more than a hundred houses), where housing was predominantly mono-familial, which was in keeping with the presence of buildings rarely over two floors high, and had four floors only exceptionally. To understand this difference, we have to understand why, in Lyons, the buildings were conceived for several households from the late fifteenth century. One result from the study of the *Nommées* of 1493 is that the distribution of the households is remarkably similar in old houses and in new ones as mentioned in the source:

---

71 They were supported by protruding stones still present on a dozen houses. Similar devices were present as well at Mâcon, where one house still bears them, and at Avignon, as described by Dickens when he travelled to the city in 1845. See Charles Dickens. *Pictures from Italy.* London: Bradbury & Evans, 1846. One finds them in several Italian cities too, like Orvieto.

72 Livio Fornara. Genève. Jean Guillaume (ed.). *La maison de ville à la Renaissance. Actes du Colloque de Tours (1977).* Paris: Picard, 1983, 43–44; 157–158.

Table II.1 Distribution of households in old and new 'e-houses' in 1493
('E-House' is here an entry in the source, corresponding to a property. The entries could correspond to several buildings described as houses, probably meaning that these houses were generally mono-familial medieval constructions. Henceforth 'e-house' will be used to distinguish between an entry in the source and a house as described in the entry. An e-house may comprise several houses, and in some rare cases corresponds to a part of house)

Number of households per building in 1493	in new 'e-houses'	percentage	in old 'e-houses'	percentage
1	118	57.6	1,077	57.4
2	42	20.5	446	23.8
3	20	9.8	168	9.0
4	10	4.9	95	5.1
5 and over	14	6.8	90	4.8
Total	= 205		= 1,876	

This implies that the existing houses were very probably modified in order to answer the market demand, and in accordance with new ways of dwelling, in parallel to the building of new constructions aimed at more or less the same market. The trend towards houses inhabited by several households is perceptible, but only just, in the higher proportion of houses with five households or more in the new buildings. Overall, the new houses had on average ten percent more inhabitants than the older ones:

Table II.2 Households in old and new 'e-houses' in 1493

Age of 'e-houses' in 1493 (entire city)	number	number of households	households per 'e-house'	occupied by owners
Extant	1,876	3,538	1.89	1,075
New	212	444	2.10	118
Under construction	46	36 (15 still empty)		14
Total	2,134	4,018		

The amount of 4,018 households implies a population of roughly 20,000 inhabitants or over, as the size of the households was generally high, over five, in boom periods like this one.

These figures have to be understood more thoroughly. The total number of e-houses had grown by 25 percent in 1493 compared to 1446 (1,700). This increase of 430 entries between the *Nommées* of 1446 and 1493 is due for about 60 percent to the e-houses qualified as 'new' in 1493, which were possibly constructed in the previous decade, and to about 175 e-houses built between 1446 and, say, 1480. It was due in the main to the reoccupation of abandoned plots in the exterior quarters of the city, as it seems that the fabric of the central areas remained compact and for the most part fully occupied during the late medieval crisis, especially between 1400 and 1450. The number of households in the e-houses of the peripheral areas, which were inhabited mainly by people on low incomes, was in general only one. The increase in the number of households per building was in fact probably more marked in the central areas (see Fig. III.5), where the houses under construction were predominantly located (this changed soon after when many new developments were carried out in the periphery), and where the new houses often had a large number of inhabitants. In addition, many of the houses described as 'new', and especially those which we have reason to believe were still under construction, were certainly not yet fully occupied. The houses built in that period all conform to the new typology of buildings, which was probably a recent development in the late-fifteenth century. In 1493 its full effects were only beginning to be visible.

The way the population increased in an extant built-up fabric can also be understood by comparing the *Nommées* in 1406 and 1493, when facts about the city were recorded in the same way, namely, by registering information e-house after e-house in a spatial order. This information may be reconstructed as follows:

Table II.3 E-houses and households in the west part of Lyons, to the west of the River Saône (*Côté royaume*), in 1406 and 1493[73]

Number of households per e-house	Number of e-houses in 1405–06	Percentage of households in 1405–06	Number of e-houses in 1493	Percentage of households in 1493
1	612	76%	423	35%
2	48	15%	181	34%
3	7		72	
4	5	9%	37	31%

73 In 1406 only the west bank of the River Saône is fully documented.

Table II.3 E-houses and households in the west part of Lyons, to the west of the River Saône (*Côté royaume*), in 1406 and 1493 *(Continued)*

Number of households per e-house	Number of e-houses in 1405–06	Percentage of households in 1405–06	Number of e-houses in 1493	Percentage of households in 1493
5	4		21	
6	1		9	
7	3		4	
8	0		2	
9	0		0	
10	0		1	
11	0		1	
12	0		1	
Total	680	(796 households)	753	(1,385 households)

The end of the fifteenth century was clearly a period of development for multifamilial housing. In the part of the city to the west of the River Saône, the number of e-houses grew by about 10 percent, but the number of households increased from about 800 to 1,385, a gain of about 74 percent, which would imply a population in 1405 of around 11,000 for the city as a whole, at least if one assumes the same population ratio for the two banks of the River Saône. But this calculation must be qualified by recognizing that the records of 1405 contain no information regarding some of the poorest people in the eastern part of the city, for whom the register e-house per e-house has been lost.

The situation in 1405 must also be placed in a historical perspective, as the population was probably at that time significantly under the high point reached in the early fourteenth century. This means that in 1405 the houses, when not abandoned, were not as densely occupied as they were a century earlier. The population was probably comparable in 1493 to what it was in the early fourteenth century, but the replacement of the old medieval fabric was conducted using a new building type which tended progressively to replace the older one, which is still largely unknown. The evolution was extremely rapid from the end of the fifteenth century, as a population peak can be estimated in the mid-sixteenth century at some 50,000 inhabitants, as we will see below.[74]

One finds usable data subsequently, in the 1597 census,[75] the object of an in-depth study by Olivier Zeller. But unfortunately, this occurred when the population had fallen to about 30,000 inhabitants. Mono-familial houses, when their number can be calculated, were still very present at this date, even in the center of the city: 19/50 (38 percent) in the Grenette quarter,[76] 34/108 (31 percent) in the Cordeliers quarter, 30/113 (27 percent) in the St-Pierre quarter, thus attaining similar levels to 1493. So the central areas kept a proportion of mono-familial houses of about one third, which was also true of the Rue Neuve quarter. By contrast, in the St-Vincent quarter, located at the north-west limit of the city, the ratio was 61/93, which is approximately two thirds. If the resistance of the mono-familial model was still strong, it was increasingly replaced by multi-familial buildings: 28 of 108 buildings in the Cordeliers quarter housed more than three households (26 percent), 21 percent in the Rue Neuve quarter, 18 percent in the Grenette quarter, 14 percent in the St-Pierre quarter, and only six percent in the St-Vincent quarter. Multi-familial housing had clearly become an important reality throughout the city, maybe beginning in the most central areas in the fourteenth century, then strongly developing in the late fifteenth century. In the sixteenth century, this model was extended to less central locations.

But the similarity between 1493 and 1597 is not the result of continuity and may even be misleading, for the city had by then lost one third of its inhabitants or more. To fully understand the evolution, we have to evaluate the situation at the demographic peak of the 1550s. The total number of houses given in a fiscal document of 1551 is 3,449,[77] which is 33 percent more than the 2,574 houses (not e-houses, cf. table II.1) of 1493. The population in 1551 can be approximately estimated by assuming an average of 3 households per house and 4.5 persons per

74 Richard Gacon, *Grand commerce et vie urbaine au XVIe siècle*. Paris, Mouton, La Haye: SEVPEN, 1971, 2: 346, proposes 60 to 70,000 inhabitants, which seems too high, the error likely lying in the fact that he bases his estimation on the number of inhabitants per house in 1709, now known to be higher.

75 Olivier Zeller, *Les recensements lyonnais de 1597 et 1636: démographie historique et géographie sociale*, Lyon, Presses Universitaires de Lyon, 1983.

76 The quarter is an administrative subdivision of the city into 35 to 38 sectors, which occurred in the Renaissance period. The total number varied only slightly.

77 AML CC 40 – 41. Gacon, *Grand commerce*, 2: 345. I thank Olivier Zeller for checking the *Nommées*. The figure corresponds here nearly only to real individual buildings, differing from the e-houses of 1493 because in 1597 the great majority of the entries deal with one only building, which could have in some cases been constructed on a plot where there were several medieval houses previously.

household, which gives a total of about 45,000 to 50,000. The 875 new houses that appeared between 1493 and 1551 are nearly all located in the new developments on the periphery and are generally low-rise, principally mono-familial and bi-familial.

The fabric of the city in 1551 can be considered approximately equivalent to what it was in 1597, as only limited new areas were subdivided for new plots and only a few dozen new buildings were produced between these dates.[78] So we have to understand how maybe 15,000 or 20,000 more inhabitants could occupy the same buildings a few decades earlier. Olivier Zeller explains this depopulation by the political crisis of the wars of religion and the Ligue, making it clear that the bulk of the loss was due to poor people (*menu peuple)* who left the city, mainly servants and workers.[79]

We can further develop the answer to this question by considering the situation documented in the census of 1636, when the population had once again reached the level of the mid-sixteenth century, and also a later inquiry of 1677.[80] The sources become much more abundant on the production of new buildings after 1617, so the relationship between buildings and households can be examined more thoroughly in this period.[81] The population increase between 1597 and 1636 is significantly greater in the peripheral districts: 47 percent more in the St-Georges quarter and 64 percent more in the Bourchanin quarter, which more or less makes up for the preceding decrease between 1551 and 1597. In other sectors, like the Grand'Côte quarter, the population tripled. Here the densification was intense thanks to the production of new buildings with more floors and many raisings, which the alignment authorizations document very well. Many silk workers dwelled in this area. The St-Vincent quarter also offers a good illustration of this process. In 1677, it still counts 58 mono-familial houses (29 percent, compared to 65 percent in 1597), of a total of 198 buildings, of which 62 are occupied by four households or more (31 percent, compared to 6 percent in 1597). The persistence of the mono-familial model is still strong in this area, probably because of the conservation of old houses, as found in Rue Bouteille, but many new buildings were also produced, more than doubling the total number of the entries in the survey (from 93 to 198). In this area, the sixteenth-century buildings, exemplified by some still extant structures, had only one floor,

78 But this is maybe a too conservative figure.

79 Zeller, *Les recensements*, 234.

80 AML, CC 4187, municipal accounts.

81 There is no register of new constructions before 1617, the year when the practice was instituted by the *Consulat*.

whereas those built in the first half of the seventeenth century had two to three floors.

By contrast, the number of households per building in the quarters where they already had four floors in the sixteenth century, like Pêcherie and Grenette, increased only slightly from 1597 to 1636. In an intermediary situation, that of the St-Pierre quarter, the increase is more marked from 1597 to 1636, and again from 1636 to 1677, with almost no variation in the number of buildings. In this quarter the new families lived in new-built houses with four floors, which replaced older ones. The same phenomenon is documented in the Grenette quarter between 1636 and 1677, where the number of houses increased only slightly, but the number of households by 60 percent. There as well, the new buildings were higher, and the old ones were modified in order to answer the growing demand. The Cordeliers quarter is a case in point: the number of buildings grew from 108 in 1597 to 112 in 1677, but the number of households more than doubled from 281 to 566. The ratio of households per house increased here from 2.6 to 5.1. Significantly, 60 buildings were reconstructed in the quarter in the period, and 25 were raised: respectively 53 percent and 22 percent of the buildings extant in 1677. The correlation here is very clear between demographic growth and building production. But what is the cause of what? The production of a building is due to the decision of a person or of an institution, who aims at a market with capital gain in mind, especially when demand is high, though capital gains can also be realized by increasing the cost of rent. Therefore, an individual decision may not directly answer the general demand of the market, but globally the decisions taken by many investors can produce the new dwelling space required. The way gains are realized, building for renting or only increasing the rents, is a first variable in the process. We will see in PART III that another one is the variable propensity of investors to build for the poor and that the proximity of owners to their property may also have played an important role.

The overall evolution was certainly complex. Nevertheless, the multiplication of the number of buildings (or houses) corresponded neatly to an increase in the population. New developments were a first solution to answer the increased demand, and they were numerous in the late fifteenth and early sixteenth centuries. But another solution was dominant in Lyons during the seventeenth century, when only a few new buildings were produced on new ground:[82] densification, achieved by raising the extant houses and reconstructing them with additional floors. Many new buildings were produced to house the in-

82 The difference with Lille and probably Marseilles, cities considerably extended in the same period, is clear. In Lille, the houses were predominantly mono-familial.

creased population, but the demographic level in 1636 was only equivalent to, or slightly above, what it was around 1550. In the five quarters that can be compared between 1597 and 1677, the ratio of households per building increased from 2.22 to 3.88, with the number of buildings multiplying by 1.42 and households per building by 2.49. This implies that in these five quarters the population growth between these two dates is of a factor close to or above 3.5. Applied to the whole city, this could imply a little over 100,000 inhabitants at Lyons in 1677, which actually seems a little high in comparison to the data collected by Olivier Zeller from the parish records, and because only a small number of quarters are documented. The increase in the number of houses was actually possible only in the peripheral areas like the St-Vincent quarter, were it went from 117 in 1551 to 198 in 1677. Conversely, the Cordeliers quarter had 107 houses in 1551, 108 in 1597 and 112 in 1677, and the St-Pierre/Platière quartier had the same number of houses (113) in 1551 and 1636. These two quarters show a remarkable stability in the most central areas.

Another clue about where the inhabitants lost between 1550 and 1597 were living before they disappeared from the city is given by the number of buildings in the St-Vincent quarter, which fell from 117 to 93 during this period,[83] which can very likely be explained by the conjoining of formerly separate houses into a single property and not the destruction of buildings, for no abandonment or ruin is mentioned in the archival record. The adjustment of the building stock when the population was diminishing was probably perceptible mainly in the peripheral areas. This was true also of the second half of the sixteenth century, but in a much more moderate way than during the great medieval crisis when many houses simply disappeared.

In the central areas the houses had been rebuilt, generally with four floors, between 1480 and 1560. The number of households in these areas was on average certainly superior to four, which is coherent with the trend recognisable in the 1493 data. It's also important to bear in mind that many of the residents lost between 1550 and 1597 were servants, and that, as will be examined in PART III, the tenants of these centrally located houses were generally members of the middle and upper classes who would have employed servants to help them in their economic activities; and, as these were in decline, many servants would have been laid off.

So, between 1550 and 1597, the central quarters lost a significant part of their population, maybe one third or more, and, when the population rose to its pre-

83 This a clear example of uniting two or more houses in an 'e-house', which illustrates the possible confusion between buildings and properties in the records.

vious peak again around 1636, the new inhabitants dwelled in majority in the peripheral quarters. The central areas remained stable – the number of houses built in the early seventeenth in the St-Jean and Change quarters was low, though there were some raisings – and the more distant ones were densified considerably, with new ground being built upon only in the most peripheral locations. As a consequence of these developments, the average floor area per inhabitant was certainly considerably greater in the 1630s compared to the mid-sixteenth century, and the prosperity of streets like Rue Juiverie and Rue St-Jean around the Change, probably became more marked at the time. This pattern of recovering the previous demographic peak through densification and development of peripheral sectors, with central ones keeping more or less their reduced population and not growing significantly, can be recognized after other major occurrences of population loss. In general, the recovery implied an extension of urbanization in the periphery and a densification of the less dense areas. This happened for example in the recovery that occurred after 1740, but only for high social milieus (see PART III).

The buildings produced until 1630 to 1640, according to the sixteenth century dominant type, were generally rather small and corresponded to the average plot dimension common in the sixteenth century, with a frontage width of 7–8 m. The width of the new plots was drawn accordingly, in some subdivisions: around 7.5 m for Rue des Bouchers (Rue Hyppolite-Flandrin) in 1509; 7.5 m in Rue Noire in 1518; and 7.5 m in Rue Confort in 1530 and in the large aborted development to the south of Place Bellecour in 1559–60.[84] It was 7.2 m in the lower Grand'Côte in 1505–35. The plots of Rue Bellecordière, subdivided in 1540, had a width of 8.9 m, the maximum known for the period. The minimum was at the Fossés de la Lanterne subdivision in 1550 (the area of the former northern town ditch where Place des Terreaux was formed a little later), at 5.8 m.[85] The building typology in the early seventeenth century was clearly in continuity to that of the sixteenth century (Fig. II.3). The main difference was that the staircases were now right-angled instead of spiral. The decors were also modernized, and had fully embraced the classical style.

Another important innovation of the new, late fifteenth-century building type was its standardized "boutiques", which meant that the façade at street level was composed of arcades for shops, which in turn opened onto an activity room on the ground-floor. This was the end of a process which would appear to

84 As seen above, the size of the plots had been fixed at 22 feet. This is equivalent to one beam of twenty feet, an ideal length frequently applied in the buildings, plus the width of a party-wall.
85 *Terreaux* means precisely ditches. Gauthiez, La topographie, fig.1.

have begun in Lyons with the general inspection of the streets in 1395,[86] when about 440 benches (Latin: *banchas*) were examined in the city-center and their alignment modified and made more regular. In the Middle Ages, benches were a standard piece of equipment used for trade and handcrafts, taking the form of permanent private objects placed along the façade in the public space of the street. The 1395 inspection makes it clear that they were increasingly seen as a nuisance at the time. This certainly explains why a few decades later, in 1446 and in 1493, their number was very low,[87] as they had been systematically removed. Their use in the late fifteenth century was limited to butchery and, in a few instances, to drapery. The systematic mention of the shops (*boutiques*) in the early sixteenth century *Nommées*, with each house being qualified according to its number of *boutiques*, indicates their newly acquired importance, as a general novelty in the new street-scape made of hundreds of new buildings. The medieval bench placed in the street was thus systematically replaced by a private space placed at the ground-floor of the building.

The new building type was drawn according to this requirement, maybe accompanied by a still unknown by-law. This development created an incentive to add a new floor to the average house, to compensate for the need for a room dedicated to economic activities at the street level. Thus it was that the spread of the boutiques catalyzed the transformation of buildings not initially built with them in mind. In the century from 1550 to 1650, many façades were remade at the street level to accommodate boutiques, as mentioned in many authorizations given by the *Consulat*, and as are still visible in many extant buildings like those at the corner of Rue Lanterne and Rue Luizerne, where late sixteenth-century boutiques were added to a building constructed a few decades earlier, and Place de la Trinité, where boutiques were added to a late fifteenth-century house in the 1660s.[88] The significance of this is twofold: first, it means that some new buildings in the sixteenth century had not yet been fitted with boutiques, particularly in secondary streets; and second, that the need for economic and commercial spaces grew considerably when the population developed in the sixteenth and seventeenth centuries and accordingly spread to many secondary streets, thus calling for even recently constructed buildings to be adapted so as to include boutiques, a common phenomenon in the seventeenth century.

---

86 AML DD 18, the document, copied in the late seventeenth century, counts 84 pages.

87 On the River Saône west side, only fourteen benches are mentioned in 1493, used by butchers. Conversely, in 1406, only 19 *ouvreurs* are mentioned in the same area. *Ouvreurs* are the equivalent of the boutiques mentioned systematically in the early sixteenth century.

88 As a result, the ground-floor façade is more recent than the frontage.

In all, the period from 1480 to 1560 saw the generalization in the central areas (St-Jean, St-Paul, Grenette, Platière, Mercière, St-Nizier) of a dominant building type (Caniggia's *tipo portante*) adapted to the size of the medieval plots, and which replaced the previously dominant medieval type.[89] Instead of mono-familial houses placed mainly along the street, the new dominant type was made of two or three buildings parallel to the street, connected by passageways englobed in the buildings and allowing for access to a first courtyard, and in some rare occurrences also a second. In the courtyards, a spiral staircase provided access to the upper floors, and, thanks to galleries placed along its side, to a buildings at the rear of the plot. This arrangement was carefully adapted to the available plots, which were at times united so as to form larger houses. It was also systematically adopted in the new developments and incorporated into the modifications of existing houses. The variations of the type consist mainly in variations of the number of floors, from one to five above the ground-floor, depending on the value of the land. Lower numbers of floors can be found in the new developments of the periphery, higher ones in the old central areas. Local circumstances, like being located at a crossroads, implied other variations, as did the introduction of the right-angled staircase in the late sixteenth century.

After the loss of between 30 and 40 percent of the population between 1550 and 1597, the new inhabitants arriving after 1597 were not generally accommodated in existing buildings, but in new ones produced in the peripheral quarters and which replaced – sometimes on a massive scale – gardens or the previous urban fabric, which was still often medieval. A consequence of the high building investment level between 1600 and the mid-seventeenth century is the considerable increase in available square meters for the average inhabitant, especially the more well-off ones, a situation probably more marked in the old central areas, which had been built previously to a high level of density and only slightly modified over the period, but whose population did not return to its mid-sixteenth-century peak until maybe a century.

89 The analysis of the *Nommées* makes it clear that the number of properties along the streets did not vary significantly from the late fourteenth century to the early sixteenth.

II.2.4 Seventeenth century: the invention of a new building type of multi-familial housing (or apartment-building)

A new type of multi-familial building appeared in the early seventeenth century, unequivocally exemplified in a new construction in 1624 Rue Leynaud (n° 15). This new type became dominant in the following decades, which means that it had by that point become well suited to the requirements of the majority of investors. Its conception was significantly different from the previously dominant type of multi-familial dwelling, as it was made of one single building placed along the street, thicker towards the rear of the plot, accompanied by smaller wings bordering the lateral plot limits, which formed a courtyard larger than in previous constructions. The apartments were accessed by a doorway opened in the center of the façade and giving on an alley or corridor, linking the street to the courtyard, and behind which the staircase was located. This staircase, with straight flights of steps, was now fully included in the building and no longer protruded outside. Each landing opened out onto the courtyard, without joineries (as in the previous architectural types featuring spiral staircases, the common spaces were open). The ground-floor was still conceived as a space set aside solely for economic activities, whether in the form of shops, workshops, merchant's premises, or warehouses. The masonry of the shop bays giving onto the street was generally wide open, and could be closed thanks to large wooden panels which opened inwardly. In some secondary streets and close to the ports used for water transportation, like at Port Neuf de Neuville established in 1684 on the River Saône, or at Place de la Douane, the ground-floors intended for warehouses had only one large aperture on the street, accompanied by barred windows on one or two sides. This sort of design was adopted for the Chartreux buildings, Quai de Saône around 1700. It is clearly associated with the storing of goods, with a close relationship to the navigation on the River Saône in this instance.

The landings, placed over the alley leading to the courtyard, give access to a number of apartments, generally with two doors oriented towards the street. In larger buildings, two more doors giving onto the landing are oriented laterally, and in some rare examples there are four doors in the direction of the street (like at n° 24 Rue Lanterne, 1693). These doors offer potential access to as many apartments per floor, but the maximum number of flats is rarely fully exploited, like at n° 24 Rue Lanterne, where there were seemingly only four apartments per floor, instead of the six theoretically possible. The rooms of a single floor were separated by load-carrying walls, but a door-frame was generally placed also in these walls; it could be either closed by a thin wall or equipped with a communication door in order to form a larger apartment. Each room, as it may form a single dwelling, was equipped with a fire-place where it was possible to cook.[90] The upper floors, the fourth one and later the fifth or the sixth, were more often subdivided into one-room apartments for the poorest.

The dwelling pattern of the women seems to have been particular, especially for the single women and widows. The upper floors were often occupied by poor female households, women alone or with children, or associated women of different generations, among them widows. The place of women in the dwelling space is in that respect particular, but the sources are too scarce to give a precise idea of their situation when they were not married. As is well documented in 1677 (though there are also hints of such a situation in the medieval *Nommées*), some gathered in buildings occupied only by women, sometimes accompanied by a single male household. This latter dwelling organization mainly concerned rather well-off women and illustrates the possibility for women with enough money, generally widows, to form a distinct form of sociability in respect to housing, sometimes associating a man for protection. In general, women opted when possible for protective dwelling solutions, as when several generations were united in the same poor apartment. The early nineteenth-century censuses give a fuller image of this sociability, but the age of the women, in contrast with the men, is not given in this source. Many probably young women working for silk weavers lived in groups of two or three on the top floor. This varied from the general way of dwelling of poor bachelor males on the same floors, who would have lived alone.

The height of the ceiling diminishes the higher the floor. It was frequently between 3.5 and 4 m on the second floor. The ground-floor tended to become, in the late seventeenth century, high enough to accommodate a mezzanine (*entresol*), which could be inhabited by the tenant of the shop over which it was placed, or a warden. The *entresols* became dominant in the eighteenth century, and contributed to the architectural individualization of the lower part of the façade, which formed a strong base underlined by a thick stone cordon separating it from the second floor and drawn with arcading.[91] The central floors were treat-

---

90 The main use for the fireplaces was cooking. The seventeenth century fireplaces were very inefficient for heating and the combustible wood rather expensive. See Jean-Pierre Gutton. Le peuple a-t-il droit à la chaleur? Le cas de Lyon au XVIIIe siècle. Philippe Guignet (ed.). *Le peuple des villes dans l'Europe du Nord-Ouest (fin du Moyen Âge-1945)*. Lille: Centre de Recherches sur l'Histoire de l'Europe du Nord, 2002, t. I, 313–322. Seventeenth-century fireplaces are very rare today, because they were systematically replaced from the mid-eighteenth century by fireplaces made only for heating. Some subsist at n° 24 Rue Lanterne, third floor.

91 The *entresol* and the ground-floor still feature heavily in the way people in Lyons number the floors. The 'first' floor is generally placed over the *entresol*, which is actually the true first floor.

ed more simply. For the same surface area, one generally paid ten percent less for each additional floor. The first and second floors over the ground-floor and the mezzanine had the highest ceilings and rental values[92]. This is where the richest people dwelled, but also the owners themselves, though as time passed they tended to move further away (see III.2.4). The social level decreased the higher one went, until one arrived at the poorest on the last floor, often directly under the roof in the early nineteenth century. The fourth and fifth floors had slightly lower ceilings, but nevertheless were not designed as attics. A few of the buildings constructed in the late seventeenth century had windows forming *oculi* at the highest floor. The roof space in the seventeenth and eighteenth century was generally a loft, but it was modified from the mid-eighteenth century in the case of many buildings in order to install roof-windows and accommodate dwellings for workers. The living conditions in these roof-apartments were very poor. The available height under the tiles did not always make it possible to stand fully erect, and the heat in summer could be unbearable, as could the cold in winter. Conditions were more benign when the last roof floor was raised by a few feet to form an attic. Modifying the upper part of the extant buildings was probably one of the main ways to accommodate the growing population in the second half of the eighteenth century, when it peaked at about 135,000 inhabitants. The increase was composed largely of poor silk-weavers.

The architecture of the buildings had been extremely repetitive in the late fifteenth century and the first half of the sixteenth, leading to successions of low shop arcades in yellow lime stone from the nearby Mont d'Or, with a late gothic decor. The same was true in the seventeenth century, but with rounded arched shop bays in grey stone from the same region, and with classical mouldings. The frontages had to be white-washed when newly built or refurbished. All windows had a compulsory cross-mullion, which had been abandoned elsewhere, in Paris and Rouen for example, in the early seventeenth century. The obligation stayed as late as the 1690s and had probably, for the archbishop Camille De Neufville De Villeroy, a signification as a papal sign, as this form, clearly archaic in seventeenth-century France, had been known in Italy as the Guelf window in the fifteenth to sixteenth centuries. In all, the streetscape was extremely standardized. The ground-floor shops were generally vaulted, and their wooden ceiling replaced by stone, from the early seventeenth century, to protect the rest

92 The height under the ceiling was frequently close to 4 m or over, in the second half of the seventeenth century, at least for the first and second floors. It was much lower for the last floor, where the silk-weavers were working.

Figure II.5 Example of the multi-familial building type which appeared in the 1620s
Building authorized to Pierre Dervieux, one of a series of three (15 march 1685, AML DD 37).

of the building from fire, avoiding its propagation to the upper floors.[93] They were closed by large wooden doors, open during the day inside the buildings so as not to impede the public space of the street, at least by the sixteenth century. This compulsory practice was often reaffirmed in the alignment authorizations.

93 The same reason led to the replacement, in the early seventeenth century, of many wooden floors over the boutiques or the cellar, by stone vaults.

Figure II.6 Multi-familial building type as it developed in the eighteenth century
Building authorized to Pierre Grassot, Quartier St-Clair (Doctor in medicine and Master Surgeon, 6 Aug. 1761, AML DD 54).

The Palais St-Pierre, a large and magnificent new construction undertaken by the nuns of St-Pierre abbey on Place des Terreaux from 1656, of which the façade on the square was paid by the *Consulat* to obtain a better contribution to the architectural ensemble of the square, had a spectacular design. The ground-floor was occupied by large shops with two floors placed above for dwelling space. The rooms of the nuns themselves were located at the rear around a large cloister, as well as over the shops and their associated dwellings, on the third and fourth floors. This disposition of a palatial abbey placed over 'englobed' houses (24 in total) was certainly inspired directly by Palazzo Pamphili in Rome, on Piazza Navona, completed in 1650, and so was the design of the façade of the abbey itself, as can be ascertained through a comparison of the two buildings. Pamphili had been designed to conserve large parts of the previous buildings on its site, only the façades of which were rebuilt to produce a large and magnificent frontage.[94] This was intended to keep the income from the rents of the shops and the attached dwellings. The Jesuits at the Grand Collège, in a building constructed around 1604 (today rue de la Bourse), and the Antonins in the 1640s (on the River Saône Quay), had already adopted this solution for their new buildings at Lyons.

The façades were rather abundantly decorated and classical in style from the 1640s to the late seventeenth century, but they changed considerably after the turn of the century. The same change could be seen in every large city in the French kingdom (Rouen,[95] Lille,[96] Paris,[97] Strasbourg, Bordeaux,[98] etc.). It consisted in the simplification of the façades to the point where nearly no decor was allowed, except around the main door. The window frames were to conform to the 'French way', i.e., they were narrower than before, underlined by a plain flat cordon of grey stone, with no cross-mullion, and with a lintel which was either flat or more usually curved. From the mid-eighteenth century on, the older cross-mullions were systematically removed – very few are still present in the city (principally in courtyards in windows opening on staircases) – and the decor progressively reappeared, first in a rococo guise in the mid-century, and from the 1760s with a neo-classical design.

Before the normalization conducted by the King's architects from around 1700, the architectural design of the buildings often alluded to various classical references, especially from Italy, like at Palais St-Pierre. In 1670, Dusoleil, lord of Pierre-Bénite, produced a large construction on the new Trinity square, giving it the shape of a late Renaissance Italian palace. The seven large buildings erected from 1658 on the west side of Rue St-Dominique (nowadays Rue Emile-Zola) were intended for rich aristocrats and civil servants, in the spatial context of the aristocratic Place Bellecour to the south and of the royal mint in Rue du Port du Tem-

---

94 Gauthiez, Les logiques. Gauthiez, Zeller, Beautifying.

95 Quenedey, *L'habitation*; Gauthiez, Les maisons.

96 Parent, *L'architecture.*

97 Jean-François Cabestan. *L'immeuble à Paris au XVIIIème siècle, la conquête du plain-pied.* Paris: Picard, 2004; Jean-François Cabestan. La naissance de l'immeuble d'appartements à Paris sous le règne de Louis XV. Daniel Rabreau (ed). *Paris, capitale des arts sous Louis XV.* Bordeaux: William Blake and co/Arts and Arts, 1997, 167–195; Jacques Fredet. *Les maisons de Paris.* Paris: Editions de l'encyclopédie des nuisances, 2003, 3 vols.

98 Chantal Callais, Thierry Jeanmonod. *Bordeaux patrimoine mondial. Tome 1. La fabrication de la ville.* La Crèche: Geste éditions, 2012.

ple to the north-west. The façades were heavily transformed later on, but their French or rather Parisian inspiration is obvious. These buildings were somewhat hybrid, as in the meantime they tried to conform to the model of the Parisian *hôtels particuliers*, with a main access large enough to let coaches pass,[99] but they were nevertheless multi-familial, including apartments of several hundred square meters. In Rue Juiverie, some other high class houses were designed in an Italian manner in the 1640s. The subtlety of the varying architectural styles and influences and their significations unfortunately largely escapes us today.

II.2.5 Typological variations and evolutions

Generally, the production of a multi-familial building type required the fusion of two previous plots, which led to a partial transformation of the plot pattern in some areas of the city. In the Rue de l'Enfant-qui-Pisse, nine plots extant in 1493 were reduced in 1692 to five, thanks to the fusion of pairs of plots. The same phenomenon occurred also at Rue Pizay. The width of the new multi-familial type was remarkably constant, which points to the strength of the model. The three new buildings constructed by Dupuis in 1659 on Rue Pêcherie had an average width of 14 m, and the seven new ones produced by Perrachon Place Bellecour in 1665–1674 averaged 17.5 m.[100] In 1728, in a new subdivision Rue Vaubecour, where building sizes could be freely established, five had a width of 16.5 m. The very fact that this measure corresponds to double the average of a sixteenth century plot means that the new building type had probably been conceived with a view to adapting the extant plot pattern. Another reason for the uniting of two plots and the building of only one construction on the area thus created, was that the surface dedicated to the staircase could be reduced by a factor of two. Understandably, the new buildings of the higher social classes were larger: 19 m for three new buildings by the daughters of Perrachon de St-Maurice on the Rue St-Dominique (nowadays Rue Emile-Zola) in 1714, around 20 m in the new St-Clair quarter from 1750, up to a maximum of 25.5 m at the façades forming the east and west sides of the royal Place Bellecour a few years after 1720.

The trend in the eighteenth century was to construct larger buildings, with fewer smaller constructions. The increase of building size provided a strong in-

99 This is when the private coaches increased in number, becoming a status symbol of the upper classes.

100 Bayard. *Villes et campagnes.*

centive to create adequate plots, which was easiest to do in new developments like the east side of Rue Zola, subdivided in 1714, and the St-Clair quarter. Like in 1658 on the west side of Rue Zola, the buildings had large entrances for coaches. It was much more difficult to find adapted plots for such architectural programs in the dense extant urban space. Successive acquisitions of plots were necessary, and this sometimes involved combining plots traversing between two parallel streets. This is what Roux did between Rue Désirée and Rue Puits-Gaillot in 1741, with an average plot width of 17 m, and Tolozan between Rue du Plâtre and Rue Longue in 1762, with a width of 22–25 m; understandably, this sort of realization remained rare.

The conception with a central staircase at the extremity of a corridor coming in from the street, a defining element of the new type of seventeenth-century building, appeared in 1605, Place du Grand-Collège, in a house by Ratton (the house sign was the *Tambour*), but other solutions were also tried and tested to find the most rational and economic position of the staircase(s) in relation to building(s). In 1668, Leaud, a carpenter known to have produced several buildings, designed a house between Rue Pizay and Rue de l'Arbre-Sec (fig. II.7),[101] with a building on each street and a third one in the middle of the plot in between. On each street the width was about 15 m, but two staircases per building were present, as if it had been designed according to the old typical plot width of 7.5 m, each vertical series of apartments necessitating a proper staircase. But the general plan of the constructions corresponds to the new type, and the third building – the depth of the three buildings being about 13 m – is accessed thanks to galleries linking it to the other buildings, with no proper staircase(s). Here, the ratio of staircases per unit of superimposed apartments is 4:6. This was not very economical, as in the sixteenth-century type it was 1:2.

On Leaud's neighboring plot immediately to the west, in 1753 Chazelle produced a layout fully obeying the canon, with two buildings, one on each street, whose depth was 18 m for a width of 14 m. No space was allowed for a third building in between. One staircase was provided per building, for a ratio of 1 staircase to 4 apartment series superimposed (1:4). This is remarkably rational and economical, but considerably limited the natural light available in the interior parts of the buildings. The 1693 building at n° 24 Rue Lanterne, already alluded to, had a potential ratio of one staircase for six apartment series (1:6), with a depth of 18 m. It was difficult to do more (or rather economically better) without making the parts of the apartments more distant from the façade unpleasant to live in. Actually, the buildings produced with a depth of 18 m were rare, and

101 AML, DD 30, alignments.

Figure II.7 Remarkable examples of new buildings with new ideas for their layout in seventeenth and eighteenth centuries
A: Leaud's building in 1668.
B: Chazelle's building in 1753.
At the top, **C:** the Missionnaires of St-Joseph buildings around a large common courtyard, in 1698.

the standard between the mid-seventeenth century and the early nineteenth was generally around 14–15 m (which corresponds to the standard given in the *Encyclopédie*). The depth was later reduced to about 10 m, particularly from the mid-nineteenth century, after awareness of the need for light and air in dwellings had emerged in the late eighteenth century.

There was another variant of the dominant type: a central staircase linking galleries that provided access to several apartments or rooms distributed around a courtyard. An example from the early seventeenth century can still be seen at n° 1 Rue Bouteille, for poor dwellings. Some buildings in the eighteenth century, generally on wide square plots, were conceived according to this layout, like the one by Desraisses, at the corner of Rue Ste-Catherine and Rue Ste-Marie-des-Terreaux, in 1734–36, where one large staircase gave access to dwellings on the four sides of the courtyard. Here the building has a very limited depth of about 8 m, but the dwellings had windows only on one side. In such cases the apartments located overlooking the courtyard, with no visibility from or to the street, generally comprised only one room each, and they were intended for relatively poor people.[102]

This pattern could also fit the needs of large inns. The rear building of the Auberge de l'Ecu de France, Rue Lanterne, today visible from Rue de Constantine, was conceived in this way in the early eighteenth century. The Desraisses building, at least for the rooms looking out only over the courtyard, could also have been built partly as an inn, as Desraisses was the owner of the neighboring *Auberge de la Croix Verte* ('Green Cross Inn'), which he had rebuilt in 1732.

The new conception of the buildings developed in the early seventeenth century certainly had a strong economic rationale, with better accesses implying an improved ratio of occupied space to overall surface area, and probably also – though the calculation would need to be undertaken – of the total length of walls compared to the usable surface, as the buildings were now more compact. The same economic pressure, when the population grew again after the peak of the late seventeenth and the loss of about 20 percent in the following decades, led to floors being added either to extant houses, or to projects for new ones. From the 1760 to the 1770s, the number of floors of the new buildings over the ground-floor was at least five, often six, and sometimes seven. A maximum was reached in the early 1820s, with an exceptional ten floors for a construction at the rear of Rue Leynaud in 1820, inside a block, with a height of about 35 m.[103] The maximum height of the authorized constructions along the streets was lim-

102 The dominant building type at Turin in Italy and Pinerolo in the late eighteenth and early to mid-nineteenth century seems to be a derivation of this layout. A large and thick bourgeois building followed the street line, and a passage in its center gave access to the staircase of the main building and to a large courtyard of which two lateral sides (or three in some case) were lined with one-room or two-rooms apartments accessed by walk-ways.

103 It is located on a steep hill and because of that has only eight floors on its north side.

ited in the 1820s to 25 m, and still later, from the mid-nineteenth century, to 20.5 m, which corresponds to a ground-floor, four further floors, plus a fifth one with roof windows (*lucarnes*). This is when the recent preoccupation with health, nourished by medical reports in the 1840s, was taken into account in the municipal by-laws and in the practice of architects and investors. As a consequence, buildings henceforth had limited height, a depth of about 10 m, and the streets of the new developments were also much enlarged. Hygienism also called for larger windows. The maximal ratio of the surface of the windows compared to the whole surface of a façade is a little over 50 percent, at n° 1 Place d'Albon, a building erected in 1850. This is quite remarkable because this building was heated, whereas the houses of the previous centuries with a high ratio of window surface (though only about 30 percent) were generally not heated.

II.2.6 The new type and its assemblage properties

We saw that the assemblage properties of an architectural type were an important parameter for its definition. The new seventeenth-century building type, like its predecessor, was designed to give rise to series of similar buildings, assembled thanks to common party-walls through which, in principle, no doors or windows were present. This coincided in reality, with the fact that the bulk of the construction was now placed only along the street, and had as a consequence that a new idea could develop for the role of the courtyard. The result of this idea was perceptible in the previously studied Leaud and Chazelle buildings between Rue Pizay and Rue de l'Arbre-Sec in 1668 and 1753, where the courtyards tended to be larger. In 1698, the St-Joseph convent produced a remarkable series of four use units, unfortunately demolished in 1855, on a combination of plots whose previous buildings had burnt down (Fig. II.7, C). This redevelopment was made possible by placing on the perimeter of the whole area a succession of four entrances giving access to four apartments on each floor (when the type could be fully implemented, which was not possible at the corners), along three streets (Rue Pizay, Rue du Garet and Rue Lafond). The total length of the frontages was 111 m. The depth of the four units of building, drawn according to the standard type and adapted to the contour of the block, was also standard, 15.2 m,[104] but they enclosed inside the plot a very large rectangular common courtyard, the first of its kind to appear in Lyons. It was followed later by

104 This is about 50 feet, and another example of rounded figures in the design of buildings, as is the common use of twenty feet beams between load-bearing walls.

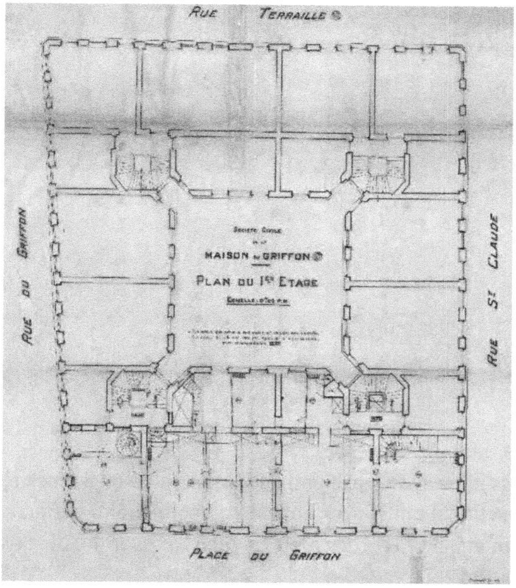

Figure II.8 Building by Lenoir and Miège, silk ware merchants, 1830, Rue Griffon, forming a block with a square central courtyard
Each landing gives access to four or five potentially independent rooms or apartments (© AML, 1 S 265)

other examples, but the opportunities to build such an ensemble were actually very rare because of the densely occupied plot pattern, the result being that actual occurrences were also rare. The shape of the courtyard was not dictated by the line of the streets around, but formed a perfect rectangle. Some rare blocks were later built or rebuilt according to this pattern. The building constructed by Lenoir and Miège in 1830 replaced about ten older houses between Rue Terraille, Rue St-Claude, Rue du Griffon and Place Romarin.[105] The four staircases were designed to give access to a maximum of four apartments each.

A similar solution was adopted for a block between Rue Ste-Catherine, Rue Ste-Marie-des-Terreaux, Rue d'Algérie and Rue Terme, for a building named *Hôtel du Parc*, after a complete demolition occurred in 1858 to 1859.[106] This solution was also used on a large scale in the urban renewals of the Quartier Grolée from 1890,[107] and on the east bank of the River Rhône around 1890, where several large blocks were drawn with standard building types lining the streets

105 AML 1 S 265, plan of the first floor measured in 1937.
106 AML 315 WP 002, 8 Feb. 1859.
107 Plan AML 2 S 0430_3, block K, ground-floor.

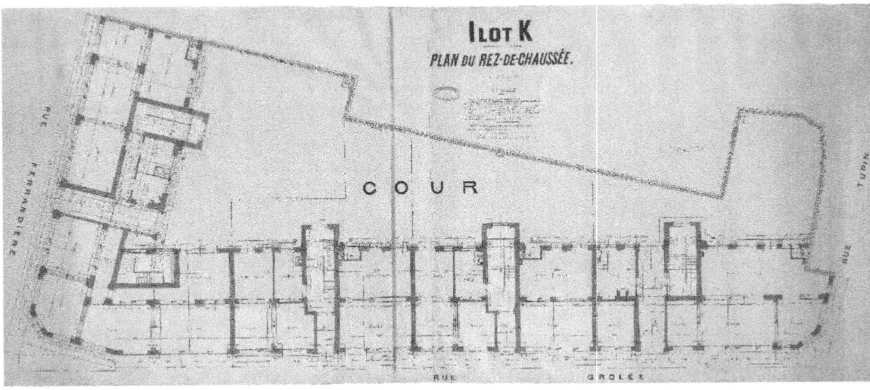

Figure II.9 Urban renewal Rue Grolée 1890, plan of new block K
The design is made of functional units accessed by a staircase and a lift assembled on a block to line the streets (© AML 2 S 0430). Three functional units are identical and correspond perfectly to the type, two are adaptations to a location at a corner. They are designed to cover the block's entire length.

around them and large interior private squares, on blocks also cleared of their previous buildings.[108] This form had already been adopted for some blocks in the extension of Geneva from the end of the 1850s.[109]

A remarkable fact emerges from these designs, in which the previous plot pattern is erased and plays no role. The conception is determined only by the general form of the block and the typological determination of the architecture, but with buildings still aligned on the surrounding streets. This is obviously a major step towards the urban form that developed from the early twentieth century, as proposed by the modernists, when the alignment along limits of the blocks was abandoned, though this is a story that lies outside the scope of this book.

---

108 Anne-Sophie Clemençon. *La fabrication de la ville ordinaire. Pour comprendre les processus d'élaboration des formes urbaines, l'exemple du domaine des Hospices civils de Lyon. Lyon-Guillotière, Rive gauche du Rhône, 1781-1914.* Lyons: Université Lyon 2, 1999 (unpublished PhD dissertation), ill. 180; Bernard Gauthiez. La rénovation urbaine au centre de Lyon au XIXe siècle, une histoire en trois phases. Jacques Comby (ed.). *Peurs dans la ville, urbanisme et sécurité dans l'agglomération lyonnaise XIXe-XXIe-siècle.* Rennes: Presses universitaires de Rennes, 2015, 23–69; 56–57 and fig. 11.
109 Gilles Barbey, Armand Brulhart, Georg Germann, Jacques Gubler. Genève. *INSA – Inventaire Suisse d'Architecture 1850-1920, 4. Delémont, Frauenfeld, Fribourg, Genève, Glarus.* Bern: Société d'histoire de l'art en Suisse, 1982, 360; 372–373.

II.2.7 The typological adaptation of older buildings

The reconstruction of a building, or its production in a new urban development, allows for the full implementation of the dominant building type in a given period. But its conception also guides the transformation of extant houses conducted with more limited means. The building is in this context not replaced, but adapted, and the resulting object may keep some features of an older type and in the meantime also be made closer to the new one in a hybrid combination.

The development of the Renaissance type was often the product of successive buildings, linked with galleries, according to a relative chronology that can be summarized as follows:

- Phase 1: previous building, of medieval type, located on the street;
- Phase 2: new building at the rear of the courtyard, with an associated staircase;
- Phase 3: rebuilding of the front part located on the street with a gallery linking it to the added rear part.

The transformations of buildings in the modern period followed some regular patterns. In many cases, two extant buildings were united to form a larger unit, one of the staircases was demolished and a communication door was established through the party-wall. Sometimes a new right-angle staircase replaced the two previous spiral ones. Often a new façade with an up-to-date design replaced two older ones. The building at n° 8 Rue de la Platière, still extant, whose façade was remade at the ground-floor in 1636, was later modified in this way in 1668, when only one staircase was built to replace the two previous ones, and a new façade was designed. The new unit was often raised by one or two additional floors.

A precisely measured plan was drawn in 1852 before the redevelopment of the block between Rue Mercière to the west, Rue Chalamont to the south, and Rue des Trois-Carreaux to the east.[110] This rare plan (for Lyons) of a 'metamorphized' area, first developed in the early Middle Ages, allows for the comparison between the content of the building authorizations and the actual layout of the buildings once modified or reconstructed, in an area where the new building type, which appeared after 1600, could not be fully developed (Fig. II.10). Unfortunately, only the layouts can be compared to the authorizations, for the buildings were destroyed in 1854.

110 AML 2 S 427.

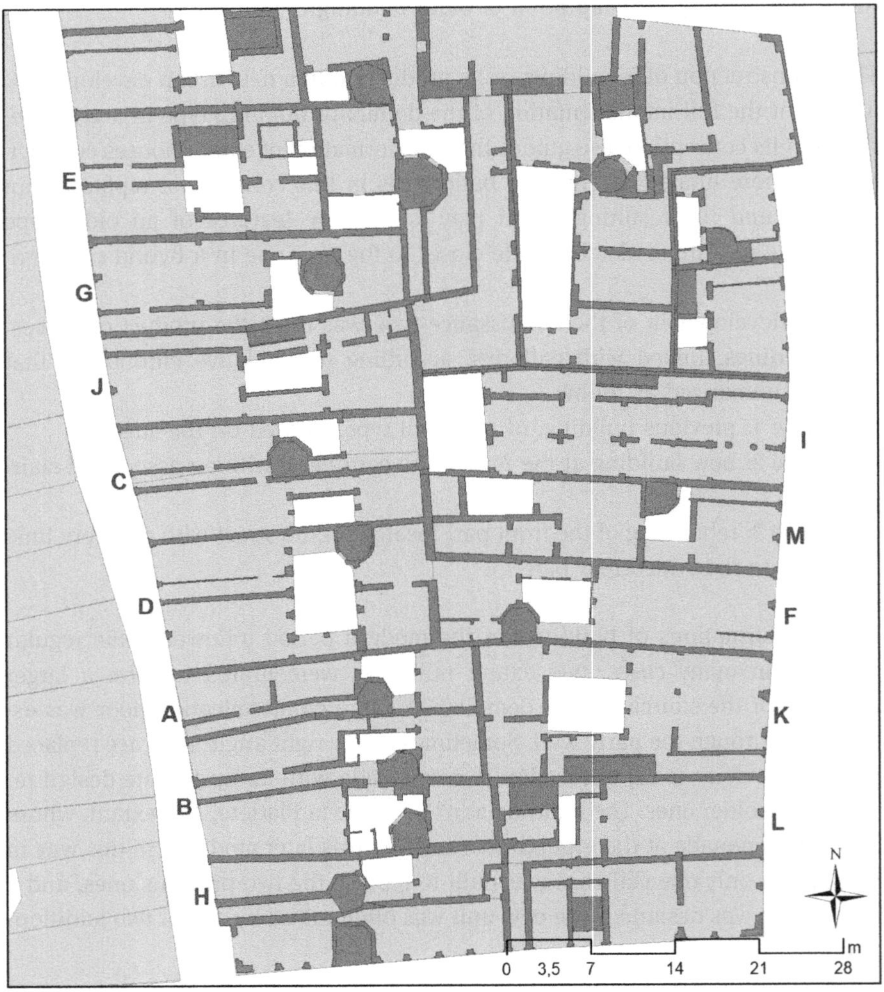

Figure II.10 Transformations of the buildings in the block between Rue Mercière to the west, Rue Chalamont to the South and Rue des Trois-Carreaux to the east, identified on a measured plan made in 1852 before its redevelopment, an example of metamorphized urban fabric

The transformations of the fabric of the area, which took place principally in the seventeenth century, can be detailed. The west side of Rue des Trois-Carreaux had been rebuilt on a new line with an important set-back in the early nineteenth century. (Gauthiez from AML 2 S 427). In the comments below, the letters correspond to features on the plan:

– Buildings conforming to the Renaissance architectural type: **A.**

- Buildings modified to conform to the new type: **B:** two A type buildings united by the rebuilding of a common façade, the removal of one of the two previous entrance alleys, the opening of a door through the party wall, and with a raising of one floor, 22 Oct. 1641.
- **C** and **D:** Two A types united by rebuilding a common façade and removal of one of the previous staircases, **C:** 10 Mar. 1637 and 12 June 1640; **D:** Aug. 1634, 8 Jan. 1635 and 22 Oct. 1641.
- **E:** two A type buildings united by the rebuilding a common façade and a new straight staircase replacing the two previous ones, 28 Aug. 1646.

The multiple dates for a single building represent the steps of the transformation, which were not made as part of a single project, but on several different occasions by not so rich proprietors. This process was very frequent, but is generally difficult to document in the absence of accurate plans showing the details of the structures. Such plans are unfortunately rare for Lyons.

In a single plot, some other modifications are simpler adaptations to new circumstances:

- **F** – **G** – **H** and **I:** the reconstruction of a façade and at least part of the front building, with no documented transformation of the rear part, **F:** 8 Feb. 1605; **G:** 18 Nov. 1636 and 26 Feb. 1637; **H:** 26 May 1696; **I:** 8 Aug. 1811.
- **J** – **K** – **L** and **M:** reconstruction on the same plot with a straight staircase, without the possibility fully to conform to the new type, **J:** 10 Apr. 1637 and 4 Mar. 1640; **K:** 18 Aug. 1757; **L:** 10 Mar. 1807; **M:** 8 Aug. 1811

Several transformations of this sort were carried out according to the new multi-familial type.

This analysis shows that it is possible to get to a deep understanding of the urban fabric in its morphological aspects, when the following conditions are present:

- The methodology of spatial analysis (developed in PART I):
- The reconstitution of the city plan, plots, building, architectural structures, using the same geometry over time, in order to place at the same location the shared and invariant spatial features.
- A system allowing for the location of information, the succession of the proprietors, especially from such sources as building authorizations.
- The use of the alignment authorization registers, compiled in a database, and the location of the authorizations in a GIS shapefile.

Conceptualization:
- Determination of the pertinent geographical and material units, conceived as construction-units.
- Understanding and identifying the dominant building types and their variants.
- Identification of the forms corresponding to small modifications and adaptation of buildings. This implies a morphological decomposition of the building layout and elevation in parts corresponding to a building fully produced according to a type and parts corresponding to transformations.

At n° 28–30 Rue Lanterne, when the façades of two houses were united at the ground-floor in 1692, the interior layouts were retained. In such cases, the different spacing of the windows on different floors is due to conserved structures and floor plans. The varying placement of the windows is a frequent indication of the presence of two buildings, now forming a single property unit, united under a new common façade.[111] The building of a fully united façade in place of two previous ones is another frequent transformation. Such a transformation was carried out, together with the removal of a staircase, at n° 8 Rue Lainerie (previously Rue de la Boucherie-St-Paul), authorized 30 April 1737.[112] The arcades on the ground-floor can be changed with no modification of the upper façade, which, counter-intuitively, makes the ground-floor look more recent than the rest of the building, as occurred at Place de la Trinité, authorized on 18 March 1666 (today n° 2 Montée du Gourguillon), modifying a house constructed there in the late fifteenth century.

In a special occurrence, n° 15 Rue des Trois-Maries, the arcades of the demolished building, constructed around 1500, were carefully placed to one side, with the stones being individually numbered and then re-used in the otherwise fully new construction authorised on 20 March 1738.[113]

In addition, many features present in modern times are very difficult to document because they were removed or modified in the late eighteenth and

111 This can explain some of the variation in building numbers between censuses or fiscal surveys.

112 The surrounding wall of the other staircase was not removed, but the steps were removed to form a small room.

113 The four arcade vaults were numbered A, B, C and D before being demolished, and their stones numbered with roman figures.

nineteenth centuries.[114] A short list of these transformations gives an idea of their importance:

- Transformation of a roof space into a habitable floor, with or without a raising of less than a full floor.
- Raising of one or two floors.
- Addition of roof windows.
- Modification of the façade: change of the decor (For example, in 1852, of the Desraisses building constructed in 1734).
- Modification of the ground-floor arcades, either through replacement with a more modern form or mere transformation. As a consequence, the lower part of the frontage is newer than the upper one.
- Widening and lowering of the windows, addition of pig-iron railings and lambrequins[115] to hide the venetian blinds when folded.
- Removal of the cross-mullions after they were no longer compulsory from the mid-1690s to install window *à la française*. From the late eighteenth century the joineries were set back at the rear of the window frames to leave space for venetian blinds. The joineries were previously placed directly on the façade plan or only one or two inches further back.
- Installation of wooden shop fronts, often with glazing, replacing large plain shop doors. This occurred from the late eighteenth century onwards.
- Changing of the door joinery.
- Closing of the access spaces, especially of the staircases, with joineries and glazing.
- Changing the staircase, from spiral to straight.

Of course, the typology is better understood from the constructions built with no or limited constraints, for example in the new subdivisions, where the plot widths were determined with a building type in mind, and in series of buildings constructed on large plots. It is to a lesser degree possible to build an ideal architectural type on the old plot pattern. When it is possible, it will occur through transformations effectuated step by step instead of a full clearing of two previous plots. But these transformations aim to adapt houses to new ways of dwelling, new technologies and aesthetics. They are only small modifications, Caniggia's

114 It would be possible to document them, but the authorizations are lost among the thousands of others in the contemporary registers, which still wait to be constituted in a database.
115 Openwork board in wood or pig-iron, placed at the top of the window-frame to hide and protect the blind when folded-up.

mutazioni capillari, an understanding of which is crucial if we are to grasp the generally rather sudden emergence of a new building type[116].

II.2.8 The origins of the building types present at Lyons

The new dominant multi-familial building type which appeared in Lyons during the boom period between 1480 and 1560, and which was used systematically throughout the city, was actually also dominant at Geneva and Chambéry, 100 km from Lyons to the north-east and the south-east respectively as the crow flies. It was also present at Turin as well (250 km to the south-east on the other side of the Alps), and at Rome in some rare instances. It did not differ greatly from what was built in Paris (450 km to the north-west) and Rouen or other large French cities like Dijon (200 km to the north). So it was probably an imported dominant type, whose origin is yet unknown. Nothing points to a local origin.

By contrast, the development in the early seventeenth century of a new dominant building type occurred in parallel to the adaptation of existing buildings according to the same logic, but also, quite remarkably, alongside some alternative forms which bear testimony to local quests to discover the most rational layout of rooms, accesses and staircases, such as the building by Leaud (see II.2.4). This new dominant type evidently emerged in response to strong demand for numerous small dwellings. Also at this time, the average size of a new building was growing, corresponding to bigger units of investment, probably in the context of the rapid development of silk weaving.

A comparison with Rouen, a city studied by Jean-Pierre Bardet and by the present author,[117] gives some clues that may help explain the development of massive multi-familial housing in Lyons. In Rouen in 1773, there were 10,925 houses for about 70,000 inhabitants, which meant about 6.4 inhabitants per house. In Lyons, there were about 3,500 houses for approximately 135,000 inhabitants in the late 1780s, which meant about 39 inhabitants on average per house. One major factor explaining this difference was probably the average wealth of the tenants. In Lyons, at the end of the eighteenth century, 57.7 percent

116 Gian Franco Caniggia. *Lecture de Florence.* Brussels: Institut Supérieur d'Architecture Saint-Luc, 1994, 17, n. 8; Gauthiez, *Espace urbain*, 304.

117 Jean-Pierre Bardet. *Rouen aux XVIIe et XVIIIe siècles, les mutations d'un espace social.* Paris: SEDES, 1983. Bernard Gauthiez. La logique de l'espace urbain, formation et évolution, le cas de Rouen. Paris: Ecole des Hautes études en Sciences Sociales, 1991 (unpublished PhD thesis).

of the households inhabited a dwelling with a rental value inferior to 100 livres, compared to the 22.5 percent at Rouen inhabiting dwelling spaces with a rental value inferior to 108 livres. The difference is less for the higher value dwellings: 71.8 percent at Lyons under 200 livres, compared to 53 percent at Rouen under 216 livres.[118]

Clearly, multi-familial housing was a solution for the dwelling of the poorer members of the population – hence its greater part at Lyons. Those inhabiting dwellings with a rental value under 100 livres, typically corresponded in Lyons to the silk-weavers, but there was probably also a less obvious economic explanation. As we saw earlier, the multi-familial nature of the building pattern in Lyons developed in a first phase in the early sixteenth century, accompanied by a new dominant building type, and became dominant from the 1640s according to a new and different type. At Lyons, the growing size of the new constructions, corresponding to growing average financing units, became possible thanks to a capitalistic economic development which gave rise to a dwelling pattern adapted to the low wages, notably of the silk industry, on which the city's wealth was based. Wealth was thus confined to only a small part of the population (see PART III), especially people of the higher classes. In contrast, the average early seventeenth century building looked like a raised house, which it sometimes was. Over the course of time, the proportion of low incomes exceeded sixty percent and wealth became concentrated. As a consequence, whilst the average building grew in size, the average number of new constructions decreased accordingly. The concentration of real estate property and economic wealth reached an extreme in 1789.[119]

As a consequence of the growing size of the new buildings, with an increased number of floors (up to seven, generally five), and of the unifications of two previous plots to build them, the built-up area in square meters in Lyons, all floors taken into account, expanded by about 30 to 40 percent between 1600 and 1789, although the population had more than tripled, from around 40,000 to around 135,000 inhabitants. This means that each inhabitant had an average available floor surface two to three times smaller when the French Revolution occurred than in 1600, a decrease which would have particularly affected the poor.

Actually, it seems probable, given the current state of our knowledge, that the new seventeenth-century building type was invented in Lyons under partic-

---

118 Bardet. *Rouen*, vol. 1, 167, vol. 2, 34 table 17 and 116 table 91. Maurice Garden. *Lyon et les Lyonnais au XVIIIe siècle*. Paris: Les Belles Lettres, 1970, 197.

119 For Paris, see Cabestan, *L'immeuble*.

ular circumstances. Before the 1680s it was not present in Paris, where it remained still very rare in the following decades, becoming dominant only from the mid-eighteenth century.[120] In Rouen, the houses remained massively mono-familial until the late eighteenth century.[121] It is still impossible to determine whether the new type was invented *ex nihilo* and then spread to the point where it came to dominate the market, or whether it developed progressively from the multiple small modifications identified and so well exemplified by the buildings in the block between Rue Mercière and Rue Grenette (Figure II.10). The cases already discussed, in this same block, make one think that the latter scenario was what actually occurred, leading in a few decades to the complete realization of the new type. In the seventeenth to eighteenth centuries, real estate increasingly became a financial asset, as well as, as we will see presently, a personal investment with a weaker affective dimension. An important consequence was the production, where possible, of series of buildings of a larger size than that produced in the sixteenth century.

The logics of the two successive dominant building types in Lyons are quite different. The earlier one, dating from the Renaissance, in a gothic or a classical style, catered for multi-familial housing by piling up familial units in accordance with a planned layout that may already have existed in the late fourteenth century (though this still has to be ascertained). The doubling of the number of apartments meant that a new building at the rear was necessary, and this in turn entailed further modifications like galleries and staircases. The new type in the seventeenth century came about quite differently. The functional unit, defined by one entrance and its associated staircase, was generally larger than before and typically corresponded to two previous functional units (if one considers that the basic unit in the sixteenth century had one apartment per floor, or two apartments united by a gallery). The functionality did not differ from one period to the next, as the functions were not predetermined and the different spaces could be used in various ways. This nevertheless called for some standard equipment, like fireplaces in every room so that it could be used as an entire dwelling (this held foremost every room except those on the ground-floor). The assemblage properties of the successive types are also similar, as each building was conceived to be neighbored by two similar ones, with lateral blind party-walls on either side. But the seventeenth-century type allowed for the appearance of a quite novel arrangement, which consisted in placing buildings along the streets around a block, allowing for the clearing of a large common space

120 Cabestan, *L'immeuble*.
121 Bardet. *Rouen*, vol. 1, 172.

or courtyard at the center, a layout occasionally explored until the early nineteenth century, which also anticipated developments in the later nineteenth century. The massing of the construction directly on the street, with buildings of greater depth, liberated the interior space of the block. This was a major step on the way to modern (i.e., twentieth century) thinking about the relationship between architecture and urban space. The slab buildings produced in the large housing ensembles from the 1930s to the 1970s were made of the assemblage of functional units made of staircases and lifts giving each access to two or four apartments. But the modern buildings did not allow for the possible union or separation of rooms on the same floor, as was made possible by the doorframes present in the walls of the seventeenth- to nineteenth-century buildings, which are much more plastic in their adaptative potential.

The multi-familial building type in Lyons, which developed in the early seventeenth century, has all the main defining traits (morphology, assemblage properties and relationship to plot pattern, plasticity, even materials) of the building type qualified in historiography as 'Haussmannian', in reference to what was produced in Paris at the time of Baron Haussmann's transformation of the city. But a precise comparison has to be made between the situations in Lyons and Paris.[122] Firstly, this type of building developed much earlier in Lyons than in Paris; one has to wait until 1683 to find a Parisian building designed like those of Lyons. So it is nonsense to qualify the *immeubles* in Lyons as *haussmanniens*, even during and after the Second French Empire. The local tradition was strong and independent, except for the decor, which was largely drawn from examples from Italy and later on from Paris.[123] Secondly, in Paris, the need to multiply the number of dwellings produced in a single operation was generally met, in the seventeenth century, by juxtaposing them in series of cells drawn according to a layout already present in the Renaissance tradition, with straight staircases and several floors. The series of buildings constructed by the St-Germain-l'Auxerrois chapter of canons in 1669 Rue de la Ferronnerie, or by the Blanc-Manteaux convent in 1640, were produced in this way.[124] But this way of building was unknown in Lyons, though frequent elsewhere, with an example found even in Rome, built by the French of St-Louis-des-Français church in 1712.[125] The mutualization of the staircases developed in the eighteenth

122 Gauthiez, Les transformations.

123 Cabestan, *L'immeuble*, 47

124 Boudon et al., *Système*, 279–280; the huge amount of data gathered by Boudon et al. in this study is difficult to use in this regard, because the precise chronology of the buildings is generally not available and the investors are not systematically dealt with.

125 Gauthiez, Les logiques, 376, n. 298.

century in Paris, with, as in Lyons, minimal space dedicated to walls and accesses, and a maximization of usable and thus rentable space. This comparison, made from limited empirical material, shows that a more thorough parallel study between several cities would lead to a finer understanding of where the dominant architectural types developed, in which circumstances, according to what chronologies, as well as how they could have been imported from one city to another by some sort of diffusion process. This would require one not to limit one's study to the architectural traits, but to seek also to understand the relationship between building conception, building production, and demography, rent amounts and wealth levels, as well as the logics of investment, which will be the subject of Part III.

The study of building typology in Lyons provides evidence of a specific temporality, marked by the development of two clearly new different dominant types, the first in the late fifteenth century and the second in the first decades of the seventeenth. The first of these developments was present in many cities at the same time, and was due to the importation of a building type from elsewhere, a type whose origin is unknown. In this case, the new type corresponded exactly to a well-known historical period, the Renaissance. The development of the second new type in the early seventeenth century occurred in a different context, and did not correspond to a separation between commonly demarcated historical periods. In this case, it was arguably a local invention, and the passage from a typological period to another one was largely independent of large scale politics and social trends. The temporalities of historical and typological periods are thus quite separate in this latter instance.

Part Three: Temporalities of urban fabric production

III.1 Temporalities and urban morphology

Urban morphology, as developed over the past few decades, has made important advances both in the field of theory, notably thanks to the works of scholars like Conzen, Whitehand and others, and to the empirical study of many towns and cities. Both directions call for further research. On the empirical side, for example, the history of town planning is far from being complete, simply because many towns have not yet been analysed. On the theoretical side, bridging the divide with historical studies is a necessity, both to better understand the time scales and processes of urban change and to introduce more thorough economic, fiscal, and sociological analyses. Quantification represents a second important possibility for future research. Another is to investigate information at the scale of the building in order to map buildings and cities through time using Geographic Information Systems.

This explains why I collaborated with my friend and colleague, the historian Olivier Zeller, on what was for us a challenging project. The idea was simple: to map the transformation of a city at the scale of the building, with each construction-unit being precisely characterized in space and time, and then to make a 'film' of the transformation. Is it possible, we wondered, to go beyond the traditional mapping of cities at those moments imposed by the sources, usually a precise year, simply because this or that plan was itself drawn up at a precise date? I earlier proposed the metaphor of the sausage. The sausage is as long as the length of time in question, and the layout of a city at a given time is equivalent to a cross-section of the sausage, just as the present may be regarded as a cross-section corresponding to the present moment in time. But what if I also reconstruct the fibres of the sausage, such that I can then cut it at any moment, which implies knowledge of all the fibres that compose it? The 'fibre' is here a building, existing along a segment of time.[1] This research program was steadily implemented over the years, encountering technical difficulties and methodological bottlenecks which had to be overcome.[2] The choice of Lyons as a case study

1 The physician Max Tegmark uses a comparable image to represent the 'universe-lines' of objects in the four dimensions of space, with 'spatio-temporal tubes' (*Notre univers mathématique, en quête de la nature ultime du réel.* Paris: Dunod, 2014, 453–454 [In English: *Our mathematical universe: my quest for the ultimate nature of reality.* Alfred A. Knopf/Random House, 2014].

2 The main ones were the substance of papers mentioned in the bibliography.

https://doi.org/10.1515/9783110623062-005

site was selected, partly because the city had fortunately kept continuous records from 1617 onwards of its building licenses, with the only significant gap being between 1763 and 1789, and partly because I lived there and knew the city well. There then followed the long and somewhat fastidious work of trawling through the archival records to build a database including all building licenses, whether for new buildings, transformations, or raisings. At present, the database is complete for the period from 1617 to about 1830, though some work is still to be done for the period after 1830. In total, 14,000 authorizations have been recorded. Another major task was to build a geographical reference frame for all information, which required the development of a GIS (see II.1.1). The following step was to map the authorizations.

III.1.1 A 'film' of the building production over three centuries

As the building authorizations were for objects which resulted from retraceable social processes,[3] it was possible to reconstruct, in the form of a film, the transformation of the urban fabric, while also providing a useful tool for investigating the logics of that transformation: its locations, the social milieus, and the uses. This film could also be made more accurate by cross-referencing the social data with the available data on the building activity. This film of the production of new buildings highlights periods and places of higher and lower intensity for the construction industry. It also discloses some scale effects not present in the preceding analyses, especially the way the emergence of new buildings often occurs in groups. When one house was replaced, the neighboring houses were also often rebuilt, or at least renewed, in subsequent years. This process was certainly encouraged by the *Consulat* administration, as many places affected by this process were streets which it wanted to widen and/or embellish. This process concerned about fifty percent of the new constructions and façade renewals, maybe more.

Another effect of the rebuilding may become visible through mapping the widening of streets, in line with the obligation to set the new façade further back in order to gain between 0.3 m and more than 6 m of public space (from one foot to twenty feet) (Fig. I.4). The Consulate street policy was constant and very efficient in that respect. General street widening occurred in response to the increasing traffic of coaches and carriages, and was also intended to ease traffic jams. This change took place from the late sixteenth and early seven-

3 Gauthiez, Des unités.

teenth centuries, becoming standard from the 1660s. It probably corresponds to a great shift in the way commercial goods were transported, from the use of mainly mules and donkeys in the Middle Ages, and then, progressively, from the Renaissance onwards, to more and more carriages, including heavy ones. This shift probably represented a major step towards the Industrial Revolution. Lyons developed very early as a great industrial city, with an economic activity centered on silk-weaving.[4]

This mapping of the construction-units as defined in PART I is clearly very efficient when it comes to determining and interpreting the planning policy of the municipality. As of today, more than ninety percent of the transformations (new buildings, transformations of extant ones) mentioned in the authorization deeds have been mapped for the period between 1640 and 1828, and about sixty percent for the period between 1617 and 1640, at which time the information was less consistent. The huge number of objects to map was nevertheless limited, since, as we saw in PART II, housing in Lyons was already largely multi-familial from the sixteenth century, so the numbers of properties and fiscal entries of the surveys based on them was relatively small, not exceeding 3,500 for the whole town. It could have been much more, in the case of Rouen for example, where housing was predominantly mono-familial and where the number of buildings was nearly three times as great (10,925 in 1773, suburbs included).[5] The number of houses in the suburbs was comparatively small in Lyons, probably only several hundred.[6]

The sources have also been tentatively explored for the late fifteenth century, including the 1493 *Nommées*. It seems that the sixteenth century archives could partly fill the gap between this period and the early seventeenth century, via mentions of new houses in the fiscal surveys, but their exploration remains to be carried out and their data mapped. The period after 1830, if one wants to deal with the city as a whole, has not yet been covered, with the exception of the old central areas, though records do exist. The scale of the city becomes difficult to grasp at this point, because of the considerable number of objects to analyse. To give an idea of the scale of the work to be carried-out, Nicolas Ferrand has dealt with the 1950 – 2005 period, considering only the planned developments and subdivisions in the agglomeration of Lyons. He mapped more than

4 Gauthiez, Zeller, Beautifying.

5 Bardet, *Rouen*, I: 167.

6 This figure is based on a consideration of the many houses forming ribbons along the access roads to the city, especially on the east bank of the River Rhône, as far as two kilometers away from the river.

5,000 objects,[7] to which research on the transformation of the city from about 1850 to 1950 would need to add a further 2,000 planned developments (subdivisions, new thoroughfares, urban renewals, etc.). The total number of building authorizations for buildings and transformations between 1500 and the present would be of the order of hundreds of thousands.

A problem remains for the period between 1763 and 1790, when the Bureau des Finances, a royal administration in France generally in charge of the building authorizations (*autorisations d'alignement*) in other cities, won its trial against the City of Lyons after a century-long legal action, and became responsible for its authorizations. The case was only definitively settled in 1773, but the remaining records of this period only deal systematically with the '*petite police*', i.e., just the small modifications, not the full constructions and reconstructions, though there are some exceptions. Some partial sources have been used to fill the gap, among them an incomplete series of street plans scattered in various archive files, covering the period after 1763 and bearing the date and nature of the authorizations. The still extant constructions of this period were also of great help, as it seems that the majority of the houses produced in the second half of the eighteenth century are still standing today. An explanation will be given below as to why they were so well preserved (see III.2.2.3). The reconstitution of the average production in this period has thus been possible.

III.1.2 Space, time and social scales

The film I dreamed of twenty years ago has now been made (see Appendix and Fig. III.3). Before analysing its time and space scales, it was necessary to check that all the objects produced during the period it covers were fully characterized. The authorizations database was the key to doing this. The percentage of precisely located and clearly identified building authorizations given above also allows for an evaluation of the total surface concerned. A check was also made in the field, in order to ensure that no building had been excluded. This check revealed that the building authorizations exhibit a high level of coherence with the record of the extant constructions: the corresponding works were systematically carried out soon after the authorizations were given, with only rare exceptions, and in the records there exist written authorizations relating to every extant building from the period after 1617.

7 Ferrand, Approche morphologique.

The analysis of building production and its pattern as it evolved during the three centuries studied reveals several categories of phenomena defined by both a spatial scale and a temporal scale. Their description and understanding requires a triple definition as a spatial unit, a temporal interval, and a social process. These construction-units correspond to the following temporal logics:

- The annual cycle.
- Groups of neighboring reconstructions and façade modifications carried out over a period ranging from one year to two decades.
- Long duration logics of the location of new constructions, covering distinct periods of fifty to eighty years.
- A very long duration evolution differentiating the modern period (1450–1800) from the medieval one before 1450, but also from the nineteenth and twentieth centuries.

These logics are first identifiable on the graph of yearly building production:

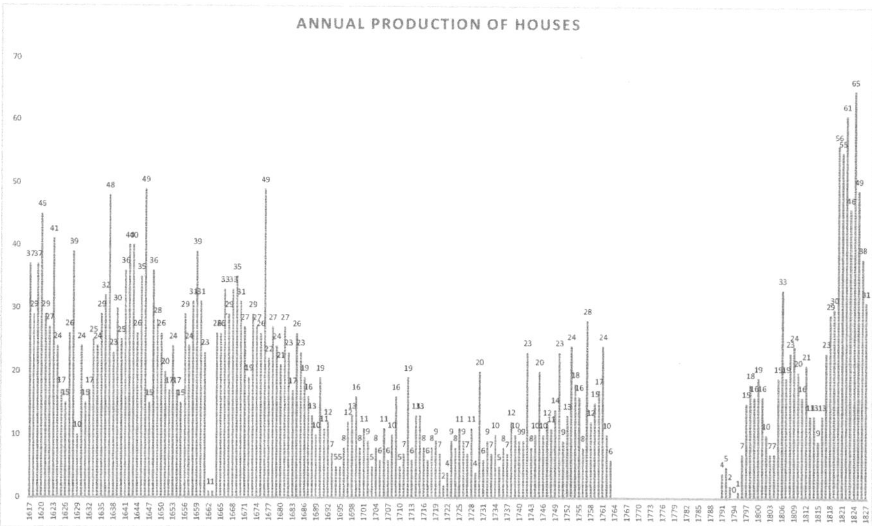

Graph III.1 Constructions per year from 1617 to 1828 (The gaps in 1661–63 and 1763–89 are due to absence of serial information in the archival record.)

III.1.2.1 The year scale

At the level of a single year, single buildings appear very neatly. They correspond to the actions of individuals or organizations, the goals of which are closely determined by personal, familial and contingent causes. No spatial structure is legible on the map of yearly building production, except of course the shape and location of the new buildings. In addition, the number of produced objects varies greatly from one year to the next. Building a film of the transformation based on this annual scale (one image per year) gives no clear idea of the urban space logics involved. The location logic is specific to each investor, and could potentially be the object of a parallel study involving analyses of family or personal wealth management and familial history, especially with regard to marriage and children[8].

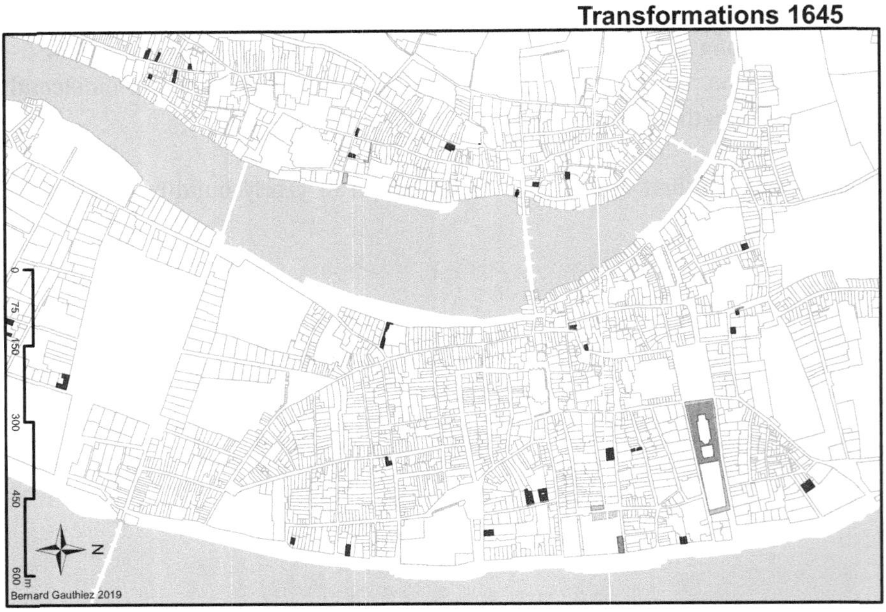

Figure III.1 Example of mapping at the scale of the year: buildings of the year 1645

The year was nevertheless an important cycle in the social life of the city. This can be studied through the precise dates of the authorizations, divided here by month for four different decades both with an important number of constructions and separate along the period studied, 1628 – 1627, 1665 – 1674, 1750 – 1759 and 1808 – 1817.

The graphs of the four decades between 1628 and 1817 are rather similar, but also show unexpected differences. The principal peak for construction work to begin is in March in 1618 to 1627, in April in 1665 to 1674. A lower peak appears

8 See the example of the investments of Perrachon de St-Maurice in Bayard, Ville et campagne.

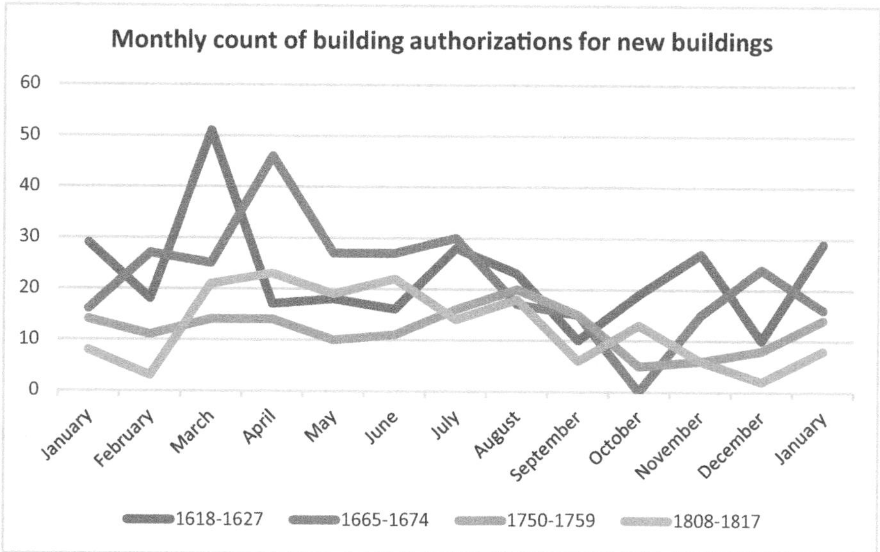

Graph III.2 Monthly count of authorizations for new buildings in four decades of the seventeenth and eighteenth centuries

in July in both periods, whereas in 1750 to 1759, July is the main peak. The decades 1618 to 1627 and 1665 to 1674 are similar again, with the first peak occurring a month later for the second period, and a third peak in November for the first period and December for the second. The graph of 1750 to 1759 does not show the same structure. Explaining the change can be made only very tentatively as we lack the necessary data. It seems that in the seventeenth century activity grew neatly – which is not a surprise, after winter, in March-April, with a near cessation in October. The full cessation in 1665 to 1674 for this month is puzzling, it is certainly significant as it occurred during a rather intense construction period and for ten successive years. Some activity also occurred from November to January, probably the demolition of the older extant buildings on the plots earmarked for construction (the great majority of new constructions were replacements), the clearing of the plots, the digging of the cellars and the preparation of the new construction site. In many cases, these processes probably began only at the end of winter and were immediately followed by the construction itself. The difference between the early and later seventeenth century could be hypothetically explained as an impact of the longer winters of the Small Ice Age.[9]

9 There is no available study on the seventeenth-century climate in the region of Lyons. A larger

The construction activity seems relatively equally spread throughout the year during the 1750s. The larger size of buildings produced in that period would have required works of longer duration, and in consequence the lesser importance, as far as the season is concerned, of the timing of their beginning. It also varied only slightly in the 1810s, but with a smooth decrease from a peak in late winter-early spring to a yearly low in December. Generally, with the exception of the 1750s and probably the end of the eighteenth century when the constructions were bigger, the rhythm of the yearly construction activity was relatively equivalent for two centuries, from 1617 to 1830. The building permits were given when activity grew very fast at the end of winter, and were at their lowest at the end of summer and again in December. The changing seasons were clearly a very potent factor in determining the timing of building activities.

Unfortunately, no data regarding the precise timing of the construction works of these private buildings has been kept in the archival records, so no direct data is available about the process other than the date of the authorization. The duration of the building work can nevertheless be estimated thanks to indirect information: the authorization to put a sign on a house the construction of which had been authorized previously. The precise location of the house signs authorized by the municipality is difficult because of the general lack of neighbors mentioned in these deeds. In consequence, there are only a small number of cases where, for a single building, both the authorization for construction and an authorization for a sign to hang over the main door once the house is completed are available. Unfortunately, the placing of such signs largely disappears from the authorization records in the eighteenth century.

view is given in Geoffrey Parker. *Global crisis. War, climate change and catastrophe in the seventeenth century.* New Haven, London: Yale University Press, 2017: 6–13.

Table III.1 Time span between the beginning of a construction and the placing of a sign on the completed building

Name of proprietor	Operation	Date	Date of sign	Time elapsed[10]
Badelon	whitening	31 May 1672	26 Jun. 1672	12 m 26 d
Bagnon	house construction	27 Jan. 1687	22 Jun. 1688	16 m 26 d
Barnier	façade (new house?)[11]	20 May 1703	19 Oct. 1705	27 m 29 d
Charnozat	house construction	15 Nov. 1661	22 Apr. 1664	29 m 7 d
Chilaguet	whitening	20 May 1679	1 Feb. 1680	8 m 12 d
Cousin	house construction	11 May 1688	30 May 1690	23 m 19 d
Demurard	whitening	16 Apr. 1711	13 Sep. 1711	3 m 27 d
Deville	whitening	20 Oct. 1690	14 Dec. 1690	1 m 24 d
Fillion	house construction	19 Jan. 1649	17 Mar. 1650	13 m 28 d
Gelas	house construction	3 Feb. 1678	07 Feb. 1679	12 m 6 d
Girardet	house construction	10 Dec. 1676	30 May 1679	17 m 20 d
Grateloup	house construction	25 Feb. 1681	14 Jan. 1683	22 m 17 d
Jacquand	raising	26 Mar 1669	10 Sep. 1669	5 m 15 d
Jacquemet	raising	31 Jul. 1668	7 Feb. 1669	6 m 7 d
Jannin	raising, new frontage	2 Aug. 1696	2 July 1697	11 m
Lelong	house construction	10 Feb. 1678	30 Jun. 1679	16 m 18 d
Célestins convent	shop bay	11 Aug. 1678	19 Jan. 1679	5 m 4 d
Célestins convent	large building construction	6 Mar. 1721	15 Feb. 1725	47 m 9 d
Loubat and Dumoulin	house construction	7 May 1658	2 Sep. 1659	15 m 25 d

10 In months and days.

11 The word façade is sometimes employed in the building authorizations to mean a full reconstruction. This is due to the fact that, legally, the authorization deals only with the limit between private and public spaces.

Table III.1 Time span between the beginning of a construction and the placing of a sign on the completed building *(Continued)*

Name of proprietor	Operation	Date	Date of sign	Time elapsed[10]
Marquet	house construction	14 Mar. 1669	29 Jan. 1671	22 m 12 d
Mellier	house construction	5 Oct. 1691	9 Jun. 1693	20 m 4 d
Panthot	house construction	31 Dec. 1668	21 Nov. 1669	10 m 21 d
Quinson	house construction	18 Mar. 1681	1 Apr. 1683	24 m 13 d
Satre	house construction	17 Jul. 1665	18 Mar. 1666	8 m 1 d
Simonnet	house construction	30 Jul. 1676	11 Aug. 1678	24 m 12 d
Vaubertrand	house construction	2 Mar. 1649	19 Jan. 1651	22 m 17 d

As this table makes clear, the duration depends on the type and importance of building work carried out:

- *Whitening:* from 1 month 24 days to 12 months 26 days (probably in that case heavier repairs were involved, much more than a simple whitening).
- *Raising:* 5 months 15 days; 6 months 7 days; 11 months with the remaking of the façade.
- *Full construction:* minimum duration 8 months (probably the transformation of an extant building, not a full reconstruction); three occurrences of around 12 to 13 months, which is one full year; three occurrences of 16 to 18 months, i.e., one year and a half; six occurrences of around 20 to 24 months, two years. The Célestins convent building on the River Saône Quay, intended for dwellings, took about four years to construct, it was very large, with a total length of 106 m.

Although the figures are not statistically very significant, one can note that the works were apparently completed mainly in January to February, June, and September, which is one or two months before the peaks for the authorizations. This could be because the construction works were carried out in succession by a single builder-entrepreneur or mason, with an interval of one or two months to prepare the following construction operation. These elements allude tantalizingly to both a year-round organization of building production, with different tasks according to the seasons, and to an organization specific to every entrepreneur. This organization undoubtedly intended to maintain a continuous activity throughout the year.

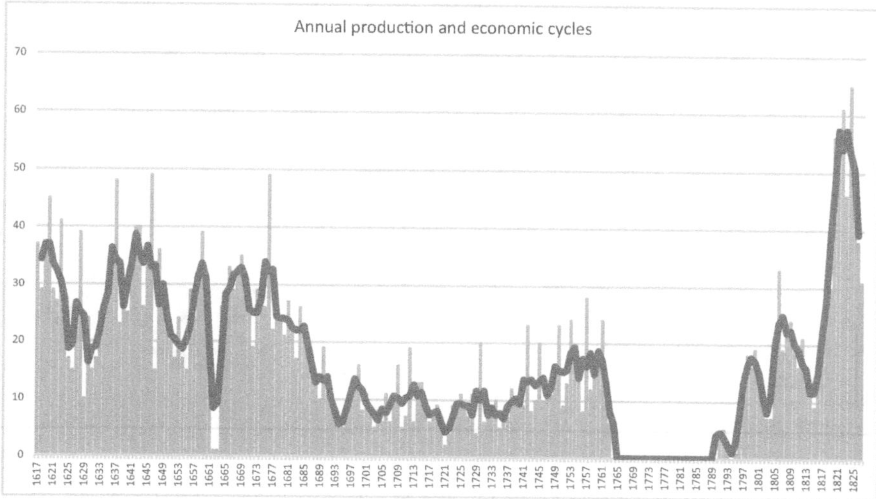

Graph III.3 Annual building production between 1617 and 1827, with a triennial mobile average (The lack of data explains the gaps in 1661–63 and from 1763 to 1789.)

III.1.2.2 The several year cycle and the grouped rebuilding of neighboring houses

Another time scale appears, defined by the succession of highs and lows in the production graph, probably as a consequence of economic cycles. The cartography has been tempted at this time scale (one image per cycle), but it does not clearly show any particular spatial pattern, so it is not presented here.[12] But considering the time length of a decade gives striking results, as groups of neighbor-

12 The reason for this is simple. The cycles are not very marked in the pluri-annual variation, although some years were clearly very bad. One could try a mapping corresponding to pluri-annual cycles, but this would mean varying durations for the cycles mapped, and some cycles would contain very few new buildings. As a consequence, this would not be spatially very significant.

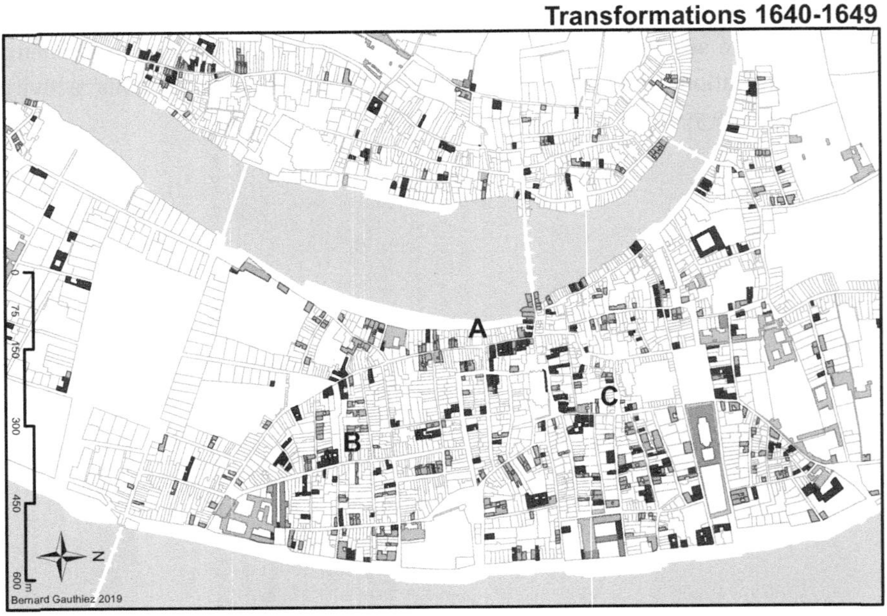

Figure III.2 New constructions during the decade 1640–1649
New buildings of the decade are mapped in dark blue (private buildings) and dark green (religious and public), new buildings of the two previous decades in pale blue (private buildings) and pale green (religious and public). New streets and public spaces in dark orange and pale orange.

ing buildings were produced over a period of a few years in every decade. This was as true in 1493 as in later centuries.[13]

The map of new buildings appearing in the 1640s clearly shows the grouping of many new constructions. The buildings produced in the twenty years before have been mapped with a paler shade and allow for a better understanding of the phenomenon. On the map (Fig. III.2), some groups are neatly visible, such as Rue Mercière (**A**), Rue de l'Hôpital (**B**) or Rue Malpertuis (**C**). The other groups are rather blurred by the fact that each one has its own complex temporality.

This phenomenon is also clearly visible on the map of new constructions and buildings under construction in 1493 (Fig. III.5). Grouped re-building actually includes several different phenomena:

13 This had already been identified in my study on Rouen, albeit on the basis of much less precise information. Gauthiez, *La logique*, 493.

- Synchronic rebuilding according to one only authorization given to several owners on the same day, like Rue des Trois-Carreaux in 1647 (three houses), Rue de l'Enfant-qui-Pisse in 1692 (four houses), Rue Raisin in 1737 (three houses).
- Rebuilding in rapid succession of as many as ten houses, like Rue Neuve c. 1700.
- Slow rebuilding, neighbor after neighbor, like Rue St-Jean between 1726 and 1744, where only two houses were fully rebuilt, and the other houses were given a new set-back façade with a new design.
- Buildings following a subdivision (like Rue St-Dominique in 1658, seven houses).

The purposes could vary: to give an orderly frontage to a street section, as occurred in 1692 Rue Lanterne; to compensate for the instability induced in one building by the destruction of its neighbor (since the party-wall was structurally shared), as occurred in Rue Grenette in the early nineteenth century; or, in many cases, to widen a street like Rue St-Jean in the eighteenth century. Of course, these aims related to the architectural landscape, public security, and traffic, and they were often associated with one another and accorded a high priority. Over these timespans of a few years, various groups of individuals played different roles, and the economical context played also a determining role. But local circumstances and the individuals involved were probably foremost.

It is possible to make the film previously alluded to in such a way that each frame corresponds to a decade (Appendix). Tests showed that an image every ten years provides a good compromise between clear visibility of the phenomena involved and the economic cycles, which lasted from four to ten years and are neatly legible on the graph presenting the new building authorizations. To get a better understanding of what happened, the new streets and squares are represented on the maps in darker colors, and a representation of the preceding twenty years has also been added in a paler shade in order to exhibit the spatial dynamics more clearly.

The question of the best time sequence for the images is a difficult one. This is due to the fact that it is not an actual film, showing a single object and simulating movement. The period which could be mapped spread over 280 years, from 1620 to 1900. The analysis of the images allow for the recognition of well-known features, like, for example, an urban fringe of convents in the 1620s, some rare new planned developments that occurred in the 1650s, an intense urban renewal occurring in the period between 1850 and 1870 and more sparsely later, but already also present in a small block in 1706 (by the canons of the St-Nizier collegial church).

The building of city facilities, like two large hospitals and the City Hall in the 1620s and 1640s, were also locally determined. They required hierarchical decisions and actions at the political level of the city. At still larger space and time scales, structural logics could play the determining role, as occurred when the Counter-Reform movement led to the creation of many convents in former private properties around the city, a phenomenon clearly visible in the 1620s, when the ground value was still low and thus made their installation much easier; or when the city center was almost completely renewed, beginning in the 1850s, a process which continued until the 1890s. These phenomena were due to the action of central, hierarchical organizations (the Church, the City), able to act on this large-scale over decades, according to strong political and ideological targets, in the first case the religious control of the population, in the second the eviction of the poor from the city center to establish a business district and to gentrify the area.

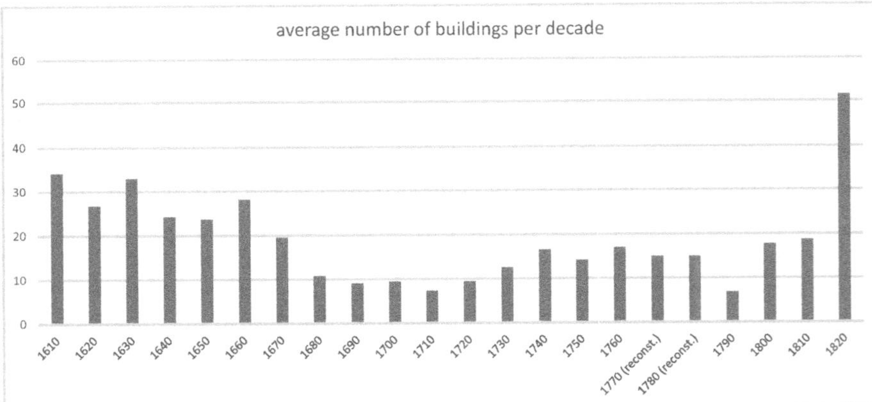

Graph III.4 Building in Lyons (1610–1830): decennial rhythms

III.1.2.3 Long duration periodicity

Another scale of time, space and society appears when one looks at the graph of long-term building production (Graph III.3), as it can be decomposed into separate logics running for several decades. The mapping of these logics reveals some striking features.

The pictures in fig. III.3,1–4 show a succession of periods affected by varying powerful phenomena concerning the entire city, as well as interactions between center and periphery:

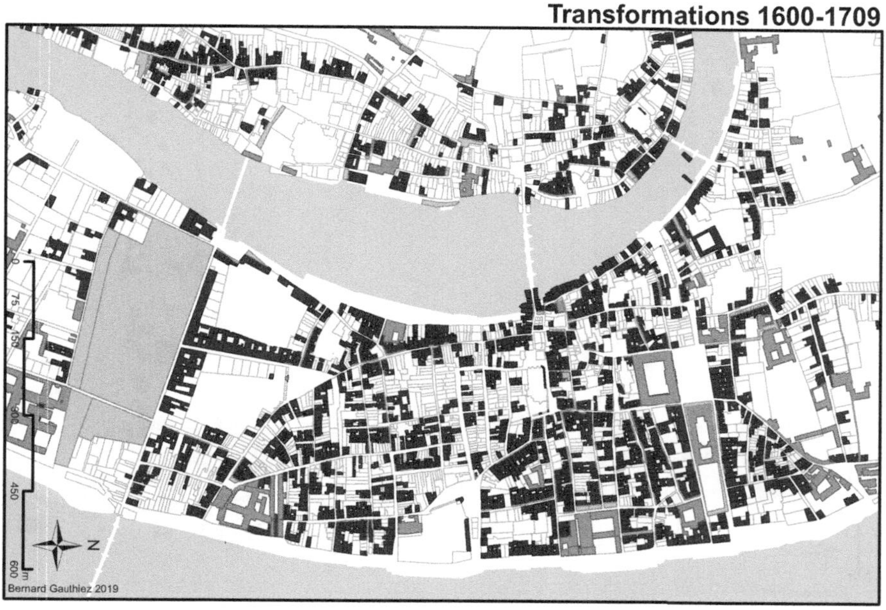

Figure III.3-1 4 images of the building activity at Lyons on the long duration, from the early seventeenth century to 1900
A: from 1600 to 1709

1600 – 1709:
The densification of the central areas was rather isotropic, as it concerned every part of the city, either rich or poor, which means that the wealth was at least partly shared by many potential investors, allowing some middle-class people to build new houses. The period was also characterized by the creation of numerous new convents and the construction of huge facilities like two large hospitals (Charité and Hôtel-Dieu), a public college (the Jesuits) and a new City Hall. The geographical extension of urbanization was very limited. Densification dominated, accompanying the population growth from 30,000 to 100,000 inhabitants.

1710 – 1789:
The new buildings were predominantly located in the wealthiest areas, either the aristocratic quarters to the south, around the Place Bellecour created around 1685, or to the north-east around the City Hall, where a gentrification process followed its completion in 1656, slowly at first, but more rapidly after 1740. In this latter area, the quarters concerned were not new, but their population was progressively replaced. A new subdivision appeared to the north-east in 1750, the Quartier St-Clair (largely outside the map, see III.2.2), dedicated to higher eco-

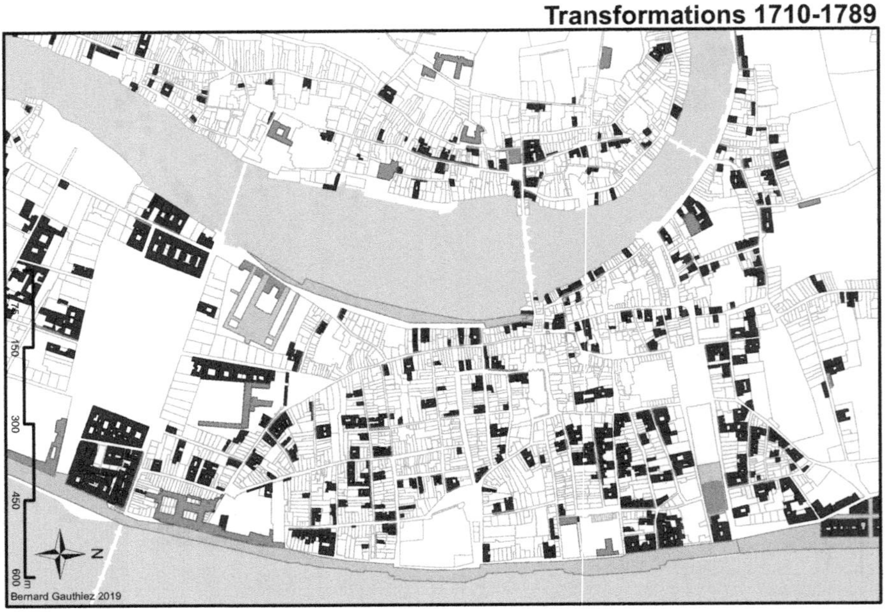

Figure III.3-2 B: from 1710 to 1789

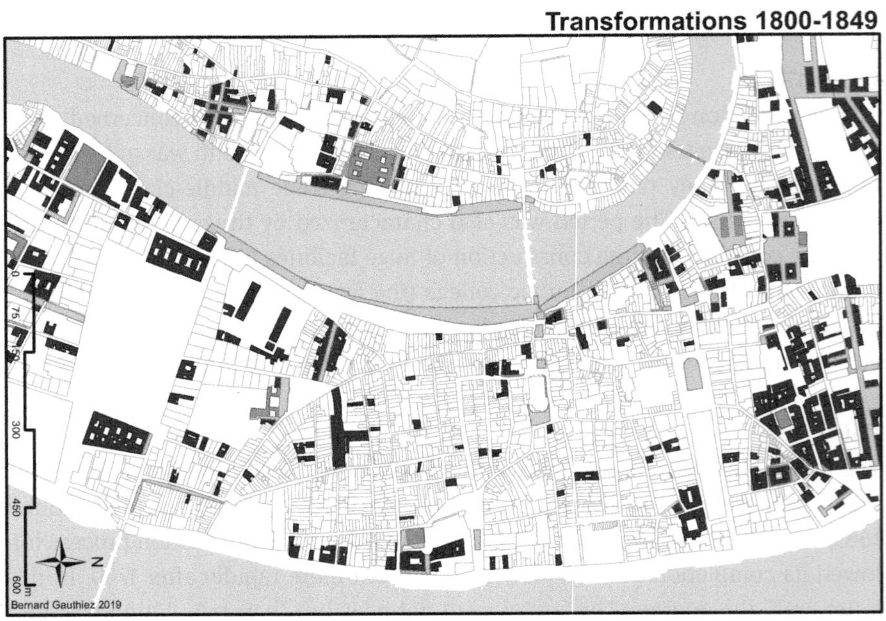

Figure III.3-3 C: from 1800 to 1849

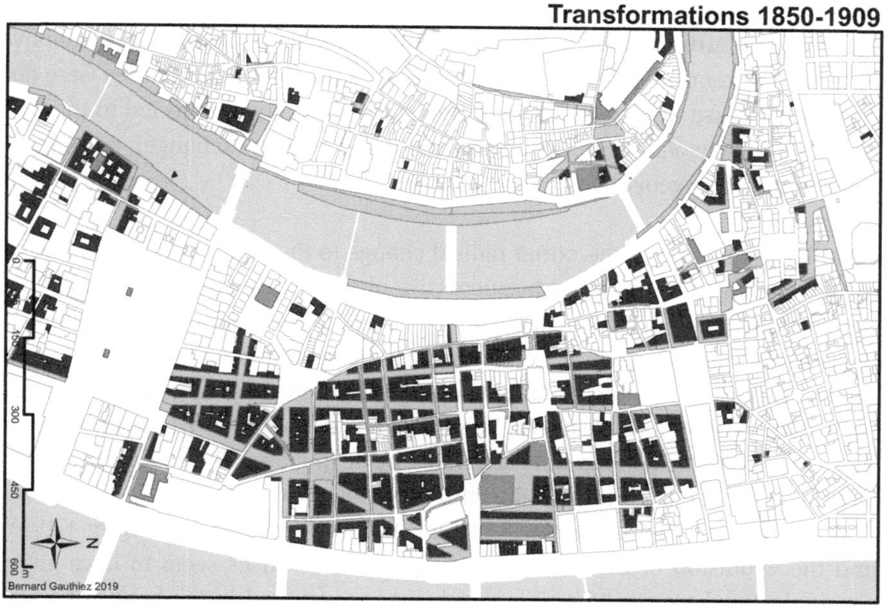

Figure III.3-4 D: from 1850 to 1909

nomic and social groups. The geographical extension of urbanization was again very limited, with densification allowing for the addition of another 30 to 40,000 inhabitants. Almost no new buildings were intended for the lower, working-class. The 1790s are not taken into account as they were dominated by the reconstruction works following the bombings that occurred during the siege of 1793, a catastrophic event of no long-term significance in this context.

1800 – 1849:

Nearly no rebuilding occurred in the old quarters of the city in this period, whether between the Saône and the Rhône rivers, or on the west bank of the River Saône. This lack of rebuilding occurred in parallel to their rapid impoverishment. All new investments went to peripheral areas, to the south in the new Perrache sector (outside the map), to the east beyond the River Rhône (outside the map), and to the north, firstly in connection with the previously established business quarter around the City Hall, and secondly to the north for the silk weaving workshops (partly outside the map, see the example III.2.3.1), mainly in subdivisions of religious precincts established in the seventeenth century.

1850 – 1899:
The growth of urbanization continued rapidly (outside the map), but the impoverishment of central quarters led to their renewal. In consequence, they were destroyed en masse to make room for a new business center connected to the City Hall and the new Palais du Commerce (including a stock-exchange), but also to provide new bourgeois housing.

What is striking here is the rather radical change to the logics in building investment, which are characterized by successive phases, each with a strong identity. Bernard Guy, a physicist colleague, talked of '*phase transitions*' when looking at these maps. These long-term trends can also be seen in the cases of Paris and Rouen. This pattern could no doubt also be found in other large French cities, be it with varying local features. The question is, therefore, what can explain these changes? The periods were separated by deep crises. The end of the seventeenth century and the early eighteenth are known for their succession of famines, the wars of the last decades of King Louis XIV's reign (ending in 1715),[14] and the expulsion of the Protestants in 1685. These crises seem to have given rise to a city where wealth was increasingly concentrated in the hands of a significantly reduced number of families. At Lyons, the workers insurrections in 1744, 1745 and 1786 must be considered in this context.[15] The development of the silk industry was probably accompanied by a growing impoverishment of a significant part of the population, whose dwelling conditions grew progressively worse.

The crisis of the French Revolution, beginning in 1789, is also well known. At Lyons, it corresponded to deteriorating local relations between the well-off and the workers, with a small percentage of the population living in large newly constructed heated apartments facing a mob of workers inhabiting old houses, often in cramped conditions just below the roofs. Its end saw first the reconstruction of the buildings damaged or demolished during the 1793 siege by the Convention army,[16] followed by a rapid extension of the city in parallel with the advent of a new economy benefiting wider social groups. Quality housing became available for the majority of the population thanks to strong investment in building works, whether in the form of new constructions or renovations. As a conse-

14 Gauthiez, *La logique.*

15 Olivier Zeller. Géographie des troubles et découpage urbain à Lyon (XVIème-XVIIIème siècles). *114ème congrès des sociétés savantes, Paris 1989. Les espaces révolutionnaires.* Paris: Editions du Comité des Travaux Historiques et Scientifiques, 1990, 43 – 59.

16 This particular period explains why it has not been taken into account to establish the maps (Appendix, 1790 – 1799).

quence of the general enrichment, one counts about 6,000 rentiers at Lyons, many of them benefiting from real estate property, in the mid-1860s, at which time the population of the city as a whole was 320,000 inhabitants.

The change occurring around 1850 had other causes. Investment in real estate on the periphery was preferred as it was very difficult to replace the urban fabric in old quarters, notably because of the high income possible from renting out crowded houses, but also because the law did not make expropriation easy. This changed markedly with a new law on expropriation for public utility in 1840, intended for railways and roads, but used also for new streets in the old urban fabric. At the same time, the awareness of growing private and public health problems in the old quarters, along with the risk of insurrections like those of 1831 and 1834, called for political intervention. In the light of these problems, city politicians decided, with great continuity of purpose from 1846 to the 1900s (the last renewals occurred in the 1980s), to destroy the old and impoverished quarters. The poor inhabitants of these areas were dislodged and replaced by middle- and upper-class people.

In light of the above, we can see that three scales are present in the transformation of urban space through time. They associate a time duration, a space dimension, and a social level of organization and action:

- The year / individuals and single organizations / single buildings.
- The decade or economic cycle / groups of individuals and local institutions / groups of neighboring buildings and clusters of buildings sharing the same function.
- The half century or century / high-level state (or religious) organization, or large-scale economic trend / urban-scale transformation logic.

These scales have their own changing logics of transition from one phase to another. A transformation at the level of the economic cycle or the scale of the decade is local and obeys specific rules: the interest of several investors to act in a concerted manner or a tendency for a proprietor to act because their neighbors have already acted. This represents a form of energy limited by local possibilities. Such local changes seem to behave like spreading wildfires, being halted by houses whose proprietors don't want to sell to make way for a reconstruction, by newly built ones not in need of modifications, by insufficient funds, or even by the disappearance of a contractor who had convinced several proprietors to rebuild or renovate; for it seems that some contractors could have encouraged neighboring proprietors to act together at the same time or in quick succession. This phenomenon of grouping new constructions often exhibits some characteristics of a so-called emergent phenomena, as it was generally not initially planned. It was, however, the result of strong motivations (the will and money of the proprietors, contractors, *Consulat*), and it came spontaneously to an end when the available energy was consumed or had become insufficient, or when the renovation had allowed it to achieve the standard set by the dominant type to a local group of houses of an old building type.

This can be synthesized in a cross table presenting three variables: time scale / level of social organization / space transformation scale:

Table III.2 The scales logics of urban space production / transformation

Agent ► Time scale ▼	**Individuals / single organisations**	**Groups of individuals / groups of organizations / City politics / economic short cycles**	**State politics / geopolitical change / centennial economic trend**	**society scale**
1–2 years	Single buildings	Single investor		
5 to 20 years	Large public and religious buildings and compounds	Groups of neighboring buildings / Urban fringe / Boom of construction / New planned developments	Territorial facilities / Major symbolic buildings and facilities	Exceptional realizations / City shaping
50 to 100 years	Maintenance / Reconstruction	Establishment of Public facility systems	Urban renewal / Convents of the Counter-Reform / Urban segregation of investment / Urban growth phase / De-urbanization	Consolidation / City featuring
500 to 1,000 years		Religious compounds maintenance and reconstruction		Rise and fall

III.1.2.4 Long-term trends and demography

Mapping over time implies the attachment of quantitative information to each object and each time sequence. It is then possible to calculate on the decennial scale the evolution of investment in new buildings, their average size and their quantity, which may be compared to the extant buildings. Comparing this data with the known evolution of population, some interesting facts appear which can only be understood at the scale of several centuries.

The number of buildings produced per decade, compared to the number of extant buildings, reveals an initial interesting fact. This ratio was historically at its highest level during the half century between 1493 and 1551, around 1.2 to 1.5 percent annually. The total number of houses is known at both dates: 2,574 in 1493 and 3,460 in 1551. But, if the increase is clearly of 886, the figure counts mainly new buildings produced in the decades after 1493 in new planned developments, but it doesn't include the replacement of old medieval houses. The new buildings constructed in the period immediately before 1493, described then as 'new', (considered on the graph as a decade) were mainly replacements. Of the approximately 2,300 houses extant in 1493, excluding the 256 new houses from the total figure of 2,574,[17] about 600 had been constructed between around 1450 and 1480, which implies a rather high rate of annual new constructions of about 1.0 (of which only a few houses remain). Probably over 1,000 medieval houses (built before 1450), maybe more, were replaced in the half century until 1551. So, the new buildings produced in the decades after 1493 comprised of a lot of replacements and many constructions in new planned developments. There were of course highs and lows, although the graph (Graph III.5) shows only a sort of plateau, because we have no detailed information regarding the variation of the production activity during the decades between 1493 and 1551. Nevertheless, production was clearly exceptionally high during the Renaissance, with maybe 1900 new houses produced, i.e., high levels of over 1.5 percent of new buildings annually in some periods. Such a level was seen again only in the 1820s and is quite remarkable in the contest of long-term trends.

Unfortunately, the production between 1551 and the 1610s cannot be quantitatively reconstituted. Its level was undoubtedly low, as the few remaining buildings of this period indicate. The production level was again high in the early seventeenth century, at about 1.0 percent of new buildings annually, a figure which then steadily declined until the 1710s.

Production in the seventeenth and eighteenth centuries consisted mainly of replacements. It increased again before plateauing between 1740 and 1789, with a slight increase of the proportion of buildings located in new developments (10 percent of the total of new buildings between 1720 and 1800). It is interesting to note that the decennial average for the replacement rate of the extant buildings could vary between approximately 0.2 and 1.0 percent per year. In the long-term, this would represent an average age for the buildings of between 50 and

17 Supposing that the new houses in 1493 were essentially built after 1480 and that the stock of housing in 1480 was made of the 1700 medieval houses counted in 1446 plus about 600 built in the meantime.

250 years. Today, the replacement rate of buildings within the perimeter of pre-industrial Lyons is extremely low, under 0.2 percent per year. This entails an increase in average age, the basic reasons for which are quite specific to the present: the area is undergoing a gentrification process and is subject to protection as a world UNESCO heritage site.

The late seventeenth-century crisis is known to have been very profound and to have lasted a long time. The surprise here is that it began before the events of the early 1690s (epidemic and famines), with no identified explanation (one explanation could be the expulsion of Protestants from France in 1685). When the situation improved, the concentration of investment funds in the hands of the upper social classes dominated the building scene. Fewer buildings were erected, but their size increased.

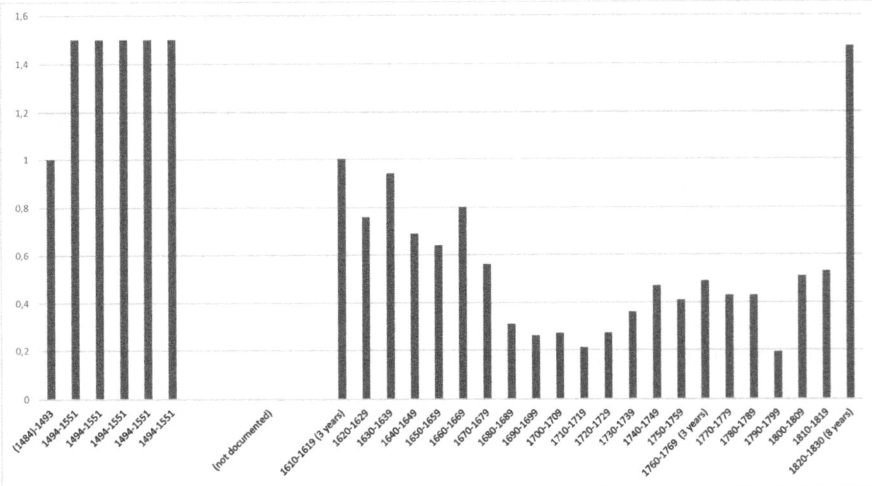

Graph III.5 Average annual ratio of new constructions compared to the number of extant buildings

The growth of average building size had already begun during the seventeenth century, but at a slow pace. It came about largely because of the emergence, from the 1620s, of the new type of multi-familial housing building examined above (II.2.4), which comprised one main building along the street, with a single central staircase providing access to two to six apartments on each floor.

The trend, visible from 1600 to 1800, towards increasing the size of buildings is also due to the concentration of investment money, which was higher when the economy was low, and accompanied the generalization of a new type of building, which was easier to implement in newly developed areas, although

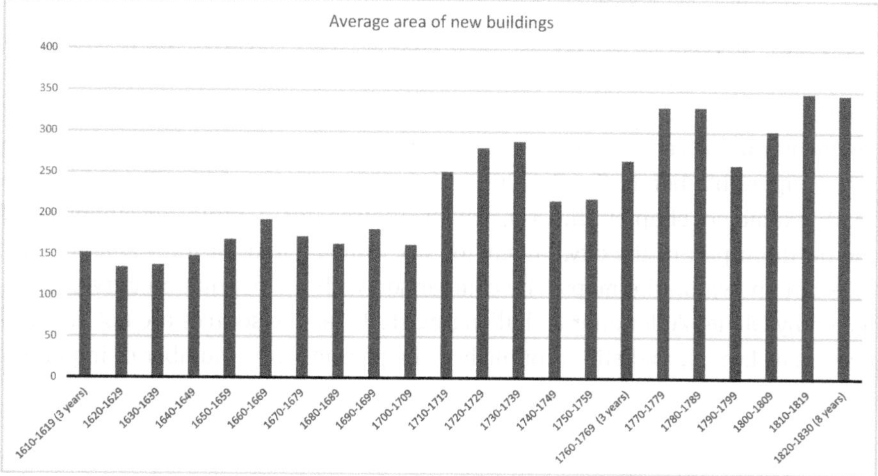

Graph III.6 Average area of the new buildings from 1610 to 1830, in square metres

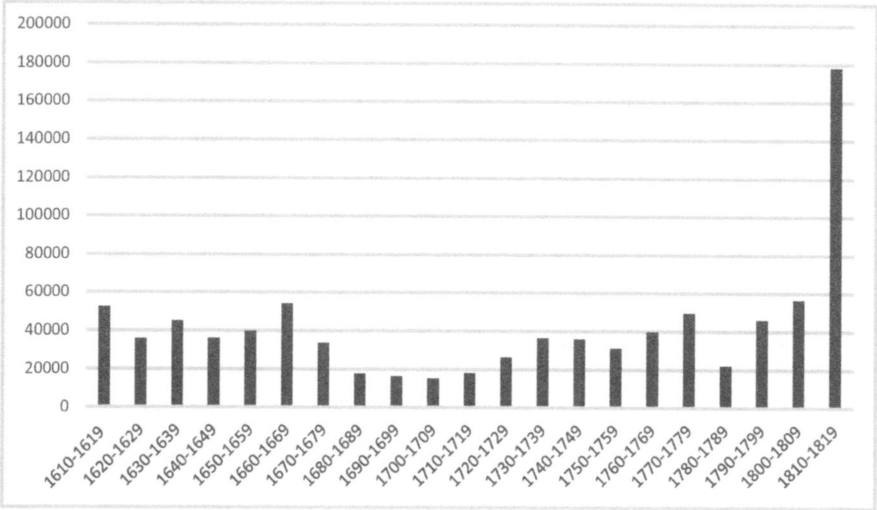

Graph III.7 Buildings surface total production per decade, in square metres (The figures for the 1610s and 1760s are extrapolated from the three known years of these decade. The level of the 1790s corresponds to the reconstruction after 1794.)

in the crowded historic center it became more and more difficult to find room for it, as it generally required the unification of two previous houses and plots. It is also important to note that the beginning of the seventeenth century allowed many more people to invest in their own building than was the case in later times, and the eighteenth century saw a growing concentration of money, increasingly invested in aristocratic buildings to the neglect of the dwellings of the poor. This situation needs further socio-economic study if it is to be fully explained. It changed in the early nineteenth century, when building investment again became accessible to low or middle class investors, often organized in ways impossible before the Revolution (see the example of Rue Pierre-Blanc in 1820, examined chapter III.2.3.1), which allowed for a rapid development of the northern part of the city, largely for silk workers, and for the spread of suburbs not shown on the maps. The comparison with the population curve, established by Olivier Zeller after a challenging study (as the sources are not very numerous at Lyons), and still unpublished, helps establish a number of important facts.

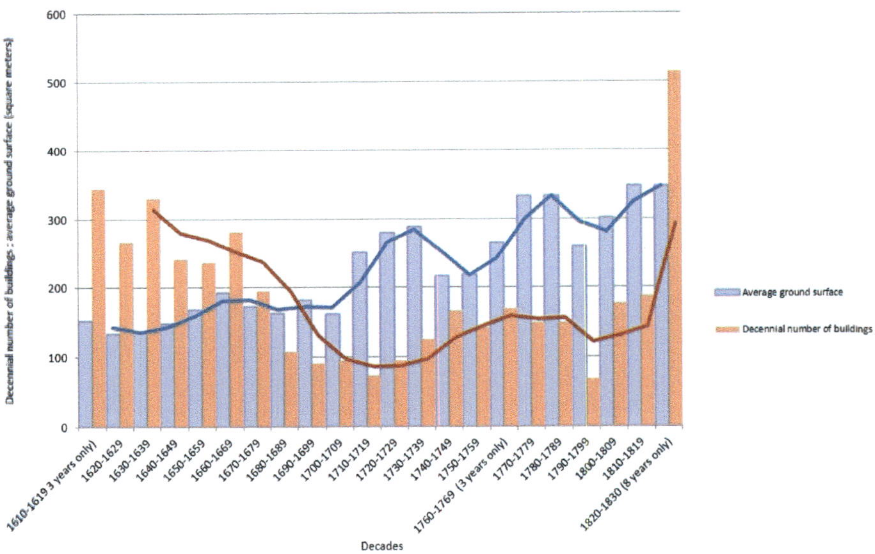

Graph III.8 Parallel between the number of constructions per decade and their average size: opposite trends

One of the most evident, visible in the first half of the seventeenth century, in the decades before 1789 and in early nineteenth century, is the lag between the beginning of a new period of high building investment and a period of population growth occurring, in all three cases, about 20 years later. This is striking as the population level after a drop has taken several decades, when the situation had improved, to get back to its former high level. This implies that many new buildings were constructed although the population had not fully recovered.

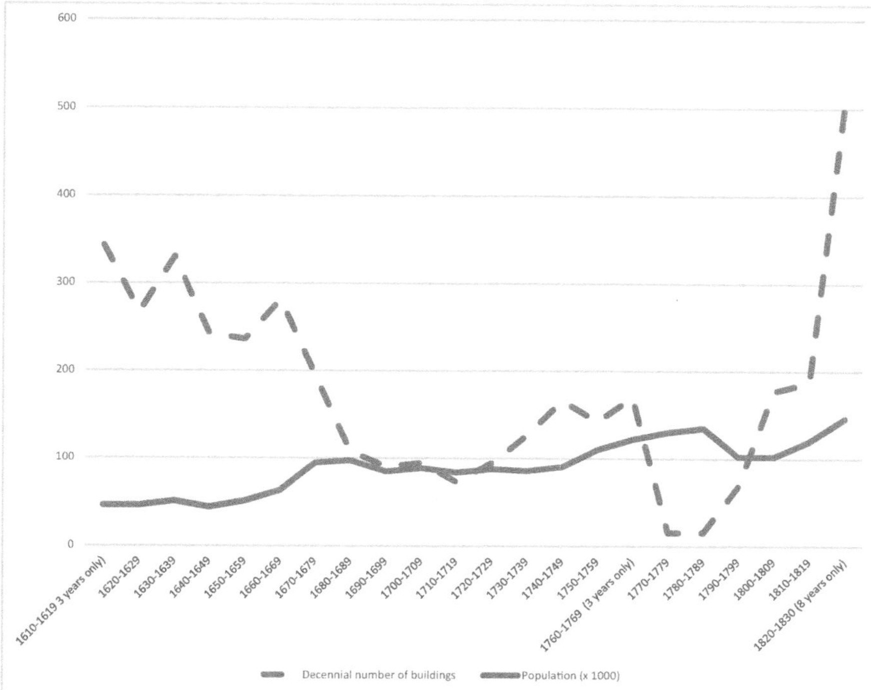

Graph III.9 Parallel between population curve and number of buildings per decade

The great variation in the population level has to be emphasized. There's no general determinism accounting for its evolution. The low of 1597 (30,000) was one third below the high of the 1550s (45 to 50,000), a level which was regained only in the 1630s, after three decades of intense building. A new high in the late seventeenth century (about 100,000) was followed by a low (83,000) in the early 1720s and regained only towards 1750. The Ancien Regime maximum was reached a little before 1789 (at about 135,000), although building activity had not been intense in the previous period. A new low after 1793 (less than 100,000) was followed by a long phase of growth, but the 1789 level was regained only in early 1820s, again after two decades of strong building activity.

This implies that there is no direct link between the population level and building activity, but also that both the population level and the logics of investment in new buildings (social categories of investors, target market) varied greatly through time. When the urbanization process is in its resumption phase, it doesn't prioritize areas that had previously been more or less abandoned, but rather the more economically active sectors. A cycle of growth/decline typically follows these phases:

A. High building activity within already urbanized areas (this happened in the late fifteenth century, in 1600 to 1680, and in 1850 to 1900). A new building type can appear in such circumstances (late fifteenth century, early seventeenth).
B. New developments at the periphery of urbanized areas. The population level of the previous demographic peak is regained (1500 to 1550, 1720 to 1750, 1820 to 1850). The first new developments tend to be small, but can be followed by larger urban schemes, some of which may be aborted, as occurred in the 1560s to the south of Place Bellecour or in the late eighteenth century with respect to the Perrache and Morand projects.
C. Densification of the built-up fabric of particular central areas (generally the richest). Building activity is carried out mainly on the periphery for entirely new constructions. The previous demographic high is exceeded (for example 1750 to 1790). This phase does not always occur.
D. Decline with low building activity. Demographic de-densification in all quarters (1580 to 1600, 1710 to 1720, 1790s). Such a phase can provoke the stasis of developments undertaken in the previous logic of high investment, which happened to the south of Place Bellecour and in the Morand and Perrache quarters after 1789.
E. Abandonment of buildings in peripheral areas (this occurred only in the late Middle Ages and late Roman period).
F. De-urbanization of central areas (this occurred only in the late Roman period and early Middle Ages).

III.2 The social agents of change: who builds, for whom

Understanding the transformation of urban space implies the identification of agents responsible for the production of a new urban fabric, particularly investors. The social grouping of these agents is obviously of importance, and so is their role among the population. This makes it important to understand their objectives, which include:
- Contributing to their own field of economic activity (for example, a mason, a carpenter, etc.).
- Investment in real estate and creation of new incomes through rents or capital gain through sales.
- Facilitation of a given activity (like silk-weaving in late sixteenth century and early nineteenth century)
- Profiting from a gentrification process in a given area.

These objectives are multiple and generally overlap. One also has to understand the functioning of the real estate market, not, from the point of view adopted here, with respect to property deeds, but rather with respect to investment in new buildings. What is the market aiming at: selling after construction, or renting? Answering these questions requires particular data. Qualitative data may shed light on a single building operation, on a subdivision, or perhaps even on a larger development. The action of the agents involved in the transformation may also be studied. Quantitative data are also necessary to understand wider logics. It will be useful to identify the social group to which the construction agents belong, as it will provide a better understanding of the significance of the new constructions, including their economic and social dynamics. Separating social groups among the urban population may reveal different behaviors with respect to property ownership and investment in new buildings. The different groups identified may then be compared to the status of the houses, whether old, new or under construction.

The available sources that might provide this data are not numerous at Lyons. The *Nommées* in 1493 allow for a general and detailed overview. The *Nommées* were a fiscal survey of the entire city, carried out house after house, registering proprietors, dwelling households, their activity and social status, the age of the building, and often giving information allowing one to deduce that the construction was not in fact completed. Some similar data are available for the year 1677, which can be compared to the building authorizations of the previous years, but only four quarters are adequately characterized in this record. Much the same enquiry could have been very interesting for 1597, when another survey of the city was produced, but it gives no information on the age of the constructions, especially the newest ones. However, it is probable that new houses were rare then, given the context of a reduced population compared to the mid-sixteenth century. The few quarters characterized in 1636 can also be included in this comparison, but the difficulty of locating the building authorizations before the 1640s compromises their utility. The next data set allowing for a precise parallel to be established between proprietors, households and building age dates from more than a century later, in 1808. But a close study of this source has not been carried out because about 30,000 households would have to be examined. Beside these quantitative data, qualitative analyses are also possible.

The sources that make it possible to understand the logics of the production of urban space in the sixteenth to eighteenth centuries require a lengthy investigation of the archival records, which are not, in the case of Lyons, especially fertile. As a consequence, our understanding of these logics is currently still fragmentary and patchy. This type of study would be much more feasible for the nineteenth century, as the sources are more or less complete, but this would require a huge research investment as the quantities involved are enormous, with tens of thousands of buildings and households detailed in each archival record (building authorizations, fiscal surveys and censuses). Nevertheless, the present study of the modern period sheds some new light on the understanding of the evolution of a city. Another part of the enquiry will deal with the analysis of urban developments, subdivisions, and, later on, also the larger schemes of the late eighteenth century. These operations targeted a specific market and involved particular investors.

III.2.1 From the late fifteenth century to the mid-sixteenth

The sources allow for a clear identification of the new subdivisions carried-out over this period. Some of them can be analysed in detail in 1493. The general situation of dwelling in houses in 1493 and later can also be studied according to the social groups of owners. The social groups of owners are:

1. Nobles.
2. Officers and doctors.
3. Merchants: drapers, bathers, printers, booksellers, bankers, mercers, goldsmiths ...
4. Little *officiers:* solicitors, priests, canons, sergeants, wardens, writers, apothecaries, artillerymen, *bourgeois* (people with a particular statute)[18]...
5. Food, cloths, and accommodation: butchers, bakers, grocers, cheese-mongers, innkeepers, millers, pastry makers, fishermen, second-hand clothes dealers, wine-growers ...
6. Building activity: masons, carpenters, ironmongers/locksmiths (*serruriers*), joiners, tile-makers.
7. Craftsmen: needle-makers, armourers, barbers, laundrymen, embroiderers, papermakers, hat-makers, breeches makers, rope-makers, shoemakers, belt-makers, dressmakers, spur-makers, founders, polishers, glove-makers, blacksmiths, parchment-makers, furriers, potters, resellers, saddle-makers, shearers, coopers ...
8. Textile: dyers, silk-weavers, wool weavers ...
9. Journeymen and transportation: packers, carters, workers, sailors ...
10. Men of unknown status.

18 Olivier Zeller. *La bourgeoisie statutaire de Lyon et ses privilèges. Morale civique, évasion fiscale et cabarets urbains (XVIIe-XVIIIe siècles).* Lyons: Editions lyonnaises d'art et d'histoire, 2016.

11. Women of unknown status (mainly widows).
12. Owned directly by the church or public institutions (*biens de mainmorte*).

These groups have been determined from the categories separated by Bardet and Zeller, adapted to take the unknown professions into account, with two groups added for men and women.[19] The distinction of the building trade professions was fundamental to this research and has therefore also been added. The widows whose late husband's profession is given in the source have been classified accordingly.

One can observe, first of all, that the number of owners inhabiting one of their own properties is about 70 percent in the *Nommées*. All in all, many city dwellers owned their own house, which is remarkable. Thirty-five percent of the households were proprietors of a house (owning 70 percent of the houses), which is a high proportion compared to the situation in successive centuries, as we shall see. The social group of the little officers was over-represented among the proprietors, at 18.7 percent compared to their demographic importance of 9.7 percent. Groups like merchants, those involved in building, food and accommodation, and single women (mostly widows) owned a number of houses that corresponded approximately to their overall weight in the total population. Merchants were slightly more numerous among owners, women slightly less so. The rich women were generally widows.[20] Two groups show a greater discrepancy: craftsmen-textile workers and journeymen-transportation, who were considerably under-represented among the proprietors. These were actually poor groups. Men whose social status is unknown were over represented: the likely explanation here is that some of them were members of the nobility or of higher social classes, and so, since they were known as powerful or rich people, it was not necessary to stipulate their socio-economic category. Were their category known, it would probably considerably increase the percentages for groups 1 and 2.

When considering the number of owned houses as a percentage, the effect of the social group is significantly amplified. Merchants, for example, accounted for 10 percent of the population, but 12.4 percent of the proprietors, owning 19.1 percent of the houses. The four richest social groups accounted for a little over 20 percent of the population, but 35 percent of the proprietors, and they owned 45 percent of the houses (information about the unknown men and

19 Bardet: *Rouen*, I: 235; Zeller: *Les recensements*, 349.

20 The proportion of widows is difficult to calculate, as some widows seem not to have been qualified as such.

Table III.3 Owners, dwellers in old houses, new ones, and those under construction, in 1493

Social group*	Nb house-holds	% total	Nb owners	%	Nb owned houses	%	Houses per owner	New houses owned	% of new houses owned	Households in new houses	% of house-holds in new houses	Houses in construction	% of houses underway
1	1	0.03	23	1.5	87	3.4	3.8	2	0.8	0	0	2	6.2
2	31	0.8	25	1.6	76	3.0	3.0	10	3.9	7	1.6	0	0
3	375	10.0	189	12.4	493	19.1	2.6	80	31.0	86	19.2	8	25.0
4	362	9.7	285	18.7	503	19.5	1.8	53	20.7	44	9.8	7	21.9
5	341	9.1	130	8.5	216	8.4	1.7	18	7.0	26	5.8	2	6.2
6	191	5.1	84	5.5	112	4.4	1.3	12	4.7	22	4.9	5	15.6
7	1,132	30.3	285	18.7	339	13.2	1.2	30	11.7	130	29.0	4	12.5
8	205	5.5	44	2.9	55	2.1	1.3	4	1.6	28	6.2	2	6.2
9	469	12.6	102	6.7	125	4.9	1.2	4	1.6	24	5.3	0	0
10	366	9.8	263	17.2	414	16.1	1.6	35	13.7	51	11.4	2	6.2
11	261	7.0	76	5.0	112	4.3	1.5	8	3.1	31	6.9	0	0
12			19	1.2	42	1.6	2.2	0	0	0	0	0	0
Total			1,525		2,574			256		449		32	

women would undoubtedly increase these percentages). Conversely, the poorer groups formed about 50 percent of the population, with 28 percent of them proprietors, but they owned only 20 percent of houses – and these were smaller houses than those owned by the richer proprietors. Intermediary groups comprising professions specialized in food/accommodation and building show a fairly constant percentage. Their wealth was average, but they formed only 13 percent of the population and accounted for the same percentage of owned houses.

The new houses formed 10 percent of the total (256 compared to 2,574). Here, the difference with the older houses is striking. The merchant group accounted for nearly 20 percent of the proprietors of these new houses, as opposed to 10 percent of the older ones. The owning of new and old houses was about the same percentage for the little officers, but also for the various building professions, the textile workers, the craftsmen and the unspecified women. Most of the active forces in the economy were represented in equivalent proportion in old and new houses, but the richest were over-represented in the new constructions, and the poorest under-represented.

The merchants owned more than 30 percent of the new houses, the little officers 20 percent, compared to 10 percent each for the old houses. The properties owned by the building professions showed no significant difference between new and old houses (although they were considerably over-represented as proprietors of houses not yet completed). The poorest groups were considerably less present as owners of the new houses: 12 percent for craftsmen, as opposed to 30 percent for the old houses, 1.6 percent for the textile professions as opposed to 5.5 percent, and 1.6 percent for the journeymen as opposed to 12.6 percent. Unspecified female proprietors were also less present as owners of new houses; conversely, unspecified males were more present. These figures show clearly that new buildings were predominantly owned by the higher social groups, and in a much greater proportion than was the case regarding the older houses. In 1493, the four wealthiest social categories owned 55 percent of the new houses, as opposed to 35 percent of the old ones. They obviously sought to invest in these new assets. Conversely, the poorest, who accounted for 28 percent of the proprietors of the old houses, accounted for only 13 percent of the proprietors of the new buildings, and these were of a small size. They could not in general afford to invest in new constructions.

Some information is available about houses under construction, but not yet completed. Their number can only be estimated (about 32), as their particular status was not systematically recorded, though it can be inferred by details present in the source. Less than 20 percent of their proprietors belonged to poor social groups, with 53 percent belonging to members of richer groups, which is consistent with the percentages for the new houses. More remarkable is the fact that nobles were more present here, at 6 percent, and even more remarkable is that the building professions represented more than 15 percent of the owners of the houses under construction, even though they accounted for only 5 percent of the population and possessed only 5 percent of the old and new houses. This suggests that they were investing directly in new constructions to sell them once completed to richer individuals. And this in turn suggests that they were acting as entrepreneurs, generating the new activity in their economic domain. It could also be that they acted as substitutes for investors during the construction phase, some of whom preferred not to be involved in the production process.

So the analysis of the situation in 1493 provides evidence of some of the fundamental mechanisms of building production, which were likely also present to varying degrees in subsequent times:

- New buildings were predominantly produced for the richest social groups.
- They were possessed by social groups richer than the proprietors of older houses, which indicates a process of concentration of real estate wealth.
- Investors in new houses were also among the richest groups.
- Building professions were over-represented among investors in new houses during the construction process, for they aimed both to generate more activity in their economic field and to retain a larger part of the capital gains generated in the process.

Moreover, the new houses respected a logic of investment predominantly in already well-off areas, which is coherent with the relative percentages of the social groups involved. In the late fifteenth century, this arguably contributed to an increased segregation of social groups within the urban space.

The principal spatial patterns are the concentration of new houses in the wealthier areas between St-Paul Church and St-Jean Cathedral on the west bank of the River Saône and a general movement of new constructions affecting also the poorer quarters, but to a lesser extent

Several groups of joint new houses, which implies concerted action, appear on the map (Fig. III.4.): Rue Bourgneuf (**A** on the map, seven houses), on the street towards Confort Gate (**B**, four houses), on the Saône Bridge (**C**, five houses), and on Rue St-Jean (**D**, two groups of four houses each). No proprietor in these groups of new houses was a member of the building professions, and we do not know who built these new houses. This is in contrast with a group of five joint houses under construction (**E**) at the eastern extremity of Rue Grenette. Along with the subdivision created by Chanu which will be examined later on, what we see here is the production of urban space in the making: the replace-

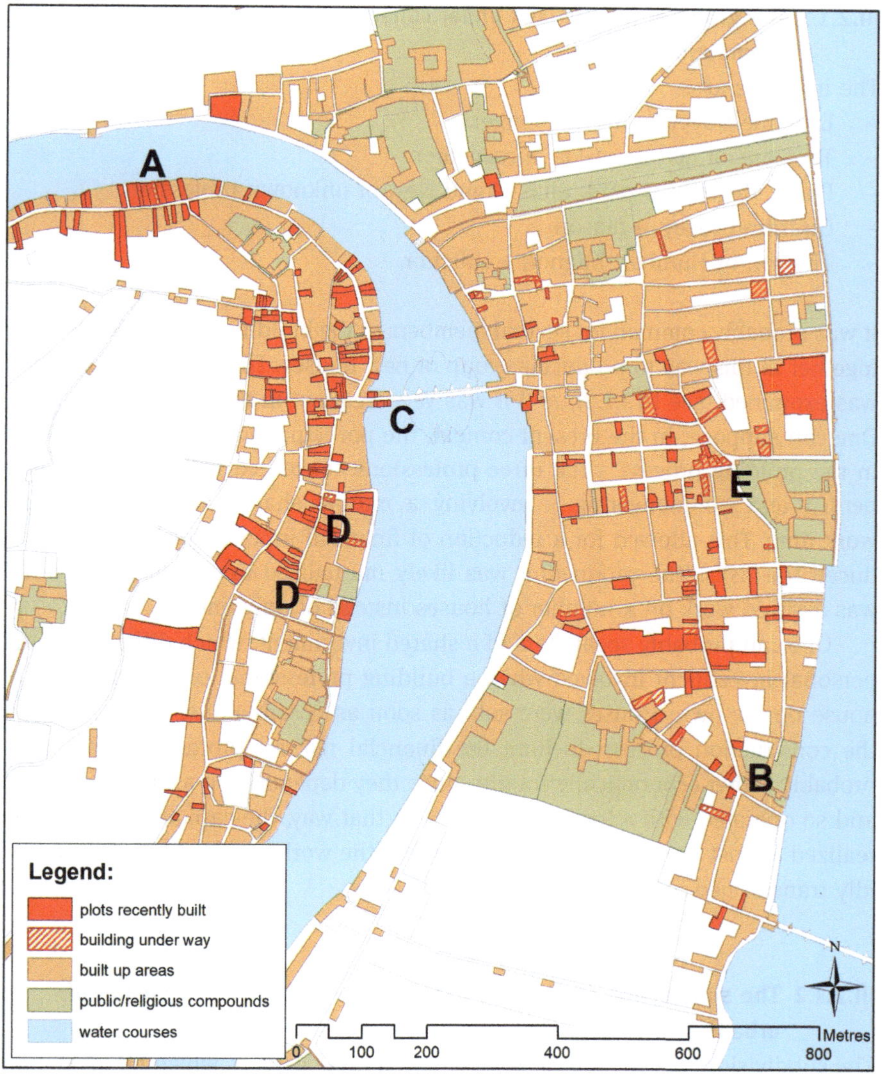

Figure III.4 Map of the houses described as 'new' in 1493
The large patches indicate new houses in a garden. In orange: built-up areas in 1550.

ment of the old fabric in the case of the new groups of houses and a geographical extension of urbanization in the case of the new subdivision.

III.2.1.1 The group of five houses under construction in Rue Grenette: an example of renewal

The investors are:
- Estienne Noyerie, an ironmonger.
- The sons of Mathieu Glas, a carpenter.
- Pierre Mege dit Giraud, alias Grand Nez, of unknown profession.
- Girardin Cossey, a mason.
- The son of Humbert Mignot, a solicitor.

It was probably common for several members of the building professions to work together in this way to produce a group of new houses. This scale of production was examined (see III.1.2.2), and it was very frequent in the making of the city. One can suppose, in the present context, the participation of each professional in the building process – the three professions concerned being masonry, carpentry, and ironmongering – involving a mutual sharing of know-how and work time. This allowed for a reduction of financial inputs, which in return reduced the risks. The production was likely mutualized and each professional was assured work on a number of houses instead of only one.

One can probably speak here of a shared investment, which differs from the personal investment involved when a building professional produces an entire house on his own. Houses were sold as soon as possible after or even during the construction process, to limit the financial risk for professions that were probably rather economically fragile, since they depended on a varying market, and so operated with a logic of no-stock. In that way, the capital gain could be realized almost immediately and the input of the workforce and know-how rapidly transformed into capital.

III.2.1.2 The subdivision of Chanu's garden, illustrating the extension of urbanization

The subdivision by Chanu took the place of a large garden, which he divided in two by means of a new street located between Rue Confort and Rue de l'Hôpital, and lined on both sides by plots for new houses. It was the first significant new subdivision after 1450. The new street was later named Rue Paradis. The ground was formerly owned by a Dodieu, then a Leviste, both of them members of eminent families in the city in the fifteenth century. The number of plots initially created was 27, of equal size, with a width of 6.6 m (twenty feet) on Rue Confort.[21]

21 The name given the plots at Lyons in the late Middle Ages was *pie* (piece of land).

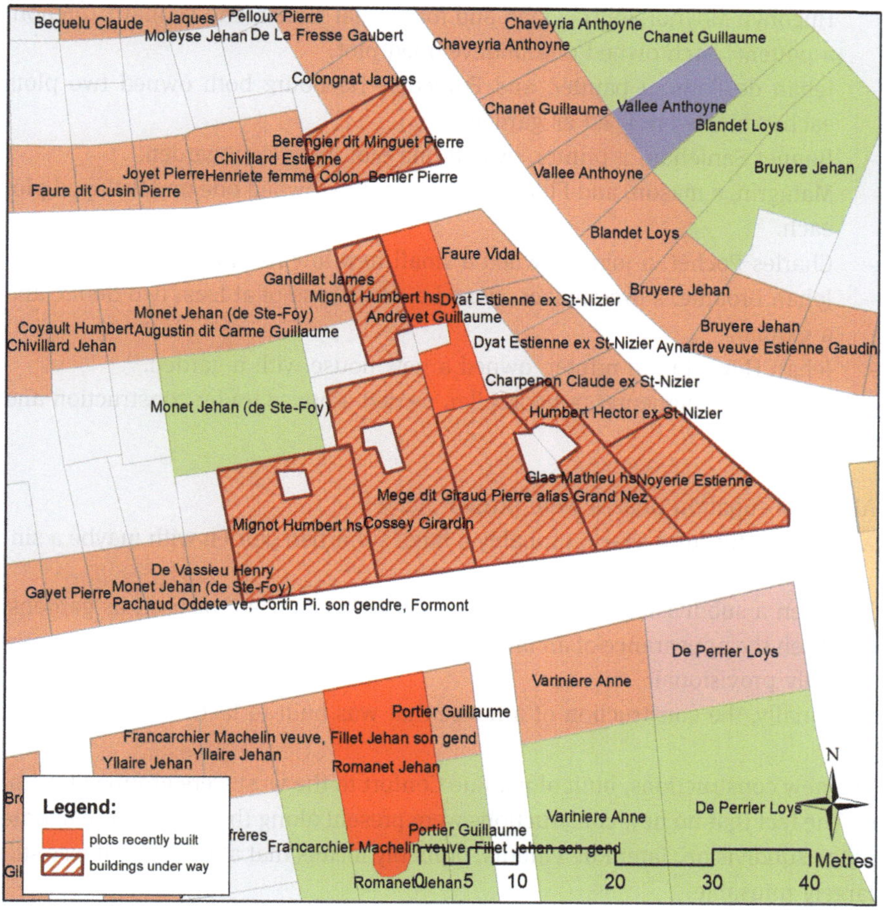

Figure III.5 Detailed map of the group of new constructions under way in 1493 Rue Grenette

Chanu himself kept five plots. The state of occupation of the plots in the survey gives a good idea of how a piece of land went from being a garden to being occupied by houses, from being rural to being urban:

- The five plots kept by Chanu were described as being ‘for house and garden’ (*pour maison et jardin*); they were waiting to be sold and developed.
- Guillaume Lenfant and Guillaume Carme dit Augustin, a goldsmith, each owned four undeveloped plots.
- George Georgaillon and his wife Jane, both writers, each owned one undeveloped plot.

- Hugonyn Moynot, journeyman and former hat-maker, and Léonard Torchon, a potter,[22] each owned one undeveloped plot.
- Jehan de Paris, a painter, and Françoise De Bourg both owned two plots each, which were used as gardens.
- Bonnet Sanjehan, a printer, owned one plot, used as a garden.
- Matagrin, a mason, and Florentin, a locksmith, owned one undeveloped plot each.
- Charles Pochet, a joiner, owned a small new low-rise house.
- Jehan Broallie, a dressmaker, owned a new house of at least two floors, and a garden.
- Jehan Huguetan, a printer, owned a new house with a garden.[23]
- Guillaume Seigneuret, a bookseller, owned a house under construction and a garden.

All the occupation phases were present here:

A. First a still rural space, probably a large suburban garden with maybe a single house on the street.
B. Then a subdivision into plots that were either unused, or used as gardens.
C. Then the appearance of an initial light construction, a shack or shelter, probably provisional.
D. Finally, the construction of a house that was built to last.

The new constructions, built along Rue Confort to the west were grouped together. The fact that no new constructions were present along the street in the middle of the subdivision, later Rue Paradis, probably means that at that time it was still largely unusable.

Representatives of the building activities encountered previously were also present on the site. One mason, one locksmith, and a painter each owned an undeveloped plot, and a joiner had already built a small construction.

Another phenomenon, common elsewhere, is also worth noting: several associated professions were present in a single space, namely, two printers, a bookseller, two writers (public writers or accountants). In Lyons at the end of the fifteenth century, these professions were at the cutting edge of modernity. In this case, they sought new houses in a place free of the constraints of the old urban fabric and allowing for an optimized professional activity. A comparable

22 Torchon was proprietor of a house close by, on Rue de l'Hôpital.

23 The size of this plot is larger than the other plots of the subdivision, which were of an equal size and width. This could tell us that the new house was built at the place of an old one, which would have been attached to the garden before its subdivision.

situation was developing at the same time at the intersection of Rue Misère and Rue Bourgneuf in the St-Paul parish, one of the main sites of the printing industry in Lyons, which also possessed a concentration of new houses, this time in an already urbanized area.

The subdivision can also be examined as a succession of social processes:

- Fully rural space (as yet undocumented).
- Suburban garden and house of a well-off family (Dodieu, and Le Viste).
- Capital gain by LeViste when the land was sold to an investor, Chanu.
- Capital gain by Chanu when he sold the plots to would-be builders.
- Capital gain by investors from within the building trade when they sold the newly built houses.

III.2.1.3 The investment logics of major proprietors in the late fifteenth century

The logics of production of new houses in 1493 can be examined looking at the real estate assets of some major proprietors:

François Du Pré:

A merchant, he was the biggest proprietor in Lyons and the son of Robinet Du Pré. His real estate properties, comprising 48 houses, 44 *hommées* of vineyard,[24] three barns (*granges*),[25] and five butchery benches, were such that they could easily have represented his most important source of income. The vineyards were located around the city, and the houses concentrated in an area between St-Paul Church to the north, the Change quarter to the south and River Saône to the east. These locations were probably due to chance investment opportunities, as is suggested by the fact that they are not neighboring. Nevertheless, they are concentrated in a particular quarter, and the fact that all the seven new houses he owned were also in the area, suggests a particular interest in the more financially profitable new constructions that this area afforded. He was therefore an important investor in real estate, but we do not know if he directly financed the new constructions, or whether he bought them from others. The area was one where many people of the highest social milieus lived, and so was probably also where the potential capital gain was highest. There were 55 new houses in the same sector in 1493, the highest concentration of building investment in the city.

24 About 1,79 hectares. *Hommée* is a measure of surface area, corresponding to 431 m^2 in Lyons.

25 Which can be translated as 'warehouse'.

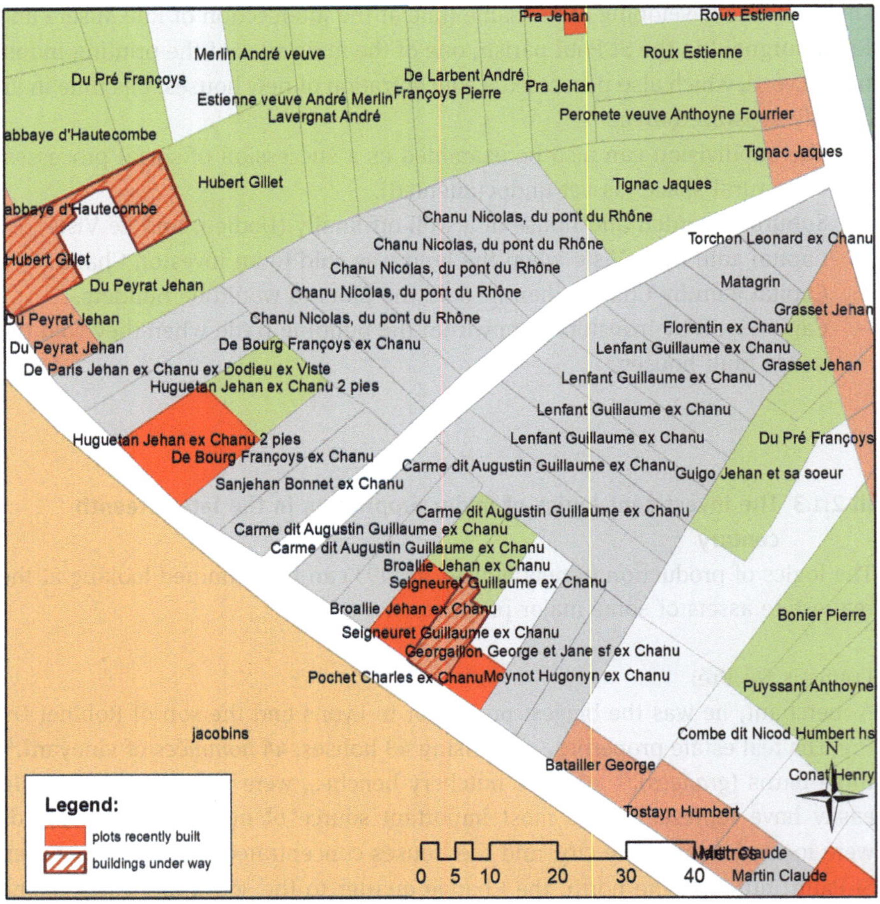

Figure III.6 Map of Chanu's subdivision begun in 1493 or a little earlier
The subdivision was intended for twenty-seven plots (grey). Three houses were already built, one was underway. Chanu's subdivision is an example of the subdivisions carried out in suburban properties previously used as places for *otium* by great families.
The green areas are mentioned as garden in the *Nommées*.

The Baronnat family:
The proprietor members of the Baronnat family were Guillaume, a merchant, Jacques, Jehan, bourgeois, and Léonard, a doctor and keeper of the accounts (probably of the city). This was one of the most significant families of the Lyons oli-

garchy, a family who had built its fortune in commerce and public offices.[26] The pattern of their investment in real estate was similar to Du Pré's: their 14 houses were all located in the same area, including all three of their new houses, located at Montée du Change (this house is still extant, at the corner of Rue Juiverie) and Place de la Boucherie St-Paul.

Pierre and Jean Salla:[27]
Their family was also from a very high social milieu. They owned 13 houses, of which six were located in the same quarter. Only one of them was new, on the Saône Bridge, in a very profitable area.

Barthélémy Bellièvre, solicitor (*notaire*):[28]
He was proprietor of eight houses located in varied places throughout the city, all old. Bellièvre was obviously little interested by investment in new houses, although he added some new parts to his house in Rue Gourguillon, where he built, probably later, a belvedere.[29]

The De Villars family:[30]
Half of the houses of the *De Villars*, André, Anthoyne, Camyon, all three qualified as bourgeois, and Pierre, a merchant, were concentrated to the north of Place de l'Herberie, at the eastern end of the Saône Bridge. Two of these houses were new.

Claude and Loys Taillemont:
Their investments were located predominantly on the eastern bank of the River Saône, where they owned 17 houses. Four of them were placed face-to-face on the two sides of Rue Mercière, with seven others in the same area. They only owned old houses.

Many proprietors tried to acquire houses facing each other on the same street, which thus became a rather common pattern. An example is a rather modest proprietor, Pierre Faure dit Cusin, a stocking-maker, who owned four houses,

---

26 René Fédou. Baronnat (famille). Jean-Pierre Gutton (ed.). *Les Lyonnais dans l'histoire*. Toulouse: Privat, 1985, 176 – 8.

27 Jean-Pierre Gutton. Sala (Pierre). Jean-Pierre Gutton (ed.). *Les Lyonnais dans l'histoire*. Toulouse: Privat, 1985, 366.

28 Fédou. Bellièvre (famille). *Les Lyonnais*, 180.

29 Which is still extant today in Place de la Trinité.

30 Fédou. Villars (famille). *Les Lyonnais*, 397.

Rue Vendrant. Two of them were adjacent and they faced a third one on the other side of the street. Pierre Faure probably invested the gains made from commerce in real estate.

These examples show the significant investment of the great families of Lyons in real estate, which was also true in the subdivisions produced up until the mid-sixteenth century (Fig.III.8):

- (**A** on Fig. III.8) Jehan Caille, a doctor, and Pierre Vive, were developers of a subdivision in 1510 – 12, at the Montée du Garillan (a piece of land formerly belonging to Bleterens Rivoyre lord of Romaigny),[31]
- (**B**) Nicolas Chanu, Rue Paradis in 1492 – 93.
- (**C**) Claude Thomassin, consul and *Capitaine* of the city, developer in 1500 of a new street which the *Consulat* allowed him to name after himself.[32]
- (**D**) Guillaume De Legue, from the Dauphiné, who subdivided the south side of Rue Noire in 1519 (see II.2.2).
- (**E**) The children of Pierre De Villeneuve (doctor, lieutenant of the *Sénéchal* of Lyons) for the north side of Rue Noire.
- (**F**) Loys Teze for the south side of Rue Port-Charlet.
- (**G**) Françoys de Gennas, a merchant, along the River Rhône to the south of Rue Gentil and for the north side of Rue Mulet.
- (**H**) Françoys Du Pré, a merchant, subdivided his vineyard between the Terreaux and Rue Romarin.
- (**J**) Pierre and Jehan Salla, both bourgeois, sold their vineyard to Jacques and Barthélémy Boyer, who began subdividing it in 1509, establishing a new street in the middle, today's Rue Hippolyte-Flandrin.[33]
- (**K**) Claude le Viste, a doctor, subdivided a vineyard into plots lining a new street, Rue des Epies (= *des pies*, which means 'street of the plots').
- (**L**) Claude Champier, between Rue du Plat and the River Saône.
- Symon Faure, a merchant, between Bellecour and the River Rhône.
- (**M**) Jaquemo Torneon, new subdivision of the block between the Mint and the River Saône.[34]

Some convents also subdivided parts of their properties:

- (**N**) The Augustinians subdivided the north side of their precinct in 1509, along what is nowadays Rue Sergent-Blandan.

---

31 Becker and al., *Le musée Gadagne*, 101.

32 AML BB 24, f° 230 r°, 28 Jan. 1500. Fédou. Thomassin (famille). *Les Lyonnais*, 382.

33 Gauthiez. La topographie, 31 and n. 11.

34 This block was previously a property of the Antonins hospital, with 11 houses for the poor, in ruin in 1493.

- (**O**) The Jacobins in c.1509 subdivided Rue Confort and in 1540 Rue Bellecordière, which was created at the time and today forms the southern part of Rue de la République.
- (**P**) The Antonins, on the southern side of Rue du Port-du-Temple.[35]
- (**Q**) The nuns of the Déserte convent subdivided the south-east part of their precinct, beginning in 1505.[36]
- The abbey of Cluny sold its tenement between Rue Tramassac and Montée St-Barthélémy in 1572, and it was subdivided immediately afterwards.[37]

These subdivisions were of course motivated by potential capital gain in a period when the demand for undeveloped grounds to build new houses was high because of demographic pressure and the high availability of capital. Françoys De Gennas and Françoys Du Pré probably bought gardens and vineyards at the periphery of the city precisely with a view to realize such gains. The subdivision of peripheral houses and gardens by some rich families was undertaken for the same reason: financial gain. This mechanism predominantly benefitted families who were already rich, via a process common also to different periods.[38] Figure III.7 shows the expansion of urbanization. It was made principally by new subdivisions around the already built-up areas. The growth was significant in the sixteenth century (from **A** to **O**). It led to a last important subdivision, the larger one by far, to the south of Place Bellecour, began in 1559 (**P**), but it was a failure as it developed only in the seventeenth century, allowing for the establishment

35 The Antonins sold a garden where they formerly owned another series of houses, also for the poor, and also in ruin. At the time, they kept only the houses which they owned on the north side of the street. These houses were sold and rebuilt a little later.

36 Josette Barre. *La colline de la Croix-Rousse, histoire et géographie urbaine*. Lyons: Editions lyonnaises d'art et d'histoire, 1993, 41, mentioning Joseph Pointet. *Histoire des propriétés et maisons de la Croix-Rousse du XIVe siècle à la Révolution*. Lyons, 1926.

37 Archives départementales de la Saône-et-Loire, H 22 (Inventaire général des titres de l'abbaye de Cluny, 1er vol., written in the early seventeenth century), f° 297 r°. The house of Cluny, named "la Bombarde", was not a priory, but only the representation of the abbey in the city of the overarching archbishopric. It was in a poor state of repair, and the city, in 1560, already wanted to establish a better link with the hill of Fourvière, trying at that time to widen the Montée St-Barthélémy, just to the north of Cluny's house, and which would have cut through a part of that house. The Montée du Chemin-Neuf answered this desire in 1562, in the form of a new street linking the lower quarter of St-Jean to the upper one on the Fourvière hill, passing right through the precinct of the house of Cluny. The decision to sell the rest of its land was taken in 1564 by the abbey of Cluny, with the sale occurring on 29 April 1572, to Lambert Pinet, for 3,000 livres.

38 This happened in the nineteenth century when large suburban domains were subdivided for urbanization to the east of the city: the Monplaisir estate in 1826, the Montchat estate in 1858, and so on.

of aristocratic mansions and several convents. In the seventeenth century, only small scale subdivisions occurred (**aa** to **ee**). The growth resumed from the mid-eighteenth century (**1** to **9**), at first by rather small operations like at St-Clair, soon followed up by very ambitious projects of extension to the south (Perrache quarter) and the east (Morand's project). But these developments took place principally in the nineteenth century.

III.2.2 The seventeenth and eighteenth centuries

Table III.4 New buildings per social group, 1617–1763

Social group	(parallel: new buildings owned in 1493)	New buildings produced in 1617–1661	Percentage of the production	New buildings produced in 1662–1697	Percentage of the production	New buildings produced in 1698–1763	Percentage of the production
1	0.8	56	4.3	22	unknown	60	8.3
2	3.9	59	4.6	29	unknown	50	6.9
3	31.0	211	16.4	23	unknown	173	23.9
4	20.7	174	13.5	43	unknown	105	14.5
5	7.0	78	6.1	4	unknown	25	3.4
6	4.7	91	7.1	26	unknown	68	9.4
7	11.7	126	9.8	13	unknown	32	4.4
8	1.6	71	5.5	9	unknown	14	1.9
9	1.6	9	0.7	1	unknown	1	0.1
10	13.7	274	21.3	501	64.5	79	10.9
11	3.1	64	5.0	47	6.0	30	4.1
12	0.0	76	5.9	59	7.6	88	12.1
Total		1,289		777		725	

The 'unknown' is due to insufficient data in the archival records.

We have little information about the level of wealth of the investors. Cross-referencing the list of the *échevins* (members of the city *Consulat*) with the list of the building authorizations is one way to fill this lacuna.

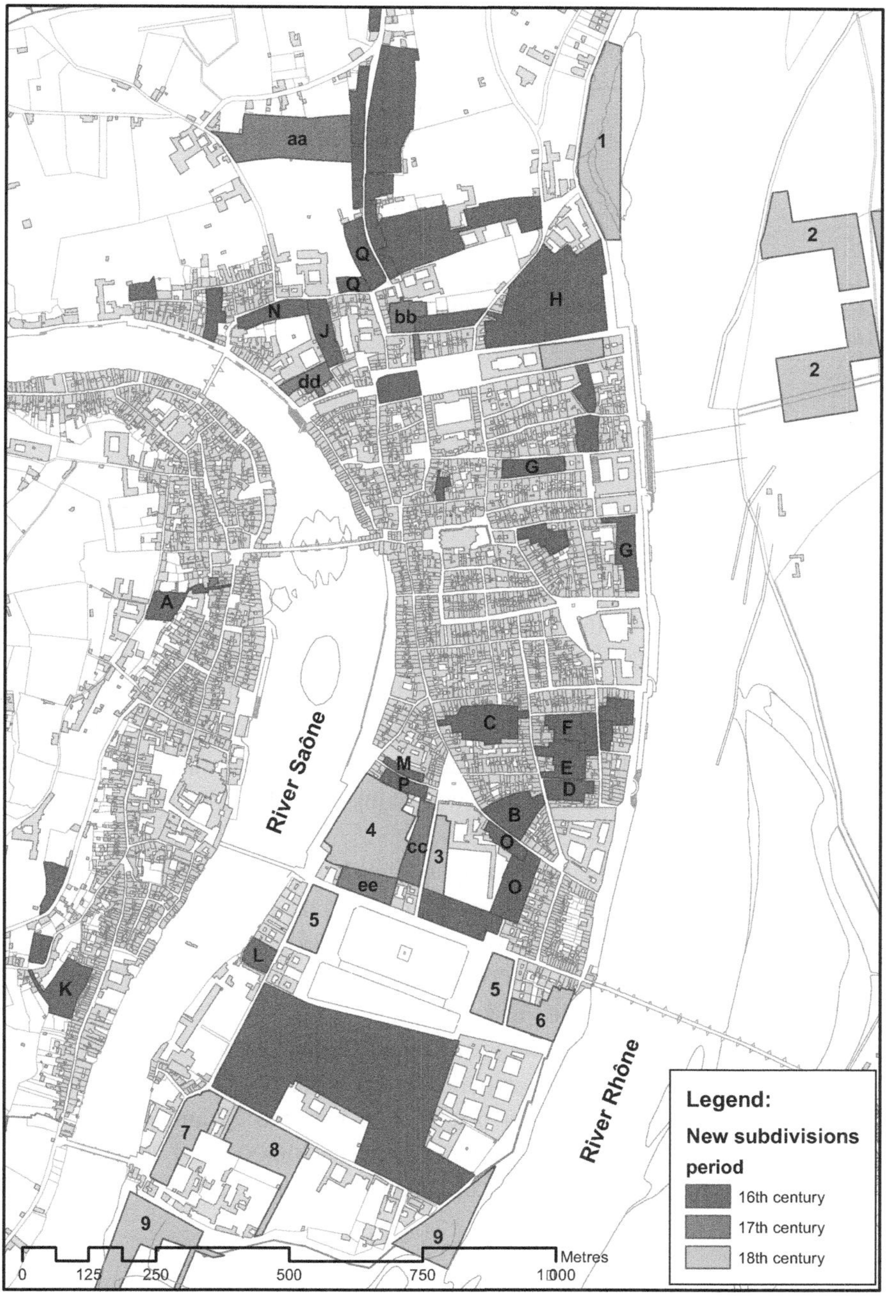

Figure III.7 Map of the new subdivisions in Lyons, sixteenth to eighteenth centuries

Table III.5 New buildings by members of the *Consulat* families (the *prévôts* were the mayors, heads of the *Consulat*)[39]

Period	Number of *échevins*	*Echevins* who built houses	Percentage	Of which produced when they were *échevins*	Number of *prévôts*	*Prévôts* who built houses	Percentage
1617–1661	109	44	40	10	19	6	32
1662–1697	89	32	36	4	16	4	25
1698–1763	142	37	26	9	9	2	22

The proportion of *échevins* families who built new houses is high and illustrates a comportment common to many in their social group. The *échevins* came systematically from one of the four richest social groups. But their situation was probably not stable. The percentage of *échevin* families constructing new houses seems to have diminished over time, which is also true for the *prévôts*. This could mean a decrease of the average level of wealth of people forming the *Consulat*. Another possibility is that their opportunities to get richer during their charge as *échevin* or *prévôt* decreased, as they were subject to closer social and political control.

Another hint regarding the correspondence between the level of wealth and the number of houses built is given when one uses the inquiry made in 1677 into the wealth of the inhabitants of Lyons, which makes possible a tentative classification of wealth brackets.[40] The comparison with the houses built by the corresponding families is detailed in graph III.10.

The role of wealth in building investment is clear. Between 40 and 70 percent of families with a wealth superior to an order of 200,000 livres built a new house in the three decades before 1677; between 25 and 40 percent of those possessing fortunes of the order of between 100,000 and 200,000 livres; and between 10 and 20 percent of those possessing between 25,000 and

39 I am grateful to Olivier Zeller to have allowed me to use his list of *échevins* and *prévôts*.
40 The classification was built from heterogeneous data, differing from quarter to quarter (real estate wealth in some cases, sum which can be afforded to the compulsory municipal loan in some others, etc.), so the result is possibly questionable. But the trend is incontrovertible.

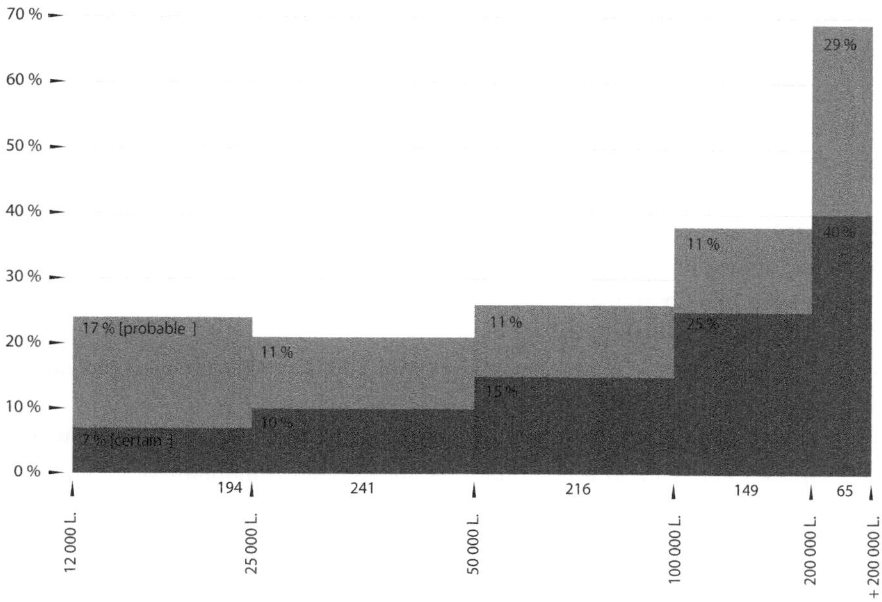

Graph III.10 Proportion of families having produced new construction(s), according to their level of wealth in 1677 (Th. Egger del., data B. Gauthiez)

50,000 livres. Clearly, only a very small section of the population could afford the capital needed to build a new house. This trend is confirmed by scattered elements concerning levels of wealth in the population. One example is the study of the masters of the silk-weaving trade between 1617 and 1763, designated each year by the *Consulat*.[41] Again, the list established using the registers of the *Consulat* deliberations has been cross-referenced with the list of the building authorizations. About 400 masters of the silk-weaving trade were listed, of which only 35 invested in a new building. These persons were generally merchant-fabricants – those who provided materials and placed orders with the weaving workshops, and not actual heads of the workshops themselves. Less than ten percent of them invested in new houses, which is very few bearing in mind their importance in creating wealth in the city during this period.

Counting the number of proprietors relative to the number of households gives another indication of the overall trend. The figures were approximately the following:

41 AML, BB series.

- In 1493: 35 percent of households were owners (for 2,574 houses containing 4,018 households, and comprising about 20,000 inhabitants).
- In 1551: 22 percent of households were proprietors (2,250 among the 3,260 taxpayers listed in the source, for 3,460 houses. With a ratio of 3 households per house and 4.5 persons per household, the city numbered about 45,000 habitants).[42]
- In 1677: 15 percent (787 owners for 1,160 houses in ten quarters for which the data are available. For 3,500 houses and an average of 4.3 households per house given in the documented quarters, this implies that the city had about 70,000 inhabitants).[43]
- In 1698: 10 percent (1,800 for a population of about 90,000 habitants, at 4.5 persons per household).[44]
- In 1709: 7.5 percent (1,512 for 2,669 houses in 28 documented quarters, which suggests about 1,890 for 35 quartiers and 100,000 inhabitants).[45]
- In 1789: 5.7 percent (1,700 for a population of 135,000 inhabitants, at 4.5 persons per household and an average of 8.5 households per house).[46]

These data clearly establish the progressive decrease of the number of proprietors and of their relative proportion in the population, and thus also a growing concentration of real estate in the hands of the few. The number of houses went from about 2,500 in 1493 to 3,500 in the mid-sixteenth century, with only very limited variation thereafter. The proportion of owners dropped from about 35 percent in 1493 to 5.7 percent in 1789. This progressive decrease was continuous throughout the seventeenth and eighteenth centuries, and concerned increasingly large buildings, which were higher and had more floors (going from three to five, six and sometimes even seven), and larger surface areas (double the area in the 1770s compared to the early seventeenth century), which further reinforced

42 AML CC 40 – 41. Many of the payers in the 1551 *Nommées* were also owners, and some names reappear in different quarters. Some owners were not listed, probably because they were too poor to be taxed.

43 Tax list in 1677.

44 Tax for the lanterns 1698. Precise counting of the number of owners and of their proportion among the households is never possible, because some names appears in several instances in the list, and one doesn't know if it is the same person or because no detail is given regarding the surname or the profession, but the degree of imprecision is low as these uncertain cases represent less than one percent of the total. The way the same name is spelt, as it may vary, can also reduce the accuracy of the count. Similar difficulties are present in all the sources used here to count the number of proprietors, until the early nineteenth century.

45 Partial census in 1709.

46 *Vingtième* (1/20th) tax list in 1789.

the overall trend. Average usable surface in square meters doubled or trebled in the seventeenth century, then decreased, not in parallel to the evolution of the total population, but the richest had progressively more space, and the poor less.

The growing wealth of investors in the modern period corresponded quite precisely to larger investments. The selling contracts in late eighteenth century give a good idea of the relative value at that time of buildings produced in previous periods. In the late eighteenth century, the average value was more than 100,000 livres for the large buildings of the St-Clair quarter constructed after 1750 (see III.2.2.2); 60,000 to 80,000 for the biggest buildings constructed in late seventeenth century (to be compared to the levels of wealth given above); 40,000 for those constructed in the early seventeenth century; and 20 to 30,000 for those of the early sixteenth century.

The increasing size of the buildings probably also explains the decrease in the number of building authorizations, which was much higher in the seventeenth century. Comparing the graphic representation of the new constructions with that of the number of inhabitants helps one understand the counter-intuitive lack of connection between the two.

Several periods with distinct characteristics can be distinguished. Up until the beginning of the 1690s, demographic growth was accelerating, in parallel with a high level of building production. The population plateaued in the 1690s, at about 100,000 inhabitants, and the production of buildings collapsed in this period to less than one third of its previous level. The population diminished slowly thereafter for a few decades. The production of new buildings grew again in the 1740s, followed ten years later by a similar movement in the population. A population peak occurred in the 1780s, at about 135,000 inhabitants, although building production declined in the middle of the decade. The correlation between the two curves is strikingly feeble. One explanation is the growing concentration of investment capacity in a smaller number of hands. Another significant factor is the market for which new buildings were produced, which we can know, at least partly, by comparing the buildings authorizations list with the municipal loan enquiry carried out in 1677, and again in 1788, the date of an *Indicateur* (gazetteer) listing the names of about 6,000 inhabitants of some social importance.[47] For this later date, it is necessary to compare various different sources of data about the new buildings identified, for the authorizations registers disappeared from the record after 1763.

---

47 *Indicateur alphabétique des curiosités, établissements réguliers et séculiers; des personnes de qualité, officiers et judicature, police et finances; notables, bourgeois, négociants, gens d'affaires et principaux artistes de la ville de Lyon, avec les noms des rues et des maisons de leurs demeures.* Lyons: Faucheux, 1788.

Dwellers in the new buildings of the Rue Neuve quarter, 1677.

The number of houses in the Rue Neuve quarter was 109 in 1677, of which nine had been built during the previous decade. Most of the inhabitants of the new houses worked in the textile trade, as silk weavers and associated professions. They often represented more than half of the tenants, as was the case in the houses owned by the Jésuites and De Jussieu, which were inhabited each by three silk-weavers and two dyers, or a house owned by Janon and Compain, where there were four silk-weavers, a glove-maker, a carter and a widow. This quarter was at that time one of the main ones for Lyons' silk-weavers, who were actively encouraged to set up therein. Indeed, the new constructions were clearly aimed at this market, in the context of an active development of the silk trade at Lyons. Within the quarter itself, some houses did not conform to this general trend, like the one belonging to Ratton's heirs, in which one encountered the quarter's *Caporal* (a public officer in charge of the administration of the quarter, under the command of a *Capitaine*), a turner, a shoe-maker, two bourgeois, a merchant, and a bookseller (facing Jesuits College).

One of the houses, owned by the Hôtel-Dieu, was a good example of what happened later in the same area, when gentrification became active from the mid-eighteenth century onwards. In 1677, its inhabitants comprised five silk-weavers and five associated professions, plus a silk dyer, a carpenter (perhaps specialized in the construction and maintenance of looms), a turner (idem), a shoemaker (the only professional maybe not involved in the silk industry), and two widows. The house was rebuilt by the Hôtel-Dieu in 1750.[48] We know its inhabitants in 1788 from the *Indicateur:* several drapers, two merchant-fabricants, a trader of silk wares, an accountant, and a doctor. The other inhabitants are unknown. The change following the reconstruction was radical, as a new social reality of well-off inhabitants replaced a former population of craftsmen from lower social milieus. Interestingly, the inhabitants of another building located close-by, also owned by a Ratton, and already reconstructed in 1671, also underwent much the same social shift to a higher class of tenant. By 1788, it was inhabited by three traders, a merchant, a doctor, and a merchant-fabricant of silk-fabrics. It is also important to realize, however, that this quarter does not necessarily provide an exact image of the whole city, only a few of whose districts are sufficiently documented in the archival source in 1677.

An interesting feature of these two cases is their parallel evolution, whereby the reconstruction of a house is accompanied by a change in the socio-economic

48 AML DD 53. The initials "H D", for "Hôtel Dieu", are still legible over the doorframes of the building.

status of their tenants, a change which is similar in the unreconstructed houses of the same quarter.

One also finds, in the seventeenth century, entrepreneurs playing an important role in the organization of house-building. Three names in particular appear on several occasions in the building authorizations of the period. The first is Claude Chana, who built at least seven new houses as investor and entrepreneur, in 1637, 1642, 1646, 1657, 1664, 1670 and 1685.[49] He was first described in the sources as a master mason, and it is as such that he was chosen as one of the two principal contractors at the City-Hall construction site from 1646, along with Jacques Daurolles (who also invested in some new houses). He was in charge in 1672 of the new buildings of the Rue des Augustins. In 1685, at the end of his life, he was described as an architect, which seems to bear testimony to the fact that his career as a contractor, entrepreneur and investor enabled him to improve his professional and social status. He was acting as a de facto designer of the buildings he invested in (and probably also of many others made for other investors, on which he could have worked as a contractor). Here the practice led to the title, which was not due to any academic formation. His son Jean also took up the profession of his father. He was in charge in 1681 to 1682 of the construction of the west aisle of the St-Pierre abbey, and was described at the time as *master architect and mason.*[50] His initials (J.C. for Jean Chana) were placed over one of the main doors of the buildings on Rue des Augustins, where he had undoubtedly worked with his father ten years earlier.

The second name is Jean L'Habitant, who built three new houses for himself in 1727, 1736 and 1740 as investor. In 1753, Jacques Marie L'Habitant, probably Jean's son, also built a house. Jacques-Marie was at that point described as an *architecte et bourgeois,* which implies that he was living from his rents, probably the rents his father had patiently constituted with his investments. The third is Corneille Leau, whose name appeared (see II.2.4) in association with a particularly interesting design for a house-plan. He was a carpenter, and his career as investor in mid-seventeenth century was also important.

III.2.2.1 The series in seventeenth- and eighteenth-century production

New subdivisions were rare in the seventeenth century, although the population grew considerably during this period. Those subdivisions that did occur were: a) the west side of Rue St-Dominique (today Rue E.-Zola) in 1658, for seven build-

49 In 1685, the Chana mentioned is probably the son of Claude, Jean.
50 ADR 27 H 69.

ings of a very high social standing in the area of the aristocratic Place Bellecour, and in proximity to the Royal Mint at Rue du Port-du-Temple; and b) the Rue des Augustins in 1672. One of the more striking aspects of civil constructions in the second half of the seventeenth century is the series, of which there are no known examples previously at Lyons.[51] These are made of several buildings, often identical in form, designed within a single architectural project. Examples include:

- Three buildings by Dervieux, a silk merchant, Rue de Flandres in 1685 (Fig. II.5), of which two are still extant.
- Three by Dupuis, a banker, on Rue Pêcherie in 1685, still extant.
- An ensemble built by Christophe Boesse, treasurer of France and knight, in 1659 Rue Poulaillerie, Rue de la Gerbe and Rue des Forces, with a façade length of 123 m for four entrances, and which in 1709 lodged 20 households and 150 inhabitants (still extant).
- Six by Perrachon de St-Maurice, a noble, on the north side of Place Bellecour, in 1665.[52] (n° **ee** Fig. III.8), of which five are still extant.

The approximate value of these series, at the end of the eighteenth century, was about 200,000 livres for Dervieux's and Dupuis's, and double that for Perrachon's and Boesse's, which made them huge investments.

The new type of multi-familial building was perfectly suited to such important investments and their associated market, optimizing architectural structure and suppleness of use. The amount of land required was much greater than for the existing average building of the time, and so it necessitated the unification of several plots, either by heritage or through acquisition. Dervieux and Dupuis had to acquire a number of smaller plots, but Boesse and Perrachon were able to develop spaces still used as large gardens, which had by that time become extremely rare in the city center. Religious establishments in the seventeenth century also participated directly in real estate production, designing series of houses, whereas in the sixteenth they had tended simply to sell their land directly to others. Acting as developers, they could better realize the value of those parts of their precincts on which they decided to built. These series include:

- Three large buildings produced by the Antonins hospital in 1665, after a fire, at the Rue Mercière (15 m of frontage each), still extant.[53]
- In 1672, the Augustinians convent built a series of houses, accompanying the creation of Rue des Augustins through the southern part of their precinct,

51 They were probably rather common in the Middle Ages, as the lists in the *Nommées* make it appear, in 1406 and 1493.

52 Bayard, Ville et campagne.

53 All the dates are from the registers of the AML DD series, Gauthiez, Zeller, Un SIG historique.

with 107 m of façade length and five entrances. Claude Chana and his son Jean were in charge of this operation (n° **dd** Fig. III.8), still extant.
- The Joséphistes convent produced a series of houses in 1698, after a fire (see II.2.6), between Rue des Ecloisons and Rue Pizay (111 m of façade length, four entrances for buildings around a central common rectangular courtyard), demolished in 1854.[54]
- The St-Nizier chapter in 1706 constructed a big building (so not exactly a series of houses, but the difference is not always clear-cut between a big building with several entrances and a series) forming nearly a whole block, to replace eleven small houses rented by its canons, between Rue Gentil, Rue de la Gerbe and Rue des Forces (three entrances), still extant.
- The Célestins convent in 1720 produced a long building with a classical architecture at the Quai des Célestins (façade 113 m), partly extant.
- The Feuillants convent produced a series of buildings in 1739 (façade 92 m), still extant.

These series of buildings or large buildings were designed with a common objective: to optimize rental income from buildings designed as efficiently as possible. The goal was common both to religious institutions and to private investors. The presence among investors listed above of Dervieux, a silk merchant, is not surprising as silk merchants were among the richest people in the city and acted frequently as bankers in the silk trade. This form of investment became dominant from the late seventeenth century in Lyons, and by the end of the eighteenth century it had almost completely crowded out other reasons for the production of new buildings. Furthermore, the dominance of financial logic led to investments being made that served only the highest social milieu.

Interestingly, many of these series and big buildings are still extant today, with a ratio of conservation much higher than for the other productions of the time. This is probably due to their adaptation to higher social milieus and to the fact that they were not superseded by taller or bigger architectural types that might have taken their place.

III.2.2.2 The production of buildings in the late eighteenth century

The data available for the end of the eighteenth century allow for a good understanding of the modalities of the production of new buildings and, in a somewhat less precise way, of the market they were aiming at.

54 This is the first known occurrence of a building with a large common courtyard.

Who builds at the end of the eighteenth century?
Building production can be understood thanks to two important urban development projects. One, begun in 1749, was a rather small new quarter to the northeast of City Hall: Quartier St-Clair.[55] The second one is the quarter known as "Perrache", named after a sculptor-architect who undertook its development at the end of the 1760s. Lacking systematic information about building authorizations after 1763, quantitative analysis may focus instead on the extant buildings, which is necessarily partial as in some instances they have been demolished (fortunately this concerns only a few cases), and from the administrative record of real estate sales (*Contrôle des actes*).

***St-Clair quarter* (1 on Fig. III.8)**
The St-Clair Quarter derived from a small operation taking place nearby. In 1742, the St-Pierre abbey sold a plot on which they were due to build five houses, near St-Clair city Gate,[56] to a group of four people, among them Jacques-Germain Soufflot, a Royal architect. The building authorization was requested only in 1748 by Soufflot, along with Millanois, a merchant and possibly the main financer, for the building of a series of three houses of a total length of 57 m (19 m each). The buildings are still extant today, though they had to be repaired in 1807, after the siege of the city in 1793.[57] In 1749, Soufflot and Millanois, in association with a third person, Munet, also an architect, founded a company to finance a new quarter at St-Clair on a site to the west side of the River Rhône, which had to be fully reclaimed from the river bed, and bordered by a new quay which would be used as a new royal road to Geneva. They would develop new streets and plots, and retrocede public spaces to the city. The project was ratified by the Conseil d'Etat in Paris on 22 October 1749.[58] The first two buildings were authorized in 1756, a third one only in 1760, after which the rhythm of new constructions accelerated. The buildings in 1756 were for Millanois himself and François Drivon, a carpenter and entrepreneur. Roux, an architect, built a beautiful construction in 1760, followed by a house for the surgeon, Pierre Grassot, another one for the architect, Antoine Rater, and in 1762 a large building for

55 Alain Charre, Catherine Servillat. L'entreprise du quartier St-Clair. *L'œuvre de Soufflot à Lyon*. Lyons: Presses universitaires de Lyon, 1982, 21–26. This study is predominantly of the architectural conception. See also Pierre Claude Reynard. *Ambitions tamed. Urban expansion in Pre-Revolutionnary Lyon*. Montreal: McGill-Queen's University Press, 2009.
56 ADR 3 E 599. Plan AML 3 S 163.
57 AML DD 53.
58 AML BB 315, DD 256; Archives Nationales (Paris) E 2301.

the joiner, Philibert Lombois.[59] The loss of the authorizations from the archival record makes it impossible to precisely date later constructions of new buildings within this project, but the *Vingtième* tax list in 1789 gives the names of the proprietors of the houses in that year, at which point all the plots had been developed. Of the 32 properties listed, the brothers, Antoine and Jean-Baptiste Rater, owned two, including four buildings,[60] which they probably built themselves (these buildings are different from those authorized for Anthoine Rater in 1761, which he had sold, and different also from the one the brothers had sold to the bookseller Rosset in 1780).[61] Roux, an architect, owned two buildings, Munet one, and Loyer, also an architect, another one. Two more architects – Ledras and Michel – lived in the quarter in 1788, but their role in its construction is unknown. The former was probably a colleague of Rater, maybe working for him; the latter was maybe an associate of Munet. The Rater brothers evidently had a certain importance in the construction of the quarter. They acquired two more plots, which they sold undeveloped to Blanchet in 1779, and another which they sold to Etiennette Taillard in 1778.[62] Soufflot himself had also built several new houses, as in 1781 Jeanne Soufflot, his sister, sold to Marie Combe, the widow of Lora, 450,000 livres worth of buildings in the quarter, which is a considerable amount and could correspond to the property owned in 1789 by Montluel de Jussieux, made of four buildings (defined as use-units with their own entrance).[63] The architect Jean-Antoine Morand also played a significant role in the development of the new quarter. He bought, along with his wife, a first plot to Soufflot, Millanois and Munet in 1757, then a second one in 1764 to the *échevin* Genève, and a third one in 1766 to Munet. They constructed new buildings on the three plots, which they sold in 1763 to 1764 to the merchant-fabricant Courajod and in 1767 to Pitiot, in that case for 250,000 livres. Morand also built as an architect for Pierre Grassot, the surgeon.[64] Looking at the quarter as a whole, the architects Soufflot, Rater, Roux, Munet, and Morand, directly built

---

59 AML DD 55.

60 A single property may include more than one building. The plot is not equivalent to the building.

61 ADR 10 C 1295, f° 156v°-157r°, 3 Sept. 1780, for 100,000 livres.

62 ADR 10 C 1295, 23 March 1779, 11,000 livres, which corresponds to an unbuilt plot; 18 Jul. 1778, for 14,000 livres, f° 172r°-173v°.

63 ADR 10 C 1295, 21 April 1781. The correspondence can be established from the value in the *Vingtième* (1/20th) tax list, in which the real estate values seem to be systematically under-estimated in comparison to the sale transactions ones. In this case, Montluel de Jussieux's property is valued at 60,000 livres.

64 Henri Hours, Michel Nicolas. *Jean-Antoine Morand, architecte lyonnais 1727-1794*. Lyons: Archives Municipales de Lyon, 1985, 6.

more than one third of the constructions (actually big multi-familial buildings) in the area, and for a while also possessed a significant portion of the other plots. They also probably worked as architects for other investors, like Grassot. Our information is unfortunately insufficient to derive exact knowledge of their participation in the construction of the St-Clair quarter, which they had initiated, and from which they acquired considerable wealth, at least in the case of Soufflot, Rater, and also Morand.

The success of the St-Clair operation led Jean-Antoine Morand soon afterwards to develop a new quarter on the east bank of the River Rhône, on land facing this new St-Clair quarter, starting in the late 1760s (**2**, Fig. III.8).[65] But Morand faced strong opposition from the proprietor of nearly all of the land concerned by his project, namely the Hôtel-Dieu, and had to abandon it after the development of a first rather small area, named *Pré Morand*. His idea was continued from the 1780s by the Hôtel-Dieu itself, under the supervision of another architect, Decrénice, using a modified layout. But as building activity was low in Lyons before the French Revolution, this new quarter developed mainly after 1815.

The Perrache quarter (9, Fig. III.8)

The *Quartier Perrache* is better known.[66] Antoine Michel Perrache, like Morand, had worked under the direction of Soufflot at the Grand Théâtre in the mid-eighteenth century.[67] Supported by the Consulat, he founded a company in 1770 to finance his project for a new development to the south of the city, in a marshy area,[68] which was agreed upon by the Conseil d'Etat.[69] As in the case of St-Clair, he was adding to previous subdivisions carried out in the area, namely Rue Vaubecour developed in 1728, Rue d'Auvergne in 1740 (**7** and **8**, Fig. III.8), as well as some earlier development projects.[70] The project also required reclamation and embankment works to be carried-out along the River Rhône (and later also along the River Saône). These were both extensive and expensive, and took many years to complete. A new bridge made it possible to cross the River Saône to the south.

---

65 Hours, Nicolas, *Jean-Antoine Morand*, 10 – 16.

66 Felix Rivet. *Le quartier Perrache (1766-1946)*. Lyons: Audin, 1951. The development, which still needs a thorough reassessment, is studied here only in respects to its agents.

67 AML BB 322, 1755.

68 ADR 1 C 154.

69 AML BB 339.

70 Susanne Rau. Guillaume-Marie Delorme. Projet pour la jonction de l'isle Mogniat à la ville de Lyon (1738). Erfurt: Universität Erfurt, 2015, https://www.academia.edu/19542808/, accessed October 2019.

The bridge and the quay along the River Rhône were a part of the new Languedoc royal road. This operation was a major financial failure for a variety of reasons: the tremendous costs involved, the destruction of the bridge during the break-up of ice on the River Saône in the winter of 1780, and the weak real estate market of the 1780s, which was made worse by fierce competition both with the St-Clair quarter and with Morand's and Rigod de Terrebasse's projects at the time (the latter is examined below). It is nevertheless interesting to examine the operation through the estate transfers and investments involved. The *Contrôle des Actes* mentions 36 transfer deeds in the Perrache area between 1777 and 1785,[71] beginning with sales by Antoine-Michel Perrache in the name of his company, later by his widow, Marie-Anne, from May 1779, and later still by the shareholders (*intéréssés*) of the company, from 1782. All these sales were of undeveloped plots, with the exception of a building sold to Valin de la Mothe in 1780 for 80,000 livres, and another more modest one to Pierre Monier for 40,000 livres.[72] The company built only a few new constructions, all near or on Place Grollier (today Place Gailleton), where in 1789 it still had its head office, located on the corner of the quay (still extant). The plots were sold to at least four architects (Antoine Durand, Raymond Tourreau, Jean Morel and Ennemond Brillon), one mason (Pierre Thibaudier), and one carpenter (Albertin). None of these names was encountered at St-Clair, which probably also tells us something about competition between investors, with no-one apparently buying or constructing on both sites. Of these investors, only Jean Morel would appear to have built a house, which numbered among the ten extant in 1789.

The great majority of the other professions represented in the transfer acts of the plots, as well as their eventual constructions, both at St-Clair and at Perrache, were among the wealthiest social categories. But members of the building trade also had a strong presence, whether as regards plot ownership alone or also the practice of building on owned plots and then reselling with capital gains when the market was higher. At St-Clair, the market was buoyant because of the proximity of City Hall, in a context of rapid gentrification. This allowed some members of the building trade to enter the ranks of high society, thanks to huge capital gains in real estate. Roux, for example, also became *Secrétaire du Roi* (secretary of the King) and Soufflot, who had initiated the new St-Clair quarter, and who a little later became stockholder of Morand's and Perrache's companies, was named in 1773 *Contrôleur général des édifices et embellissements*

71 ADR 10 C 1295. This source is a compendium of the deeds registered by the solicitors. The previous acts have not been studied.

72 These two buildings are still extant on the quay of the River Rhône, near Place Grollier.

publics de la Ville de Lyon (General Inspector of the Buildings and Public Embellishments of the city of Lyons) by the *Consulat*.[73] In Lyons, he was also architect of the new grand Hôtel-Dieu, and in Paris Architect of the King.[74] Such a high patronage, directly connected to the milieu of the royal court in Paris, probably provided a significant boost to the various projects in which he was involved.

Outside the St-Clair quarter and the Rigod de Terrebasse development, the prospect for capital gains was less obvious. The sale value of plots also suggests that speculation was involved. The Perrache company sold plots at about one livre per square foot in 1779,[75] one and a half livre per square foot in late 1781,[76] one livre again at the beginning of 1783, before lowering the price to a half livre in June 1785.[77] One measures here the growth of demand, followed by its collapse. There were no new sales by the company after the mid-1780s. It is in this depressed context that the Count of Laurencin, one of the prominent shareholders of the company and its director from 1783,[78] launched his own project on a part of the Perrache project perimeter. He bought at least 18 plots, mainly from April 1785 onwards, comprising of a small house built by an architect, Morel, and another one by a pork-butcher, Revert. He also bought 16 others plots, still unbuilt, or featuring only a shack (*baraque*), like the one he bought from the architect Brillon, his last acquisition, in July 1786.[79] The price he paid was generally much higher, between 1.5 and 2 times higher than the price of the plots when previously sold to his sellers by the Perrache company, which is possibly explained by the fact that many of these earlier buyers had already built a shack on their plot, or a fence, or had begun to fill the land.

Laurencin concentrated his acquisitions along a street on which he constructed several large houses in a rather modest architectural style, and which are listed in the 1789 tax-list (and are still standing today). The street, which later bore his name, Rue Laurencin, benefitted from the proximity of Place Grolier where the Perrache Company offices were located. His initial project, if one considers the number of plots he bought, was probably much larger, but was interrupted first by the deep crisis which preceded the French Revolution, and then by the Revolution itself. De Laurencin, as director of the Perrache Company, lived in the company's building on Place Grolier in1788.

---

73 AML BB 341.

74 He is famous for the building of the Ste-Geneviève abbey church in Paris.

75 ADR 10 C 1295, 26 Feb. 1779.

76 ADR 10 C 1295, 3 Sept. 1781.

77 ADR 10 C 1295, 18 Feb. 1783; 26 June 1785.

78 Rivet, *Le quartier Perrache*, 16.

79 ADR 10 C 1295, 29 July 1786, for 18,950 livres.

Laurencin has a precursor in the form of Aimé-Julien Rigod (or Rigaud) de Terrebasse (a merchant who became Treasurer of France, then Honorary President of the Bureau of the Finances), who constructed a remarkable ensemble of buildings in 1772 to 1774 and which formed the north side of the Place de la Charité, looking out to the east over the River Rhône Quay, (**6**, Fig. III.8). Rigod built 270 m of façade length of luxury buildings, at a social level comparable to St-Clair, but largely occupied by aristocrats.[80]

III.2.2.3 For whom were new buildings produced at the end of the eighteenth century?

There are no systematic sources of information regarding the households inhabiting the houses of the city in the eighteenth century, except partly for the year 1709 and then again after 1789, which is of no avail for the period which interests us here. But as we saw, the *Indicateur* published in 1788 gives a list of about 6,000 persons of importance in the city, also specifying the proprietor of the building they inhabited. Lower class professions were omitted, but the highest social categories were prominent: aristocrats, rentiers, bankers, merchants, etc. (i.e., the four highest social categories defined in II.2.3).

The persons listed as dwelling in Rigod's buildings in 1788 were:[81]

- Category 1: ten (four nobles and six *sans état*, i.e., without status, probably nobles).
- Category 2: ten (nine high officers).
- Category 3: four (a banker, a chocolate fabricant, an iron seller, and Gros, the architect of Rigod's buildings?).
- Category 4: 18 (16 bourgeois = rentiers, a school-mistress, an officer at the Charité Hospital).
- Category 7: two (both saddlers).

At St-Clair, the list is:

- Category 1: 11 *sans état* and *échevin*.

---

80 On the projects of new developments at the periphery of the city in the late eighteenth century, see Susanne Rau. The urbanization of the periphery: a spatio-temporal history of Lyon since the eighteenth century. Sebastian Dorsch, Susanne Rau (eds.). Space/time practice and the production of space and time. *Historical Social Research/Historische Socialforschung*, special issue 38 (2013), 150 – 175; and Bernard Gauthiez. Trasformazione dei valori urbani tra settecento e ottocento: il caso di Lione. *Storia urbana* 71 (1995): 149 – 170.

81 Rigod de Terrebasse in 1789 was still owner of two of the biggest buildings. His own dwelling was in the most prestigious location, on the corner of Place de la Charité and the Rhône Quay.

- Category 2: 13 (including four consuls representing foreign States).
- Category 3: 73 (including five architects, Loyer who was also an owner, Antoine and Jean-Baptiste Rater, also owners, the architects Ledras at Rater's, Michel at Munet's).
- Category 4: 101 (bourgeois principally, designers for the silk-wares, etc.).
- Category 5: three.
- Others: six.

These lists do not have statistical significance, but they clearly show that these buildings were aimed at people of the highest social milieus. Rigod's buildings had a higher proportion of aristocrats, who often worked in offices of the state, all of which is not surprising, given that the area around Place Bellecour had since the seventeenth century been the core quarter for Lyons' aristocracy, and that the *Intendance* – the offices of the state's representative in the city, the *intendant* – was situated nearby. St-Clair was inhabited by professions related to large-scale commerce, both national and international, including many brokers and several foreign representatives who acted as major intermediaries between the production of silk-wares, the merchant-fabricants and their associated designers and book-keepers, and the main markets for luxury goods.

Building for the poor?

In all, the available sources from the eighteenth century give rather a clear idea of who invested in new houses (members of the highest social milieus) and for whom (mainly the same social classes). By contrast, only limited data exist concerning investments in the building of dwellings for the thousands of families of silk-weavers, whose role was foremost in the production of wealth in Lyons. Modest buildings devoid of décor, with a form comparable to the new ones in the richest areas, but with no or nearly no decor, appeared only after the Revolution. Many of them were built in the 1820s on the slopes of the Croix-Rousse hill, to the north of Place des Terreaux and City Hall, with layouts adapted for the looms used to weave silk. In particular, their ceiling height was considerable, close to four meters, as was also common in bourgeois buildings, albeit for different reasons (one example of the production of buildings for silk-weavers will be examined below). Investment in buildings for the poorer social categories consisted of:

- Raisings and modifications of the roof space to adapt it for dwellings, with roof-windows and a few feet of raised walls. Many existing buildings exhibit such tiny transformations intended for workers and poor people, notably the many women who worked as warpers (*ourdisseuses)*. These living conditions were very common in the early nineteenth century, as has been documented by censuses.

- Frontages rebuilt in the 1770 to 1780s when the *Consulat*, in Rue St-Jean and Rue St-Georges, intervened to widen these major streets to create more public space. Either just a new façade was constructed to replace the previous one, but with a setback, or an entirely new building was erected, as happened at the south-west corner of Place du Change. In both cases, the construction was not of a high quality, without decor, or reused elements from the demolished fabric, including door joineries and the stone frames of doors and windows.

This bricolage reflects the impoverishment of an area that was formerly one of the richest in the city, but which had by the 1780s been overtaken by silk workshops. The location of the workshops, whose families were supplied by the municipality with food during a great crisis in 1786 to 1788, shows this situation.[82] The location of these workers, in old houses and far from the city government, is quite different from the locations of the societies of merchant-fabricants (the biggest ones are mapped Fig. III.8), and of the silk brokers, the commanding professions of the *Grande Fabrique*, the silk industry at Lyons, which were placed around the City Hall, often in newly built constructions. Although the population of the city continued to grow between 1750 and 1789, the proportion of new buildings made specifically to accommodate silk-workers was so limited that not a single one has been identified. The production of new buildings was intended for the richest only. The poorest, who formed the great majority of the city's inhabitants, could only dwell in old existing houses, increasingly subdivided and poorly maintained, and in cramped dwelling spaces located under the roofs. While the objective of this book is not to explore growing tensions before the French Revolution, one of these tensions is nevertheless visible here: the concentration of real estate wealth in the hands of the richest and investment in constructions also aimed only at the richest.

A glimpse of the situation during the French Revolution

Only a few new buildings were produced after the beginning of the 1780s, and very few after 1789. Demolitions resulting from the bombings of the siege in 1793 were followed by a few dozen full reconstructions and about four hundred repairs of varying importance. These operations were mainly carried out in 1794,

82 AML HH 165.

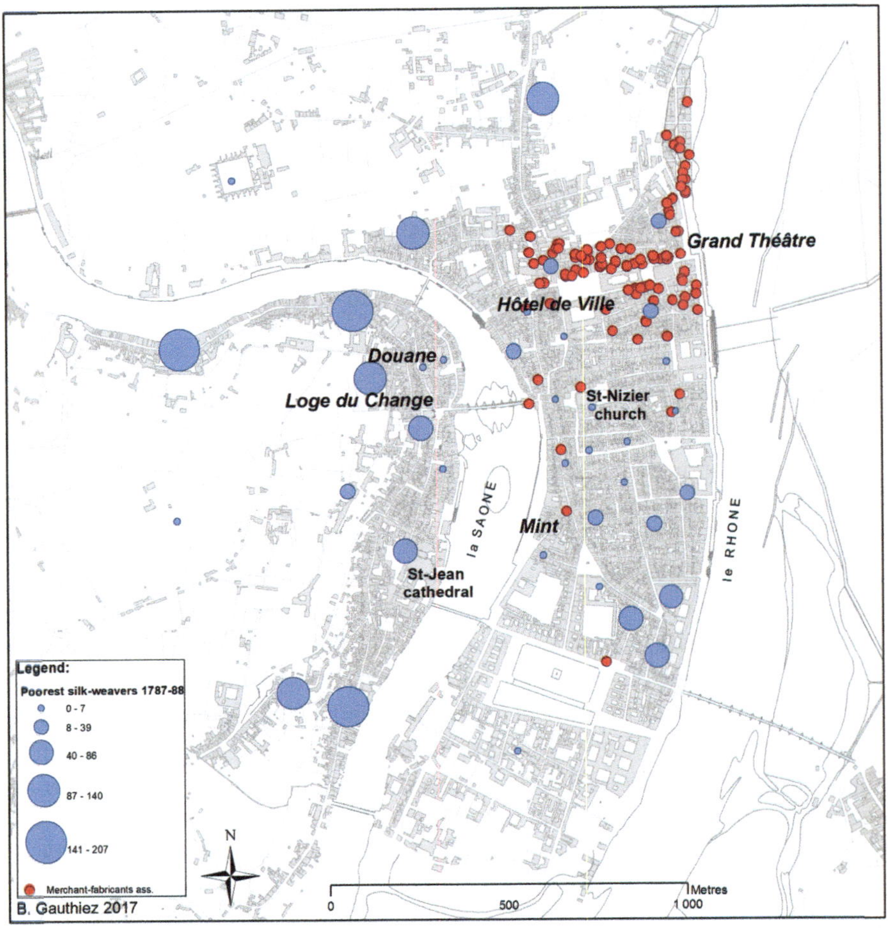

Figure III.8 Map of the situation of poor and rich in the silk-trade during the crisis in 1787 – 88: workshops of the poorest silk weavers fed by public help during the crisis and location of the societies of merchants-fabricants

in a situation of emergency.[83] Some buildings were reconstructed in the early nineteenth century, though they are difficult to discern among the great number of new productions of that period, from the First Empire and still more after 1815.

83 The authorizations for repairing and reconstructing were particularly numerous in 1794, AML 316 WP 002. The production of the time was characterized by the absence of decor and the standardization of widened windows without cross-mullions.

An important historical document gives an idea of the way new late eighteenth-century buildings, particularly in the St-Clair, Rigod de Terrebasse and Perrache sectors, could be perceived by the non-wealthy. In 1793, the revolutionary authorities of the Convention government, which can be qualified as far left, decided, after the successful siege of Lyons by their armies, to punish its counter-revolutionary opposition. The project was to dismantle the city of Lyons, such that its name was replaced by *Commune affranchie* ('Freed commune') and its territory divided into three separate communal entities (North, South and West). These actions were accompanied by a number of projected demolitions which would entail a *damnatio memoriae.* To the destructions of the siege, notably on the River Rhône Quay and around the arsenal near Place Bellecour, which had exploded, they added the demolition of the building façades forming the east and west sides of the Place Bellecour. These exemplified proud aristocratic architecture in a classical design, and were erected in the 1720s to form an appropriate architectural setting for the statue of King Louis the XIVth. As such, they were choice symbols of the hated ancien régime. The statue was of course destroyed as well. But the demolition project was much larger. A list of 438 buildings to pull down was established at the end of 1793,[84] to which was added the demolition of another 154 buildings along the River Saône in order to enlarge its quays. These latter buildings were actually demolished from 1794 on the south side of the river (117 buildings), and later on also on the east side (37 buildings), which were only demolished in 1820 to 1822. The houses on the south bank of the river were inhabited predominantly by poor people. So 154 buildings had to be demolished to establish new wider means of access to the city, the purpose of which was to facilitate the arrival of government armies, especially in the event of a rebellion like that of 1793. Significantly, the new quay along the River Saône was given an appropriate name: *Quai de la Convention.* The list also included 438 buildings to demolish for varying reasons, all of which ultimately boiled down to the political status or behavior of their proprietors, such as being rich (which was a serious political mistake in the eyes of the Convention), being fanatical, or having acted in a counter-revolutionary way, like Rigod de Terrebasse, described as *ex noble and contre-révolutionnaire* (and guillotined 17 December, 1793). Their owners include 190 nobles, 60 rentiers, merchants, bankers, stockjobbers, solicitors, and ex-royal officers, including treasurers of France, as well as architects involved in many of the operations studied above: Roux, Morand, Loyer, Munet, and Rater. The two buildings still owned by the Perrache Company were also earmarked for demolition, as were those

84 ADR 1 L 1031.

of another company which had undertaken a new development on the Célestins convent site towards the end of the 1780s, namely, the Célestins Company, which was directed by a Parisian, Devouge.[85] Only a few buildings owned by the highest echelons of Lyons' society were absent from the list, and these were probably buildings owned by people who had helped the Convention government or who had kept a benevolent neutrality towards it and towards the poor. Such buildings were rare. The buildings of Rigod and at St-Clair nearly all had to be demolished. Of the 36 proprietors at St-Clair concerned by this demolition project, one counted ten nobles, 16 rentiers stemming from the high royal civil service (like Millanois, ex director of the Mint), commercial professions of the highest level, one merchant, one grocer, one banker, and six architects.

Nearly all these condemned 438 buildings are still standing today, which bears testimony to their adaptation to the subsequent real estate market. The same cannot be said of the houses inhabited by the poor, which have largely disappeared amid the nineteenth- and twentieth-centuries' waves of urban renewal.

The superimposition of these 438 buildings scheduled for demolition onto the map of the buildings constructed in the late eighteenth century before the Revolution show a strong correlation.[86] This close correspondence, with its implied condemnation not only of nobles, but also of other professions having profited from the building production, like developer-architects, shows that an important part of the population felt a very strong resentment against them, and especially their monopolizing of wealth and its arrogant architectural expression.

The list also shows the proportion of real estate owned by the nobles, which was difficult to establish from previous sources in which the status of the nobility is generally not mentioned, as they are generally qualified as *sans état*. It thus seems that the nobility had remained very discreet with respect to the documents previously established by the offices of the State or of the *Consulat*. This was arguably caused by a desire not to disclose information that strongly indicated the origin and reality of severe inequalities in society, which the map (Fig. III.10) indicates were deeply felt by the poor.

In all, there were 612 buildings to demolish out of a total of about 3,500: 17.5 percent of the total number would have disappeared, for a proportion of probably as much as 35 percent of the total built-up fabric, as the majority were recent large buildings. The demolition project was, however, soon abandoned, so the

---

85 Bertin, Dominique, Mathian, Nathalie. *Lyon, silhouettes*, 25–27.

86 The list did not include the façades (east and west) on Place Bellecour, which had already been demolished.

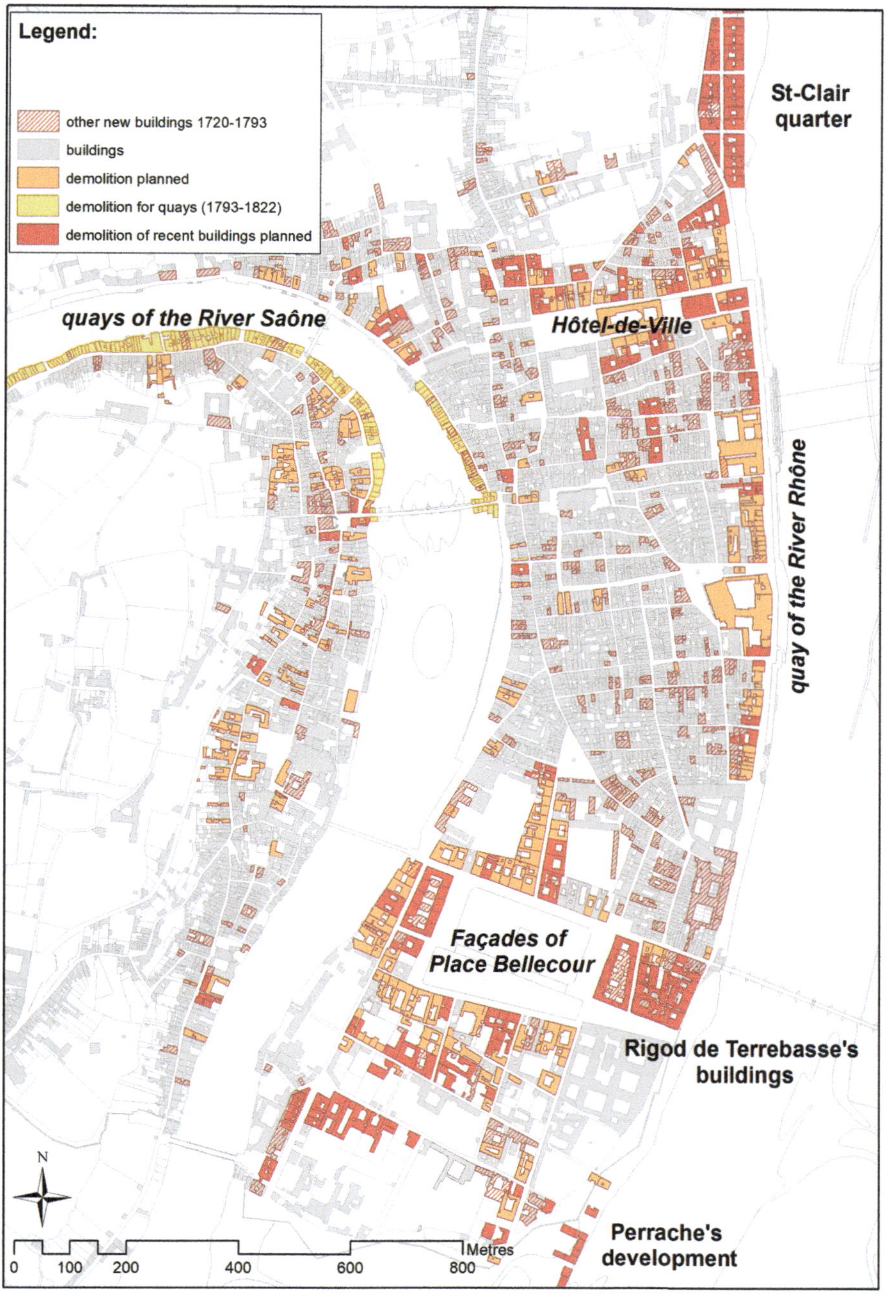

Figure III.9 Map of the buildings planned to be demolished after the siege in 1793 to punish the rebellion of Lyons against the Convention government

only buildings actually demolished were the east and west façades of Place Bellecour, whose symbolic expression was particularly significant, as well as those necessary to form the quays along the River Saône.

III.2.3 Elements of building production in the nineteenth century

The present book deals mainly with the period up until the end of the eighteenth century, which has here been thoroughly investigated. For subsequent periods, the extremely abundant sources have only been explored occasionally, generally with the aim of shedding light on some aspects of building production. A very well informed history of building production, both quantitatively and qualitatively, becomes possible from 1808 onwards, the date of the first complete municipal census.

The Revolution seems to have led to a significant modification in the distribution of real estate property. In 1808, the census makes it possible to estimate the number of proprietors at about 6.7 percent of the number of households. The population of Lyons was 108,457 habitants at this date, of which 23,097 households have been precisely counted, corresponding to 67,894 inhabitants.[87] This gives a ratio of about three persons per household. There were about 1,540 proprietors among the 23,097 counted households, which means about 2,440 in total for the city. The proportion of 6.7 percent is only slightly above what it was in 1789 (5.7 percent), but the situation was actually very different as the evolutionary trend was inverted.

Table III.6 Evolution of the number of proprietors from 1493 to 1808

Year	1493	1551	1677	1698	1709	1789	1808
Population	20,000	45–50,000	70,000	90,000	100,000	135,000	108,457
Number of households	4,018	10,000					36,660
Percentage of proprietors	35%	22%	15%	10%	7,5%	5,7%	6,7%

The structure of property ownership had only slightly evolved from the late eighteenth century, and about 30 percent of the proprietors were the same in 1789 and 1808, even – perhaps predominantly – in wealthy areas. Some new important trends were nevertheless present. In 1808, the number of new proprietors

87 AML 1808 municipal census. 921 WP 005–006–009–010.

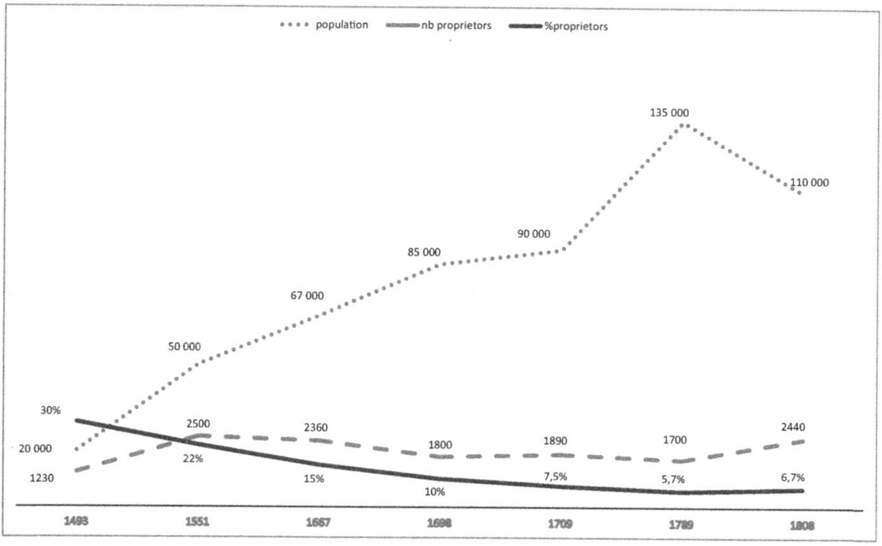

Graph III.11 Evolution of the number of proprietors from 1493 to 1808

was strikingly higher than was previously the case in the poorest areas, where multi-ownership of the same building had progressed, and in the peripheral quarters, where land was more subdivided, often into small buildings housing only one or two households, and with many new proprietors owning small plots taken from the precincts of former convents.

The expropriation of religious buildings made possible the appearance of new categories of owners, who came to possess plots and houses that were first built as shacks and then progressively replaced by multi-familial buildings. This is a process which became very important in the urbanization of the east bank of the River Rhône in the nineteenth century.

The production of new buildings in the nineteenth century can be studied in great detail after 1830, the date of the first cadastre.[88] I shall only deal here with

88 Sylvain Schoonbaert has studied the production of new buildings at Bordeaux from 1835 to 1890, giving quantities per year, but his mapping is only per *feuille cadastrale* (i.e., that part of the city covered by a cadastral map), which is very imprecise. He does not discuss the temporalities involved, and instead simply counts the number of new buildings per year. *La voirie bordelaise au XIXe siècle.* Paris: Presses de l'Université Paris-Sorbonne, 2007, 355–378. The yearly number of new constructions was considerably higher in Bordeaux than Lyons, because the average number of inhabitants per house was much lower, under ten as opposed to over 25

the old communal territory of Lyons, before its extension in 1852 to the peripheral communes of La Guillotière on the east bank of the River Rhône, La Croix-Rousse to the north, and Vaise to the north-west. The main bulk of the expansion of Lyons in the nineteenth century occurred in this space after 1830 and, conversely, renewal occurred primarily in the old center from the late 1840s onwards. Production increased considerably in the early nineteenth century, as is visible on the graph of year-on-year production up until 1830, and the city was also extended considerably over the course of this century, principally outside its former administrative limit. The building authorizations still remain to be compiled in databases for the periods subsequent to 1830. Professionals from the building trade continued to act as investors, maybe more so than previously. The role of architects as developers seems to have remained very important.

Rue Chenavard and Rue de Brest, two segments of a new thoroughfare established from 1848 onwards between Place des Terreaux and Place Bellecour, were the object of a contract passed between Benoît Poncet and Amédée Savoye, both architects, and the municipality, on 17 March 1846 for Rue de Brest, and on 18 January 1847 for Rue Chenavard.[89] Several dozens of old buildings were pulled down. Initially, the architects had intended to sell the plots along the new street once cleared, but Poncet kept several of them and built about ten new houses himself, including a series of seven neighboring ones, which was actually a construction-unit made of seven use-units defined by separate entrances and designed to form a sort of symmetrical super-architecture. He thus acted according to the same logic as his predecessors at St-Clair, but for slightly lower social milieus. This implied a remarkable financial know-how, risk being the reason why Savoye later withdrew from the operation. The potential capital gain was very high, with a multiplication up to four of the value per square meter of land or of floor space, but the investment capital – for demolitions, street works, constructions – could not be recouped until the sale or letting of a building. The success of the operation considerably enriched Poncet, and also explains why Mayor Marius Vaïsse asked him to pilot the much more ambitious thoroughfare of Rue Impériale (later named Rue de la République) in 1853. Poncet accepted becoming director of the joint-stock company (Société Anonyme de la Rue Impériale – SARI) which was contracted with the municipality for this project, and convinced his board not only to construct the new street and prepare the plots, but also to construct buildings all along it, which it did. This was a

in Lyons. The number of new constructions remains to be counted for Lyons for these same decades.

89 AML 321 WP 53; 321 WP 54.

huge economic and political success, and a major source of wealth for shareholders.[90]

One gets a glimpse in this operation of another aspect of the evolution of investment strategies in the nineteenth century: the development of joint-stock companies. This trend began with the Perrache and Morand companies in the 1770s, but also that of Devouge in the late 1780s, which aimed principally at the creation of new plots and of profits from their sale.[91] St-Clair also followed this logic, initially associating two architects and an investor providing capital, though some of the share-holders also invested themselves in numerous constructions on the plots of the development.

The capital of the SARI was shared mainly among stock-holders from Lyons. A new thoroughfare (*percée*), the Rue de l'Impératrice (today's Rue Edouard-Herriot) was planned immediately after the Rue Impériale, capitalizing on the latter's success. A contract was passed between the municipality and an international society, the Geneva based Banque Générale Suisse de Crédit Mobilier et Foncier International S.A. (BGS), created in 1852 by James Fazy, who was also head of the government of the Canton of Geneva, and whose shareholders were mostly English (London City Bank, Bank of London and Westminster, National Freehold Land, Bank of Birmingham). For both circumstantial reasons (the bankruptcy of BGS bank in 1864),[92] and structural ones (the fact that the value of the buildings to be expropriated had considerably augmented as a result of the success of the neighboring Rue Impériale), the BGS withdrew from the operation and the city decided to go ahead with the development on its own. The redevelopment of the Grolée quarter around 1890, by a company directed by Ferrand and owned by Parisian capital, was also integrated within these operations.[93] All of this allows us to see that private companies held a dominant position in building investment, and in the renewal of the old Lyons center, in the second half of the nineteenth century.

The growing importance of big capital, which is today dominant in real estate investment, doesn't preclude other operations from benefitting smaller construc-

90 See Gauthiez, *Entre Bellecour*, 47–51; and Gauthiez. La rénovation, 23–69.

91 Olivier Zeller. Enjeux d'urbanisme à Lyon en 1777. Propriétaires contre promoteurs. *Bulletin du centre Pierre Léon d'histoire économique et sociale*, 1 (1995), 3–15. Gauthiez. Trasformazione.

92 Olivier Perroux. *Tradition, vocation et progrès: les élites bourgeoises de Genève (1814-1914)*. Thèse de doctorat, Université de Genève, 2003, 11.1.5, https://archive-ouverte.unige.ch/unige:200, accessed 10 Jun. 2019.

93 Félix Rivet. *Le quartier Grôlée, Une réalisation d'urbanisme à Lyon*. Lyons: Institut des Études rhodaniennes de l'Université de Lyon, 1955.

tion companies. An example was the building of a whole block in a renewal project between Rue d'Algérie, Rue d'Oran and Rue de Constantine in 1850 by a society of associated entrepreneurs or masons called La Sécurité Générale.[94] In Rue Impériale, Poncet had kept one full block and two half-blocks to be constructed by contractors of the SARI. The goal here was to share profits with the project's partners, as occurred in some of the operations from around 1500. The entrepreneurs, G. Villatte and Pénelon, therefore built n° 33 – 35 Rue Impériale using this strategy. I have examined in a previous paper how such entrepreneurs had developed their investments through networks of professionals and partners with whom they co-invested. In the case of Villatte, this network was seemingly based on municipal employees, and in the case of another entrepreneur, Pierre Dumont, on an association with solicitors, who often acted as bankers. The role played by such agents in the production of buildings has still to be fully explored for the nineteenth century.[95]

Architects remained major orchestrators of building investment until the end of the nineteenth century. Besides Poncet, whose career extended after Lyons to cities like Rouen and Nice, one may also cite Etienne Journoud,[96] who later on played an important role in structuring the profession of architects at the national level while living and working in Paris, as well as other names like Bissuel, who was also an important investor in Lyons, and Rivière, who played an active role in developing the east bank of the River Rhône in the late nineteenth century. Journoud was a member of the team of young architects which Poncet had assembled around himself for the conception and building of the Rue Impériale/de la République ensemble. Afterwards, he adopted an interesting investment strategy, notably organizing the sharing of the profits with other professions of the building trade involved in the construction work. An example of his orchestration of the production of several buildings is that of Rue Gasparin, a new street between Place Bellecour and Place des Jacobins, created in association with Rue de l'Impératrice in the 1860s. To do this, Journoud bought two large plots at the corners of Rue Gasparin and Place Bellecour, associating two investors, Dumont, an entrepreneur already alluded to, and Touzot, a solicitor.[97] Two big buildings, identical in their architectural design, were then rapidly constructed on these plots. Further north along Rue Gasparin, he organized the production of six small buildings, undertaking the architectural design himself, and

94 AML 321 WP 37; ADR 3 P 123 – 7.

95 Gauthiez, *Lyon entre Bellecour ...*, 88 – 92.

96 Gauthiez, *Lyon entre Bellecour ...*, 93 – 95

97 Amédée Savoye was also involved as an opportunistic investor and had acquired one of these plots, but he later sold it.

leaving the investment to a joiner, Romain Pilet, an entrepreneur, Antoine Chavepeyre, and a plasterer,[98] Joseph Gilles, each of whom worked with a financer, solicitor or rentier. The financial and administrative structuring of this operation was complex, but had the significant result that some small entrepreneurs in the building trade could become proprietors and profit from the capital gains made from real estate investment.[99] This financial structure was perhaps not so different from what we presume occurred regarding the various houses of the Rue Grenette built in 1493, examined previously (see III.2.1.1), as well as, no doubt, in many other historical scenarios.

If the context of the renewal of the city-center between 1850 and 1890 was very favourable to architects and entrepreneurs, the parallel development of the east side of the River Rhône was a golden opportunity for the small contractor, many of whom worked in the renewal operation in the meantime, to invest their gains. As the municipality seems to have encouraged the displacement of the poor from the redevelopment areas towards the eastern side of the Rhône, many masons, carpenters, joiners, stone cutters, plasterers, etc., built hundreds of new small buildings in the area, described as *baraques* (shacks) in the building permits. They represented maybe about 50 percent of the builders in this other context.[100]

III.2.3.1 Rue Pierre-Blanc: a singular development of 1820

One last case will be examined, of which there is no equivalent in the seventeenth or eighteenth centuries, and maybe also in the nineteenth century. This is the subdivision of a part of the Carmélites convent precinct in 1820.[101] The subdivision was carried out by three associates: Etienne Noailly, qualified as proprietor, living n° 9 Rue Lanterne, Jean Pierre Blanc, a joiner and later also an entrepreneur, from n° 3 Rue Romarin, and Pierre Briffaud, a mason and entrepreneur as well, living nearby at n° 5 Rue des Bouchers.[102] The area to be subdivided was bought from Mme Steinmann, owner of the former convent, who kept a part of it to the north, where she had her lodgings and where

---

98 Journoud bought Chavepeyre his building after he went bankrupt, and re-sold it him after he had financially recovered.

99 Bernard Gauthiez. Les immeubles numéros 15, 17, 19, 21 et 23 de la rue Gasparin à Lyon, un exemple urbain de production complexe du bâti. *In Situ:* 2 (2002), 10, https://journals.openedition.org/insitu/1181.

100 Gauthiez, la rénovation urbaine, 49.

101 Plan AML 3 S 697, 1818.

102 AML 321 WP 006, n° 208.

many silk-weavers already rented workshops in the old buildings of the convent (79 looms in that part in 1833, which corresponds to more than 25 weavers). The new subdivision covered 1.17 hectares and was made of a central street (originally named Rue Tolozan, and later Rue Pierre-Blanc) and associated lateral plots. Several constructions were built rapidly, from August 1820 onwards, by Anselmier on a plot at the corner of Côte des Carmélites,[103] by the three subdividers on the neighboring plots, and on other plots by Chassagny, a mason-tiler, by Genestine/Genestelle (the name varies in the sources), a mason, by François Pinchon, a mason journeyman, by Anthelme Ginod, a joiner (perhaps specialised in looms), and by Antoine Rousset, a taffeta-maker. The next year (1821), there followed buildings by Lambert Plumet, a butcher, Michel Mallet, a mason, and Piroud, whose profession is unknown. On the north side of the street, the first to be developed because of its favorable exposition, the last building was constructed in 1822, by Jouvanon, at the corner of a street later named Rue de Flesselles, located at the western extremity of rue Pierre-Blanc. The great number of masons among the investors is striking, especially as they were modest individuals, building modest houses, with three-five floors and nearly no decor. The buildings on the south side were constructed in 1824 to 1825, half of them by people having already built on the north side, which suggests an accumulation of capital reinvested in new constructions, notably on the part of Ginod, Blanc and Briffaud.

The social milieu of the investors is indicated by the location of their residences when they invested in Rue Pierre-Blanc, as may exceptionally be ascertained thanks to the 1820 census (this information is never mentioned in other censuses). The wealthiest, by far, was Noailly, a well-off (but in no way rich) rentier, who paid a rather high rent of 300 francs for an apartment of six rooms,[104] which is a rather considerable number. Pierre Blanc (after whom the street was later named) lived with his son and paid 200 francs for his workshop and 100 francs for their dwelling. Pierre Briffaud lived in a very modest apartment comprising only one room rented for 30 francs, which was among the lowest rents in the city.

This subdivision immediately came to house the biggest concentration of silk-weaving looms in the city, even though the subdividers were a poor mason and two members of the middle-class. Their age is also noteworthy: Blanc was 68 and his son 34, Noailly was 52, and Briffaud 31. Again, as in so many occurrences, capital and building know-how were associated.

---

103 AML 316 WP 020 – 21.

104 The highest annual rents in the city were at that time over 1000 francs.

Figure III.10 Map of the development of Rue Pierre-Blanc in 1820–25.
Background: plan of the area bought by Anselmier in 1818 (© AML 3 S 0697).

To carry-out the subdivision, the following phases were necessary:

- Firstly, the construction of a house by each of the three associates.
- In parallel, they sold the other plots on the north side of the street, and a little later on the south side.
- They later built on the plots they had kept on the south side, one for Blanc in 1824 to 1825, and two for Briffaud, constructed in 1823 and 1825.

The financial success of this project, thanks to the immediate letting of entire buildings to silk-weavers, was such that it allowed the first investors to build new houses in the subdivision soon after their first building: the joiner, Ginot, bought a plot on which in 1820 he built a narrow house, with only three floors (this was both because he did not possess large amounts of capital and to limit the risk of no immediate income if the building remained tenantless), and in 1825 he built two much larger houses on the south side of the street (he had obviously succeeded in renting his first house). The Genestelle family of masons did the same: a first building on the north side was built by the father in 1820, and a second by the son on the south side in 1825. Ginot, aged 34, who previously paid a rent of 200 francs at Rue des Capucins, and Genestelle, aged 43, who previously paid a rent of 100 francs at Rue Bellecordière, became proprietors, dwelling in their own building, and probably also rentiers. The project was clearly a remarkable success.

Having examined who invested in this subdivision, we still have to understand how it was occupied. The 1822 census shows clearly that the buildings were rented immediately and in full by silk-weavers. The census, in a seemingly exceptional way, which probably emphasizes the peculiarity of the Rue Pierre-Blanc subdivision, tells us about the origins of the new dwellers. This allows for a comparison of their new living places with their previous ones, in particular the rents paid. Forty-one new tenants are listed for the new buildings of Ginot, Rousset, Pinchon, Genestelle, Chassagny, and Decran. All their previous addresses are mentioned, whereas previous censuses give their former activities and rents only in 18 cases. That means that many of the new tenants previously lived at someone else's residency, which would appear to be confirmed by their age: from 19 to 28, with one exception at 38, and a majority at 23 to 26 (average 24.6). Those whose former addresses can be retraced were older, averaging 36.3, and included both young and old people, some at 62, 65 and 70, accompanied by their sons of 32 and 34. Unfortunately, the age of the women is not given in the census.

The youthfulness of the newcomers, especially the first tenants, is remarkable when compared to other contexts. The average age of the silk-weavers on rue Pierre-Blanc[105] in the 1824 census is 30.1 years, compared to 44.9 years for the silk-weavers on Rue Noire, located in an old quarter of the city near the Hôtel-Dieu, and 47.9 years for the silk-weavers of Rue St-Georges (calculated for the inhabitants of the even-numbered side of the street), both of which stand out for their high concentrations of silk-weavers. This huge difference is remarkable, and shows that the new buildings of Rue Pierre-Blanc were aimed at a market of young and dynamic silk-weavers, but who came from areas where most silk-wea-

---

105 The name of the street was at that time Rue Tolozan, which is somewhat ironic as the Tolozans at the end of the eighteenth century were among those who profited the most by the money made from silk-weaving, in a period where no buildings were produced for the silk-weavers.

vers were old and poor. This social ascent is also clear in the rents paid, generally around 40 to 50 francs on Rue St-Georges, compared to between 50 and 200 francs, with many at 150 francs, which is three times as much, in the new constructions of Rue Pierre-Blanc. Only in 18 cases is it possible to compare the rents paid for old and new apartments by a tenant residing henceforth on the new street. In 16 occurrences of increased rent, the cost is multiplied by a factor of 2.14. In the remaining cases, a widow pays 75 francs instead of 125 francs, but she is now alone in her apartment, and a furniture merchant reconverted to silk weaving pays 85 francs instead of 250 francs, perhaps because he had gone bankrupt in the meantime.

A third indicator of this social ascent – in addition to the cost of rent and average age of the newcomers – is the nature of the looms used at Rue Pierre-Blanc. In 1833, the proportion of Jacquard looms was 33 percent in the old weaving areas, compared to 72 in this new one, and the average number of looms per workshop also grew, from 2.3 to 4. The equipment used was much more modern and there was more of it, allowing for bigger workshops and higher potential incomes.[106] These elements show without any ambiguity that the new constructions, which were modern, better lit and technically up-to-date,[107] were intended for a new generation of weavers, who were much younger and better equipped. These new weavers were clearly aiming to become much better off than their parents and forbears.

The sources also suggest the probable role of spatial and social proximity in the recruitment of tenants, though this could considerably vary from one building to another. The tenants of Rousset, himself a weaver of taffeta and the only investor in the new street from the silk weaving trade (and previously an inhabitant of Rue Longue), paid high rents and were already, for their majority of them, seasoned professionals. Conversely, the tenants of Pinchon, a mason from Rue Grand-Côte, were inexperienced weavers; they were younger and used relatively less modern equipment (a total of eleven Jacquard looms and seven older ones).

To conclude this rapid analysis of an exceptional – and exceptionally well documented – new development aimed at workers of the silk-weaving industry, a statistic may help us understand its important place in the general context at

106 On the situation of the silk-weaving industry at Lyons at that time, see Ludovic Frobert (ed.). *L'écho de la fabrique, naissance de la presse ouvrière à Lyon.* Lyons: Ecole Normale Supérieure Editions, 2010.

107 In comparison with the older built-up fabric elsewhere, a point on which Monfalcon insisted in 1834. See Jean Baptiste Monfalcon. *Histoire des insurrections de Lyon en 1831 and 1834.* Lyons: Louis Perrin, 1834.

Lyons. In 1833, one year before the 1834 insurrection, 810 looms were located in the buildings of Rue Pierre-Blanc, plus 210 in two neighboring buildings (including Brunet's famous building constructed in 1824), Rue de Flesselles. This may be compared to the total number of looms present in Lyons, given in the yearly census: 17,656, of which 6,566 were on the slopes of Croix-Rousse (the area in which Rue Pierre-Blanc is located), 2,718 in the Hôtel-Dieu area, 1,421 to the south of Place Bellecour, and 6,612 on the west bank of the River Saône (notably the areas of Rue St-Georges, Rue St-Jean and around the St-Paul Church). There were also 3,500 looms to the north, in the commune of La Croix-Rousse (not to be confused with the slopes bearing the same name, for the Croix-Rousse commune was on the plateau above the slopes). The new street later named Rue Pierre-Blanc thus accounted for five percent of the looms present in Lyons at a time when Lyons was the largest producer of silk wares in the world, and probably for a higher proportion of its silk production thanks to the better equipment of its weavers. This new development, led by rather modest people, was thus a considerable economic success.

When comparing this production of urban space to those that took place at the end of the eighteenth century, it is important to realize that it constitutes a rare case in which the target market was defined by its economic production. The buildings were not sold immediately after their construction, probably because of their high profitability. In 1822, all the tenants were involved in this activity of silk-weaving. This situation is quite different from that which prevailed during the second half of the eighteenth century, when no buildings were produced to answer for the need for dwelling and working spaces for silk-weavers,[108] and despite the fact that silk-weaving was at that point central to Lyons' overall economy. The Revolution, it follows, clearly made previously unknown types of investment possible, and in a way that was profitable to the trades, following the suppression of the corporations. Such moments have been rare in the history of the city. Such a situation also favored similarly oriented developments in the late fifteenth and early sixteenth centuries, for example in the milieu of the printers and booksellers, who seem to have privileged the construction and use of new houses. This was arguably true as well in the Rue Griffon area, immediately to the north of the City

---

108 The same space, usually comprising only one or two rooms, was used as both a workshop and a dwelling. It was inhabited by the family of the weaver (two thirds of them at least were married), one boy apprentice, and sometimes also several girls helping the functioning of the looms.

Hall, where new subdivisions in the mid-sixteenth century were also made predominantly for silk-weavers, though this is still poorly documented.[109]

III.2.4 The growing distance between the dwellings of proprietors and their properties

Investment in real estate seems to have become more detached from the buildings themselves in the seventeenth to eighteenth centuries, moving towards a more financial logic. This movement occurred in parallel to changes in the relative locations of the proprietors own dwellings, which can be determined from various rare sources, notably in 1493, in 1677 for some quarters, and in 1853 from a survey of the buildings to be demolished for the construction of the Rue Impérale. In 1493, the great majority of owners lived in one of their own properties, often as a single household. By 1677, of the proprietors in the Rue Buisson quarter (named also Quartier des Cordeliers), only one occupied the entirety of the building he owned (of a total of 112 buildings). There were 55 cases of buildings inhabited both by their owner and by tenants, and seven proprietors lived in neighboring properties rented from other proprietors. The survey carried out in the same sector of the city in 1853, before the demolition of about 300 buildings to make room for the new Rue Impériale, showed that the number of proprietors living close to their assets had decreased. In the block between Rue Gentil, Rue de la Gerbe and Rue Buisson, corresponding to the former Rue Buisson quarter, the number of proprietors-occupants had decreased from 18 to 11. Those who lived near their buildings were also fewer, and many lived a few blocks away or even outside Lyons. Another indicator of this phenomenon is given by the proportion of proprietors living in their own building in 1597 and 1709, which exhibits the same trend.

109 See the discussion about the reconstruction of the Justice building after a fire, ADR, 8 C 303, Apr. 1627.

Table III.7 Evolution of the proprietors dwelling in their own building, 1597–1709[110]

Administrative quarters	**Houses occupied by their owner, 1597**	**Houses occupied by their owner, 1709**	**Trend**
Pierre Scize	unknown	20 %	
Bourgneuf	unknown	quarter suppressed	
Puits du sel	33 %	quarter suppressed	
Port St Paul	23 %	33 %	43 %
Rue de Flandres	34 %	24 %	-29 %
Asnerie	unknown	18 %	
Juiverie	68 %	29 %	-57 %
Change	16 %	17 %	6 %
Grand Palais	14 %	33 %	136 %
Bœuf	33 %	Unknown	
Porte Froc	48 %	33 %	-31 %
Gourguillon	41 %	36 %	-12 %
St Georges	unknown	26 %	
Saint-Just	unknown	quarter suppressed	
Total River Saône west side	34 %	25 %	-26 %
Herberie	unknown	16 %	
Rue Mercière	unknown	20 %	
Port du Temple	unknown	41 %	
Thomassin	42 %	Unknown	
Confort	22 %	22 %	0 %
Bourchanin Bellecour	47 %	35 %	-26 %

110 I thank Olivier Zeller for his elaboration of this table and his comments.

Table III.7 Evolution of the proprietors dwelling in their own building, 1597 – 1709 *(Continued)*

Administrative quarters	Houses occupied by their owner, 1597	Houses occupied by their owner, 1709	Trend
Bellecordière	not extant as quarter	31 %	
Grande rue de l'Hôpital	unknown	15 %	
Plat d'Argent	not extant as quarter	23 %	
La Croisette	unknown	15 %	
Bon Rencontre	unknown	38 %	
Basse Grenette	24 %	26 %	8 %
Haute Grenette	38 %	9 %	-76 %
Saint-Nizier (part of)	35 %	20 %	-43 %
Rue Buisson	26 %	27 %	4 %
Rue Neuve	45 %	Unknown	
Saint-Pierre	29 %	22 %	-24 %
Le Platre (part of)	50 %	Unknown	
Lanterne	29 %	27 %	-7 %
Pêcherie	31 %	Unknown	
Terreaux	34 %	31 %	-9 %
Saint-Vincent (part of)	39 %	Unknown	
Cote St Sébastien	unknown	39 %	
Griffon	unknown	Unknown	
Total River Saône east side	35 %	24 %	-31 %
Total whole city	35 %	27 %	-23 %

The overall proportion of owner-habitants decreased from 35 percent to 27 percent, in a slow change which had begun much earlier and continued long afterwards. The situation in different quarters may have varied according to different logics, and so may not correspond to a single cause. For example, the proportion of owner-inhabitants decreased rapidly in the Rue Juiverie quarter, an area with an ancient and powerful elite population which had begun to seek dwellings closer to the City Hall. By contrast, the evolution was less pronounced in areas inhabited by middle classes, like the Rue St-Pierre and Rue de Flandres quarters, with some quarters exhibiting no change at all (Change, Confort, Rue Buisson, whose situation of property changed later, as seen above). This evolution calls for more thorough study, notably by taking account of choices made by the owning families, but at present this information is not available. The situation in the poor areas is known only at one date (1709, Pierre Scize, St-Georges, La Croisette, Côte St-Sébastien, Griffon quarters), so its evolution is unknown. The available evolution of owner-occupants is nevertheless clearly a significant source of knowledge regarding the movements of the higher social levels in the city.

To summarize, it seems that a slow global and long-term evolution of the relationship between the proprietors and their properties occurred in Lyons over the fifteenth to nineteenth centuries. This evolution, which was characterized by growing separation and distance, occurred in parallel to the concentration of property assets among a diminishing number of families. This goes against the traditional propensity of owners to live in or near their properties (hence also the traditional propensity, when possible, to acquire houses facing each other on the same street), in order to keep an eye on its occupants and to facilitate the collection of rents. As time went by, a disconnection occurred, with new management systems appearing on the scene, notably a proprietor letting to a principal renter, who in turn sublets to tenants.[111] In the nineteenth century, there appeared societies (called *régies* at Lyons) specialized in the management of buildings for one or several proprietors. Logics of real estate and dwelling became increasingly separate. Information about a single area at two different dates is certainly not enough to draw strong conclusions about the overall pattern of this evolution, but the available data does hint at a trend which may have played a significant role in the evolution of the city.

111 Olivier Zeller. Un mode d'habiter à Lyon au XVIIIe siècle: la pratique de la location principale. *Revue d'Histoire Moderne & Contemporaine*, 35 – 1 (1988): 36 – 60.

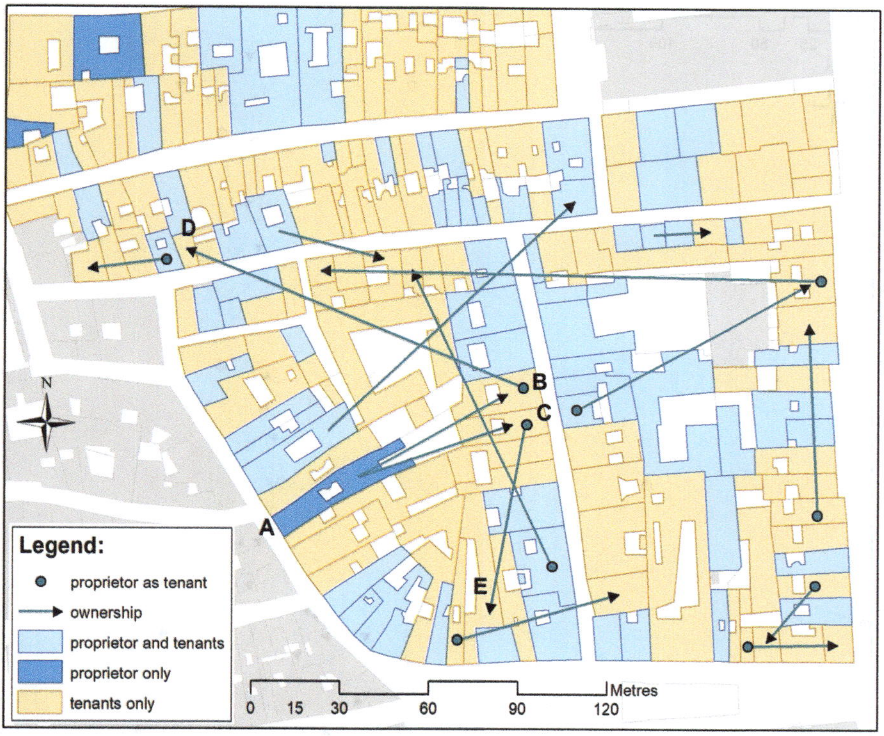

Figure III.11 Map of Rue Buisson quarter in 1677, showing the living places of the proprietors of buildings: in their own one, in their own with tenants, or nearby, as indicated by arrows. The other owners lived further afield.

Example: The owner of **A** is the only occupant of his property. He owns also **B** and **C.** In **B**, one of the tenants is proprietor of building **D.** In **C**, one of the tenants is proprietor of building **E.**

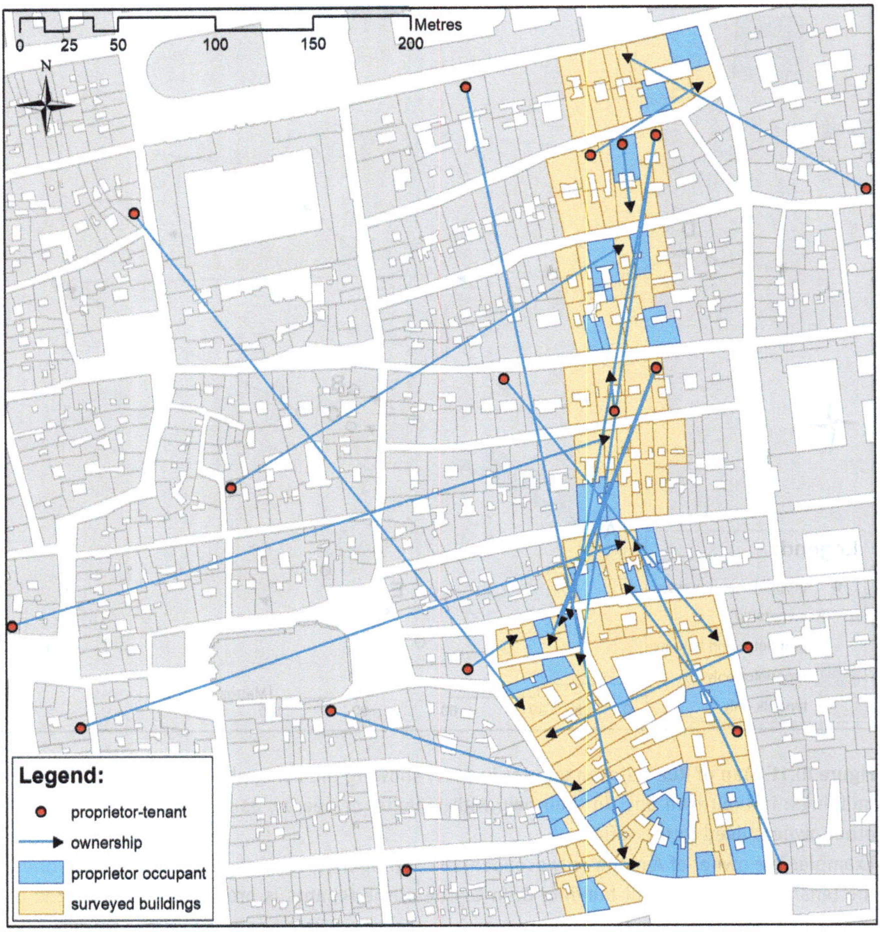

Figure III.12 Property situation in 1853 of the buildings demolished for the northern part of the Rue Impériale redevelopment in 1854 – 55. The proprietors not shown on the map lived outside the represented area.

The buildings in grey were not surveyed, so the status of the red dots on them is unknown, either proprietors tenants or proprietors occupants. No proprietor was occupying alone his building.

Conclusion and discussion

Conclusion 1: Temporalities and spatialities of the production of urban space

From the historical material we have studied over the three parts of this book, the existence of different temporalities can be inferred, each of which is associated with their own spatial and social scales. They are:

- Natural contingencies: cycles of the day and of the climatic year, which act as constraints on construction activity. These temporalities have no direct spatial implications.
- Anthropological contingencies: the week, the festivals and their annual cycle, the rhythms of a given profession and its work habits. These constraints have no spatial consequences.
- Emergent temporalities:
  - Individual buildings/houses, contextualized in a life path, the location of which is dictated by opportunities and a project corresponding to a social and familial situation. When a single family possessed two houses, it seems that they generally sought buildings located opposite one another on the same street. When capital was divided more equally between households, new constructions tended to be spread more evenly throughout the city. Conversely, in the second half of the eighteenth century, when property ownership was concentrated in the hands of a few, new constructions were grouped in areas of limited extent.
  - Groups of new constructions were sometimes organized by professionals of the building trade. The grouping is probably mainly due to the role of party-walls and to decisions of the City administration to enforce the widening of street sections. The location of grouped reconstructions share no spatial logic throughout the city, and groups are not linked in time. A group can also be determined by a new development/subdivision.
  - Transformations taking place over the long-term have their own logic, in relation to the state of society. Investors seek out particular areas, either new developments allowing for a full expression of the dominant building typology, or in gentrification spots and quarters, as occurred around the City-Hall after the mid-seventeenth century. This occurred with great force in the mid and late eighteenth century because of the concentration of investment capital in higher social milieus.

https://doi.org/10.1515/9783110623062-006

Emergent temporalities correspond to different scales of growing complexity with respect to social agents: an individual in a familial and economic context; groups of professionals in the real estate and building trade gathered together by a common interest or called on by public authorities to produce a more beautiful city-space and improve its functionality; economic cycles and long-term economic trends,[1] the logics of which are largely independent of local agents. It is, however, important to give a bit more nuance to this picture, which may be achieved by comparing the situation in Lyons with that at Rouen, another big French city. The concentration of capital in the hands of the elite was greater in Lyons that in Rouen, where the proportion of proprietors was about 17 percent in 1773, up slightly from what it was in 1713.[2] This discrepancy between Lyons and Rouen was probably due to the absence in Lyons of a more substantial bourgeois and merchant class (perhaps because Lyons was not the head city of a rich region, whereas Rouen was). In Lyons, the development of the silk weaving, a dominant activity in the late eighteenth century, favored the emergence of a sizeable population of workers devoid of any political weight in the day-to-day government of city affairs. Local factors have had – and still have – powerful effects on the evolution and character of building investment. These differences are also important factors for the development of different architectural cityscapes.

We saw that spatial scales were entangled with temporal scales as well as with the social phenomena involved. One strong spatial contingency must also be added: the dominant building typology, which it is not possible to escape. Every investor must bear this dimension in mind when planning his investment, even if it will appear perfectly natural and implicit to him, at least until it is replaced by a new dominant type, as occurred in the seventeenth century, when alternative solutions to the then dominant type were explored. Other contingencies take the form of financial possibilities, the size of the plots in an inherited plot-pattern, and availability of undeveloped land, which may theoretically make it possible to draw and establish plots appropriate to the dominant building typology. The rarefaction of opportunities to build on new land around the city, as occurred after the creation of numerous new subdivisions in the sixteenth century, was a major phenomenon in the seventeenth century. The key moment occurred around 1620, when numerous Counter-Reform convents acquired land around the already built-up areas to be founded, making consecutive purchases of neighboring plots in order to enlarge their precincts, and in so doing replacing

1 Dockès, *Le capitalisme.*

2 Bardet, *Rouen*, I: 170 – 171. The proportion was higher in the suburbs, which can be paralleled to a comparably higher proportion in Lyons in the suburbs after the French Revolution. Bardet doesn't give the proportion in 1713.

suburban bourgeois or aristocratic houses and gardens (*maisons des champs*). This certainly explains why there were nearly no new subdivision around the city after around 1600, with the notable exception of Rue Neyret, a new street established through his land by Neyret, a silk merchant, in 1619, and on which many silk workers later settled. One has to wait until the second half of the eighteenth century to see new subdivisions emerge again around the city, including of course the former religious precincts sold after they were expropriated by the state (becoming *Biens Nationaux*). Nevertheless, although the religious precincts have sometimes been described as an impediment to extending the city beyond its current limits, the absence of significant extension between 1619 and 1750 can also be interpreted as a consequence of the development of multi-familial housing, accompanied by new typological solutions which met the demand for housing resulting from the multiplication of poor households. Elsewhere, in cities like Rouen, people had higher average incomes and lived predominantly in mono-familial houses. The evolution in Lyons was probably comparable to that of port cities, where the proportion of the population living on very low incomes was significant, as was the case in Genoa and Toulon. In parallel, the concentration of real estate capital meant that the needs of the majority of the population were ignored, with investment and construction mainly satisfying the demand of the wealthiest, even if those demands were increasingly of a purely financial nature. Considering these evolutions, the idea that there was some sort of impediment to the development of new real estate in subdivisions could quite well be a mirage, as there was in fact no significant demand to develop new lands on the outskirts of the city, for these lands would have been inhabited by the poorest and all the investment capital was being used to develop central accommodation for the wealthiest. Over periods of several decades, the concentration of the poorest in multi-familial buildings, to which new dwelling space could be added under the roofs, was enough for investors. This interpretation explains why the late eighteenth century developments began by Morand and Perrache were such failures.

This doesn't imply that the poor would have not appreciated more living space – of course they would – but only that, over time, there were fewer and fewer investors who saw it financially beneficial to seek to satisfy this demand. Indeed, there was no system to correct the inequality that resulted from this purely financial investment logic before the end of the nineteenth century.

Taking a broad historical perspective, we can see that the great social and economic movements that have affected the city have had varying consequences for financial investment in houses and living quarters. The great crisis at the end of the sixteenth century was followed by an intense construction period, targeting varied social levels, an important consequence of which was that the available living surface per household significantly increased, such that by the mid-seventeenth century it was probably significantly greater than what it was in the mid-sixteenth century. The consequences of the late seventeenth century crisis were quite different. It was followed by a population decrease, though the development of the silk-weaving trade, seemingly abruptly interrupted in 1685 with the departure of the Protestants who refused to convert to Catholicism, soon established itself again thereafter. This meant the rise of a low-income population, who couldn't afford more than a single-room dwelling, or at most two, which in turn required multi-familial buildings, following a trend that had already started to appear in the previous decades. This trend also pointed towards increased concentration of capital. The great crisis of the French Revolution, which was certainly no bigger than its predecessors in demographical terms, provoked a population decrease of maybe 30 percent, which probably made the living conditions of the remaining inhabitants better (even if this was jeopardised for a moment by the projects of the Government after the siege in 1793, when hundreds of buildings were to be demolished, but in fact were not). In about 1800, when economic activity recovered, the suppression of the convents was a decisive factor in re-distributing real estate ownership in peripheral areas, leading to an increase in the number of proprietors and the construction of many new buildings in new subdivisions. The Rue Pierre-Blanc was a perfect illustration of these new possibilities.

The development of capital in the new post-revolutionary economy made possible, at least from the 1810s, the required concentration of capital for real estate investment in the town, especially for renewal operations like rue Impériale/de la République. The capital probably came initially from profits made from urbanizing the periphery, as well as from industrialization, which had in the previous decades led the elites to abandon the city center and to a concomitant depreciation of the value of its real estate. This new investment was undoubtedly the principal driver of the massive re-development of the old center, which aimed to attract clients on high incomes. It was also meant to solve the problem of workers' insurrection, which occurred in 1744, 1745, 1786, 1831 and 1834, though the general enrichment had already reduced the likelihood of these insurrections, particularly from the 1850s.

The theoretical examination of the production of space carried-out in Part I concentrated on the moment of new building production. The period examined, from the end of the fifteenth century, is rich in rebuilding and development operations in which professionals of the building trade played a major role, whether discreetly or ostensibly. Over long periods of time, the professions of the building trade – masons, entrepreneurs, joiners, carpenters, and smiths – were ever present, generating significant economic activity in their field, even if the level of activity varied. Drawing on their know-how, their time and their strength, their collaborative participation in many constructions projects, provided a flow of funds that would otherwise have to be provided by a rentier, a solicitor, or a merchant. Activity in the real estate market was in this way increased, and the risk limited. Buildings produced in this manner were generally sold immediately after completion, if not during construction. This allowed also for some investors to avoid any risk related to the construction projects themselves. This mechanism probably played a major role in the production processes, even if it is difficult to grasp in full because its agents appear only during the construction process, which is very poorly documented in the archival record.

This general strategy of building production underwent two major upheavals. The first occurred when, from the late seventeenth century onwards, architects began to act directly as investors. Some of these architects emerged from the masons-entrepreneurs, like Claude Chana, managing in some cases to undertake developments for the aristocratic and high-end sector of the market, as Jacques-Germain Soufflot did in the St-Clair quarter. Some of them became rentiers and abandoned their profession after having become wealthy, which explains their condemnation in 1793 by the Convention government of Lyons, just after the siege. Architects were in the eighteenth- and nineteenth-century major orchestrators of investment in new buildings, mounting companies to federate capital provided mainly by others, though they disappeared from the scene in the early twentieth century. This brings us to the second major upheaval, which occurred with the development of building companies. These companies were still in gestation in the eighteenth century, but they were fully operational by the mid-nineteenth century thanks to the availability of new capital arising from industrialization. Some building companies still played an important role in the twentieth century (though this is outside the period considered here), specializing less in construction than in real estate production and management, as occurred, in Lyons with Pitance and Coignet, or, in contemporary France as a whole, with Bouygues.

One of the striking results of the present research is that building production was typically not aimed at a specific economic sector, or a specific use, though there were rare exceptions, like the Rue Pierre-Blanc, which was developed at a time when silk-ware production in the city was very active, even at its apogee.[3] Gen-

3 This was the apogee within the city perimeter. The silk-ware production continued to develop outside its limits, first in La Croix-Rousse immediately to the north, then from the 1850s in farther suburbs and in areas within a radius of more than one hundred kilometers centered on

erally, the precise social and economic profile of the future occupants of a new building are not known before the building work begins, though one can suppose an active search on the part of investors to find possible tenants. Unfortunately, however, we have no information in the modern period about this important process, even though it is decisive for determining the success of the investment. The investor will keep the building in his own hands and rent it – as professionals of building trade generally do not – or sell it to realize the capital gain involved in producing a new asset. Renting is only vaguely defined in its spatial requirements, as precise demands are generally not known before construction; interiors are thus conceived to be adaptable to potentially quite varied exigencies. This explains the many possibilities of interconnections between the rooms, the numerous accesses to staircase landings, and the presence of a fireplace in each room. The plasticity of modern period buildings is quite remarkable, as they could house dwellings, workshops, independent business ventures, trades, warehouses, even small industries, the result being that many people often lived and worked in the same space. This explains why these buildings can also be easily adapted to the needs of today. The absence of a predefined functionality, with the partial exception of the ground floor, which was intended to be used as a shop and/or warehouse (though an employee frequently also dwelled in this part), is a dominant characteristic of the buildings of this period. This began to change in the nineteenth century with the emergence of functionalism, which attributed one sole function to each building, as well as with the emergence of industrialization, which required specialized buildings, and is totally different from today, when a new construction is strictly conceived and authorized for predetermined uses.

The production of new buildings increasingly aimed at the rental market, and thus with rentiers in mind, excluding productive uses. This was particularly true of the real estate market in the decades before the French Revolution. The link between the evolution of the real estate market and the progressive concentration of capital for real estate investment is clear. This link was also due to the development, in the seventeenth and eighteenth centuries, of the properties of religious orders, with about 45 new convents appearing in the period, thanks to donations or purchases of large houses and gardens in the periphery of the city, and largely financed by rents from other properties. Building investment became increasingly unproductive from the point of view of economic production, though it remained financially profitable, benefitting an ever smaller part of the

Lyons. The silk-weaving workshops nearly completely disappeared from the commune of Lyons between 1860 and 1900.

population and weighing on the economy of the city to the point where the living conditions of the majority of its inhabitants, those who contributed to its success, had become difficult and despised. One understands here how elites, whether aristocratic, economic or religious, had turned their attention towards personal profit only, becoming an obstacle to the dynamism of the city. This is probably why the modern city is commonly seen as immobile, after the remarkable Renaissance phase of growth. Behind the apparent immobility there lies an active and growing accrual of profits and capital by social groups of very limited size, who also controlled the city's politics. The modern period was actually not immobile, with the immobility we perceive being the consequence of antagonistic forces, one tending towards the development of the economy, the other towards increasing unproductive levies that suffocate it. This in turn explains the development of strong socio-political tensions, expressed notably in the insurrections of the eighteenth and nineteenth centuries.

Conclusion 2: Temporalities of urban space production compared to temporalities in other scientific domains

At the end of this exploration of the production of urban space, it is possible to attain a better idea of its temporalities in comparison with other scientific fields. It has been necessary to distinguish three registers of temporality:

A. a temporality proper to surface materiality, of a much shorter duration than the structures of the buildings.
B. a remanent temporality, in which the continuity of urban forms is achieved by the replacement of buildings and their associated material surroundings.
C. a temporality of the structure of buildings.

The quantitative analysis of building production was based solely on an examination of empirical data and dealt mainly with the structures of buildings, using archived documents, extant buildings, traces of former structures, etc. Religious and public buildings have been largely excluded, with attention focusing instead on understanding the production of the more common private constructions, the near exclusive focus of the analysis.

Urban space at a given moment presents itself as an accumulation of objects, rationally designed in themselves and eventually part of a wider plan englobing other objects as well at the urban level of design. Some of these objects will not have been modified, but others will have been, and they will generally have undergone more transformations the older they are. Transformation is irreversible: once an object has disappeared, it never reappears (it can be copied and reproduced, but it is never quite the same one, materially speaking). In this respect, urban materiality can be studied in a comparable way to geology. For example, geological materiality includes the surfaces of the earth, as superficial formations such as soils are studied by geomorphology. Vegetation could be included in this surface, but is studied separately. The structure would correspond in geology to the layers of the earth and their organization. As the study of earth materiality is spread across separate sciences, the analogy is not perfect.

Another important aspect of urban materiality is the duration of its objects and processes, which occur at different scales. One may distinguish the production of a single object in an annual cycle, the production of groups of neighboring buildings over a few years, long duration cycles of high or low production associated with different spatial configurations, and logics of very long duration, for example the different logics separating the modern period from the following period beginning in the early-to-mid-nineteenth century. Different scales of duration are also present in other fields, like in physics, where short durations also correspond to small spatial scales. Causes of this temporal complexity are either natural or cultural. Nature constrains daily and annual cycles. It acts via the evolution of climate and/or catastrophic events, nearly none of which affected the urban fabric of Lyons during the period considered: no earthquake, no volcanic eruption. Two catastrophic floods are nevertheless documented, in 1569, when in the la Guillotière suburb, on the east side of the River Rhône, many houses were destroyed.[4] The flood in 1856 also destroyed many houses, in the same area.[5] These natural constraints for building production also determine biological cycles,[6] the daily and annual cycles have also become cultural, ingrained in societies, which have added new elements woven together with constraints that were initially purely natural. The organization of construction works, for example, is in no way natural, but it does follow natural rhythms. Moreover, economic and long-duration cycles are not due to nature (except maybe the impacts of the Small Ice Age, poorly documented at Lyons, but of

4 No precise figure is available. See Guillaume Paradin de Cuyseaulx. *Mémoires de l'histoire de Lyon.* Lyons: Antoine Gryphius, 1571, 388.

5 The figures given by De Ochandiano are 1,185 houses (or dwellings?) destroyed, 648 damaged (Jean-Luc De Ochandiano. *Lyon, un chantier limousin. Les maçons migrants (1848-1940).* Lyons: Lieux-Dits, 2008, 65). The great majority of buildings destroyed by the flood were shacks (*baraques*). Constructing in rammed earth was forbidden as a result of the catastrophe.

6 Armand De Ricqlès. Le temps du biologiste. Christophe Bouton & Philippe Huneman (dir.). *Temps de la nature, nature du temps.* Paris: Centre National de la Recherche Scientifique éditions, 2018, 300.

great importance in seventeenth-century Europe).[7] Daily and annual cycles are strongly ingrained in local culture, whereas cycles of long duration are externally determined by events like the great late medieval crisis between the 1340s and the mid-fifteenth-century, the Ligue wars,[8] the wars and famines at the end of the reign of Louis the XIVth (died 1715) and the French Revolution. The accumulated tensions in local society, arising from growing inequality between the working classes and the elites, which were an important contribution to the development of the latter crisis, liberate in an analogous manner to how an earthquake releases the tension between two blocks held together only by friction forces. It is here possible to draw a parallel with the concepts of *wild random* and *mild random* as defined by the mathematician Benoît Mandelbrot.[9] Wild random corresponds to the great crises determined by forces outside the city acting at a larger spatial and political scale, or by natural catastrophes. Mild random, by contrast, corresponds rather to local, smoother variations.

The logic of groups of constructions is different from that of economic cycles, though their durations are similar. These groups are primarily determined by social forces, though sometimes also secondarily by the material weakness of the party-walls once one of two neighboring buildings has been demolished, thus calling for structural reinforcement. The materiality of the party-wall in some respects resembles a geological object. Once built through a social process, it becomes independent from this social process and may evolve in a comparable manner to a geological formation. As a general rule, microevolution is made of isolated individual transformations, whereas macroevolution arises from trends in local society (like the rapid development of a poor population of silk-weavers), as responses to major events, or to political and economic forces exerting pressure from the outside. The entanglement of temporalities at different scales, as well as of their causes, both natural and cultural, local and global, is in consequence extremely complex.

The temporalities in play are often not the same even for phenomena that in other respects appear closely related. Examples include the production of buildings, the succession of dominant building types, the relationship between owners and properties, and also, though it has not been studied here, changing trends in architectural styles. The development of a new architectural dominant type is probably never a necessity, though it will in every case be a response to

7 Parker. *Global crisis.*

8 This took place between 1585 and 1593, when the Catholic party refused Henri IV as King before he converted to Catholicism.

9 Benoit B. Mandelbrot, Adlai J. Fisher, Laurent E. Calvet. A Multifractal Model of Asset Returns. *Cowles Foundation Discussion Paper*, SSRN, n° 1164, 15 Sept. 1997.

new circumstances and needs. The new type developed at Lyons in the early seventeenth century only appeared in Paris more than half a century later, and it prospered in the capital city only after 1750. In this case, its aim was to find a better way of meeting the needs for affordable housing of thousands of people on low-income. A new building type generally appears when building production booms, which happened precisely in the fifteenth and early seventeenth centuries. In similar circumstances, the new production boom after 1945 was accompanied by the generalization of buildings whose typology was not based on a new logic governing the interior distribution of apartments, which were nevertheless increasingly complex,[10] but rather on a new way of arranging the buildings on the ground, which involved their detachment from their neighbors. A period of booming production is therefore propitious for the development of a new dominant building type, whether locally invented or imported. Conversely, during moments of low production, only slight typological variations occur. This pattern affords a striking parallel to what happens in biology. The great changes to the organizational plans of species take place in exceptional periods, generally following mass extinctions that create a space for new possibilities by opening up ecological niches. Periods of evolutionary stasis, by contrast, are analogous to the logic of tiny modifications and typological continuity of buildings that occurs when production is low.[11] But the time durations differ, being of the order of a century or a few centuries for the building types, as opposed to hundreds of thousands or millions of years for species. The coherence between a dominant architectural typology, high level production, and a stylistically individualized form of urban planning constitutes what M.R.G. Conzen called a *morphological period*.[12] From this perspective, the appearance of a new building type is similar to the appearance of a new species. This analogy is all but partial, as building typology is in general limited to a small number of types – it has become much more complex today –, which are not interrelated in any sort of ecosystem.

10 The principal novelties of the period were that the average apartment was now made of several rooms, instead of one or two previously, and that rooms were now functionally specialized (bathroom, kitchen, bedrooms, etc.).

11 Philippe Huneman. Macroévolution et microévolution. Les problèmes d'échelles de temps dans la biologie évolutive. Christophe Bouton & Philippe Huneman (dir.). *Temps de la nature, nature du temps.* Paris: Centre National de la Recherche Scientifique éditions, 2018, 343 – 70: 350.

12 Larkham and Jones, *A glossary*, 55. Conzen, himself of German origin, probably coined this concept by translating from the German word *Gestaltungsperiode*. On the origins of the concept, see Harald Uhlig. *Die Kulturlandschaft Nordostengland.* Cologne: Geographisches Institut der Universität, 1956 [Kölner geographische Arbeiten n° 9 – 10], 78 – 84.

Finally, one can wonder if the period here considered, 1450 to 1900, and covering only the area of the pre-industrial city, has any specificity compared to previous and later ones. It generally appears homogeneous, without very significant changes to the temporalities of urban space production (among them the variation of the annual temporality of the beginning of the construction works in the eighteenth century). Even the most important demographic variations, whose effects on the urban fabric are so indirect, did not exceed forty percent, and the city never shrank. The long-term growth trend has also been rather constant. Previous periods witnessed at least two major crises. At the end of antiquity, the consequences of the long crisis on urban space production are poorly known but what does seem certain is that the crisis led to the near total end of urbanization in the case of Lyons (and of many other cities as well). The second crisis, which began in the mid-fourteenth century and lasted about one century with high and lows, was marked by a shrinkage of the built-up area of Lyons of maybe twenty percent, associated to a reduction of maybe three quarters of the city's inhabitants.[13] This was due to epidemics, wars, and economic disruptions. Nevertheless, the temporal logics of periods of growth and stability of the city, as occurred during the heyday of the Roman Empire in the two first centuries of the Christian era, and again in the Middle Ages between 1100 and 1400, were perhaps comparable to those of the period 1450 to 1800. But building production is so poorly documented for these periods, notably because of what is likely to have been the short lives of common buildings (of the order of a few decades because of construction techniques and materials not allowing for durability), but also because of the difficulty of acquiring relevant information about the city and its buildings for this period, that it is hard to be certain about this. From the twelfth century, the urban fabric generally consolidated, becoming more stable as materials like stone, bricks, wood and tiles were increasingly used in bigger and stronger constructions.[14] One is also struck by the slow evolution of the proportion of proprietors among the households, which underwent a constant decrease from 35 percent in 1493 to 5.7 percent in 1789, followed by an increase to about 40 percent today.[15] Of course, the recent evolution has

---

13 The peak of the crisis was probably in the 1420s. The shrinkage took the form of many houses abandoned or whose area was transformed in gardens.

14 Gauthiez. La transformation des villes.

15 In 2011, the proportion of proprietors-occupants was 39 percent in the commune of Lyons and 48 percent in the Greater Lyon area. It had been slowly growing during the years prior to 2011. (http://www.urbalyon.org/AffichePDF/Observatoire_Partenarial_Habitat_-_profils_d-occupation_et_menages_pauvres_-_actualisation_Filocom_2011-9016, accessed July 2019). The story

made the owners closer to their property, reversing the trend of the modern period. This evolution followed a slow but rather constant line, seemingly indifferent to the crises on a long duration of three centuries and to other changes like the typological ones.

The period beginning around 1800 is clearly different because what major crises such as demographic collapse and urbanization shrinkage, did not happen, and in consequence they had no impact on the long-term development of the city. Some crises nevertheless occurred, including major economic ones, for example in the 1880s, in 1929, and during the two World Wars. They induced a fall in the urban population not exceeding approximately ten percent, which is considerably less than those occurring in the period between 1450 and 1800 (taking Lyons not as a commune, but as an entire city, and not considering variations between the center and the periphery). Furthermore, in between these crises the process of urbanization generally progressed quite smoothly, as is the case today, though on a much greater scale.

Temporalities of urban materiality production have natural and cultural causes and logics. They are natural when they inscribe human action in astronomical cycles, and with the almost geological behavior of urban materiality. The analogy also includes the parallel that can be made between the evolutions of building typology and of species, which are cultural when production (its quantities, location, conception, production processes and uses) and destruction arise from social processes, which are themselves ingrained in rhythms – both natural and cultural.

of property relations in Lyons between the early nineteenth century and today remains to be written.

Appendix: 27 images from the film of building activity at Lyons from 1620 to 1830, one image per 10 years

In order to keep a common topological frame for an easier comparison, the rivers and bridges indicated on the map are drawn according to their mid-eighteenth century form until 1860, and after 1860 to their nowadays form. As the period between 1764 and 1789 is poorly documented, the precedent image is for 1750 – 1763, followed by an image for 1764 – 1789. New buildings of the decade are mapped in dark blue (private buildings) and dark green (religious and public), new buildings of the two previous decades in pale blue (private buildings) and pale green (religious and public). New streets and public spaces in dark orange and pale orange.

Transformations 1620-1629

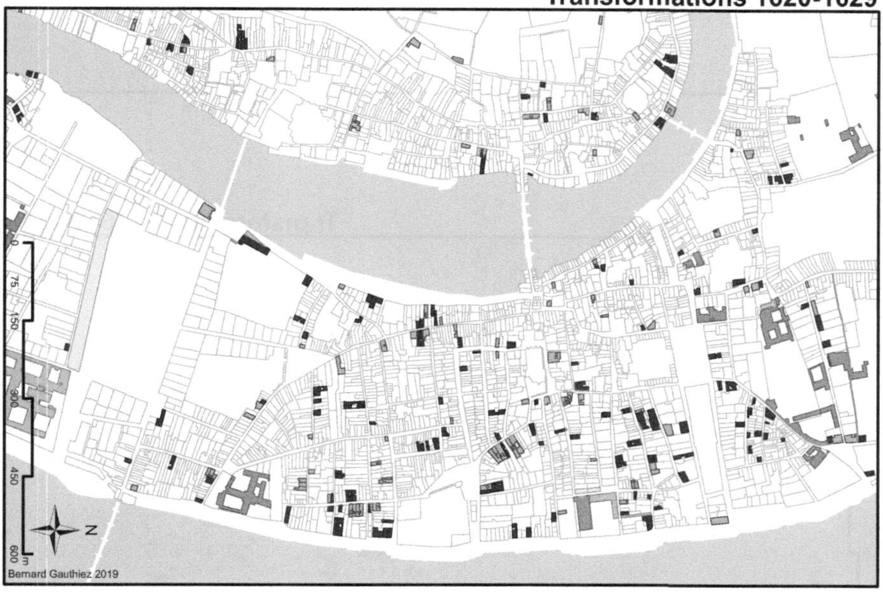

https://doi.org/10.1515/9783110623062-007

Transformations 1630-1639

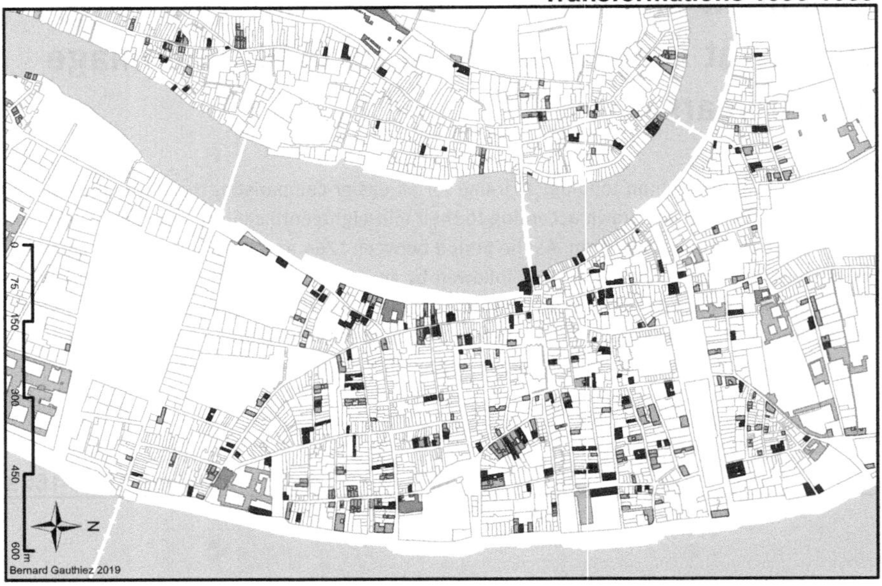

Transformations 1640-1649

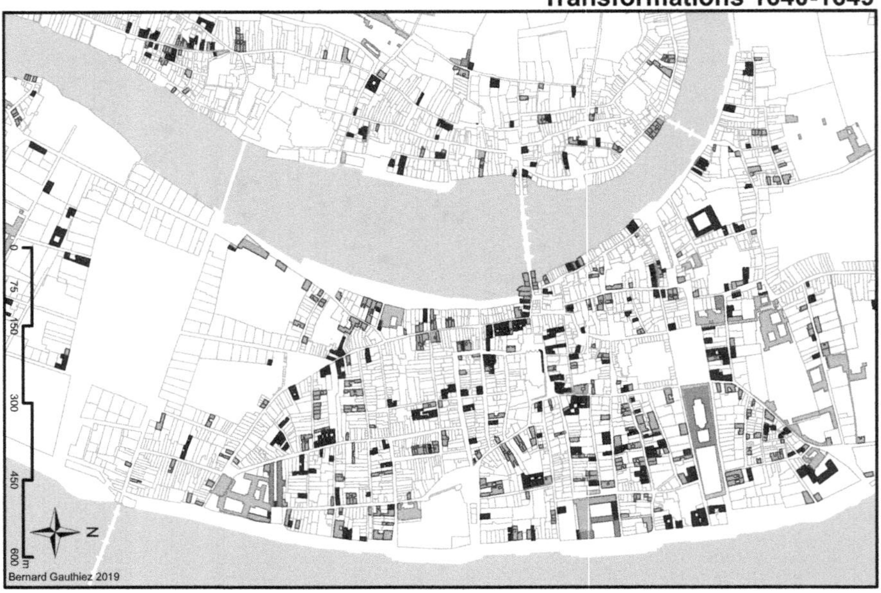

Transformations 1650-1659

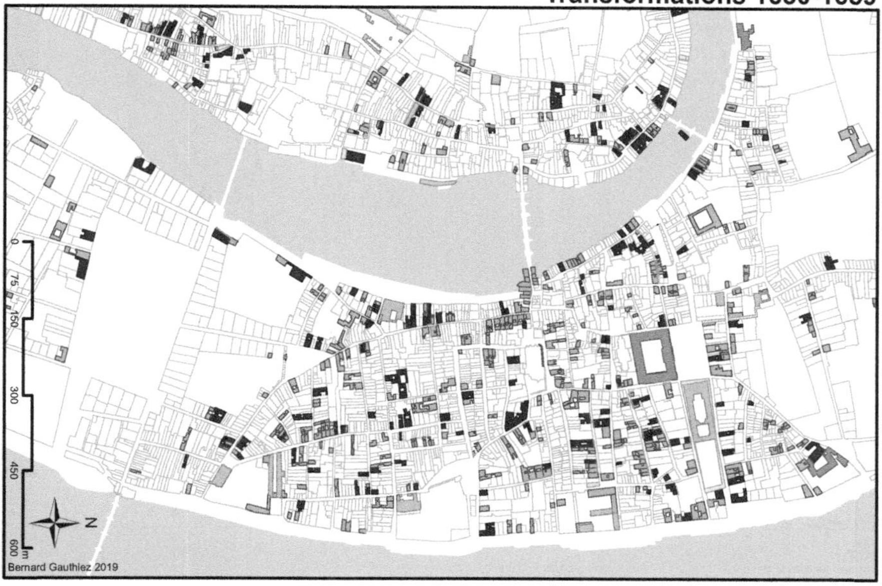

Transformations 1660-1669

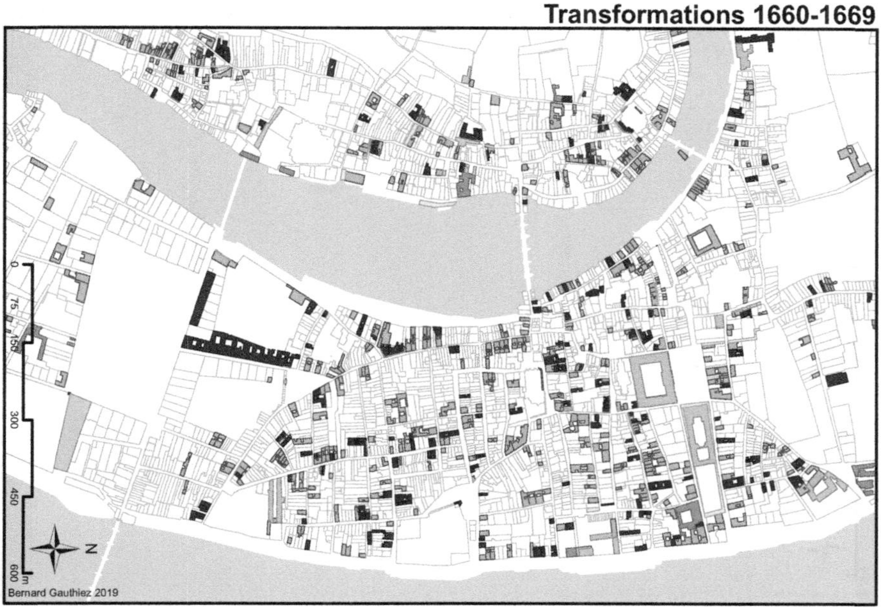

Transformations 1670-1679

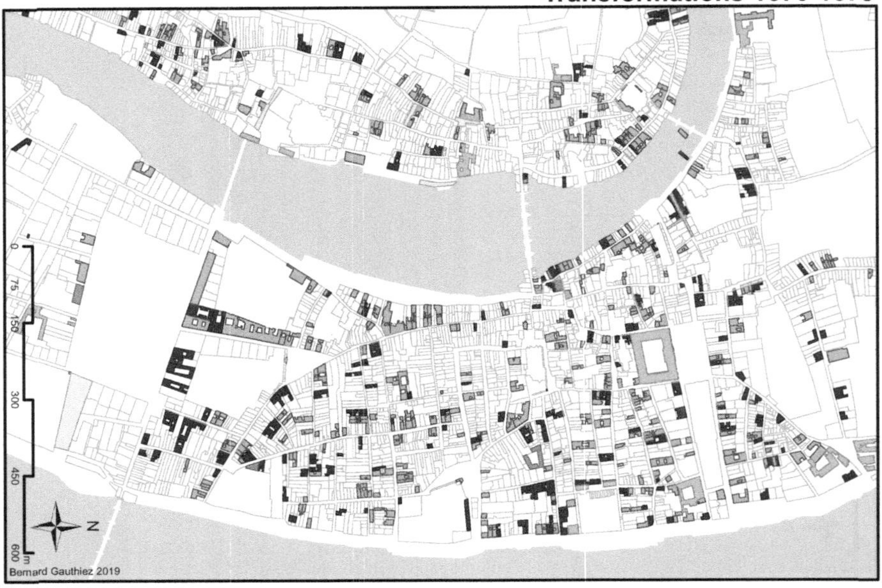

Transformations 1680-1689

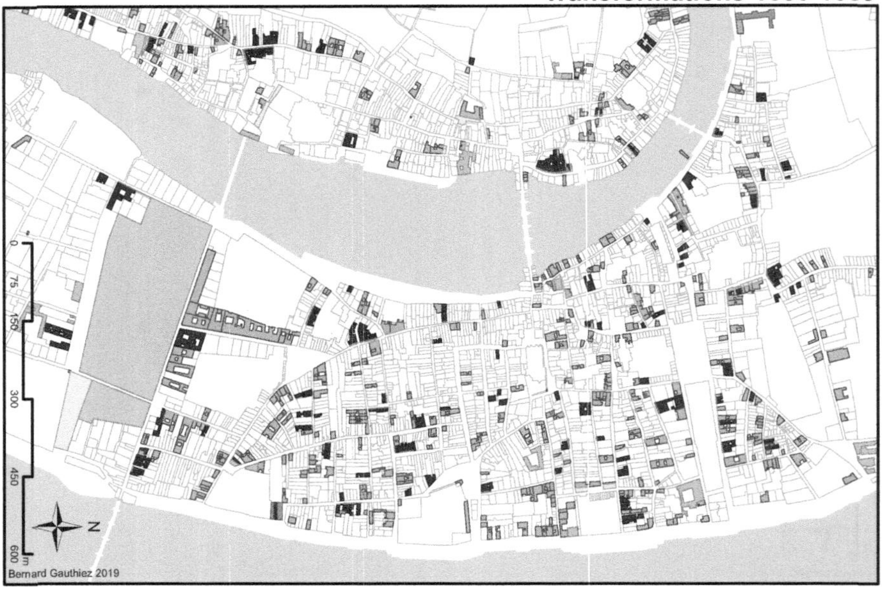

Transformations 1690-1699

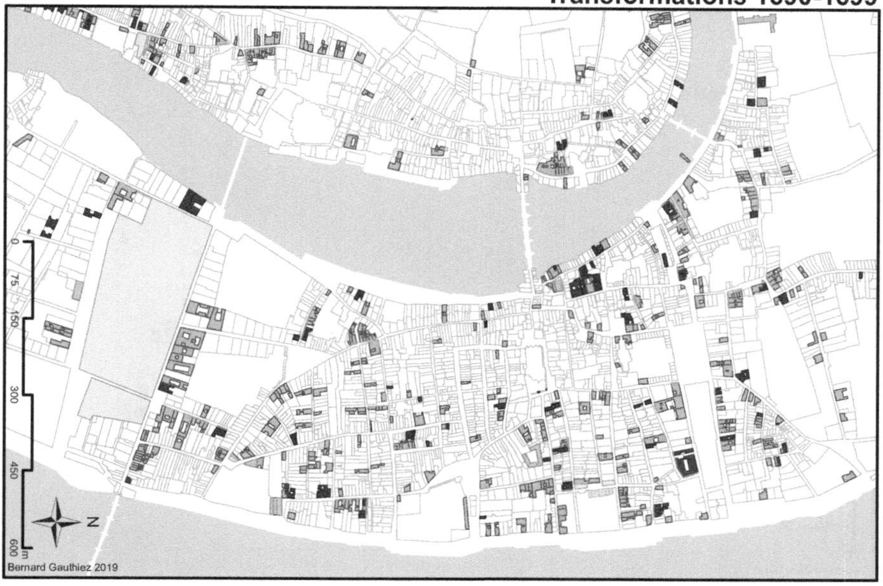

Transformations 1700-1709

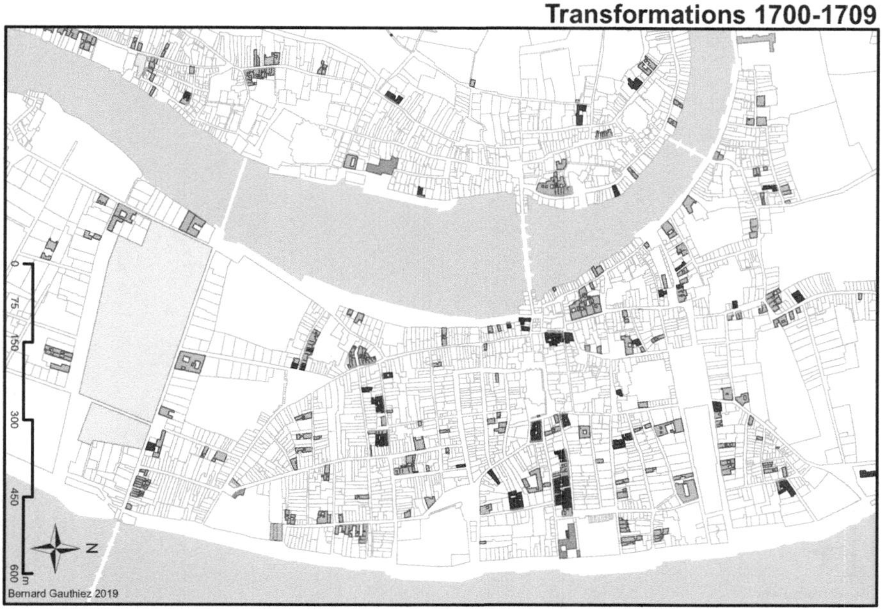

Transformations 1710-1719

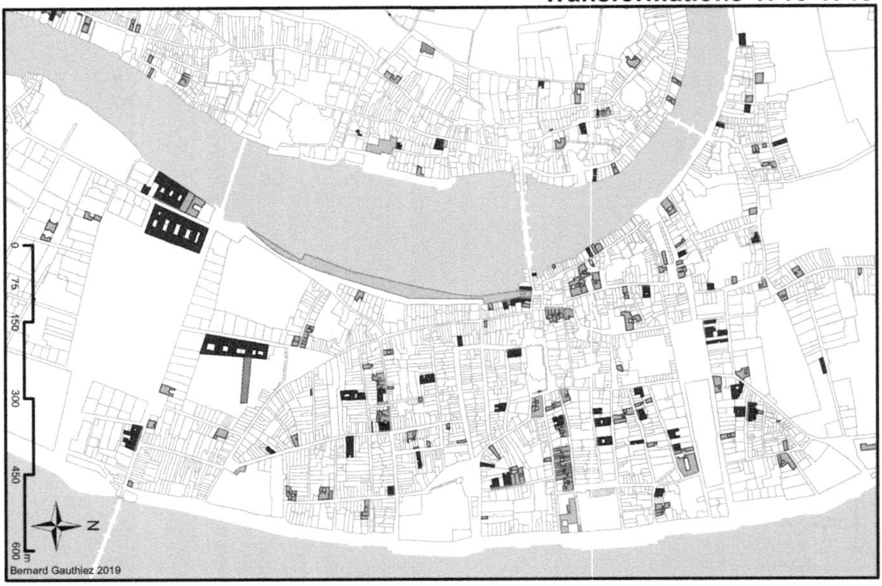

Transformations 1720-1729

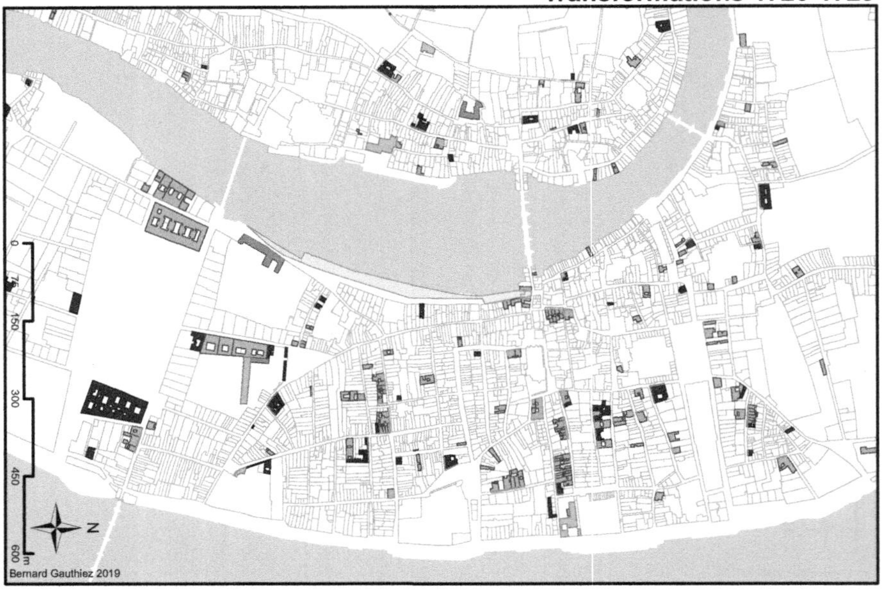

Transformations 1730-1739

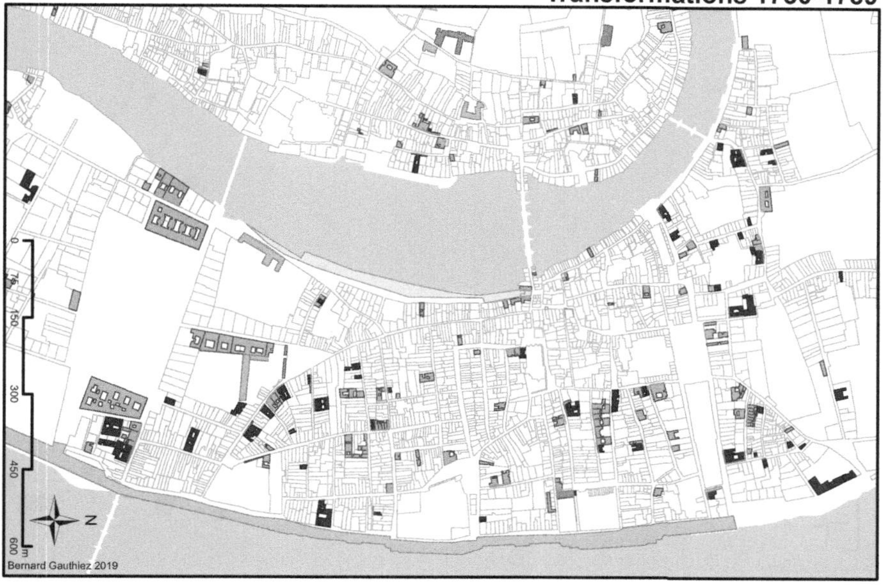

Transformations 1740-1749

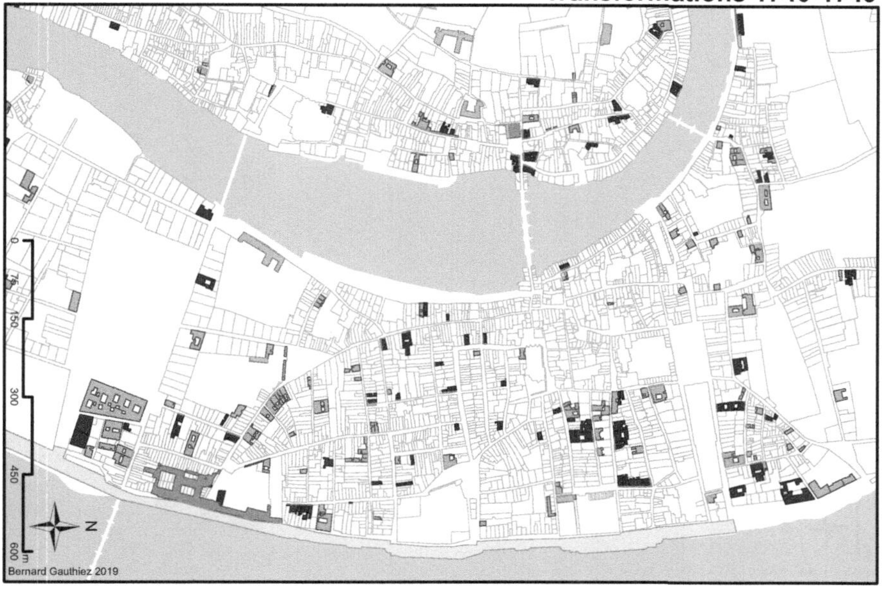

Transformations 1750-1763

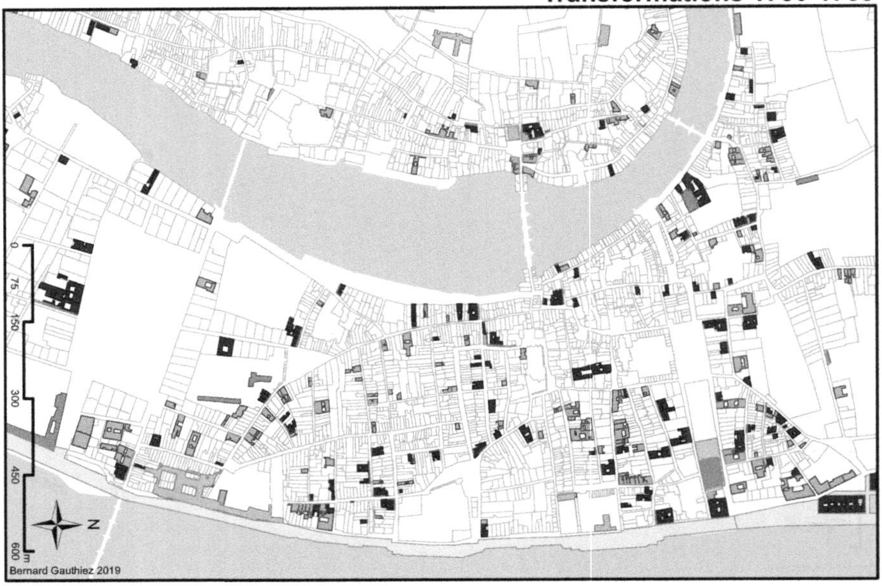

Transformations 1764-1789

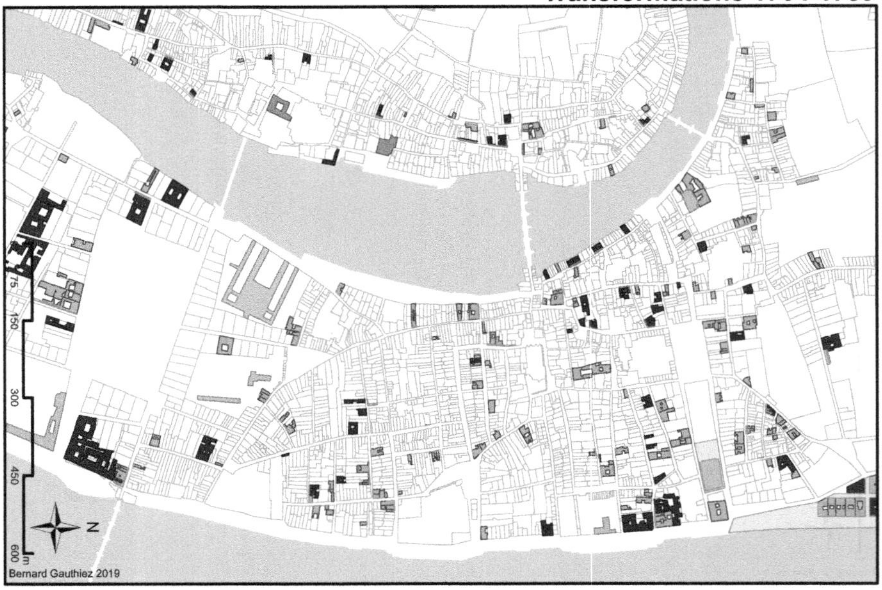

Transformations 1790-1799

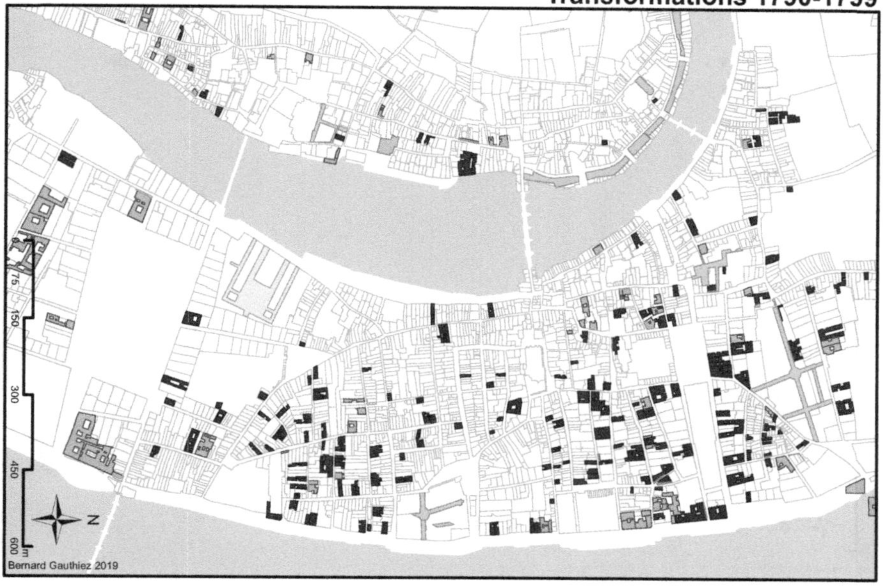

Transformations 1800-1809

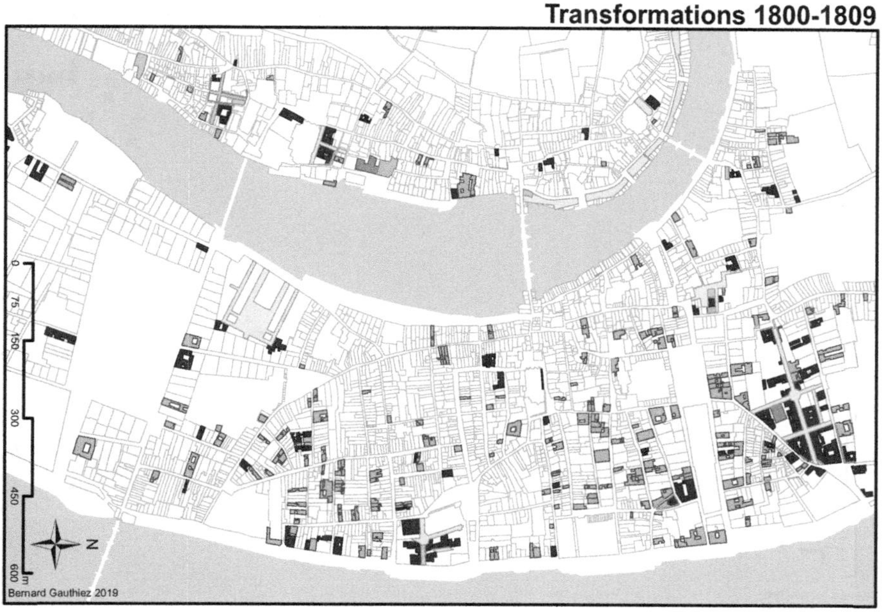

Transformations 1810-1819

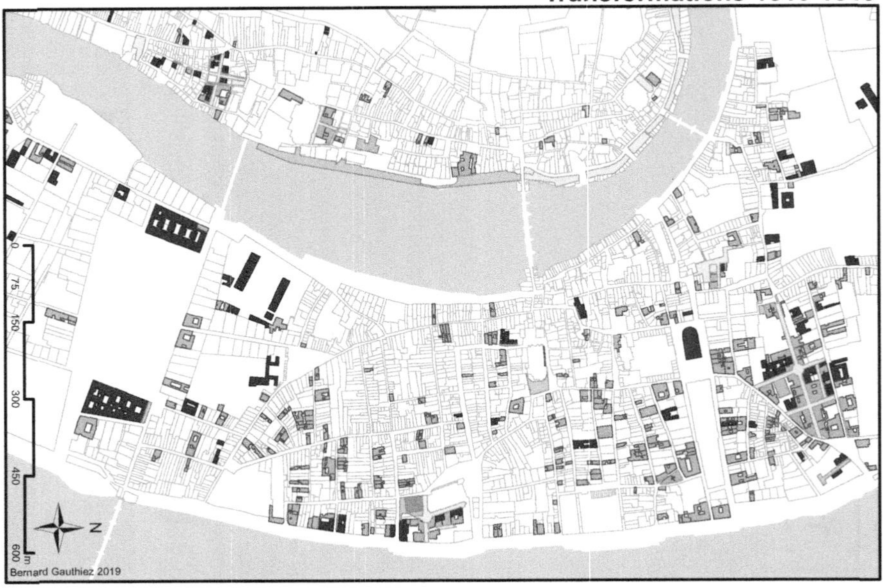

Transformations 1820-1829

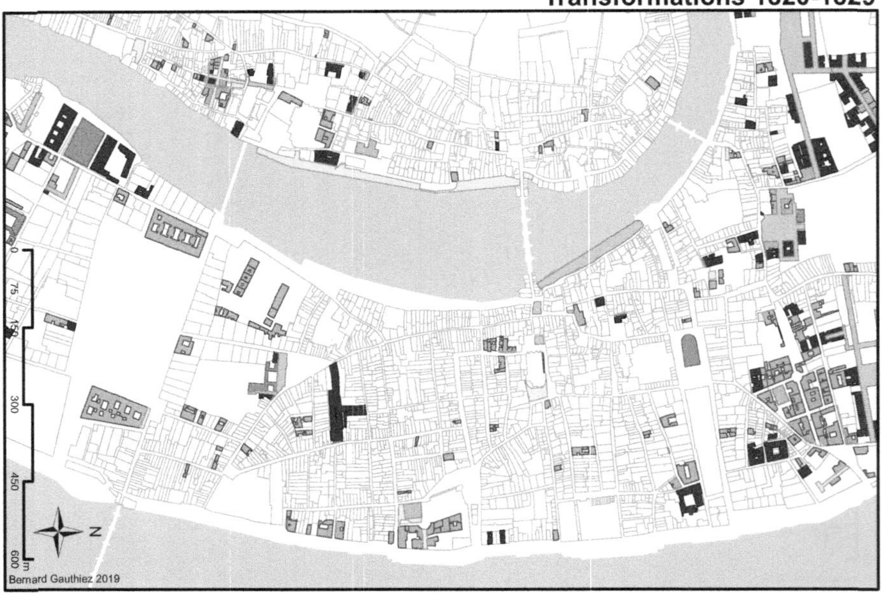

Transformations 1830-1839

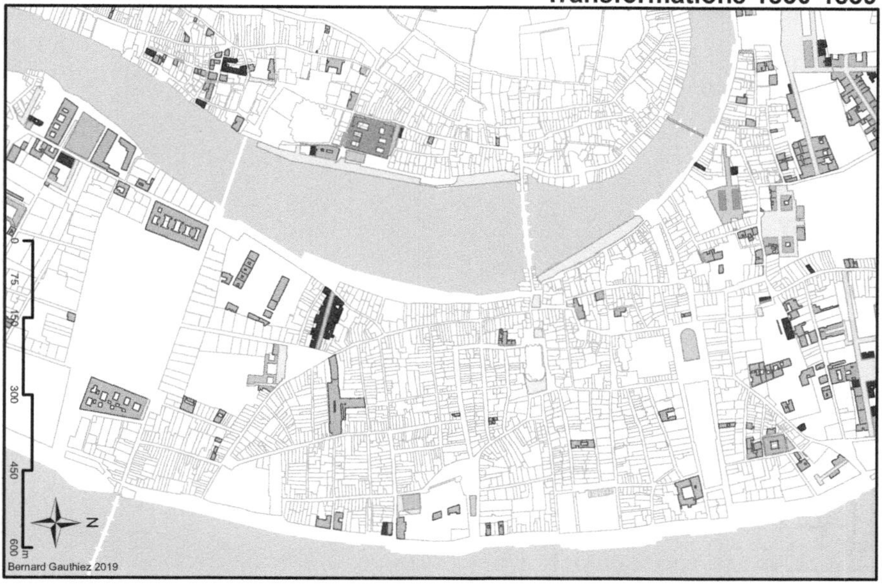

Transformations 1840-1849

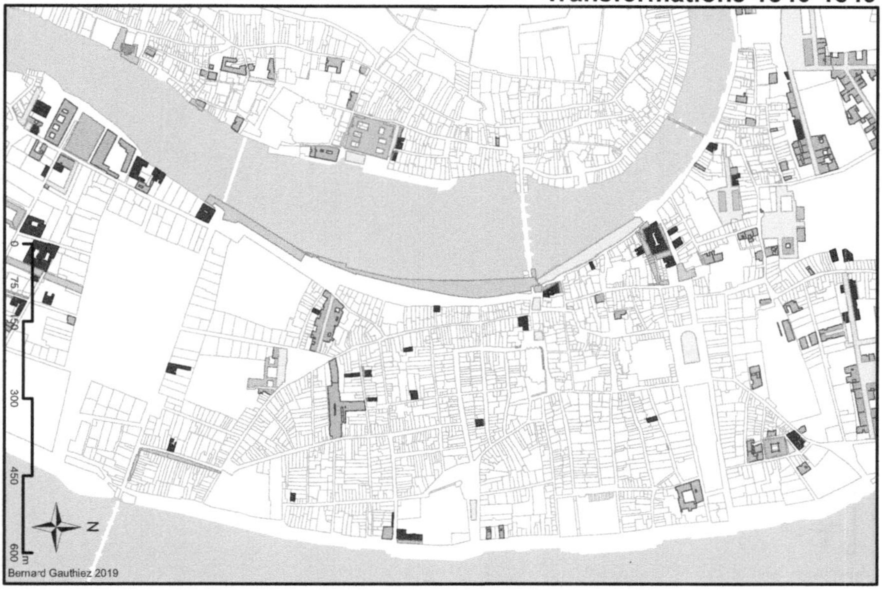

Transformations 1850-1859

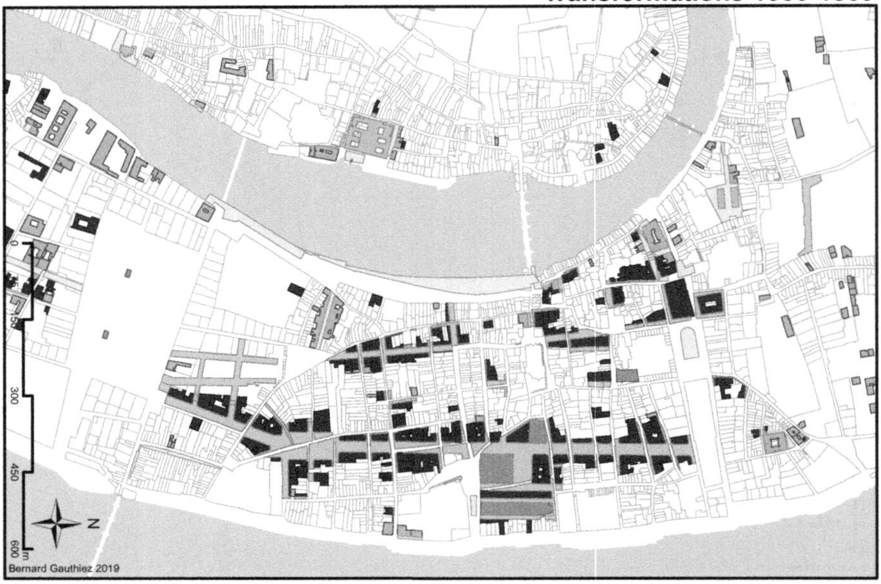

Transformations 1860-1869

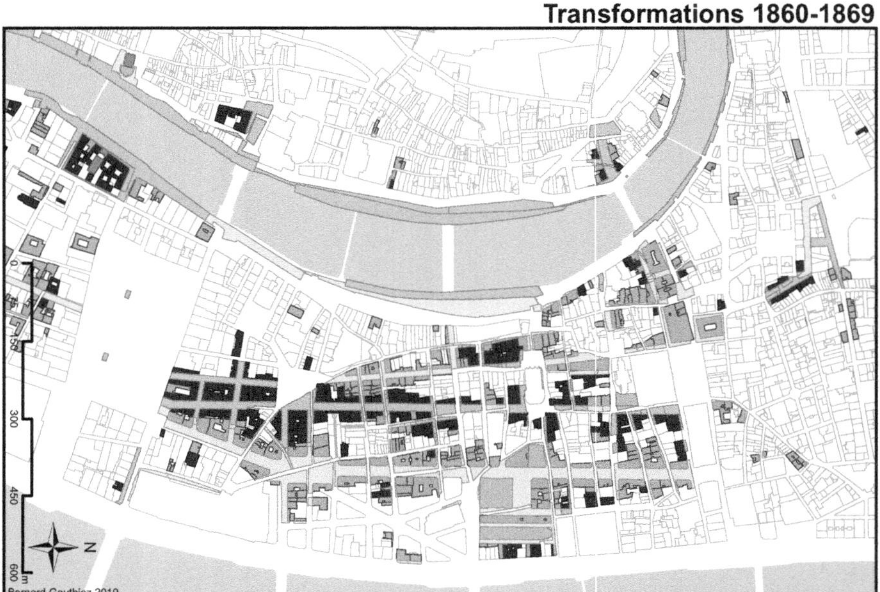

Transformations 1870-1879

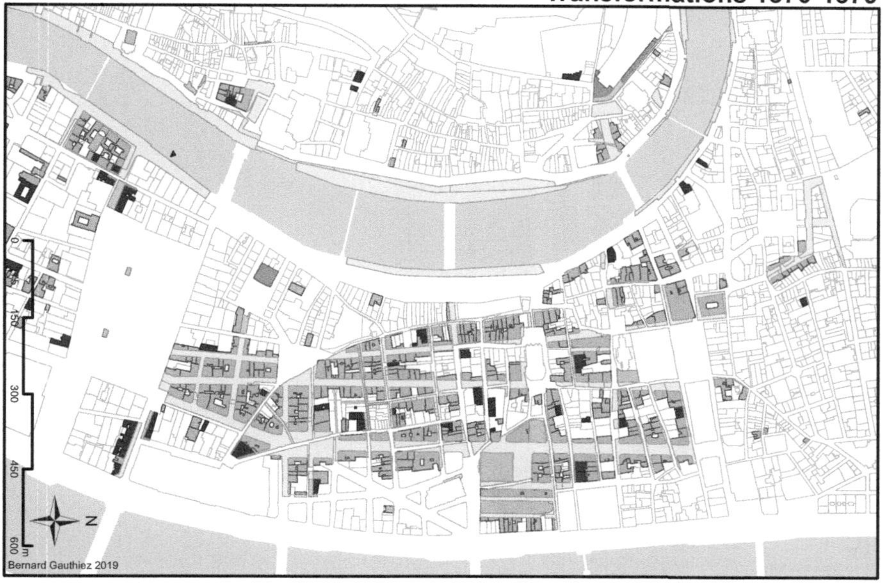

Transformations 1880-1889

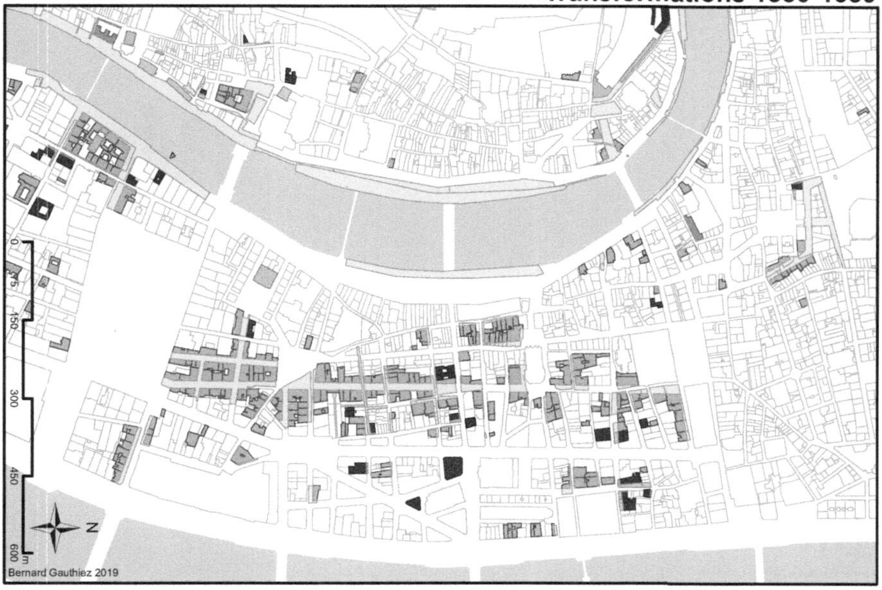

Transformations 1890-1899

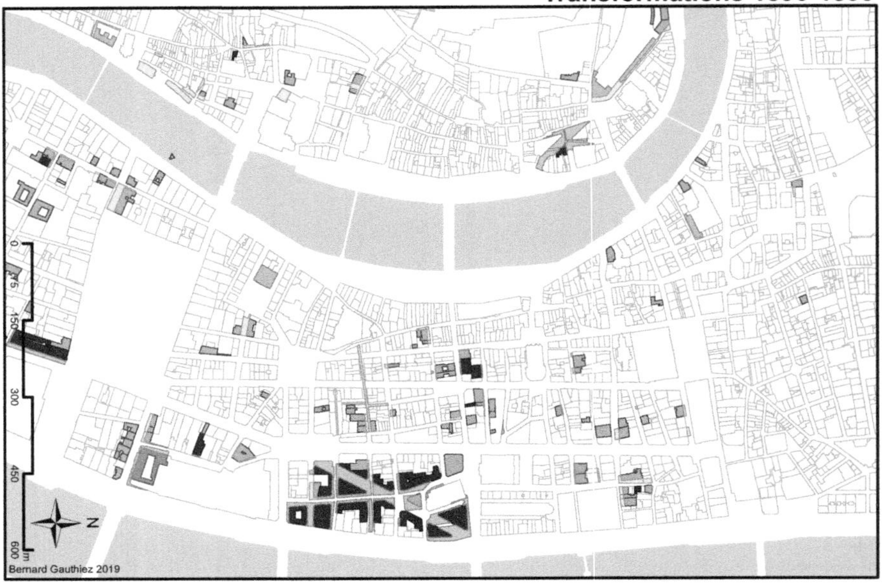

Transformations 1900-1909

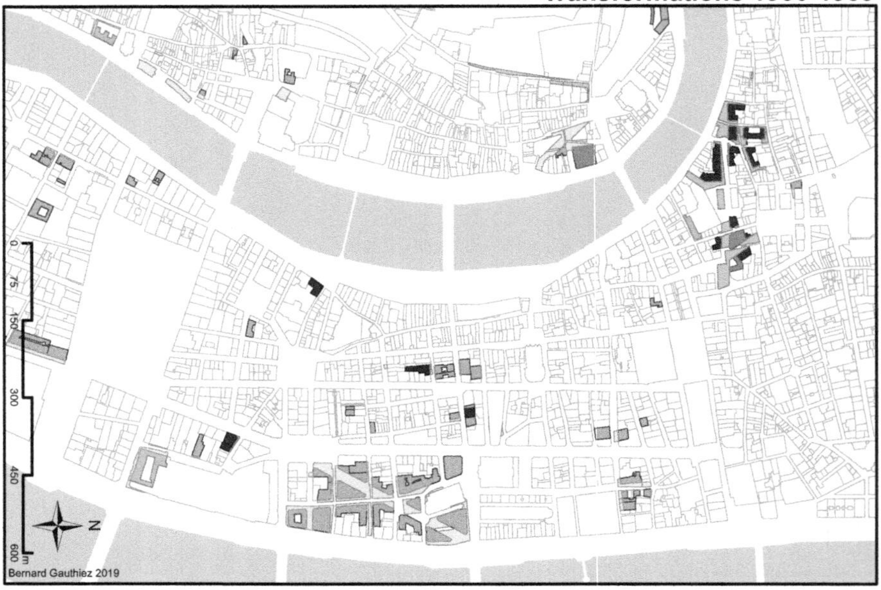

Abstract

This book explores the specific temporalities and spatialities of the production of urban space, using as a case study the French city of Lyons as it evolved from 1450 to 1900. It deals with its materiality (not with its mental representations or poetics). To achieve this aim, the first part presents the method of decomposition into production units, in particular, construction-units and planned developments. In the second part, building typology and its relation to demographic evolution are studied, while in the third part, the long-term evolution of building production and the logics that underpin it are examined from the end of the fifteenth century to the nineteenth century. The transformation of urban space is considered in its finest grain, the grain of construction-units, usually buildings, as well as in its finest temporal dimension, the year. This high level of resolution, achieved for the first time on a big city, makes it possible to understand the spatial, temporal and social logics of the processes in play. Mapping at this level is systematically carried-out using a GIS, and this in turn makes it possible to analyze the historical and social meanings of the geographical phenomena.

This study seeks a renewed understanding of the production of the urban fabric. This understanding is based on a close examination of the social processes which generate it. In this regard, the role of building trade professions emerges as very important. The temporalities of production have different scales, varying by a year or so for the production of a building, to several years for the reconstruction of groups of neighboring buildings, and up to several decades or even centuries for the logics of transformation or reconstruction of entire quarters of a city. Other temporalities concern the slow evolution of the relationship between the proprietors and their real estate over several centuries and the slow concentration of real estate capital between 1493 and 1789, a period when it reached extremes and became a major source of tension. These phenomena correspond to deep changes within society, notably the counter-intuitive relationship between demography and building production, and those that concern the distribution of wealth.

Lyons became a big city in the sixteenth century. Its study was made possible thanks to the existence of detailed archival records, which are used here for the first time to achieve the original goal of systematically mapping the entire city to the scale of a building. The scarcity of fiscal sources, which give precious and detailed information for some dates, is made up for by their spacing through time, thereby allowing for comparisons covering the entirety of the period studied. The rigorous preservation of building authorizations in archives from the early seventeenth century onwards makes it possible to obtain both the requisite

https://doi.org/10.1515/9783110623062-008

information at the level of the building or construction-unit, as well as precise dating, thus making it possible to establish a long-term series of transformations of the urban fabric which may be cross-checked and reinforced by using other sources of data.

List of Figures, Graphs and Tables

Tables

Table I.1 Number of buildings per period in the city center in 2019 (excluding public and religious constructions) —— **40**
Table I.2 Surfaces occupied in the same central sector, by period, and including religious and public buildings —— **44**
Table I.3 Average area of the construction-unit (bridges and car-parks excluded) —— **45**
Table I.4 The decomposition of lines —— **53**
Table II.1 Distribution of households in old and new 'e-houses' in 1493 —— **92**
Table II.2 Households in old and new 'e-houses' in 1493 —— **92**
Table II.3 E-houses and households in the west part of Lyons, to the west of the River Saône (*Côté royaume*), in 1406 and 1493 —— **93**
Table III.1 Time span between the beginning of a construction and the placing of a sign on the completed building —— **133**
Table III.2 The scales logics of urban space production / transformation —— **144**
Table III.3 Owners, dwellers in old houses, new ones, and those under construction, in 1493 —— **154**
Table III.4 New buildings per social group, 1617–1763 —— **166**
Table III.5 New buildings by members of the *Consulat* families —— **168**
Table III.6 Evolution of the number of proprietors from 1493 to 1808 —— **188**
Table III.7 Evolution of the proprietors dwelling in their own building, 1597–1709 —— **200**

Figures

Figure I.1 Dating of planned developments in the center of Lyons, present state (B. Gauthiez, 2019) —— **23**
Figure I.2A Dating of construction-units, center of Lyons, present state. A: dating by periods (B. Gauthiez, 2019) —— **30**
Figure I.2B Dating of construction-units, center of Lyons, present state. B: detail with explanation of the modifications (B. Gauthiez) —— **32**
Figure I.3 Place Meyssonnier and Rue Chenavard corner, a building made of many construction-units, originally medieval (B. Gauthiez, 2019) —— **34**
Figure I.4 Map of public space dating, center of Lyons (B. Gauthiez, 2017) —— **36**
Figure I.5 The street surfacing, rue Longue (B. Gauthiez, 2019) —— **39**
Figure II.1 Lyons circa 1745. A map from the Geographic Information System (B. Gauthiez) —— **72**
Figure II.2 Renaissance type buildings of the late fifteenth century and early sixteenth, Rue Juiverie (B. Gauthiez, 2019) —— **86**
Figure II.3 A building of the Renaissance type, early seventeenth century (B. Gauthiez, 2019) —— **87**

https://doi.org/10.1515/9783110623062-009

Figure II.4 Measured plan of the houses on the south side of Rue Noire, made before their demolition in c.1890 (©AML 2 S 0432) — **90**
Figure II.5 Example of the multi-familial building type which appeared in the 1620s (B. Gauthiez, 2019) — **105**
Figure II.6 Multi-familial building type as it developed in the eighteenth century (B. Gauthiez 2018) — **106**
Figure II.7 Remarkable examples of new buildings with new ideas for their layout in seventeenth and eighteenth centuries (B. Gauthiez) — **110**
Figure II.8 Building by Lenoir and Miège, silk ware merchants, 1830, Rue Griffon, forming a block with a square central courtyard (©AML, 1 S 265) — **113**
Figure II.9 Urban renewal Rue Grolée 1890, plan of new block K (©AML 2 S 0430) — **114**
Figure II.10 Transformations of the buildings in the block between Rue Mercière to the west, Rue Chalamont to the South and Rue des Trois-Carreaux to the east, identified on a measured plan made in 1852 before its redevelopment, an example of metamorphized urban fabric (B. Gauthiez) — **116**
Figure III.1 Example of mapping at the scale of the year: buildings of the year 1645 (B. Gauthiez) — **130**
Figure III.2 New constructions during the decade 1640–1649 (B. Gauthiez) — **136**
Figure III.3 4 images of the building activity at Lyons on the long duration, from the early seventeenth century to 1900 (B. Gauthiez) — **139–141**
Figure III.4 Map of the houses described as 'new' in 1493 (B. Gauthiez) — **157**
Figure III.5 Detailed map of the group of new constructions under way in 1493 Rue Grenette (B. Gauthiez) — **159**
Figure III.6 Map of Chanu's subdivision begun in 1493 or a little earlier (B. Gauthiez) — **162**
Figure III.7 Map of the new subdivisions in Lyons, sixteenth to eighteenth centuries (B. Gauthiez) — **167**
Figure III.8 Map of the situation of poor and rich in the silk-trade during the crisis in 1787–88: workshops of the poorest silk weavers fed by public help during the crisis and location of the societies of merchants-fabricants (B. Gauthiez) — **184**
Figure III.9 Map of the buildings planned to be demolished after the siege in 1793 to punish the rebellion of Lyons against the Convention government (B. Gauthiez) — **187**
Figure III.10 Map of the development of Rue Pierre-Blanc in 1820–25 (B. Gauthiez) Background: plan of the area bought by Anselmier in 1818 (c AML 3 S 0697). — **195**
Figure III.11 Map of Rue Buisson quarter in 1677, showing the living places of the proprietors of buildings: in their own one, in their own with tenants, or nearby, as indicated by arrows. The other owners lived further afield (B. Gauthiez) — **203**
Figure III.12 Property situation in 1853 of the buildings demolished for the northern part of the Rue Impériale redevelopment in 1854–55. The proprietors not shown on the map lived outside the represented area (B. Gauthiez) — **204**
Appendix 27 images of the film of building activity at Lyons from 1620 to 1830, one image per 10 years (B. Gauthiez) — **217–230**

Graphs

Graph III.1 Constructions per year from 1617 to 1828 —— **129**

Graph III.2 Monthly count of authorizations for new buildings in four decades of the seventeenth and eighteenth centuries —— **131**

Graph III.3 Annual building production between 1617 and 1827, with a triennial mobile average —— **135**

Graph III.4 Building in Lyons (1610–1830): decennial rhythms —— **138**

Graph III.5 Average annual ratio of new constructions compared to the number of extant buildings —— **146**

Graph III.6 Average area of the new buildings from 1610 to 1830, in square metres —— **147**

Graph III.7 Buildings surface total production per decade, in square metres —— **147**

Graph III.8 Parallel between the number of constructions per decade and their average size: opposite trends —— **148**

Graph III.9 Parallel between population curve and number of buildings per decade —— **149**

Graph III.10 Proportion of families having produced new construction(s), according to their level of wealth in 1677 (Th. Egger del., data B. Gauthiez) —— **169**

Graph III.11 Evolution of the number of proprietors from 1493 to 1808 —— **189**

References

Allain, Rémy. *Morphologie urbaine. Géographie, aménagement et architecture de la ville.* Paris: Armand Colin, 2004.

Arlaud, Catherine. Contribution à l'étude de l'habitat médiéval dans le quartier St-Jean à Lyon: analyse archéologique d'un immeuble n° 58 rue St-Jean. Lyons: Mémoire de maîtrise, Université Lumière Lyon 2, 1983 (unpublished paper).

Arlaud, Catherine (ed.). *Lyon, les dessous de la presqu'île.* Lyons: Ministère de la culture et de la Communication, 2000.

Arnaud, Jean-Luc. *Analyse spatiale, cartographie et histoire urbaine.* Marseilles: Parenthèses/ Maison Méditerranéenne des Sciences de l'Homme, 2008.

Bachelard, Gaston. *Le matérialisme rationnel.* Paris: Presses Universitaires de France, 1953.

Bachelard, Gaston. *La poétique de l'espace.* Paris: Presses Universitaires de France, 1957.

Baldini Lippolis, Isabella. Private space in Late Antique Cities: Laws and Building procedures. Luke Lavan, Lale Özgenel, Alexander Sarantis (eds.), *Housing in Late Antiquity, From Palaces to Shops.* Leiden, Boston: Brill, 2007, 197–237.

Ballet, Pascale, Dieudonné-Glad, Nadine, Saliou, Catherine (eds.). *La rue dans l'Antiquité, définition, aménagement, devenir.* Rennes: Presses universitaires de Rennes, 2008.

Barbey, Gilles, Brulhart, Armand, Germann, Georg, Gubler, Jacques. Genève. *INSA – Inventaire Suisse d'Architecture 1850–1920, 4. Delémont, Frauenfeld, Fribourg, Genève, Glarus.* Bern: Société d'histoire de l'art en Suisse, 1982.

Bardet, Jean-Pierre. *Rouen aux XVIIe et XVIIIe siècles, les mutations d'un espace social.* Paris: SEDES, 1983.

Barre, Josette. *La colline de la Croix-Rousse, histoire et géographie urbaine.* Lyons: Editions lyonnaises d'art et d'histoire, 1993.

Barthes, Roland. *Mythologies.* Paris: Seuil, 1957.

Barthes, Roland. *L'aventure sémiologique.* Paris: Seuil, 1985.

Bayard, Françoise. Villes et campagnes dans la fortune de Pierre Perrachon, noble lyonnais de 1642 à 1688.

Bayard, Françoise, Cayez, Pierre (eds.), *Villes et campagnes, XVe-XXe siècle.* Lyons: Presses Universitaires de Lyon, 1977, 105–131.

Bayard, Françoise. *Vivre à Lyon sous l'Ancien Régime.* Paris: Perrin, 1997.

Becker, Christine, Parron-Kontis, Isabelle, Savay-Guerraz, Sophie (eds.). *Le musée Gadagne, archéologie et histoire au cœur d'un projet patrimonial à Lyon.* Lyons: Association de liaison pour le patrimoine et l'archéologie en Rhône-Alpes et en Auvergne, 2006.

Benoist, Jocelyn. Rompre avec l'idéalisme historique: re-spatialiser nos concepts. Jocelyn Benoist, Fabio Merlini (eds.), *Historicité et spatialité. Le problème de l'espace dans la pensée contemporaine.* Paris: Vrin, 2001.

Benoist, Jocelyn. En quoi la géographie peut-elle importer à la philosophie? Jocelyn Benoist, Fabio Merlini (eds.), *Historicité et spatialité. Le problème de l'espace dans la pensée contemporaine.* Paris: Vrin, 2001, 97–116.

Bergeron, Louis, Roncayolo, Marcel. De la ville préindustrielle à la ville industrielle, essai sur l'historiographie française. *Quaderni Storici*, 27 (1974), 827–841.

Bernot, Emmanuel, Bertrand, Éric, Argant, Thierry, Carrara, Stéphane, Laidebeur, Jocelyn, Silvino Tony. Document final de synthèse de fouille archéologique, rue Monseigneur-

https://doi.org/10.1515/9783110623062-010

Lavarenne – avenue Adolphe-Max 69005 Lyon. Lyons: Service Archéologique de la Ville de Lyon/Service Régional de l'Archéologie, 2006 (unpublished paper).

Bertin, Dominique, Mathian, Nathalie. *Lyon, silhouettes d'une ville recomposée: architecture et urbanisme, 1789–1914*. Lyons: Éditions Lyonnaises d'Art et d'Histoire, 2008.

Bolle, Caroline, Coura, Geneviève, Léotard, Jean-Marc (eds.). *L'archéologie des bâtiments en question. Un outil pour les connaître, les conserver et les restaurer. The Archaeology of Buildings in Perspective. How to Better Understand, Preserve and Restore Buildings*. Namur: Service Public de Wallonie, 2014.

Bonnet Saint-Georges, Dominique. La galerie de la maison Bullioud. Jeanne-Marie Dureau (ed.). *Philibert de l'Orme, Lyonnais*. Lyons: Archives municipales de Lyon, 1993, 39–60.

Boudon, Françoise. Tissu urbain et architecture: l'analyse parcellaire comme base de l'histoire architecturale. *Annales. Économies, Sociétés, Civilisations*, 30/4 (1976), 773–818.

Boudon, Françoise, Chastel, André, Couzy, Hélène, Hamon, Françoise. *Système de l'architecture urbaine. Le quartier des halles à Paris*. Paris: Centre National de la Recherche Scientifique, 2 vols, 1977.

Bouton, Christophe, Huneman, Philippe (eds.), *Temps de la nature, nature du temps: études philosophiques sur le temps dans les sciences naturelles*. Paris: CNRS Editions, 2018 [*Nature of Time and the Time of nature. Philosophical Perspectives of Time in natural Sciences*, Cham: Springer International Publishing AG, 2015].

Brac, François P.S. Mémoire lu par M. Brac, avocat au parlement et aux cours de Lyon, ancien échevin de la même ville, dans l'assemblée de Messieurs les anciens échevins de la ville de Lyon, tenue le mercredi 30 août 1786 dans l'hôtel des exercices de la Flèche. Manuscript, La Perrière private archive, 1787.

Brogiolo, Gian Paolo, Gelichi, Sandro. *La città nell' alto medioevo italiano, archeologia e storia*. Rome-Bari: Laterza, 1998.

Cabestan, Jean-François. La naissance de l'immeuble d'appartements à Paris sous le règne de Louis XV. Daniel Rabreau (ed). *Paris, capitale des arts sous Louis XV*. Bordeaux: William Blake and co/Arts and Arts, 1997, 167–195.

Cabestan, Jean-François. *L'immeuble à Paris au XVIIIème siècle, la conquête du plain-pied*. Paris: Picard, 2004.

Cahill, Nicolas. *Household and City organization at Olynthus*. Yale: Yale University Press, 2002.

Callais, Chantal, Jeanmonod, Thierry. *Bordeaux patrimoine mondial. Tome 1. La fabrication de la ville*. La Crèche: Geste éditions, 2012.

Caniggia, Gian Franco. *Lecture de Florence*. Brussels: Institut Supérieur d'Architecture Saint-Luc, 1994.

Caniggia, Gian Franco, Maffei, Gian Luigi. *Lettura dell'edilizia di base, nuova edizione*. Florence: Alinea, 2008.

Charre, Alain, Servillat, Catherine. L'entreprise du quartier St-Clair. *L'œuvre de Soufflot à Lyon*. Lyons: Presses universitaires de Lyon, 1982.

Chauvard, Jean-François. *La circulation des biens à Venise, stratégies patrimoniales et marché immobilier (1600–1750)*. Rome: Ecole Française de Rome, 2005.

Chouquer, Gérard. Ce que le temps fait aux formes planimétriques: du péché originel de l'analyse de la morphologie agraire à sa réhabilitation. *Géocarrefour*, 84/4 (2009), 217–228.

Clarke, Jennifer. *The Barbican Sitting on History*. London: Corporation of London Records Office, 1990.

Claval, Paul. Géographie et temporalités. Philippe Boulanger, Jean-René Trochet (eds.). *Où en est la géographie historique? Entre économie et culture*. Paris: L'Harmattan, 2005, 43–62.

Clémençon, Anne-Sophie. La fabrication de la ville ordinaire. Pour comprendre les processus d'élaboration des formes urbaines, l'exemple du domaine des Hospices civils de Lyon. Lyon-Guillotière, Rive gauche du Rhône, 1781–1914. Lyons: Université Lumière, 1999 (unpublished PhD dissertation).

Clémençon, Anne-Sophie, Koyanagi, Shunichiro. Construire la ville en louant le sol. L'exemple français des Hospices civils de Lyon (de 1781 à 1914). *Dokkyo Law Review*, 2008 <halshs-01659311>.

Collart, Jean-Louis. Saint-Quentin. *Revue archéologique de Picardie* 16 (1999). Special issue: Archéologie des villes, démarches et exemples en Picardie, 67–128.

Concina, Ennio. *Venezia nell'età moderna: struttura e funzioni*. Venice: Marsilio, 1994.

Conzen, Michael Robert Günter. *Alnwick, Northumberland: a study in town-plan analysis*. London: George Philip, 1960.

Conzen, Michael Robert Günter. The use of town plans in the study of urban history. *The study of urban history*. Harold James Dyos (ed.). London: Edward Arnold, 1968, 113–130.

Cooper, Barry J. *Changing reflections on the history of geology*. London: Geological Society, Special Publications, 442, 9 Nov. 2016, 63–67, https://doi.org/10.1144/SP442.23.

Corboz, André. *Le territoire comme palimpseste et autres essais*. Geneva: Editions De l'imprimeur, 2001.

Corboz, André, Léveillé, Alain, Cassani, Yves, Mayor, Marie-Paule, Toumi-Overney, Isabelle, Hirschi, Paul. *Atlas du territoire genevois. Permanences et modifications cadastrales aux XIXe et XXe siècles*. Geneva: Georg, 1993–1999, 4 vols.

Culot, Maurice, Hennaut, Eric, Demanet, Maris, Mierop, Caroline. *Le bombardement de Bruxelles par Louis XIV et la reconstruction qui s'en suivit 1695–1700*. Brussels: Archives d'Architecture Moderne, 1992.

Cuvier, Georges. *Discours sur les révolutions de la surface du globe et sur les changements qu'elles ont produits dans le règne animal*. Paris: Dufour et d'Ocagne, 1825.

Daelemans, Frank. Les répercussions du bombardement de 1695 sur la population. Arlette Smolar-Meynart (ed.). *Autour du bombardement de Bruxelles de 1695, désastre et relèvement, Bulletin du Crédit Communal*, 199 (1997).

Dagognet, François. *Une épistémologie de l'espace concret, néo-géographie*. Paris: Vrin, 1977.

De Ochandiano, Jean-Luc. *Lyon, un chantier limousin. Les maçons migrants (1848–1940)*. Lyons: Lieux-Dits, 2008.

De Ricqlès, Armand. Le temps du biologiste. Christophe Bouton & Philippe Huneman (eds.). *Temps de la nature, nature du temps*. Paris: CNRS éditions, 2018, 291–311.

Desbat, Armand. Suppression ou élargissement de rues à Lugdunum au Ier siècle apr. J.-C. Pascale Ballet, Nadine Dieudonné-Glad, Catherine Saliou (eds.). *La rue dans l'Antiquité, définition, aménagement, devenir*. Rennes: Presses Universitaires de Rennes, 2008, 231–236.

Dickens, Charles. *Pictures from Italy*. London: Bradbury & Evans, 1846.

Dockès, Pierre. *Le capitalisme et ses rythmes, quatre siècles en perspective. Tome 1: Sous le regard des géants*. Paris: Garnier, 2017.

Dorsch, Sebastian. Introduction. Sebastian Dorsch, Susanne Rau (eds.). Space/time practice and the production of space and time. *Historical Social Research/Historische Sozialforschung*, special issue 38 (2013), 7–21.

Earle, Elias T. Property in prehistory. Michele Graziadei, Lionel Smith (eds.). *Comparative property laws global perspectives*. Cheltenham: Edward Elgar Publishing, 2017.

Eclache, Michèle. *Demeures toulousaines du XVIIe siècle: sources d'archives (1600–1630 environ)*. Toulouse: Éditions du Centre National de la Recherche Scientifique/Université de Toulouse Le Mirail, 2006.

Ellenberger, François. *Histoire de la géologie, 2 vols, Technique et documentation*. Paris: Lavoisier, 1994.

Fanelli, Giovanni. *Firenze*. Laterza: Rome-Bari, 1980.

Faron, Olivier, Hubert, Etienne (eds.). *Le sol et l'immeuble, les formes dissociées de propriété immobilière dans les villes de France et d'Italie (XIIe-XIXe siècle)*. Rome: Ecole Française de Rome, 1995.

Ferrand, Nicolas. Approche morphologique de l'urbanisation: Lyon et son agglomération de 1945 à 2005: données, outils et méthodes. Lyons, Université Lyon 3 Jean-Moulin, 2010 (unpublished PhD dissertation).

Fisher-Drew, Katherine. *The Burgundian code: book of constitutions or law of Gundobad*. Philadelphia: University of Pennsylvania Press, 1972.

Florman, Samuel C. *The existential pleasures of engineering*. London: Souvenir Press, 1994 [1976].

Fornara, Livio. Genève. Jean Guillaume (ed.). *La maison de ville à la Renaissance. Actes du Colloque de Tours (1977)*. Paris: Picard, 1983, 43–44.

Fredet, Jacques. *Les maisons de Paris*. Paris: Editions de l'encyclopédie des nuisances, 2003, 3 vols.

Fregna, Roberto. *La pietrificazione del denaro, studi sulla proprietà urbana tra XVI-XVII secolo*. Bologna: CLUEB, 1990.

Frobert, Ludovic (ed.). *L'écho de la fabrique, naissance de la presse ouvrière à Lyon*. Lyons: Ecole Normale Supérieure Editions, 2010.

Gacon, Richard, *Grand commerce et vie urbaine au XVIe siècle*. Paris, Mouton, La Haye: SEVPEN, 1971.

Galinié, Henri. *Ville, espace urbain et archéologie*. Tours: Presses Universitaires François-Rabelais, 2000.

Garden, Maurice. *Lyon et les Lyonnais au XVIIIe siècle*. Paris: Les Belles Lettres, 1970.

Gauthiez, Bernard. La logique de l'espace urbain: formation et évolution. Paris: Ecole des Hautes Etudes en Sciences Sociales, 1991, 2 vols (Unpublished PhD Dissertation).

Gauthiez, Bernard. Les maisons de Rouen, XII-XVIIIe siècles. *Archéologie médiévale*, 23 (1993): 131–217.

Gauthiez, Bernard. La topographie de Lyon au XVIe siècle. Jeanne-Marie Dureau (ed.), *Lyon, les années Rabelais (1532–1548)*. Lyons: Archives Municipales de Lyon, 1994, 23–32.

Gauthiez, Bernard. Trasformazione dei valori urbani tra settecento e ottocento: il caso di Lione. *Storia urbana* 71 (1995): 149–170.

Gauthiez, Bernard. Le rôle du contrôle de l'espace public et l'urbanisme au XIIIe siècle en France. Guy De Boe, Franz Verhaeghe (eds), *Urbanism in Medieval Europe*, 'Medieval Europe Brugge 1997' conference papers vol. 1, Zellik: Instituut voor het Archeologisch Patrimonium, 1997, 193–198.

Gauthiez, Bernard. *Entre Terreaux et Bellecour, architecture et urbanisme à Lyon au XIXe siècle.* Lyons: Editions lyonnaises d'art et d'histoire, 1999.

Gauthiez, Bernard. Les immeubles numéros 15, 17, 19, 21 et 23 de la rue Gasparin à Lyon, un exemple urbain de production complexe du bâti. *In Situ:* 2 (2002), 10, https://journals.openedition.org/insitu/1181.

Gauthiez, Bernard. *Espace urbain. Vocabulaire et morphologie.* Paris: Editions du patrimoine/Monum', 2003.

Gauthiez, Bernard. Verneuil-sur-Avre, Falaise, Pont-Audemer et Lisieux en Normandie. Bernard Gauthiez, Elisabeth Zadora-Rio, Henri Galinié (eds.). *Village et ville au Moyen-Âge: les dynamiques morphologiques.* Tours: Presses de l'Université François-Rabelais, 2003, 35–95: 64–65.

Gauthiez, Bernard. The history of urban morphology. *Urban morphology, Journal of the international seminar on urban form*, 8/2 (2004), 71–89.

Gauthiez, Bernard. Des unités pertinentes pour mesurer la ville concrète. *Histoire et mesure*, XIX-3/4 (2004): 295–316.

Gauthiez, Bernard. Un inventaire, des inventaires. *Secteurs sauvegardés, ZPPAUP et PLU patrimoniaux, actes du séminaire de Chinon.* Paris: Association nationale des villes et pays d'art et d'histoire et des villes à secteur sauvegardé et protégés/Ministère de la Culture et de la Communication, 2007, 121–128.

Gauthiez, Bernard. Lyon en 1824–32: un plan de la ville sous forme vecteur d'après le cadastre ancien. *Géocarrefour*, 83/1 (2008): 57–67.

Gauthiez, Bernard. Les plans de Lyon de 1544–1555: la cartographie des villes au XVIe siècle à repenser? *Le Monde des cartes*, 205 (2010): 119–132.

Gauthiez, Bernard. La transformation de Lyon et Paris au Second Empire: le projet du ministre de l'Intérieur De Persigny, les exécutants Haussmann et Vaïsse. Aldo Casamento (ed.). *Città nuove fondate in Italia e in Europa dal medioevo al Novecento.* Rome: Kappa, 2012: 323–344.

Gauthiez, Bernard. Les logiques multiples de la production de l'espace d'un quartier: l'exemple de la place Navone à Rome, 1450–1870. Jean-François Bernard (ed.). *Du stade de Domitien à la place Navone, histoire d'un quartier de Rome.* Rome: Ecole Française de Rome, 2014, 325–383.

Gauthiez, Bernard. Les fenêtres à Lyon, espace urbain et anthropologie, 1650–1900. Aldo Casamento (ed.). *Il Cantiere della Città.* Rome: Kappa, 2014, 221–248.

Gauthiez, Bernard. Typologie architecturale et démographie. L'habitat collectif à Lyon à l'époque moderne, 1500–1800. Mathieu Grenet, Yannick Jambon, Marie-Laure Ville (eds.). *Histoire urbaine et sciences sociales. Mélanges en l'honneur du professeur Olivier Zeller.* Paris: Garnier, 2014: 19–48.

Gauthiez, Bernard. La rénovation urbaine au centre de Lyon au XIXe siècle, une histoire en trois phases. Jacques Comby (ed.). *Peurs dans la ville, urbanisme et sécurité dans l'agglomération lyonnaise XIXe-XXIe siècle.* Rennes: Presses universitaires de Rennes, 2015, 23–69; fig. 11.

Gauthiez, Bernard. Pourquoi les remplois visibles dans l'architecture civile à Lyon aux XVIII-XIXe siècles. Entre architecture savante et identité locale. Dany Sandron (ed.). *Le passé dans la ville.* Paris: Presses universitaire de Paris-Sorbonne, 2016, 145–168.

Gauthiez, Bernard. La transformation des villes au bas Moyen Âge entre Valence et Pise. *Rodis, journal of medieval and post-medieval archaeology*, 1 (2019), 23–49.

Gauthiez, Bernard, Zeller, Olivier. Lyon aux XVII-XVIIIe siècles, la fabrique de la ville. Emilie Bajolet, Marie-Flore Mattei, Jean-Marc Rennes (eds.). *Quatre ans de recherche urbaine, 2001–2004.* Tours: Presses Universitaires François-Rabelais/Maison des sciences de l'homme "Villes et territoires", 2006, 464–466.

Gauthiez, Bernard, Zeller, Olivier. Un SIG historique sur l'espace urbain de Lyon aux XVII-XIXe siècles. Marco Panzeri, Andrea Farruggia (eds.). *Fonti, metafonti e GIS per l'indagine della struttura storica del territorio: verso il networking.* Turin: Politecnico di Torino, 2009, 39–49; 114–117.

Gauthiez, Bernard, Zeller, Olivier. Ordre textuel et ordre spatial à Lyon à l'époque moderne. Du parcours de visite au rôle nominal, une spatialité implicite. *Histoire et Mesure.* XXV-1 (2010): 197–230.

Gauthiez, Bernard, Zeller, Olivier. Lyons, the spatial analysis of a city in the seventeenth and eighteenth centuries. Locating and crossing data in a GIS built from written sources. Ekkehard Schönherr, Susanne Rau (eds.), *Mapping spatial relations, their perceptions and dynamics. The city of today and in the past.* Cham, Heidelberg, New York, Dordrecht, London: Springer Verlag, 2013, 97–118.

Gauthiez, Bernard, Zeller, Olivier. Beautifying the city and improving the streets with building permits: Lyons, 1580–1770. Terry S. Slater, Sandra M. G. Pinto (eds.). *Building regulations and urban form, 1200–1900.* London, New York: Routledge, 2018, 177–200.

Grataloup, Christian. Géographie historique et analyse spatiale: de l'ignorance à la fertilisation croisée. Philippe Boulanger, Jean-René Trochet (eds.). *Où en est la géographie historique? Entre économie et culture.* Paris: L'Harmattan, 2005.

Gregory, Ian N. *A place in history: a guide to using GIS in historical research.* Oxford and Oakville: Oxbow books, 2003.

Gregory, Ian N., Ell, Paul S. *Historical GIS: techniques, methodologies and scholarship.* Cambridge: University Press Cambridge, 2007.

Gutton, Jean-Pierre (ed.). *Les Lyonnais dans l'histoire.* Toulouse: Privat, 1985.

Gutton, Jean-Pierre. Le peuple a-t-il droit à la chaleur? Le cas de Lyon au XVIIIe siècle. Philippe Guignet (ed.). *Le peuple des villes dans l'Europe du Nord-Ouest (fin du Moyen Âge-1945).* Lille: Centre de Recherches sur l'Histoire de l'Europe du Nord, 2002, t. I, 313–322.

Halbwachs, Maurice. *La population et les tracés de voies à Paris.* Paris: Alcan, 1928.

Halbwachs, Maurice. *Morphologie sociale.* Paris: Librairie Armand Colin, 1938.

Hall, Edward T. *The hidden dimension. New York:* Garden City, 1966.

Hanson, Neil. *The Great Fire of London: In That Apocalyptic Year, 1666.* Hoboken: John Wiley and Sons, 2002.

Harris, Edward C. *Principles of Archaeological Stratigraphy.* London, New York: Academic Press, 1979&1989.

Heeling, Jan, Meyer, Han, Westrik, John, Sauren, Eugène, Hoekstra, Maarten Jan. *Het ontwerp van de stadsplattegrond [The project of urban planning].* Amsterdam: SUN, 2002.

Heinz, Marlies. *Der Stadtplan als Spiegel der Gesellschaft, Siedlungsstrukturen in Mesopotamien als Indikator für Formen wirtschaftlicher und gesellschaftlicher Organisation.* Berlin: Dietrich Reimer Verlag, 1997.

Henri Hours, Michel Nicolas. *Jean-Antoine Morand, architecte lyonnais 1727–1794.* Lyons: Archives Municipales de Lyon, 1985.

Homo, Léon. *Rome impériale et l'urbanisme dans l'Antiquité.* Paris: Albin Michel, 1951.

Hodder, Ian. *Çatalhöyük the leopard's tale, revealing the secrets of Turkey's ancient 'town'*. London: Thames and Hudson, 2006.

Huneman, Philippe. Macroévolution et microévolution. Les problèmes d'échelles de temps dans la biologie évolutive. Christophe Bouton, Philippe Huneman (dir.). *Temps de la nature, nature du temps*. Paris: CNRS éditions, 2018, 343 – 370.

Indicateur alphabétique des curiosités, établissements réguliers et séculiers; des personnes de qualité, officiers et judicature, police et finances; notables, bourgeois, négociants, gens d'affaires et principaux artistes de la ville de Lyon, avec les noms des rues et des maisons de leurs demeures. Lyons: Faucheux, 1788.

Jaucourt, Denis, Diderot, Denis (eds.). *Encyclopédie ou dictionnaire raisonné des sciences, des arts et des métiers*. Neufchâtel: 1751 – 1772, vol. 17.

Johnson, Matthew. Living space. The interpretation of English vernacular Houses. Paul Stock (ed.). *The uses of space in early modern history*. New York: Palgrave-Macmillan, 2015, 19 – 42.

Johnson, Jim, Rosenburg, Lou. *Renewing Old Edinburgh. The Enduring Legacy of Patrick Geddes*. Argyll: Argyll Publishing, 2010.

Kent, Susan. Activity areas and architecture: an interdisciplinary view of the relationship between use of space and domestic built environments. Susan Kent (ed.). *Domestic architecture and the use of space, an interdisciplinary cross-cultural study*. Cambridge: Cambridge University Press, 1990, 1 – 8.

Keyser, E. Der Stadtgrundriss als Geschichtsquelle. *Studium Generale*, 6 (1963), 345 – 361.

King, Leonard William. *The code of Hammurabi*. Paolo J.S. Pereira (ed.), 1915. www.general-intelligence.com/library/hr.pdf.

Kretzschmar, Johannes. Der Stadtplan als Geschichtsquelle. *Deutsche Geschichtsblätter*, 9 (1908), 133 – 141.

Landauer, Paul. *L'invention du grand ensemble. La Caisse des dépôts maître d'ouvrage*. Paris: Picard, 2010.

Larkham, Peter J., Jones, Andrew. *A glossary of urban form*. London: Historical Geography research Series 26, Institute of British Geographers, 1991.

Lavigne, Maryannick. Lyon, le quartier Saint-Jean. Jean Guillaume (ed.). *La maison de ville à la Renaissance. Actes du Colloque de Tours (1977)*. Paris: Picard, 1983, 37 – 41.

Lefebvre, Henri. *La production de l'espace*. Paris: Anthropos, 1974.

Levasseur, Aurelie. *Définir la rue publique du bas Moyen Âge, contribution à l'histoire du droit administratif des biens*. Dijon: Presses universitaires de Franche-Comté, 2017.

Loyer, François. *Paris XIXe siècle. L'immeuble et la rue*. Paris: Hazan, 1987.

Lussault, Michel, Levy, Jacques (eds.). *Dictionnaire de la géographie et de l'espace des sociétés*. Paris: Belin, 2003.

Lynch, Kevin. *The image of the city*. Cambridge: the Technology Press & Harvard University, 1960.

MacGuire, Randal M., Schiffer, Michael Brian. A theory of architectural design. *Journal of anthropological archaeology* 2/3 (1983), 277 – 303.

Maffei, GianLuigi. *Firenze, la casa fiorentina nella storia della città*. Padova: Marsilio, 1990.

Mallet, Françoise. L'âge des voies du centre de Marseille. *Bulletin de l'association des géographes*, 395/396 (1972), 33.

Mandelbrot, Benoit B., Fisher, Adlai J., Calvet, Laurent E. *A Multifractal Model of Asset Returns. Cowles Foundation Discussion Paper*, SSRN, n° 1164, 15 Sept. 1997.

Mantziaras, Panos. Rudolf Schwartz et l'aménagement du territoire. Jocelyn Benoist, Fabio Merlini (eds.), *Historicité et spatialité. Le problème de l'espace dans la pensée contemporaine.* Paris: Vrin, 2001.

Marconi, Paolo. *Materia e significato, la questione del restauro architettonico.* Rome-Bari: Laterza, 1999.

Marcuzzi, Max. L'écriture de l'espace dans la Géographie physique de Kant. Jocelyn Benoist, Fabio Merlini (eds.), *Historicité et spatialité. Le problème de l'espace dans la pensée contemporaine.* Paris: Vrin, 2001, 117–139.

Maretto, Paolo. *La casa veneziana nella storia della città.* Venice: Marsilio, 1986.

Mathian, Nathalie, Martinuzzi, Francis. Lyon, histoire architecturale et urbaine de la rive droite de la Saône. Lyons: Ecole d'Architecture/Agence d'urbanisme pour le développement de l'agglomération lyonnaise, 1999 (unpublished paper).

Melot, Michel, Verdier, Hélène (eds.). *Principes, méthode et conduite de l'inventaire général.* Paris: Ministère de la Culture et de la Communication, 2001.

Monfalcon, Jean-Baptiste. *Histoire des insurrections de Lyon en 1831 and 1834.* Lyons: Louis Perrin, 1834.

Monnier, François. La notion d'expropriation au XVIIIe siècle d'après l'exemple de Paris. *Journal des savants*, 3/1 (1984), 223–258.

Monroziès-Blanchard, Aurélie. Le cadastre toulousain de 1680: étude historique et statistique. *Annales du Midi: revue archéologique, historique et philologique de la France méridionale*, 115/244 (2003), 515–534.

Nières, Claude. L'Incendie et la reconstruction de Rennes. Jean Meyer (ed.). *Histoire de Rennes.* Toulouse: Privat, 1972.

Packer, James E. *The insulae of imperial Ostia.* Rome: Memoirs of the American Academy in *Rome*, 1971, vol. XXXI.

Paradin de Cuyseaulx, Guillaume. *Mémoires de l'histoire de Lyon.* Lyons: Antoine Gryphius, 1571.

Parent, Paul. *L'architecture civile à Lille au XVIIe siècle.* Lille: Emile-Raoust, 1925.

Parker, Geoffrey. *Global crisis. War, climate change and catastrophe in the seventeenth century.* New Haven, London: Yale University Press, 2017.

Pavolini, Carlo. *Ostia, guida archeologica.* Rome-Bari: Laterza, 1989.

Pereira, S. G. *A réforma urbana de Pereira Passos e a construçao da idendidade carioca.* Rio de Janeiro: Universidade Federal de Rio de Janeiro, 1998.

Perroux, Olivier. *Tradition, vocation et progrès: les élites bourgeoises de Genève (1814–1914).* Geneva: Université de Genève, 2003, https://archive-ouverte.unige.ch/unige:200.

Pinon, Pierre. L'archéologie des lotissements: quelques exemples parisiens. *Paris, formes urbaines et architectures.* Paris: Editions Recherche/IPRAUS, 1998, 15–28.

Poëte, Marcel. L'évolution du plan des villes. *Bulletin du Comité international des sciences historiques*, 20 (1933), 526–537.

Pointet, Joseph. *Histoire des propriétés et maisons de la Croix-Rousse du XIVe siècle à la Révolution.* Lyons: Imprimerie des missions africaines, 4 vols, 1926–1930.

Quatremère de Quincy, Antoine. *Dictionnaire historique d'architecture.* Vol. 2. Paris: Adrien Le Clere et Cie, 1832.

Quenedey, Raimond. *L'habitation rouennaise, étude d'histoire, de géographie et d'archéologie urbaines.* Rouen: A. Lestringant, 1926.

Rabreau, Daniel (ed.). *Paris, capitale des arts sous Louis XV.* Bordeaux: William Blake and co/Arts and Arts, 1997.
Rapoport, Amos. Systems of activities and systems of settings. Susan Kent (ed.). *Domestic architecture and the use of space, an interdisciplinary cross-cultural study.* Cambridge: Cambridge University Press, 1990, 9–20.
Rau, Susanne. Die Vielfalt des Räumlichen – Stand und Perspektiven der frühneuzeitlichen Raumforschung. *Frühneuzeit-Info*, 28 (2017), 75–86.
Rau, Susanne. The urbanization of the periphery: a spatio-temporal history of Lyon since the eighteenth century. Sebastian Dorsch, Susanne Rau (eds.). Space/time practice and the production of space and time. *Historical Social Research/Historische Sozialforschung*, special issue 38 (2013), 150–175.
Rau, Susanne. *Räume der Stadt. Eine Geschichte Lyons 1300–1800.* Frankfurt/Main: Campus Verlag, 2014.
Rau, Susanne. Guillaume-Marie Delorme. Projet pour la jonction de l'isle Mogniat à la ville de Lyon (1738). Erfurt: Universität Erfurt, 2015, https://www.academia.edu/19542808/.
Rau, Susanne. *History, space and place.* London/New York: Routledge, 2019.
Reynard, Pierre Claude. *Ambitions tamed. Urban expansion in Pre-Revolutionnary Lyon.* Montreal: McGill-Queen's University Press, 2009.
Rivet, Felix. *Le quartier Perrache (1766–1946).* Lyons: Audin, 1951.
Rivet, Felix. *Le quartier Grôlée, Une réalisation d'urbanisme à Lyon.* Lyons: Institut des Études rhodaniennes de l'Université de Lyon, 1955.
Rodriguez-Almeida, Emilio. *Formae Urbis antiquae. Le mappe marmoree di Roma tra la Repubblica e Settimo Severo.* Rome: Ecole française de Rome, 2002.
Roncayolo, Marcel. La morphologie entre la matière et le social, interview by Guy Burgel and Philippe Genestier. *Villes en parallèle*, 12/13 (1988), 42–59.
Roncayolo, Marcel. *La ville et ses territoires.* Paris: Gallimard, 1997.
Rossiaud, Jacques. Du réel à l'imaginaire: la représentation de l'espace urbain dans le plan de Lyon au XVIe siècle. Jeanne-Marie Dureau (ed.). *Le plan de Lyon vers 1550.* Lyons: Archives Municipales de Lyon, 1990, 29–46.
Rowthorn, Robert, Seabright, Paul. Property rights, warfare and the Neolithic transition. *TSE Working paper series*, 2010, 10–207.
Saliou, Catherine. Les lois du bâtiment. *Voisinage et habitat urbain dans l'Empire romain. Recherches sur les rapports entre le droit et la construction privée du siècle d'Auguste au siècle de Justinien.* Beyrouth: Presses de l'Institut Français du Proche Orient, 1994.
Saliou, Catherine. *Le traité d'urbanisme de Julien d'Ascalon. Droit et architecture en Palestine au VIe siècle.* Paris: De Boccard, 1996.
Schätti, Nicolas, Viaccoz De Noyers, Anne-Marie. L'Atlas historique de la ville de Genève, vieilles méthodes, nouveaux outils. *Patrimoine et architecture*, 14–15 (2005): 58–64.
Schlögel, Karl. *Im Raume lesen wir die Zeit. Über Zivilisationsgeschichte und Geopolitik.* Munich, Vienna: Carl Hanser, 2003.
Schoffield, John. *The building of London from the Conquest to the Great Fire.* London: British Museum Press, 1993.
Schoonbaert, Sylvain. *La voirie bordelaise au XIXe siècle.* Paris: Presses de l'Université Paris-Sorbonne, 2007.
Schwartz, Rudolf. *Von der Bebauung der Erde.* Heidelberg: Lambert Schneider, 1949.

Scott, S. P. *The Visigotic code (Forum judicum)*. Boston: The Boston Book Company, 1910. http://www.documentacatholicaomnia.eu/03d/0506-0506,_AA_VV,_Leges_Romanae_Visigotorum_[Scott_JP_Curatore],_EN.pdf.

Seneclauze, Claire. Inventaire des escaliers à vis du quartier Saint-Jean à Lyon. Lyons: Université Lumière Lyon 2 (Mémoire de maîtrise), 1975 [unpublished paper, abstract in *Travaux de l'Institut d'Histoire de l'Art de Lyon*, 4 (1978)].

Simms, Anngret, *Clarke, Howard B.*, Gillespie, Raymond (eds.). *Irish Historic Towns Atlas, vol. II: Maynooth, Downpatrick, Bray, Kilkenny, Fethard, Trim*. Dublin: Royal Irish Academy, 2005.

Slater, Terry R., Pinto, Sandra M. G. Building regulations and urban form. Terry R. Slater, Sandra M. G. Pinto (eds.), *Building regulations and urban form, 1200–1900*. London/New York: Routledge, 2018, 1–21.

Sodezza, Guillaume. Héritage et patrimoine dans l'aménagement de la vallée du Giers, vers la définition d'une nouvelle politique patrimoniale pour l'espace stéphanois. Lyons: Université Lyon 3 Jean Moulin, 2014 (unpublished PhD thesis).

Soja, Edward W. *Postmodern geographies. The reassertion of space in critical social theory*. London/New York: Verso, 1989.

Sumitaka, Harada. Notion de propriété. Traits caractéristiques du droit japonais. *Revue internationale de droit comparé*, 51 (1999), 449–452.

Tegmark, Mark. *Notre univers mathématique, en quête de la nature ultime du réel*. Paris: Dunod, 2014 [*Our mathematical universe: my quest for the ultimate nature of reality*. New York: Alfred A. Knopf/Random House, 2014].

Testart, Alain. *Avant l'histoire, l'évolution des sociétés, de Lascaux à Carnac*. Paris: Gallimard, 2012.

Thieury, Jules. *Projets de M. le maréchal de Vauban pour fortifier la ville de Dieppe (1694–1699)*. Chez A. Marais, 1864.

Toulier, Christine. *Richelieu, le château & la cité idéale*. Châteauroux: Berger M. Editions, 2005.

Uhlig, Harald. *Die Kulturlandschaft Nordostengland*. Cologne: Geographisches Institut der Universität, 1956 [Kölner geographische Arbeiten n° 9–10].

Verhaeghe, Franz. L'espace civil et la ville. Pierre Demolon, Henri Galinié, Franz Verhaeghe (eds.). *Archéologie des villes dans le Nord-Ouest de l'Europe (VIIe-XIIIe siècle)*. Douai: Société archéologique de Douai, 1994, 145–190.

Venturi, Robert, Scott-Brown, Denise, Izenour, Steven. *Learning from Las Vegas*. Cambridge: Massachusetts Institute of Technology Press, 1977.

Weber, Max. *Wirtschaft und Gesellschaft. Grundriss der verstehenden Soziologie*. Tübingen: Mohr, 1972 [1922].

Wehdorn, Manfred (ed.). *Baualtersplan Wien – innere Stadt*. Vienna: Freytag & Berndt, 2011.

Wilk, Richard R. The built environment and consumer decisions. Susan Kent (ed.). *Domestic architecture and the use of space, an interdisciplinary cross-cultural study*. Cambridge: The Cambridge University Press, 1990, 34–42.

Whitehand, Jeremy W. R. Background to the urban morphogenetic tradition. Jeremy W. R. Whitehand (ed.). *The urban landscape: historical development and management. Papers by M.R.G. Conzen*. London: Academic Press, 1981, 1–24.

Whitehand, Jeremy W. R. Recent developments in urban morphology. Dietrich Denecke, Gareth Shaw (eds.). *Urban historical geography, recent progress in Britain and Germany.* Cambridge: Cambridge University Press, 1988, 285–40.

Zeller, Olivier. *Les recensements lyonnais de 1597 et 1636: démographie historique et géographie Sociale.* Lyons: Presses Universitaires de Lyon, 1983.

Zeller, Olivier. Un mode d'habiter à Lyon au XVIIIe siècle: la pratique de la location principale. *Revue d'histoire contemporaine*, 35–1 (1988): 36–60.

Zeller, Olivier. Géographie des troubles et découpage urbain à Lyon (XVIème-XVIIIème siècles). *114ème congrès des sociétés savantes, Paris 1989. Les espaces révolutionnaires.* Paris: Editions du Comité des Travaux Historiques et Scientifiques, 1990, 43–59.

Zeller, Olivier. A l'enseigne du Chameau, manières d'habiter, manières de gérer à Lyon au XVIIIe siècle. *Cahiers d'histoire*, 38/1 (1993): 26–54.

Zeller, Olivier. Enjeux d'urbanisme à Lyon en 1777. Propriétaires contre promoteurs. *Bulletin du centre Pierre Léon d'histoire économique et sociale*, 1 (1995), 3–15.

Zeller, Olivier. *La bourgeoisie statutaire de Lyon et ses privilèges. Morale civique, évasion fiscale et cabarets urbains (XVIIe-XVIIIe siècles).* Lyons: Editions lyonnaises d'art et d'histoire, 2016.

Index of persons and places

Abreu, Mauricio de Almeida (geographer) 6
Albertin (carpenter) 179
Ancien Régime 58, 82
Anselmier (proprietor) 194 f., 234
Antiquity 60
Arlaud, Catherine (archaeologist) 82–84, 90
Avignon 91

Bachelard, Gaston (philosopher) 2
Bank of Birmingham 191
Bank of London and Westminster 191
Banque Générale Suisse de Crédit Mobilier et Foncier International S.A. 191
Barcelona 16
Bardet, Jean-Pierre (historian) 5, 120–122, 127, 153, 206
Baronnat, Guillaume (merchant) 162, 163 f.
Baronnat, Jacques (proprietor) 162
Baronnat, Jehan (*bourgeois*) 162
Baronnat, Léonard (doctor and keeper of the accounts, probably of the city) 162
Barthes, Roland (semiologist) 2, 16
Bath 42
Bayard, Françoise (historian) 42, 82, 108, 130, 174
Bellièvre, Barthélémy (solicitor) 163
Benoist, Jocelyn (philosopher) 8–10
Bern 58, 114
Biens Nationaux 207
Bilbao 15
Bissuel, Prosper-Edouard (architect) 192
Blanc, Jean-Pierre (joiner, entrepreneur) 123, 193–196, 234
Blanchet, (proprietor) 177
Blaufarb, Rafe (historian) 58
Bleterens Rivoyre (lord of Romaigny) 164
Boesse, Christophe (treasurer of France and knight) 174
Bordeaux 71, 107, 189
Bouygues, (building company) 209
Boyer, Jacques and Barthélémy (developers) 164
Briffaud, Pierre (mason, entrepreneur) 193–195
Brillon, Ennemond (architect) 179 f.
Broallie, Jehan (dressmaker) 160
Brunet (proprietor) 198
Brussels 27, 120
Bureau des Finances 128

Caille, Jehan (doctor, developer) 164
Carme dit Augustin (goldsmith) 159
Çatalhöyük 55
Catholicism 208, 213
Chambéry 91, 120
Champier, Claude (developer) 164
Chana, Claude (entrepreneur, mason, architect) 173, 175, 209
Chana, Jean C., son of Claude Chana (architect, mason) 173
Chanu, Nicolas (developer) 156, 158 f., 161f., 164, 234
Chassagny, (mason-tiler) 194, 196
Chaunu, Pierre (historian) 5
Chavepeyre, Antoine (entrepreneur) 193
Chazelle, (proprietor) 109 f., 112
Chouquer, Gérard (geographer) 50
Claval, Paul (geographer) 6
Coignet (building company) 209
Combe, Marie (widow of Loras) 177
Compain (proprietor) 172
Convention 142, 185–187, 209, 234
Conzen, Michael Robert Günter (geographer) 2, 4 f., 12, 214
Corboz, André (architecture historian) 28, 47
Cossey, Girardin (mason) 158
Counter-Reform 138, 144, 206
Courajod, (merchant-fabricant) 177

Dagognet, François (philosopher) 1, 8, 10
Daurolles, Jacques (mason, entrepreneur) 173
De Bourg, Françoise (proprietor) 160

https://doi.org/10.1515/9783110623062-011

De Gennas, Françoys (merchant, developer) 165
De Jussieu, (proprietor) 172
De Legue, Guillaume (developer) 164
De Paris, Jehan (painter)
De Villars, André, Camyon, and Anthoyne (all *bourgeois*) 163
De Villars, Pierre (merchant) 163
De Villeneuve, Pierre (doctor, lieutenant of the *Sénéchal* of Lyons, developer) 164
Decran, (proprietor) 196
Decrénice, Cire (architect) 178
Denmark 58
Dervieux, (silk merchant) 105, 174 f.
Desraisses, Etienne (inn-keeper, investor) 111, 119
Devouge (developer) 186, 191
Dieppe 27
Dijon 57, 120
Dodieu, (proprietor) 158, 161
Drivon, François (carpenter and entrepreneur) 176
Du Pré, François (merchant) 161, 163–165
Dublin 28
Dumont, Pierre (entrepreneur) 192
Dupâquier, Jacques (historian) 5
Dupuis, (banker) 108, 174
Durant, Antoine (architect)
Durkheim, Emile (sociologist) 3
Dusoleil (lord of Pierre-Bénite, proprietor) 107

Eastern Mediterranean 55
Edinburgh 24
England 5, 27–29
Erfurt Space-Time Research Group 6
Europe 3, 14, 26, 55, 57, 60, 62, 79, 103, 213

Faure dit Cusin, Pierre (stocking-maker) 163 f.
Faure, Symon (merchant and developer)
Fazy, James (banker and politician) 191
Ferrand, Stanislas (developer) 43, 191
Ferrand, Nicolas (geographer) 14 f., 127, 128 f., 239
Flanders 57
Florence 7, 20, 120
Florentin (locksmith) 160
France 2 f., 5, 13 f., 17 f., 26–28, 31, 57–59, 62–64, 70, 104, 128, 146, 174, 181, 185, 209
French Revolution 42, 58, 75, 121, 142, 178, 180, 183, 206, 208, 210, 213

Genestine/Genestelle (mason) 194
Geneva 15, 28, 91, 114, 120, 176, 191
Genève 28, 47, 74, 91, 114, 177, 191
Genoa 207
Georgaillon, Georges (writer) 159
Germany 5
Giers 28
Gilles, Joseph (plasterer) 3, 114, 193
Ginod/Ginot, Anthelme (joiner) 194
Glas, Mathieu (carpenter) 158
Google Earth 21
Grand-Lyon 24, 73 f.
Grassot, Pierre (surgeon) 106, 176 f.
Grataloup, Christian (geographer) 8
Gros (architect) 181
Guggenheim Museum Bilbao 15
Guy, Bernard (physicist) 3, 62, 142

Halbwachs, Maurice (sociologist) 3, 5 f.
Hammurabi 54
Harris, Edward C. (archaeologist) 4
Haussmann, Eugène (baron, préfet de Paris) 71, 123
Huguetan, Jehan (printer) 160

Industrial Revolution 38, 127
Institut Géographique National 21
Inventaire 29, 89, 114, 165
Italy 5, 28, 71, 91, 104, 107, 111, 123

Janon, (proprietor) 172
Journoud, Etienne (architect, investor) 192 f.
Jouvanon, (proprietor) 194

Keyser, Erich (historian) 5
Kretzschmar, Johannes (historian) 4

La Construction Lyonnaise 21

Laurencin, Espérance (count of, director of the Perrache Company, developer) 180 f.
Le Viste (proprietor) 161
Le Viste, Claude (doctor and developer)
Leaud, Corneille (carpenter, entrepreneur) 109 f., 112, 120
Ledras (architect) 177, 182
Lefebvre, Henri (philosopher) 5–8, 19
Lenfant, Guillaume 159
Lenoir, (merchant and brocker) 42, 113, 234
Lévi-Strauss, Claude (anthropologist) 5
L'Habitant, Jean (entrepreneur and mason) 173
L'Habitant, Jacques Marie, son of Jean L'Habitant ? (architect, *bourgeois*) 173
Ligue 96, 213
Lille 71, 97, 103, 107
Lombois, Philibert (joiner) 177
London 1 f., 4–6, 11, 15 f., 26 f., 37, 46, 51, 56 f., 61, 68, 70, 82, 91, 132
– Barbican Estate 26
– Cheapside 46
London City Bank 191
Loyer, Toussaint Noël (architect) 71, 177, 182, 185
Lyons
– Antonins 107, 164 f., 165, 174
– Asnerie quarter 200
– auberge de la Croix Verte 111
– auberge de l'Ecu de France 111
– Augustinians 41, 164, 174
– Avenue Adolphe-Max 43
– Basse Grenette quarter 201
– Bellecour 14, 164, 191 f., 200
– Bourchanin quarter 96
– Carmélites 193
– Célestins company 186
– Célestins convent 133 f., 175, 186
– Change area 41
– Change quarter 99, 161
– Chartreux 102
– Chemin-Neuf 165
– City Hall 25, 41, 78, 138 f., 141 f., 176, 179, 182 f., 199, 202
– Cluny, house of he abbey 165
– *commune affranchie* 185
– Cordeliers quarter 95, 97 f.
– Côte des Carmélites 194
– Croix-Rousse 41, 165 f., 182, 190, 198, 209 f., 236, 243
– Feuillants 175
– Fourvière 16, 165
– Galerie de l'Argue 24
– Gourguillon quarter 200
– Grand Palais quarter 200
– Grand Théâtre 178
– Grand'Côte quarter 96
– *Grande Fabrique* 183
– Grande Rue de l'Hôpital 201
– Grenette quarter 95, 97
– Griffon quarter 202
– Grolée quarter 191
– Haute Grenette quarter 201
– Hospices civils 43, 58, 238, 114 f.
– Hôtel-Dieu 139, 172, 178, 180, 196, 198
– hôtel du Parc 113
– Intendance 182
– Jacobins 41, 165
– Jesuits College 107, 139, 172
– Joséphistes 175
– Juiverie quarter 200
– La Croisette quarter 201
– La Déserte 25
– La Guillotière 31, 190
– Lanterne quarter 99, 201
– l'Herberie quarter 200
– Massif du Parc 43
– Mercière 101
– mint 107, 164, 174, 186
– Monplaisir 165
– Montchat 165
– Montée du Change 163
– Montée du Garillan 164
– Montée du Gourguillon 118
– Montée St-Barthélémy 165
– Morand project 150
– Musée d'Histoire de Lyon 87
– Palais du Commerce 142
– Pêcherie quarter 97, 201
– Perrache company 180, 185
– Perrache project 180
– Perrache quarter 150, 166, 178
– Perrache sector 141, 185

– Pierre Scize quarter 200
– Place Antonin-Poncet 44
– Place Bellecour 24 f., 42, 44, 81, 84, 99, 107 f., 139, 150, 165, 174, 182, 185 f., 188, 190, 192, 198
– Place d'Albon 112
– Place de la Boucherie St-Paul 163
– Place de la Bourse 25, 82
– Place de la Charité 181
– Place de la Comédie 25
– Place de la Douane 102
– Place de la République 25, 89
– Place de la Trinité 87, 100, 118, 163
– Place de l'Herberie 163
– Place des Cordeliers 25
– Place des Jacobins 25, 192
– Place des Terreaux 82, 99, 106, 182, 190
– Place du Change 40, 46, 83, 183
– Place du Grand-Collège 109
– Place Grollier 179
– Place Meissonnier 34, 45
– Place Romarin 113
– Place Sathonay 42
– plan topographique 21
– Plat d'Argent quarter 201
– Plâtre quarter 201
– Port du Temple 200
– Port neuf de Neuville 102
– Port-St-Paul quarter 200
– Porte Froc quarter 200
– Pré Morand 178
– public weight 35
– Puits-du-Sel quarter 200
– Quai Pêcherie 40
– Quay of the Célestins 175
– Quay of the Convention 185
– *règlement général d'alignement* 76
– Rhône quay 42, 181
– River Rhône 41, 113, 127, 141, 164, 176, 178 f., 181, 185, 189 f., 192 f., 212
– River Saône 40 f., 49, 74, 82, 93 f., 100, 102, 107, 134, 141, 156, 161, 163 f., 178 f., 185, 188, 198, 200 f., 233
– *Rua Palacii* 47
– Rue Bellecordière 25, 99, 165, 196
– Rue Bourchanin 25
– Rue Bourgneuf 75, 156, 161
– Rue Bouteille 96, 111
– Rue Buisson 199, 201–203, 234
– Rue Burdeau 42
– Rue Chalamont 115 f., 234
– Rue Chenavard 34, 42, 190, 233
– Rue Childebert 25
– Rue Confort 99, 158, 160, 165
– Rue d'Algérie 25, 42, 113, 192
– Rue d'Auvergne 178
– Rue de Brest 24, 190
– Rue de Constantine 25, 42, 111, 192
– Rue de Flandres 75, 174, 200, 202
– Rue de Flesselles 194, 198
– Rue de la Boucherie-St-Paul 118
– Rue de la Bourse 25
– Rue de la Charité 43
– Rue de la Gerbe 174 f., 199
– Rue Lanterne 84 f., 100, 102, 103 f., 109, 111, 118, 137, 193
– Rue de La Platière 88
– Rue de la République 25, 31, 43 f., 89, 165, 190
– Rue de l'Ancienne-Préfecture 44
– Rue de l'Arbre-Sec 109, 112
– Rue de l'Enfant-qui-Pisse 108, 137
– Rue de l'Hôpital 89, 136, 158, 160
– Rue de l'Impératrice 191 f.
– Rue des Augustins 173 f.
– Rue des Bouchers 99, 193
– Rue des Capucins 196
– Rue des Ecloisons 175
– Rue des Epies 41, 164
– Rue des Forces 174 f.
– Rue des Prêtres 48
– Rue des Trois-Carreaux 115 f., 137, 234
– Rue Désirée 109
– Rue d'Oran 25, 192
– Rue du Bœuf 62
– Rue du Bœuf quarter 200
– Rue du Doyenné 84
– Rue du Garet 112
– Rue du Jardin-des-Plantes 25
– Rue du Plat 164
– Rue du Plâtre 42, 109
– Rue du Port-du-Temple 165, 174
– Rue Edouard-Herriot 24 f., 44, 191
– Rue Emile-Zola 107 f.

– Rue Ferrachat 83
– Rue Garillan 41
– Rue Gasparin 192
– Rue Gentil 164, 175, 199
– Rue Gourguillon 163
– Rue Grand'Côte 41, 91
– Rue Grenette 122, 137, 156, 158 f., 193, 234
– Rue Griffon 113, 198, 234
– Rue Grolée 43, 114
– Rue Hippolyte-Flandrin 25, 164
– Rue Impériale 14, 24, 31, 190–192, 199, 204, 234
– Rue Jean-de-Tournes 25
– Rue Juiverie 41, 86, 88, 99, 108, 163, 202, 233
– Rue Lafond 112
– Rue Lainerie 118
– Rue Laurencin 180
– Rue Leynaud 102, 111
– Rue Longue 42, 91, 109, 197
– Rue Malpertuis 136
– Rue Mercière 115 f., 122, 136, 163, 174, 200, 234
– Rue Misère 161
– Rue Monseigneur-Lavarenne 82, 84
– Rue Mulet 164
– Rue Neuve 137, 201
– Rue Neuve quarter 95, 172
– Rue Neyret 207
– Rue Noire 89 f., 99, 164, 196, 233
– Rue Paradis 158, 160, 164
– Rue Pêcherie 108, 174
– Rue Pierre-Blanc 148, 193 f., 196–198, 208 f.
– Rue Pierre-Scize 77, 91
– Rue Pizay 108 f., 112, 175
– Rue Port-Charlet 164
– Rue Port-du-Temple 165, 174
– Rue Poulaillerie 174
– Rue Puits-Gaillot 109
– Rue Raisin 137
– Rue Romarin 164, 193
– Rue Sala 25, 42
– Rue St-Claude 42, 113
– Rue St-Dominique 107 f., 137, 173
– Rue St-Georges 40, 183, 196–198
– Rue St-Jean 40, 46–49, 83–85, 87 f., 90 f., 99, 137, 156, 183, 198
– Rue St-Sébastien 85
– Rue Ste-Catherine 111, 113
– Rue Ste-Marie-des-Terreaux 111, 113
– Rue Sergent-Blandan 164
– Rue Terme 113
– Rue Terraille 113
– Rue Thomassin 41
– Rue Tolozan 194, 196
– Rue Tramassac 165
– Rue des Trois-Maries 118
– Rue Vaubecour 42, 108, 178
– Rue Vendrant 164
– Saône Bridge 156, 163
– Saône Quay 107, 134
– St-Clair 42, 106, 139, 166, 176, 178 f., 181 f., 185 f., 190 f.
– St-Clair quarter 108 f., 171, 176, 178–180, 209
– St-Georges quarter 96
– St-Jean cathedral 64, 78, 156
– St-Jean quarter 165 f.
– St-Joseph convent 112
– St-Just 74 f., 78, 236
– St-Nizier Church 91, 137
– St-Nizier 74 f., 101, 175
– St-Paul 101
– St-Paul Church 156, 161, 198
– St-Paul parish 161
– St-Pierre Abbey 106, 107, 173, 176
– St-Pierre quarter 95, 97, 98
– St-Vincent quarter 95 f., 98
– Terreaux 14 f., 43, 164, 201, 240
– Thomassin 164, 200
– Vieux-Lyon 41, 82

Maclet, Cretin (proprietor) 34 f.
Mâcon 91
Mallet, Françoise (geographer) 37, 194
Mallet, Michel (mason)
Mandelbrot, Benoît (mathematician) 213
Mangini, Félix (industrialist, philanthropist) 43
Marcuzzi, Max (philosopher) 9
Marseilles 2, 37, 71, 97
Matagrin, (mason) 160

Mege dit Giraud, Pierre, alias Grand Nez (proprietor) 158
Mesopotamia 54
Michel, (architect) 3, 29, 54, 60, 177–179, 182, 194
Miège, (merchant and brocker, investor) 42, 113, 234
Mignot, Humbert (solicitor) 158
Millanois, Léonard (merchant, director of the mint) 176 f., 186
Ministère de la Recherche 6
Monier, Pierre 179
Mont d'Or 104
Montluel de Jussieux, François Joseph (proprietor) 177
Morand, Jean Antoine (architect, developer) 150, 166, 177–179, 185, 191, 207
Morel, Jean (architect) 179 f.
Moynot, Hugonyn (journeyman, former hatmaker) 160
Munet, Melchior (architect) 176 f., 182, 185

Nantes 71
Naples 71
Napoleon the First 58
National Freehold Land 191
Nero (Roman emperor) 56, 60 f.
Neufville de Villeroy, Camille (archbishop) 104
New-York 43, 52, 58
Neyret (silk merchant) 207
Noailly, Etienne (proprietor, rentier) 193 f.
Normandy 56 f.
Noyerie, Etienne (ironmonger) 158

Olynthos 55 f.
Onnion 55
Ordnance Survey 27
Orvieto 91
Ostia 60 f.

Pacific North-West 59
Palermo 71
Paris 1–3, 5–10, 14–17, 24, 29, 33, 37, 47, 49, 56 f., 59–61, 64, 70 f., 79, 81 f., 91, 95, 104, 107, 120–125, 142, 160, 176, 180, 189, 192, 212, 214
– Blancs-Manteaux
– Eiffel 15 f., 16
– La Défense 17
– Montmartre 16
– Notre-Dame 64
– Quartier des Halles 29, 37
– Rue de la Ferronnerie 123
– St-Germain-l'Auxerrois 123
Pénelon, (entrepreneur) 192
Perrache, Antoine Michel (sculptor, architect, developer) 150, 176, 178–180, 191, 207
Perrache, Marie Anne, widow of Antoine Michel Perrache 179
Perrachon, Pierre (lord of St-Maurice) 42, 44, 80, 108, 130, 174
Perrachon, Pierre, daughters of 108
Perrot, Jean-Claude (historian) 5
Piacenza 49
Piedmont 57 f.
Pilet, Romain (joiner) 193
Pinchon, François (mason journeyman) 194, 196 f.
Pinerolo 57, 111
Pinet 165
Piroud (proprietor) 194
Pitance (building company) 209
Pitiot, (proprietor) 177
Plumet, Lambert (butcher) 194
Pochet, Charles (joiner) 160
Pompeii 61
Poncet, Benoît (architect, developer) 31, 42 f., 190, 192
Pont-Audemer 56
Protestants 142, 146, 208

Rater, Antoine (architect) 176–178, 182, 185
Rater, Jean-Baptiste, brother of Antoine Rater 177, 187
Ratton, (proprietor) 109, 172
Rau, Susanne (historian) 5–7, 10, 178, 181
Regensburg 57
Région Rhône-Alpes 6
Rennes 1, 27, 50, 62, 114

Revert, (pork-butcher) 180
Rhône 20, 41, 49, 88, 114, 141, 193
Rigod (or Rigaud) de Terrebasse, Aimé Julien (merchant, treasurer of the Finances) 42, 44, 179–182, 185 f.
Rivière, Claude (architect) 192
Roman Empire 56, 61, 215
Rome 15, 19 f., 33, 45 f., 49, 55–57, 60 f., 63, 71, 73, 85, 88, 106, 120, 123
– Palazzo Pamphili 106
– Piazza Navona 19, 33, 106
– St-Louis-des-Français 123
– Via dei Coronari 46
Roncayolo, Marcel (geographer)
Rosset, (bookseller) 177
Rouen 5, 13, 33, 57 f., 64, 71, 77, 79, 82, 84 f., 88, 91, 104, 107, 120–122, 127, 136, 142, 153, 192, 206 f.
Rousset, Antoine (taffeta-maker) 194, 196 f.
Roux, Léonard (architect, secretary of the King) 109, 176 f., 179, 185

Sagrada Familia 16
Salla, Pierre and Jean (proprietors) 163 f.
Sanjehan, Bonnet (printer) 160
Santos (Almeida dos Santos), Milton (geographer) 6
Saône 41, 82, 102, 141, 165
Savoye, Amédée (architect and entrepreneur) 190, 192
Schwartz, Rudolf 4, 10
Sécurité Générale 42, 192
Seigneuret, Guillaume (bookseller) 160
Small Ice Age 131, 212
Société Anonyme de la Rue impériale 31, 43, 190
Soufflot, Jacques Germain (royal architect, General inspector of the buildings and public embellishments of the city of Lyons) 176–179, 209
Soufflot, Jeanne, sister of Jacques-Germain Soufflot 177
St-Etienne 28
St-Quentin 26
Steinmann, madame (proprietor) 193
Strasbourg 107

Taillard, Etiennette (proprietor) 177
Taillemont, Claude and Loys (proprietors) 163
Teze, Loys (developer) 164
Thibaudier, Pierre (mason) 179
Thomassin, Claude (consul and *capitaine* of the city, developer) 164, 200
Tolozan de Monfort, Antoine (merchant, banker) 109, 196 f.
Torchon, Léonard (potter) 160
Torneon, Jaquemo (developer) 164
Toulon 207
Toulouse 27, 58, 71, 163
Tourreau, Raymond (architect) 179
Touzot, (solicitor) 192
Turin 49, 57, 73, 84, 111, 120

Unité Mixte de Recherche 5600 VI
Université Lyon 3 6, 14, 28

Vaise 190
Vaïsse, Claude Marius (mayor of Lyons, préfet du département du Rhône, senator) 71, 190
Valin de la Mothe 179
Vauban, (Leprestre de), Sebastien (royal engineer) 13, 27
Venice 78 f., 82
Vienna 26, 31
Villatte, G. (entrepreneur) 192
Villeroy (see Neufville de Villeroy) 104
Visigoths 55
Vive, Pierre (developer) 164

Weber, Max (economist, sociologist) 3, 7
Whitehand, Jeremy W. R. (geographer) 2, 4–7, 12, 19, 38
Wilk, Richard R. (anthropologist) 17

Yalimapo 52

Zeller, Olivier (historian) 1, 5 f., 10, 19, 37, 73, 75 f., 78 f., 81, 95 f., 98, 107, 125, 127, 142, 148, 152 f., 168, 174, 191, 200, 202

Subject index

address system 6
administrative quarter 200 f.
agent 3, 5 f., 18, 75 f., 144, 150 f., 178, 192, 206, 209
allée 84, 88
architect 15, 20, 31, 42–44, 71, 88, 107, 112, 173, 176–182, 185 f., 190–193, 209
assemblage property 68

banker 152, 174 f., 181, 185 f., 192
biology 10, 214
bookseller 152, 160, 172, 177, 198
building 1, 4–8, 11, 13–25, 27, 29, 31–49, 51–53, 57, 59–61, 63–66, 68–139, 141–153, 155 f., 158, 160 f., 166, 168–200, 202–215, 217, 231–235
building activity 126, 139, 149 f., 152, 178, 217, 234
building authorization 20 f., 29, 57, 65, 75, 77, 115, 117, 126, 128, 133, 137, 151 f., 166, 169, 171, 173, 176, 190, 231
building investment 101, 142, 148, 161, 168, 191 f., 206, 210
building permit 6–8, 20 f., 31, 34, 37, 48, 61 f., 77 f., 132, 193
building production 14, 40, 79, 97, 124, 126, 129 f., 135, 138, 156, 171, 176, 186, 188, 208 f., 211 f., 214 f., 231, 235
building professions 155 f., 158
building typology 3, 68, 71, 81, 99, 124, 205 f., 214, 216, 231
building-unit 13

capital 15 f., 71, 107, 158, 165, 169, 190 f., 194, 196, 205–211, 214, 231
capital gain 41 f., 71, 97, 150, 156, 158, 161, 165, 179 f., 190, 193, 210
carpenter 109, 150, 152, 158, 172 f., 176, 179, 193, 208
celtic field 53
census 21, 31, 73, 75, 77, 79, 95 f., 103, 118, 152, 170, 183, 188, 194, 196, 198
centuriatio 56
changing rate 7
company 15, 55, 176, 178–180, 186, 190 f.
construction process 20, 68, 156, 158, 209
construction-unit 7, 9, 11–14, 19 f., 28 f., 31, 33–35, 44 f., 67, 80, 118, 125, 127, 129, 190, 231–233
construction works 132, 134, 212, 215
crises 142, 213, 215 f.
crisis 93, 96, 98, 132, 142, 146, 180, 183 f., 207 f., 213, 215, 234
cycle 10, 73, 129 f., 135, 137, 143 f., 149, 205 f., 212 f., 216

dating 2, 8 f., 18, 20, 22 f., 26–33, 35–38, 42, 66, 77, 83, 89, 122, 232 f.
densification 17, 84, 89, 96 f., 99, 139, 141, 150
development 1, 4 f., 7, 17, 19, 24–27, 38, 40–44, 53, 55, 57, 59–61, 69–71, 73, 79, 93 f., 99 f., 115, 120 f., 123 f., 126, 142, 148, 150–152, 166, 172, 176–178, 180, 191, 193, 195, 198, 206–211, 213 f., 216, 234
dominant building type 68, 82, 87 f., 90, 101, 111, 115, 118, 120–122, 213 f.
duration 6, 9, 14, 19 f., 28, 31, 46, 58, 132, 134 f., 211–213
dwelling 14, 56, 60, 78–81, 83, 92, 102–104, 106 f., 111, 119–123, 134, 148, 151 f., 181 f., 194, 196, 198–200, 202, 208, 210, 212, 233
dwelling conditions 142
dwelling space 80, 97, 103, 106, 121, 183, 207

échevin 78, 166, 168, 177, 181
édifice 29, 69, 179
'e-house' 92, 98
elites 208, 211, 213
emergence 4, 49, 54, 120, 126, 146, 206, 210
enrichment 143, 208

https://doi.org/10.1515/9783110623062-012

entrepreneur 42 f., 134 f., 156, 173, 176, 192 f., 208 f.
expropriation 59, 143, 189

film 10, 125 f., 128, 130, 137, 217, 234
functionalism 16, 80, 210
functionality 15 f., 29, 37, 58, 63, 122, 206, 210
functional unit 11, 44, 54 f., 60, 114, 122 f.

gentrification 139, 146, 150, 172, 179, 205
geographical reference frame 126
geographic information system 31, 72 f., 125, 233
geographization 4
geographizing 8, 11
geohistory 8
geology 1, 4, 8, 10, 212
Gestaltungsperiode 214
GIS 5 f., 10, 73 f., 77, 117, 126, 231
ground value 138
group of buildings 14, 29, 37, 42
group of constructions 213

historicity 7 f.
historicization 1 f., 4, 13
historicizing 8, 11, 13
household 54, 56, 78 f., 83, 85, 91–98, 103, 121, 151–154, 169 f., 174, 181, 188 f., 199, 205, 207 f., 215, 233

impoverishment 141 f., 183
industrialization 208–210
inequality 207, 213
insurrection 142 f., 197 f., 208, 211
investment 8, 15 f., 18, 41, 45, 71, 120, 122, 124, 130, 141 f., 144, 146, 149–152, 156, 158, 161, 163 f., 171, 173–175, 179, 182 f., 190–193, 198, 205–210
investment in real estate 143, 150, 163, 199
investment logic 161, 207
investor 15, 41 f., 70 f., 97, 102, 112, 123, 130, 139, 143 f., 148–150, 152, 156, 158, 161, 166, 171, 173, 175, 178 f., 190–192, 194 f., 197, 205–207, 209 f.

Jacquard loom 197
joiner 152, 160, 177, 193–195, 208

long duration 12, 129, 132, 138 f., 212 f., 216, 234
long-term 26, 138, 141 f., 144 f., 202, 205 f., 215 f., 231 f.

macroevolution 213
mapping 4–6, 8, 10, 12, 20, 22, 24, 28 f., 31, 38, 60, 73, 75–77, 125–127, 130, 135, 138, 144, 189, 231, 234
market 3, 55 f., 70, 92, 97, 122, 149, 151 f., 158, 171 f., 174 f., 179, 182, 196, 198, 209 f.
mason 134, 150, 152, 158, 160, 173, 179, 192–194, 196 f., 208 f.
materiality 1–9, 11–13, 19, 22, 45, 48–50, 52, 57, 62 f., 65, 67 f., 211–213, 231
merchant 42, 102, 113, 152 f., 155, 161–164, 172, 176, 181, 184–186, 197, 206, 209, 234
merchant-fabricant 169, 172, 177, 182 f.
metamorphism 12
microevolution 213
mild random 213
morphogenetic process 4
morphological period 214
morphotope 5
multi-familial building type 105 f., 108, 120, 123, 234
multi-familial housing 70, 79 f., 94 f., 102, 120–122, 146, 207
mutazioni capillari 120

naturality 8
new development 13, 18, 33, 41, 43 f., 46, 62, 70, 89, 93, 96 f., 101, 109, 112, 145, 150, 178, 181, 186, 197 f., 205
nommées 44, 77, 83, 88, 91, 93, 95, 100 f., 103, 127, 151, 153, 162, 170, 174
numeration system 75

palimpsest 47
party-wall 57, 61, 69, 84 f., 99, 112, 115, 122, 137, 205, 213
petite police 128

phase transition 142
planned development 12–14, 19 f., 22–24, 26, 39 f., 42, 56, 68–70, 127 f., 137, 144 f., 231, 233
planning policy 127
plan-unit 5, 12, 25
plasticity 80–81, 123, 210
plot limit 27 f., 47, 50 f., 102
plot-pattern 22, 206
plot size 70, 87
poetics 2 f., 231
poor 16, 71, 80, 83, 89, 96 f., 103 f., 111, 121, 138 f., 143, 148, 153, 155 f., 164 f., 170 f., 182, 184–186, 193 f., 197, 202, 207, 213, 234
population growth 98, 139, 148
population level 148–150
prévôt 168
printer 152, 160, 198
production of buildings 5, 26, 79, 171, 175, 182, 192, 213
production of urban space 3, 5, 10, 151, 156, 198, 205, 211, 231
production process 4, 7, 12, 18, 20, 22, 45, 53, 73, 156, 209, 216
production unit 13 f., 22, 28, 54 f., 66, 231
property right 51–60
proportion of proprietors 199, 206, 215
proprietor 15, 26 f., 35, 43, 47, 50, 74–77, 117, 133 f., 143 f., 151, 153, 155 f., 160–163, 169 f., 177 f., 181, 185 f., 188 f., 193, 196, 199 f., 202–204, 208, 231, 233–235

quantification 125

real estate 76, 87, 91, 121 f., 143, 156, 161, 164, 168, 170, 174, 176 f., 179, 183, 186, 188, 191, 193, 202, 206–210, 231
real estate market 17, 151, 179, 186, 209 f.
régie 202
remanence 45 f., 50, 53
remanent temporality 67, 211
rent 15, 74, 76, 97, 107, 150, 173, 194, 196 f., 202, 210
replacement 17, 43, 46 f., 49, 65, 90, 94, 105, 119, 131, 145 f., 156, 211
representation 3, 37, 49, 67, 74, 137, 165, 171, 231
rhythm 33, 69, 132, 138, 176, 205, 212, 216, 235
risk 60 f., 143, 158, 190, 196, 209

scale 1, 5–8, 10–14, 16, 21 f., 24, 28, 31, 33, 36 f., 45 f., 73, 79, 83, 85, 90, 101, 113, 124 f., 127–130, 138, 143 f., 158, 166, 182, 205 f., 212 f., 216, 231, 233 f.
scale effects 126
scale of the city 127
silk 38, 43, 80, 96, 104, 113, 121, 127, 148, 150, 152, 169, 172, 175, 182–184, 194–199, 207–210, 213, 234
silk industry 121, 142, 172, 183
silk merchant 174 f., 207
silk weaver 103, 172, 184, 234
silk weaving 120, 141, 197, 206
social agent 150, 206
social morphology 3, 5 f., 38
social process 2, 4 f., 7, 11 f., 51, 66, 126, 129, 161, 213, 216, 231
solicitor 152, 158, 163, 179, 185, 192 f., 209
spatial dynamics 137
spatiality 3, 5
spatializing 8, 13
spatial metaphor 8
spatial turn 6
Stadtteil 5
street policy 126
subdivision 13, 20, 22, 24 f., 27, 35, 47, 52, 69 f., 84, 87, 90 f., 95, 99, 108, 119, 127 f., 137, 139, 141, 151 f., 156–158, 160–162, 164–167, 173, 178, 193–196, 199, 205–208, 234

temporal complexity 212
temporal interval 129
temporality 3, 5, 8, 10, 39, 50, 62, 66–68, 124, 136, 211, 215
tenant 26, 29, 50, 70, 80 f., 98, 103, 120, 172 f., 196–199, 202–204, 210, 234
tessuto urbano 69
time duration 143, 214
time scale 73, 125, 135, 138, 144
time segment 9

tipo portante 68, 101
tissus urbain 69
transformation 1, 4–6, 10, 12, 14, 18 f., 22, 24, 26, 28, 31–34, 37 f., 40, 43, 47, 49 f., 59, 63–65, 71, 73 f., 78–80, 100, 108, 115–119, 123, 125–128, 130, 134, 143 f., 150 f., 182, 205, 211, 213, 215, 231–234
typology 11, 18, 42, 53, 68 f., 79, 85 f., 91, 119, 214
typology of buildings 93

unité de construction 7
urban change 125
urban fabric 3, 10, 19, 23, 29, 40, 43, 51, 68–70, 90, 101, 116 f., 126, 143, 150, 160, 212, 215, 231 f., 234
urban form 1 f., 37, 61, 68, 114, 211
urban fringe 137, 144
urban history 2, 5, 9
urban materiality 4 f., 11, 46, 61, 212, 216
urban morphology 1–3, 5, 7, 24, 38
urban space 2, 4–7, 9 f., 12 f., 16, 18 f., 22, 24, 26, 33, 37, 39, 45, 51, 57, 59–61, 65 f., 68–70, 109, 123, 130, 143 f., 150, 156, 211, 215, 231, 233

wild random 213
working class 213

Printed and bound by CPI Group (UK) Ltd, Croydon, CR0 4YY

13/09/2026

14961092-0001